Exploring Microeconomics

Second Canadian Edition

Robert L. Sexton
Pepperdine University

Peter N. Fortura
Algonquin College

Colin C. Kovacs
Algonquin College

NELSON / EDUCATION

NELSON / EDUCATION

Exploring Microeconomics, Second Canadian Edition

by Robert L. Sexton, Peter N. Fortura, and Collin C. Kovacs

Associate Vice President, Editorial Director:
Evelyn Veitch

Editor-in-Chief, Higher Education:
Anne Williams

Senior Acquisitions Editor:
Craig Dyer

Marketing Manager:
David Ward

Developmental Editor:
My Editor Inc.

Photo Researcher and Permissions Coordinator:
Nicola Winstanley

Content Production Manager:
Susan Wong

Production Service:
S4Carlisle

Copy Editor:
Liba Berry

Proofreader:
Nicole Schlutt

Indexer:
Schroeder Indexing Services

Production Coordinator:
Ferial Suleman

Design Director:
Ken Phipps

Managing Designer:
Franca Amore

Interior Design Modifications:
Nelson Gonzalez

Cover Design:
Dianna Little

Cover Image:
© Brad Wrobleski/Masterfile

Compositor:
S4Carlisle

Printer:
RR Donnelley

Library and Archives Canada Cataloguing in Publication Data

Sexton, Robert L.
Exploring microeconomics / Robert L. Sexton, Peter Fortura, Colin Kovacs.—
2nd Canadian ed. Previously published as part of: Exploring Economics. 1st Canadian ed.

Includes bibliographical references and index.
ISBN 978-0-17-650022-1

1. Microeconomics—Textbooks. I. Fortura, Peter II. Kovacs, Colin III. Title.

HB172.S49 2009   338.5
C2008-907356-8

ISBN-13: 978-0-17-650022-1
ISBN-10: 0-17-650022-7

To Cynthia, Laura, and Nicholas

P.N.F.

To Lindsay, Rowan, and Seth

C.C.K.

To Julie, Elizabeth, Katherine, and Tommy

R.L.S.

Brief Contents

Detailed Contents

About the Authors

Robert L. Sexton is Distinguished Professor of Economics at Pepperdine University. Professor Sexton has also been a Visiting Professor at the University of California at Los Angeles in the Anderson Graduate School of Management and the Department of Economics.

Professor Sexton's research ranges across many fields of economics: economics education, labour economics, environmental economics, law and economics, and economic history. He has written several books and has published more than 40 research papers, many in top economic journals such as the *American Economic Review, Southern Economic Journal, Economics Letters,* the *Journal of Urban Economics,* and the *Journal of Economic Education.* Professor Sexton has also written more than 100 other articles that have appeared in books, magazines, and newspapers.

Professor Sexton received the Pepperdine Professor of the Year Award in 1991 and 1997, and the Howard A. White Memorial Teaching Award in 1994; he was named a Harriet and Charles Luckman Teaching Fellow in 1994.

Professor Sexton resides in Agoura Hills, California, with his wife, Julie, and their three children, Elizabeth, Katherine, and Tommy.

Peter N. Fortura earned his undergraduate degree from Brock University, where he was awarded the Vice-Chancellor's Medal for academic achievement, and his Master of Arts from the University of Western Ontario in London, Ontario. He has taught economics at Algonquin College, in Ottawa, for 20 years. Prior to that, he was an economist in the International Department of the Bank of Canada, in Ottawa.

He has published articles on Canadian housing prices, Canada's automotive industry, and Canada's international competitiveness. As well, he is the author of the *Study Guide to Accompany Principles of Macroeconomics,* by Mankiw, Kneebone, McKenzie, and Rowe (Nelson Education, 4th edition), and the co-author of the statistics textbook *Contemporary Business Statistics with Canadian Applications* (Pearson, 3rd edition).

He lives in Ottawa with his wife, Cynthia, and their children, Laura and Nicholas.

Colin C. Kovacs received his Master of Arts degree from Queen's University after completing his Bachelor of Arts degree at the University of Western Ontario. He has taught economics, statistics, and finance for over 15 years at both the DeVry College of Technology, in Toronto, and Algonquin College, in Ottawa. His research papers have included *Determinants of Labour Force Participation Among Older Males in Canada,* and *Minimum Wage — The Past and Future for Ontario.*

He lives in Ottawa with his wife, Lindsay, and their children, Rowan and Seth.

Preface

Exploring Microeconomics, Second Canadian Edition, offers students a lively, back-to-the-basics approach designed to take the intimidation out of economics. With its short, self-contained learning units and its carefully chosen pedagogy, graphs, and photos, this text helps students master and retain the principles of economics. In addition, the current-events focus and modular format of presenting information makes *Exploring Microeconomics* a very student-accessible and user-friendly text. Driven by a combined 60 years of experience teaching the economic principles course, Bob Sexton, Peter Fortura, and Colin Kovacs's dedication and enthusiasm shine through in *Exploring Microeconomics*.

NEW TO THE SECOND CANADIAN EDITION

Overall Highlights

The Second Canadian Edition of *Exploring Microeconomics* is now a separate split-edition, as compared to the combined Micro/Macro first-edition text. With this edition, "In the News" features have been reviewed and replaced where needed for greater Canadian content and continued relevance. As well, all statistical information has been updated.

CHAPTER HIGHLIGHTS

Chapter 1: The Role and Method of Economics

This chapter combines the first two chapters of the first edition, thereby producing one complete introductory chapter. Topics have been carefully reviewed to eliminate any unnecessary repetition.

Chapter 2: Scarcity, Trade-Offs, and Economic Growth

Greater detail has been added to the development of both the Circular Flow and Production Possibility Curve models.

Chapter 3: Supply and Demand

This newly created chapter is solely dedicated to explaining the demand and supply curves as well as those factors responsible for shifting them.

Chapter 4: Bringing Supply and Demand Together

This newly created chapter focuses on the concepts of market equilibrium and price floors and price ceilings.

Chapter 5: Elasticity

The addition of the midpoint method to calculating percentage change has improved the rigor of the section on calculating elasticity. The addition of income demand and cross-elasticity of demand elasticities provides a more complete investigation of the topic area.

This edition also has a newly expanded section on explaining the relationship between elasticity and tax incidence.

Chapter 6: Market Efficiency and Market Failure

This new chapter provides a concise and straightforward discussion of consumer and producer surplus, including the identification of deadweight loss. As well, the chapter provides discussion of externalities, public goods, and asymmetric information.

Chapter 10: Monopolistic Competition and Oligopoly

This entirely new chapter presents the basic model of monopolistic competition; the oligopoly models include collusion and cartels, kinked demand curve, and price leadership. Adding this chapter provides a complete overview of the four market structures.

Chapter 11: Labour Markets and the Distribution of Income

In this edition, the material on land and rent, and capital and interest has been removed. Thus the chapter's focus is only on the labour market.

Chapter 12: The Environment

This edition adds an entirely new chapter on the environment, covering the basic material of externalities, pollution, public policy, and property rights.

FEATURES OF THE BOOK

The Section-by-Section Approach

Exploring Microeconomics uses a section-by-section approach in which economic ideas and concepts are presented in short, self-contained units rather than in large blocks of text. Each chapter comprises approximately six to eight bite-sized sections, typically presented in two to eight pages, that include all of the relevant graphs, tables, applications, boxes, photos, definitions, and cartoons for the topic at hand. Our enthusiasm for and dedication to this approach stems from studying research on *learning theory,* which indicates that students retain information much better when it is broken down into short, intense, and exciting bursts of "digestible" information. Students prefer information divided into smaller, self-contained sections that are less overwhelming, more manageable, and easier to review before going on to new material. In short, students will be more successful in mastering and retaining economic principles using this approach, which is distinctly more compatible with modern communication styles.

But students aren't the only ones to benefit from this approach. The self-contained sections allow instructors greater flexibility in planning their courses. They can simply select or delete sections of the text as it fits their syllabus.

Learning Tools

Key Questions   Each section begins with key questions designed to preview ideas and to pique students' interest in the material to come. These questions also serve as landmarks for students: If they can answer these questions after reading the material, they may go forward with confidence.

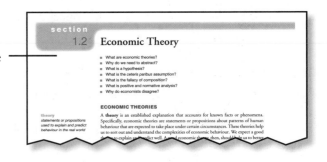

Section Checks   Section Checks appear at the end of each section and are designed to reinforce the key questions. Key points summarizing major ideas give students an opportunity to check their understanding before proceeding.

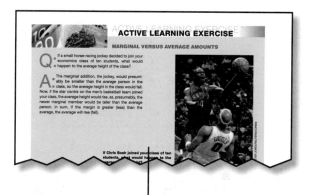

CHAPTER ONE | *The Role and Method of Economics*

Section Check

1. In the long run, firms can vary inputs that are fixed in the short run, such as plant size and equipment.
2. At low output levels, when all inputs can be varied, some firms will experience economies of scale, where their per-unit costs are decreasing as output increases.
3. Firms that expand all inputs beyond a certain point will encounter diseconomies of scale, incurring rising per-unit costs as output grows in the long run.
4. In intermediate output ranges, firms may exhibit roughly constant returns to scale; in this range, their per-unit costs remain stable as output increases.
5. Input prices, taxes, technology, and regulation can shift the cost curves.

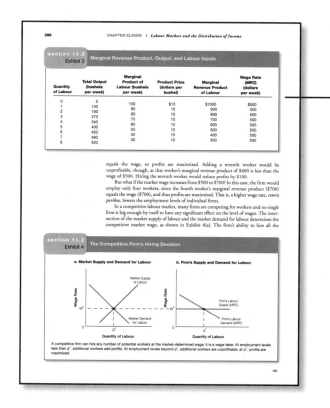

Exhibits   Graphs, tables, and charts are used throughout *Exploring Microeconomics* to illustrate, clarify, and reinforce economic principles. Text exhibits are designed to be as clear and simple as possible and are carefully coordinated with the text material.

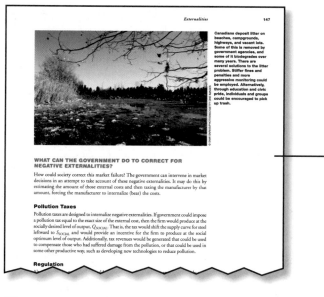

Active Learning Exercise   Active learning exercises are scattered throughout the text as a way of reinforcing and checking student comprehension of important or more difficult concepts. Students can check their work against the answer, providing them with immediate feedback and encouragement in the learning process.

Photos   *Exploring Microeconomics* contains a large number of colourful pictures. They are not, however, mere decoration; rather, these photos are an integral part of the book, for both learning and motivation purposes. The photos are carefully placed where they reinforce important concepts, and they are accompanied by captions designed to encourage students to extend their understanding of particular ideas.

In the News Boxes   In the News boxes focus primarily on current events in Canada and abroad that are relevant and thought-provoking. These articles are placed strategically throughout the text to solidify particular concepts and to help students find the connection between economics and their lives.

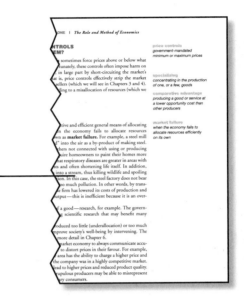

Marginal Key Terms   When key terms and concepts are first introduced within the text, they are highlighted in boldface and the definitions appear in the margin for ease of student learning.

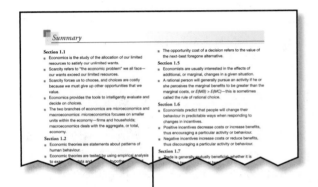

End-of-Chapter Summaries   Each chapter ends with a point-form summary that highlights the most important concepts of the chapter. The summary points are grouped by sections for quick and easy review of the chapter.

End-of-Chapter Key Terms and Concepts   There is a list of the key terms and concepts at the end of each chapter that allows students to test their mastery of new concepts. Page references are included so students can easily find key terms within the chapter.

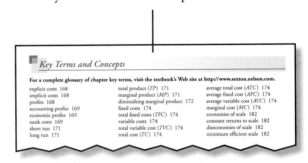

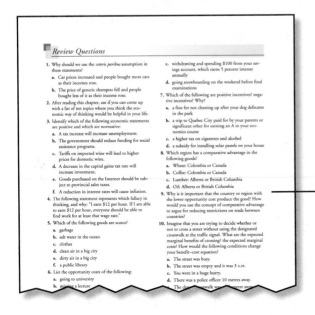

End-of-Chapter Review Questions   Questions at the end of the chapter allow students to test their understanding of chapter concepts. Some of the questions are designed for review whereas others are designed to help students extend their thinking about core concepts.

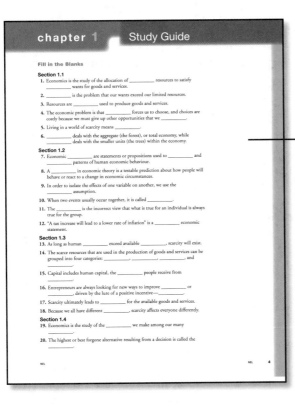

Self-Contained Study Guide   Providing added value for the student, each chapter concludes with a 6–12-page study guide that includes Fill in the Blanks, True or False, and Multiple Choice questions as well as Problems. The Study Guide questions for each chapter have been organized into sections that correspond to the relevant section in the chapter.

SUPPLEMENTARY MATERIALS

Student Web Site

The Student Web Site at **http://www.sextonmicro2e.nelson.com** provides access to many learning tools. The Student Web Site allows students to access PowerPoint presentations, online quizzes, and other resources they can use to test their understanding of key economic concepts.

Supplements for the Instructor

Computerized Test Bank   ExamView allows for quick test creation. All items in the test bank are available in computerized test bank software format. Questions and answers may be added, edited, or deleted. Instructors can easily vary the sequence of questions in order to create multiple versions of the same test. Answer keys are generated quickly with each version of the test. The program is available for both Mac and Windows.

A Word version of the test bank is available for those instructors who wish to take advantage of this option. Both the Computerized Test Bank and the Word version are available on the Instructor's Resource CD-ROM.

Instructor's Manual and Test Bank   Prepared by Gary Tompkins, University of Regina, the Instructor's Manual follows the textbook's concept-by-concept approach in two parts: chapter outlines and teaching tips. The Teaching Tips section provides analogies, illustrations, and examples to help instructors reinforce each section of the text. The answers to the end-of-chapter review questions can be found in the Instructor's Manual. The Test Bank, prepared by Tatjana Brkic, Red River College, includes approximately 150 test questions per chapter, consisting of multiple-choice, true/false, and short-answer questions.

Lecture Presentation in PowerPoint   Prepared by Alanna Holowinsky, Red River College, this PowerPoint presentation covers all the essential sections presented in each chapter of the book. Graphs, tables, lists, and concepts are animated sequentially, much as one might develop them on the blackboard. Additional examples and applications are used to reinforce major lessons, and instructors may adapt or add slides to customize their lectures. These are available on the Instructor's Resource CD-ROM and from the Instructor's Web site.

Instructor's Web Site   The Instructor's portion of the Web site to accompany *Exploring Microeconomics* contains electronic versions of many of the valuable instructor resources described previously. Adopters of the textbook may obtain a password from their local sales representative for access to Word versions of the Instructor's Manual and Test Bank along with other valuable teaching resources.

Instructor's Resource CD-ROM   Included on the CD-ROM are the key supplements designed to aid instructors:

- Instructor's Manual
- PowerPoint presentation slides
- Computerized Test Bank
- Printable Test Bank for ease of use.

Acknowledgments

Producing the Second Canadian Edition of *Exploring Microeconomics* has truly been a team effort. We would like to thank the editorial, production, and marketing teams at Nelson Education for their hard work and effort. First, our appreciation goes to Anne Williams, editorial director, who has provided the vision and leadership for both editions of the text.

We would like to extend special thanks to Katherine Goodes, senior developmental editor at My Editor Inc., for her helpful advice and constant encouragement. This book reflects her hard work and effort. Thanks also to Susan Wong, content production editor, and all the marketing and sales representatives at Nelson Education Ltd.

We are grateful to our families for their patience and encouragement.

Finally, we would like to acknowledge the reviewers of the First Canadian edition, listed below, for their comments and feedback:

Bruno Fullone, *George Brown College*
Russell Turner, *Fleming College*
Aurelia Best, *Centennial College*
Jim Butko, *Niagara College*
Geoffrey Prince, *Centennial College*
Carl Weston, *Mohawk College*

Their thoughtful suggestions were very important to us in providing input and useful examples for the Second Canadian Edition of this book.

P.N.F.
C.C.K.

Economics: A Brief Introduction

- Why study economics?
- What is economics?
- What is scarcity?
- What distinguishes macroeconomics from microeconomics?

WHY STUDY ECONOMICS?

As you begin your first course in economics, you may be asking yourself why you're here. What does economics have to do with your life? Although there are many good reasons to study economics, perhaps the best reason is that many issues in our lives are at least partly economic in character. For example, a good understanding of economics would allow you to answer such questions as: Why do 10 A.M. classes fill up quicker than 8 A.M. classes during registration? Why is teenage unemployment always higher than adult unemployment? Why are the prices of prescription drugs so high? Will higher taxes on cigarettes reduce the number of people smoking? Why do professional athletes make so much money? Why do North American auto producers like tariffs (taxes) on imported

The front pages of our daily newspapers are filled with articles related to economics—either directly or indirectly. News headlines might read: "Gasoline Prices Soar; Stocks Rise; Stocks Fall; Prime Minister Vows to Increase National Defence Spending; Health-Care Costs Continue to Rise."

cars? The study of economics improves your understanding of these and many other concerns.

Another reason to study economics is that it may teach you how to "think better"—economics helps develop a disciplined method of thinking about problems. Although economics may not always give you clear-cut answers, it will give you something even more powerful: the economic way of thinking. The problem-solving tools you will develop by studying economics will prove valuable to you both in your personal and professional life, regardless of your career choice. A student of economics becomes aware that, at a basic level, much of economic life involves choosing among alternative courses of action—making choices between our conflicting wants and desires in a world of limited resources. Economics provides some clues as to how to intelligently evaluate these options and determine the most appropriate choices in given situations.

ECONOMICS—A WORD WITH MANY DIFFERENT MEANINGS

Some individuals think economics involves the study of the stock market and corporate finance, and it does—in part. Others think that economics is concerned with the wise use of money and other matters of personal finance, and it is—in part. Still others think that economics involves forecasting or predicting what business conditions will be like in the future, and again, it does—in part.

A Unique Way of Looking at Human Behaviour

Economics is a unique way of analyzing many areas of human behaviour. Indeed, the range of topics to which economic analysis is applied is quite broad. Many researchers have discovered that the economic approach to human behaviour sheds light on social problems that have been with us for a long time: discrimination, education, crime, divorce, political favouritism, and many more. In fact, economics is front-page news almost every day, whether it involves politicians talking about tax cuts, inflation, interest rates, or unemployment; business executives talking about restructuring their companies to cut costs; or the average citizen trying to figure out how to make ends meet each month. Economics is all of this and more.

Growing Wants and Scarce Resources

economics
the study of the allocation of our limited resources to satisfy our unlimited wants

resources
inputs used to produce goods and services

the economic problem
scarcity forces us to choose, and choices are costly because we must give up other opportunities that we value

Precisely defined, **economics** is the study of the allocation of our limited resources to satisfy our unlimited wants. **Resources** are inputs—such as land, human effort and skills, and machines and factories—used to produce goods and services. The problem is that our wants exceed our limited resources, a fact that we call scarcity. Scarcity forces us to make choices on how to best use our limited resources. This is **the economic problem:** Scarcity forces us to choose, and choices are costly because we must give up other opportunities that we value. This economizing problem is evident in every aspect of our lives. Choosing between a trip to the grocery store or the mall, or between finishing an assignment or going to a movie, can be understood more easily when one has a good handle on the "economic way of thinking."

ECONOMICS IS ALL AROUND US

Although many things that we desire in life are considered to be "noneconomic," economics concerns anything that is considered worthwhile to some human being. For instance, love, sexual activity, and religion have value for most people. Even these have an economic dimension. Consider religion, for example. Concern for spiritual matters has led to the development of institutions such as churches, mosques, and temples that provide religious and spiritual services. These services are goods that many people desire. Love and sex likewise have received economists' scrutiny. One product of love, the institution of the family, is an important economic decision-making unit. Also, sexual activity results in the birth of children, one of the most important "goods" that humans desire.

Even time has an economic dimension. In fact, perhaps the most precious single resource is time. We all have the same limited amount of time per day, and how we divide our time between work and leisure (including perhaps study, sleep, exercise, etc.) is a distinctly economic matter. If we choose more work, we must sacrifice leisure. If we choose to study, we must sacrifice time with friends, or time spent sleeping or watching TV. Virtually everything we decide to do, then, has an economic dimension.

Living in a world of scarcity means trade-offs. And it is important that we know what these trade-offs are so we can make better choices about the options available to us.

ECONOMICS IS A SOCIAL SCIENCE

Like psychology, sociology, anthropology, and political science, economics is considered a social science. Economics, like the other social sciences, is concerned with reaching generalizations about human behaviour. Economics is the study of people. It is the social science that studies the choices people make in a world of limited resources.

Economics and the other social sciences often complement one another. For example, a political scientist might examine the process that led to the adoption of a certain tax policy, whereas an economist might analyze the impact of that tax policy. Or, whereas psychologist may try to figure out what makes the criminal mind work, an economist might study the factors causing a change in the crime rate. Social scientists, then, may be studying the same issue but from different perspectives.

MACROECONOMICS AND MICROECONOMICS

Conventionally, we distinguish two main branches of economics: macroeconomics and microeconomics. **Macroeconomics** deals with the **aggregate,** or total economy; it looks at economic problems as they influence the whole of society. Topics covered in macroeconomics include discussions of inflation, unemployment, business cycles, and economic growth. **Microeconomics,** by contrast, deals with the smaller units within the economy, attempting to understand the decision-making behaviour of firms and households and their interaction in markets for particular goods or services. Microeconomic topics include discussions of health care, agricultural subsidies, the price of everyday items such as running shoes, the distribution of income, and the impact of labour unions on wages. To put it simply, microeconomics looks at the trees whereas macroeconomics looks at the forest.

macroeconomics
the study of the whole economy including the topics of inflation, unemployment, and economic growth

aggregate
the total amount—such as the aggregate level of output

microeconomics
the study of household and firm behaviour and how they interact in the marketplace

Section Check

1. Economics is a problem-solving science.
2. Economics is the study of the allocation of our limited resources to satisfy our unlimited wants.
3. Our unlimited wants exceed our resources, so we must make choices.
4. Economics is concerned with reaching generalizations about human behaviour.
5. Macroeconomics deals with the aggregate, or total, economy.
6. Microeconomics focuses on smaller units within the economy—firms and households, and how they interact in the marketplace.

Economic Theory

- What are economic theories?
- Why do we need to abstract?
- What is a hypothesis?
- What is the *ceteris paribus* assumption?
- What is the fallacy of composition?
- What is positive and normative analysis?
- Why do economists disagree?

ECONOMIC THEORIES

theory
statement or proposition used to explain and predict behaviour in the real world

A **theory** is an established explanation that accounts for known facts or phenomena. Specifically, economic theories are statements or propositions about patterns of human behaviour that are expected to take place under certain circumstances. These theories help us to sort out and understand the complexities of economic behaviour. We expect a good theory to explain and predict well. A good economic theory, then, should help us to better understand and, ideally, predict human economic behaviour.

ABSTRACTION IS IMPORTANT

Economic theories cannot realistically include every event that has ever occurred. This is true for the same reason that a newspaper or history book does not include every world event that has ever happened. We must abstract. A road map of Canada may not include every creek, ridge, and valley between Calgary and Halifax—indeed, such an all-inclusive map would be too large to be of value. However, a small road map with major details will provide enough information to travel by car from Calgary to Halifax. Likewise, an economic theory provides a broad view, not a detailed examination, of human economic behaviour.

© RYAN MCVAY/PHOTODISC/GETTY ONE IMAGES

How is economic theory like a map? Because of the complexity of human behaviour, economists must abstract to focus on the most important components of a particular problem. This is similar to maps that highlight the important information (and assume away many minor details) to help people get from here to there.

DEVELOPING A TESTABLE PROPOSITION

hypothesis
a testable proposition

The beginning of any theory is a **hypothesis,** a testable proposition that makes some type of prediction about behaviour in response to certain changes in conditions. In economic theory, a hypothesis is a testable prediction about how people will behave or react to a change in economic circumstances. For example, if the price of compact discs (CDs) increased, we might hypothesize that fewer CDs would be sold, or if the price of CDs fell, we might hypothesize that more CDs would be sold. Once a hypothesis is stated, it is tested by comparing what it predicts will happen to what actually happens.

Using Empirical Analysis

empirical analysis
the use of data to test a hypothesis

To see if a hypothesis is valid, we must engage in an **empirical analysis.** That is, we must examine the data to see if the hypothesis fits well with the facts. If the hypothesis is consistent with real-world observations, it is accepted; if it does not fit well with the facts, it is "back to the drawing board."

Determining whether a hypothesis is acceptable is more difficult in economics than it is in the natural or physical sciences. Chemists, for example, can observe chemical reactions under laboratory conditions. They can alter the environment to meet the assumptions of the hypothesis and can readily manipulate the variables (chemicals, temperatures, and so on) crucial to the proposed relationship. Such controlled experimentation is seldom possible in economics. The laboratory of economists is usually the real world. Unlike a chemistry lab, economists cannot easily control all the other variables that might influence human behaviour.

FROM HYPOTHESIS TO THEORY

After gathering their data, economic researchers must then evaluate the results to determine whether the hypothesis is supported or refuted. If supported, the hypothesis can then be tentatively accepted as an economic theory.

Economic theories are always on probation. A hypothesis is constantly being tested against empirical findings. Do the observed findings support the prediction? When a hypothesis survives a number of tests, it is accepted until it no longer predicts well.

VIOLATION OF THE *CETERIS PARIBUS* ASSUMPTION

One condition common to virtually all theories in economics is usually expressed by use of the Latin expression ***ceteris paribus.*** This roughly means "let everything else be equal" or "holding everything else constant." In trying to assess the effect of one variable on another, we must isolate their relationship from other events that might also influence the situation that the theory tries to explain or predict. To make this clearer, we will illustrate this concept with a couple of examples.

ceteris paribus
holding all other things constant

Suppose you develop your own theory describing the relationship between studying and exam performance: If I study harder, I will perform better on the test. That sounds logical, right? Holding other things constant *(ceteris paribus),* this is likely to be true. However, what if you studied harder but inadvertently overslept the day of the exam? What if you were so sleepy during the test that you could not think clearly? Or what if you studied the wrong material? Although it may look as if additional studying did not improve your performance, the real problem may lie in the impact of other variables, such as sleep deficiency or how you studied.

Researchers must be careful to hold other things constant *(ceteris paribus).* For example, in 1936, cars were inexpensive by modern standards, yet few were purchased; in 1949, cars were much more expensive, but more were bought. This statement appears to imply that people prefer to buy more when prices are higher. However, we know from ample empirical observations that this is not the case—buyers are only willing to buy more at lower prices, *ceteris paribus.* The reason people bought more cars at the higher prices was that several other important variables were not held constant over this period (the *ceteris paribus* assumption): the purchasing power of dollars, the income of potential car buyers, and the quality of cars to mention just a few.

CONFUSING CORRELATION AND CAUSATION

Without a theory of causation, no scientist could sort out and understand the enormous complexity of the real world. But one must always be careful not to confuse correlation with causation. In other words, the fact that two events usually occur together (**correlation**) does not necessarily mean that one caused the other to occur (**causation**). For example, say a groundhog awakes after a long winter of hibernation, climbs out of his hole, sees his shadow,

correlation
two events that usually occur together

causation
when one event brings on another event

People tend to drive slower when the roads are covered with ice. In addition, more traffic accidents occur when the roads are icy. So, does driving slower cause the number of accidents to rise? No, it is the icy roads that lead to both lower speeds and increased accidents.

fallacy of composition
the incorrect view that what is true for the individual is always true for the group

positive analysis
an objective testable statement—how the economy is

and then six weeks of bad weather ensue. Did the groundhog cause the bad weather? It is highly unlikely.

Perhaps the causality may run in the opposite direction. Although a rooster may always crow before the sun rises, it does not cause the sunrise; rather, the early light from the sunrise causes the rooster to crow.

Why Is There a Positive Correlation Between Ice Cream Sales and Crime?

Did you know that when ice cream sales rise, so do crime rates? What do you think causes the two events to occur together? Some might think that the sugar "high" in the ice cream causes the higher crime rate. Excess sugar in a snack was actually used in court testimony in a murder case—the so-called "Twinkie defence." However, it is more likely that crime peaks in the summer because of weather, more people on vacation (leaving their homes vacant), teenagers out of school, and so on. It just happens that ice cream sales also peak in those months because of weather. The lesson: One must always be careful not to confuse correlation with causation and to be clear on the direction of the causation.

THE FALLACY OF COMPOSITION

One must also be careful with problems associated with aggregation (summing up all the parts), particularly the **fallacy of composition.** This fallacy states that even if something is true for an individual, it is not necessarily true for many individuals as a group. For example, say you are at a concert and you decide to stand up to get a better view of the stage. This works as long as no one else stands up. But what would happen if everyone stood up at the same time? Then, standing up would not let you see better. Hence, what may be true for an individual does not always hold true in the aggregate. The same can be said of arriving to class early to get a better parking place—what if everyone arrived early? Or studying harder to get a better grade in a class that is graded on a curve—what if everyone studied harder? All of these are examples of the fallacy of composition.

POSITIVE ANALYSIS

Most economists view themselves as scientists seeking the truth about the way people behave. They make speculations about economic behaviour, and then (ideally) they try to assess the validity of those predictions based on human experience. Their work emphasizes how people *do* behave, rather than how people *should* behave. In the role of scientist, an economist tries to observe, objectively, patterns of behaviour without reference to the appropriateness or inappropriateness of that behaviour. This objective, value-free approach, utilizing the scientific method, is called **positive analysis.** In positive analysis, we want to know the impact of variable A on variable B. We want to be able to test a hypothesis. For example, the following is a positive statement: If rent controls are imposed, vacancy rates will fall. This statement is testable. A positive statement does not have to be a true statement, but it does have to be a testable statement.

However, keep in mind that it is doubtful that even the most objective scientist can be totally value-free in his or her analysis. An economist may well emphasize data or evidence that supports his hypothesis, putting less weight on other evidence that might be contradictory. This, alas, is human nature. But a good economist/scientist strives to be as fair and objective as possible in evaluating evidence and in stating conclusions based on the evidence.

NORMATIVE ANALYSIS

Like everyone, economists have opinions and make value judgments. When economists, or anyone else for that matter, express opinions about some economic policy or statement, they are indicating in part how they believe things should be, not just facts as to the way things are. **Normative analysis** expresses opinions about the desirability of various actions. Normative statements involve judgments about what should be or what ought to happen. For example, one could judge that incomes should be more equally distributed. If there is a change in tax policy that makes incomes more equal, there will be positive economic questions that can be investigated, such as how work behaviour will change. But we cannot say, as scientists, that such a policy is good or bad; rather, we can point to what will likely happen if the policy is adopted.

normative analysis
a subjective, non-testable statement—how the economy should be

POSITIVE VERSUS NORMATIVE STATEMENTS

The distinction between positive and normative analysis is important. It is one thing to say that everyone should have universal health care, a normative statement, and quite another to say that universal health care would lead to greater worker productivity, a

In The **NEWS**

FEDERAL GOVERNMENT URGED TO KEEP FOCUSED ON DEBT CUTS

BY ERIC BEAUCHESNE

Despite years of federal budget surpluses, the interest charges on the nation's $501-billion debt still run at about $35 billion a year, or $95 million a day, say Canada's chartered accountants.

The Canadian Institute of Chartered Accountants, amid a flurry of last-minute, pre-budget appeals . . . , urged Finance Minister Ralph Goodale to limit spending and keep cutting the debt in [the 2005] budget.

"With a minority government facing increased spending pressures and an annual debt service cost approximating $35 billion, the federal government should not forget that the interest meter is still running at a pace of $95 million each day," David Hope, chair of the institute, said . . . .

Almost 20 cents of every dollar in federal revenue still goes toward interest payments on the debt, noted the group.

"This is similar to an individual earning $50,000 a year being obligated to pay a $9,600 interest bill at the start of each year," it said.

The accountants calculated that Ottawa will save $50 million a year in reduced charges for each $1-billion reduction in interest-bearing debt.

"We have seen good progress on paying down the debt, but the total debt still accounts for almost 40 per cent of annual GDP," Hope said. "There remains a long way to go to reach the government's 25 per cent of GDP target."

The accountants, in calling for increased debt reduction, urged the government to do more than just restrain spending. It also wants Ottawa to improve its accountability of expenditures.

"Even if the government were to keep future spending essentially constant in per-capita terms there would be very little latitude for new initiatives in the next two years," it said.

Meanwhile, a report by a right-wing economic think-tank urged Goodale to focus on improving productivity and economic performance, as well as controlling spending.

The Fraser Institute recommended stringent controls on new spending, prioritizing existing expenditures, a multi-year tax relief program—including elimination of the federal capital tax—reductions in corporate and personal income taxes and reforms in the way services are delivered.

"Since 1997, the year Canada finally balanced its books, there have been continued excessive spending increases, a lack of meaningful tax relief, and avoidance of competitiveness and productivity-related issues," said institute economist Jason Clemens. "The depth of new spending has been truly startling."

It calculated that since the government balanced its books in 1997, program spending has increased by $42.1 billion or 39.8 per cent, outstripping by a wide margin the 6.8 per cent increase in population and 15.8 per cent rise in inflation.

SOURCE: Eric Beauchesne. "Feds urged to keep focus on debt cuts." *The Windsor Star.* February 19, 2005. p. A19. Material reprinted with the express permission of: "CANWEST NEWS SERVICE", a CanWest Partnership.

CONSIDER THIS:
When the Canadian Institute of Chartered Accountants urged the finance minister to cut the debt and to limit spending in the upcoming budget, it was expressing its opinion about economic policy. This is an example of normative analysis.

testable positive statement. It is important to distinguish between positive and normative analysis because many controversies in economics revolve around policy considerations that contain both. When economists start talking about how the economy should work rather than how it does work, they have entered the normative world of the policymaker.

DISAGREEMENT IS COMMON IN MOST DISCIPLINES

Although economists differ frequently on economic policy questions, there is probably less disagreement than the media would have you believe. Disagreement is common in most disciplines: Seismologists differ over predictions of earthquakes or volcanic eruption; historians can be at odds over the interpretation of historical events; psychologists disagree on proper ways to rear children; and nutritionists debate the merits of large doses of vitamin C.

The majority of disagreements in economics stem from normative issues, as differences in values or policy beliefs result in conflict. As we discussed earlier in this chapter, economists may emphasize specific facts over other facts when trying to develop support for their own hypothesis. As a result, disagreements can result when one economist gives weight to facts that have been minimized by another, and vice versa.

Freedom Versus Fairness

Some economists are concerned about individual freedom and liberty, thinking that any encroachment on individual decision making is, other things equal, bad. People with this philosophic bent are inclined to be skeptical of any increased government involvement in the economy.

On the other hand, some economists are concerned with what they consider an unequal, "unfair," or unfortunate distribution of income, wealth, or power, and view governmental intervention as desirable in righting injustices that they believe exist in a market economy. To these persons, the threat to individual liberty alone is not sufficiently great to reject governmental intervention in the face of perceived economic injustice.

The Validity of an Economic Theory

Aside from philosophic differences, there is a second reason why economists may differ on any given policy question. Specifically, they may disagree as to the validity of a given economic theory for the policy in question. Suppose two economists have identical philosophical views that have led them to the same conclusion: To end injustice and hardship, unemployment should be reduced. To reach the objective, the first economist believes the government should lower taxes and increase spending, whereas the second economist believes increasing the amount of money in public hands by various banking policies will achieve the same results with fewer undesirable consequences. The two economists differ because the empirical evidence for economic theories about the cause of unemployment appears to conflict. Some evidence suggests government taxation and spending policies are effective in reducing unemployment, whereas other evidence suggests that the prime cause of unnecessary unemployment lies with faulty monetary policy. Still other evidence is consistent with the view that, over long periods, neither approach mentioned here is of much value in reducing unemployment, and that unemployment will be part of our existence no matter what macroeconomic policies we follow.

ECONOMISTS DO AGREE

Although you may not believe it after reading the previous discussion, economists don't always disagree. In fact, according to a survey among members of the American Economic Association, most economists agree on a wide range of issues, including rent control, import tariffs, export restrictions, the use of wage and price controls to curb inflation, and the minimum wage.

Scarcity

- What is scarcity?
- What are goods and services?

KNOW A FEW PRINCIPLES WELL

Most of economics is really knowing certain principles well and knowing when and how to apply them. In the following sections, some important tools are presented that will help you understand the economic way of thinking. These few basic ideas will repeatedly occur throughout the text. If you develop a good understanding of these principles and master the problem-solving skills inherent in them, they will serve you well for the rest of your life.

SCARCITY

As we have already mentioned, economics is concerned primarily with **scarcity**—how we satisfy our unlimited wants in a world of limited resources. We may want more "essential" items like food, clothing, schooling, and health care. We may want many other items, like vacations, cars, computers, and concert tickets. We may want more friendship, love, knowledge, and so on. We also may have many goals—perhaps an A in this class, a university education, and a great job. Unfortunately, people are not able to fulfill all of their wants—material desires and nonmaterial desires. And as long as human wants exceed available resources, scarcity will exist.

scarcity
exists when human wants (material and nonmaterial) exceed available resources

SCARCITY AND RESOURCES

The scarce resources used in the production of goods and services can be grouped into four categories: labour, land, capital, and entrepreneurship.

    Labour is the total of both physical and mental effort expended by people in the production of goods and services.

labour
the physical and human effort used in the production of goods and services

land
the natural resources used in the production of goods and services

capital
the equipment and structures used to produce goods and services

human capital
the productive knowledge and skill people receive from education and on-the-job training

entrepreneurship
the process of combining labour, land, and capital together to produce goods and services

goods
items we value or desire

service
an intangible act that people want, like treatment from a doctor or a dentist

Land includes the "gifts of nature" or the natural resources used in the production of goods and services. Trees, animals, water, minerals, and so on are all considered to be "land" for our purposes, along with the physical space normally thought of as land.

Capital is the equipment and structures used to produce goods and services. Office buildings, tools, machines, and factories are all considered capital goods. When we invest in factories, machines, research and development, or education, we increase the potential to create more goods and services in the future. Capital also includes **human capital,** the productive knowledge and skills people receive from education and on-the-job training.

Entrepreneurship is the process of combining labour, land, and capital together to produce goods and services. Entrepreneurs make the tough and risky decisions about what and how to produce goods and services. Entrepreneurs are always looking for new ways to improve production techniques or to create new products. They are lured by the chance to make a profit. It is this opportunity to make a profit that leads entrepreneurs to take risks.

However, entrepreneurs are not necessarily a Bill Gates (Microsoft), a Ted Rogers (Rogers Communications), or a Paul Desmarais (Power Corporation). In some sense, we are all entrepreneurs when we try new products or when we find better ways to manage our households or our study time. Rather than money, then, our profits might take the form of greater enjoyment, additional time for recreation, or better grades.

GOODS AND SERVICES

Goods are those items that we value or desire. Goods tend to be tangible—objects that can be seen, held, heard, tasted, or smelled. **Services** are intangible acts for which people are willing to pay, such as legal services, medical services, and dental care. Services are intangible because they are less overtly visible, but they are certainly no less valuable than goods. All goods and services, whether tangible or intangible, are produced from scarce resources and can be subjected to economic analysis. If there are not enough goods and services for all of us, we will have to compete for those scarce goods and services. That is, scarcity ultimately leads to competition for the available goods and services, a subject we will return to often in the text.

EVERYONE FACES SCARCITY

We all face scarcity because we cannot have all of the goods and services that we desire. However, because we all have different wants and desires, scarcity affects everyone differently. For example, a child in a developing country may face a scarcity of food and clean drinking water, whereas a rich person may face a scarcity of garage space for his growing antique car collection. Likewise, a harried middle-class working mother may find time for exercise particularly scarce, whereas a pharmaceutical company may be concerned with the scarcity of the natural resources it uses in its production process. Although its effects vary, no one can escape scarcity.

Section Check   SECTION CHECK

1. We all have many wants and goals.
2. Scarcity exists when our wants exceed the available resources.
3. Scarce resources can be categorized as: land (all of our natural resources), labour (the physical and mental efforts expended in the production of goods and services), capital (the equipment and structures used to produce goods and services, the productive knowledge and skills people receive from education and on-the-job traning), and entrepreneurship (the process of combining land, labour, and capital into production of goods and services).
4. Goods and services are things that we value.

Opportunity Cost

- Why do we have to make choices?
- What do we give up when we have to choose?
- Why are "free" lunches not free?

SCARCITY AND CHOICES

We may want nice homes, two luxury cars in every garage, wholesome and good-tasting food, a personal trainer, and a therapist, all enjoyed in a pristine environment with zero pollution. If we had unlimited resources, and thus an ability to produce all of the goods and services anyone wanted, we would not have to choose among those desires. If we did not have to make meaningful economic choices, the study of economics would not be necessary. The essence of economics is to understand fully the implications that scarcity has for wise decision making. This suggests another way to define economics: *Economics is the study of the choices we make among our many wants and desires.*

TO CHOOSE IS TO LOSE

We are all faced with scarcity and, as a consequence, we must make choices. Because none of us can "afford" to buy everything we want, each time we do decide to buy one good or service, we reduce our ability to buy other things we would also like to have. If you buy a new car this year, you may not be able to afford your next best choice—the vacation you've been planning. You must choose. The cost of the car to you is the value of the vacation that must be forgone. The highest or best forgone opportunity resulting from a decision is called the **opportunity cost.** For example, time spent running costs time that could have been spent doing something else that is valuable—perhaps spending time with friends or studying for an upcoming exam. Another way to put this is that "to choose is to lose" or "an opportunity cost is an opportunity lost." To get more of anything that is desirable, you must accept less of something else that you also value.

opportunity cost
the value of the best forgone alternative that was not chosen

THE OPPORTUNITY COST OF GOING TO UNIVERSITY OR HAVING A CHILD

The average person often does not correctly consider opportunity costs when thinking about costs. For example, the cost of going to university is not just the direct costs of tuition and books. It also includes the opportunity cost of your time, which for many people is the greatest part of their costs. Specifically, the time spent going to school is time that could have been spent on a job earning, say, $25 000 a year. And how often do people consider the cost of raising a child to the age of 18? There are the obvious costs: food, visits to the dentist, clothes, piano lessons, time spent at soccer practices, and so on. But there are also other substantial opportunity costs incurred in rearing a child. Consider the opportunity cost if one parent chooses to give up his or her job to stay at home. Then, the time spent in child-rearing is time that could have been used making money and pursuing a career.

IS THAT REALLY A FREE LUNCH, OR A FREE LIBRARY?

The expression *"there's no such thing as a free lunch"* clarifies the relationship between scarcity and opportunity cost. Suppose the school cafeteria is offering "free" lunches today. Although the lunch is free to you, is it really free from society's perspective? The answer is no, because some of society's scarce resources will have been used in the preparation of the lunch. The issue is whether the resources that went into creating that lunch could have been used to produce something else of value. Clearly, the scarce resources that went into the production of the lunch like the labour and materials (food-service workers, lettuce, meat, ploughs, tractors, fertilizer, and so forth) could have been used in other ways. They had an opportunity cost, and thus were not free. Whenever you hear the word "free"— free libraries, free admission, and so on—an alarm should go off in your head. Very few things are free in the sense that they use none of society's scarce resources. So what does a free lunch really mean? It is, technically speaking, a "subsidized" lunch—a lunch using society's scarce resources, but one for which you personally do not have to pay.

In The NEWS

THE COST OF ELECTRICITY

BY WILLIAM WATSON

What's a thing worth? It's a question philosophers have worried about at least since Plato. We economists have a partial and in many ways unsatisfactory answer, but at least it's an answer: One measure of a thing's worth is what people are willing to pay for it.

Take electricity. In Quebec, we produce lots of electricity and don't actually charge ourselves very much for it: a little over six cents per kilowatt/hour for residential customers (as of April 2004) and even less for big industrial users. Nearby U.S. cities pay a lot more: over 15 cents in Boston, over 18 cents in New York.

So what's Quebec's electricity worth: six cents, which is what we charge ourselves for it, or almost three times that, which is what Americans would pay for it?

Why, people say, should we charge ourselves much more than our cost of producing a valuable natural resource that supports energy-intensive industry that hires lots of local people and pays them good wages?

"For the money," is the answer to that one. Suppose Hydro-Quebec did charge American rates for energy that costs less than six cents to produce. Its profits would soar— by more than $5 billion, according to its own estimates. That money could be used to reduce taxes or public debts or to finance spending on health or education or anything the gov-

ernment fancied. If [Quebecers] had lower taxes, better roads, a health-care system people could depend on, better universities and so on, wouldn't that create jobs?

Would hikes in electricity prices hit poor people disproportionately? Maybe they would, but to prevent that we could provide rebates to poor people that cover the higher costs they'd face. Would that defeat a key purpose of higher prices, namely getting people to economize on their use of a valuable scarce resource, which is what energy is? It might, a bit. But think about it. If I gave you $500 to compensate for the increase in your energy bill, would it be rational for you to take the $500 and spend it all on now much higher-priced energy? Probably not. What's more likely is that you would substitute away from energy and buy other things.

SOURCE: Adapted from William Watson, "Higher Electicity Prices Make Cents," *Ottawa Citizen*, March 22, 2005, p. A13. Reprinted with permission from the author.

CONSIDER THIS:
The real cost of electricity is its opportunity cost, which is the benefit Quebecers give up by consuming it themselves rather than selling it to Americans, who would pay up to three times the price.

Section Check

1. Scarcity means we all have to make choices.
2. When we are forced to choose, we give up the next highest-valued alternative.
3. Opportunity cost is what you give up when you make a choice.

Marginal Thinking

- What do we mean by marginal thinking?
- What is the rule of rational choice?
- Why do we use the word "expected" with marginal benefits and costs?

CHOICES ARE PRIMARILY MARGINAL—NOT ALL OR NOTHING

Most choices involve how *much* of something to do, rather than whether or not to do something. It is not *whether* you eat, but *how much* you eat. Hopefully, the question is not *whether* to study this semester but instead *how much* to study this semester. For example, "If I studied a little more, I might be able to improve my grade," or "If I had a little better concentration when I was studying, I could improve my grade." This is what economists call **marginal thinking** because the focus is on the additional, or marginal, choices. Marginal choices involve the effects of adding to or subtracting from the current situation. In short, it is the small (or large) incremental changes to a plan of action.

Always watch out for the difference between average and marginal costs. Suppose the cost to an airline of flying 250 passengers from Edmonton to Montreal was $100 000. The average cost per seat would be $400 (the total cost divided by the number of seats— $100 000/250). If ten people are on standby and willing to pay $300 for a seat on the flight, should the airline sell them a ticket? Yes! The unoccupied seats earn nothing for the airline. The airline pays the $400 average cost per seat regardless of whether or not someone is sitting in the seat or not. What the airline needs to focus on are the additional (marginal) costs of a few extra passengers. The marginal costs are minimal—slight wear and tear on the airplane, handling some extra baggage, and ten extra inflight meals. In this case, thinking at the margin can increase total profits, even it if means selling at less-than-average cost of production.

Another good example of marginal thinking is auctions. Prices are bid up marginally as the auctioneer calls out one price after another. When a bidder views the new price (the marginal cost) to be greater than the value she places on the good (the marginal benefit), she withdraws from further bidding.

In trying to make themselves better off, people alter their behaviour if the expected marginal benefits from doing so outweigh the expected marginal costs—this is the **rule of rational choice.** The term *expected* is used with marginal benefits and costs because the world is uncertain in many important respects, so the actual result of changing behaviour may not always make people better off—but on average it will. However, as a matter of rationality, people are assumed to engage only in behaviour that they think ahead of time will make them better off. That is, individuals will only pursue an activity if expected marginal benefits are greater than the expected marginal costs, or $E(MB) > E(MC)$. This fairly unrestrictive and realistic view of individuals seeking self-betterment can be used to analyze a variety of social phenomena.

marginal thinking
focusing on the additional, or marginal, choices; marginal choices involve the effects of adding to or subtracting from the current situation, the small (or large) incremental changes to a plan of action

rule of rational choice
individuals will pursue an activity if the expected marginal benefits are greater than the expected marginal costs

Zero Pollution Would Be Too Costly

Let's use the concept of marginal thinking to evaluate pollution levels. We all know the benefits of a cleaner environment, but what would we have to give up—that is, what marginal costs would we have to incur—in order to achieve zero pollution? A lot! You could not drive a car, fly in a plane, or even ride a bike, especially if everybody else was riding bikes too (because congestion is a form of pollution). How would you get to school or

What would you be willing to give up to eliminate the rush-hour congestion you face? Think of the number of hours drivers waste each year sitting in traffic in Canada's largest cities. It costs the Canadian economy hundreds of millions of dollars a year in lost wages and wasted fuel.

work, or go to the movies or the grocery store? Everyone would have to grow their own food because transporting, storing, and producing food uses machinery and equipment that pollutes. And even growing your own food would be a problem because many plants emit natural pollutants. We could go on and on. The point is *not* that we shouldn't be concerned about the environment; rather, we have to weigh the expected marginal benefits of a cleaner environment against the expected marginal costs of a cleaner environment. This is not to say the environment should not be cleaner, only that zero pollution levels would be far too costly in terms of what we would have to give up.

Optimal (Best) Levels of Safety

Just as we can have optimal (or best) levels of pollution that are greater than zero, it is also true for crime and safety. Take crime. What would it cost society to have zero crime? It would be prohibitively costly to divert a tremendous amount of our valuable resources towards the total elimination of crime. In fact, it would be impossible to eliminate crime totally. But it would also be costly to reduce crime significantly. Since lower crime rates are costly, society must decide how much it is willing to give up: The additional resources for crime prevention can only come from limited resources, which could be used to produce something else possibly valued even more.

The same is true for safer products. Nobody wants defective tires on their cars, or cars that are unsafe and roll over at low speeds. However, there are optimal amounts of safety that are greater than zero too. The issue is not safe versus unsafe products but rather *how much* safety consumers want. It is not risk versus no-risk but rather *how much* risk are we willing to take? Additional safety can only come at higher costs. To make all products perfectly safe would be impossible, so we must weigh the benefits and costs of safer products. In fact, according to one U.S. study by Sam Peltzman, a University of Chicago economist, additional safety regulations in cars (mandatory safety belts, padded dashboards) in the late 1960s may have had little impact on highway fatalities. Peltzman found that making cars safer led to more reckless driving and more accidents. Although the safety regulations did result in fewer deaths per automobile accident, the total number of deaths remained unchanged because there were more accidents.

Reckless driving has benefits—getting somewhere more quickly—but it also has costs—possibly causing an accident or even a fatality. Rational people will compare the marginal benefits and marginal costs of safer driving and make the choices that they believe will get them to their destination safely. We would expect that even thrill-seekers would slow down if there were higher fines and/or increased law enforcement. It would change the benefit–cost equation for reckless driving (as would bad brakes, bald tires, and poor visibility). On the other hand, compulsory seat belts and air bags might cause motorists to drive more recklessly.

Section Check

1. Economists are usually interested in the effects of additional, or marginal, changes in a given situation.
2. People try to make themselves better off.
3. People make decisions based on what they expect to happen.
4. The rule of rational choice states that individuals will pursue an activity if they expect the marginal benefits to be greater than the marginal costs, or $E(MB) > E(MC)$.
5. The optimal (best) levels of pollution, crime, and safety are greater than zero.

Incentives Matter

- Can we predict how people will respond to changes in incentives?
- What are positive incentives?
- What are negative incentives?

PEOPLE RESPOND TO INCENTIVES

In acting rationally, people are responding to incentives. That is, they are reacting to the changes in expected marginal benefits and expected marginal costs. In fact, much of human behaviour can be explained and predicted as a response to incentives. Consider the economic view of crime. Why do criminals engage in their "occupation"? Presumably because the "job," even with its risks, is preferred to alternative forms of employment. For criminals, the benefits of their actions are higher and/or the opportunity costs of them are lower than is the case for noncriminals. In some cases, criminals cannot get a legitimate job at a wage they would find acceptable, so the cost of crime in terms of other income forgone may be quite low. At other times, the likelihood of being caught is small, so the expected cost is negligible. Also, for some, the moral cost of a crime is low, whereas for others it is high. The benefits, in terms of wealth gained, are clear. If the expected gains or benefits from committing a crime outweigh the expected costs, the activity is pursued. For most policy purposes, the primary concern is not what causes the level of crime to be what it is but, rather, what causes the level of crime to change. Changes in the crime rate can be largely explained in terms of such a benefit–cost framework. If the benefits of crime rise, say, in the form of larger real "hauls," and/or if the costs fall due to a reduced likelihood of being caught or of being imprisoned if caught, then economists would expect the amount of crime to rise. Likewise, economists would expect the crime rate to fall in response to increased police enforcement, stiffer punishments, or an increase in the employment rate. Whether or not this analysis tells the complete story is debatable, but the use of the economic framework in thinking about the problem provides valuable insight.

POSITIVE AND NEGATIVE INCENTIVES

Almost all of economics can be reduced to incentive [$E(MB)$ versus $E(MC)$] stories, where consumers and producers are driven by incentives that affect expected costs or benefits. Prices, wages, profits, taxes, and subsidies are all examples of economic incentives.

ACTIVE LEARNING EXERCISE

DO INCENTIVES MATTER?

Q: The penalty for drug trafficking in Singapore is death. Do you think there would be more drug traffickers in Singapore if the mandatory sentence were five years with parole for good behaviour?

A: Singapore's tough drug-trafficking penalty would clearly impact the cost–benefit ratios of would-be smugglers. Lighter sentences would probably result in more drug smuggling because the overall cost of breaking the law would be reduced.

positive incentives
incentives that either reduce costs or increase benefits resulting in an increase in the activity or behaviour

negative incentives
incentives that either increase costs or reduce benefits resulting in a decrease in the activity or behaviour

Incentives can be classified into two types: positive and negative. **Positive incentives** are those that either increase benefits or reduce costs and thus result in an increased level of the related activity or behaviour. **Negative incentives,** on the other hand, either reduce benefits or increase costs, resulting in a decreased level of the related activity or behaviour. For example, a tax on cars that emit lots of pollution (an increase in costs) would be a negative incentive that would lead to a reduction in emitted pollution. On the other hand, a subsidy (the opposite of a tax) to hybrid cars—part electric, part internal combustion— would be a positive incentive that would encourage greater production and consumption of hybrid cars. Human behaviour is influenced in predictable ways by such changes in economic incentives, and economists use this information to predict what will happen when the benefits and costs of any choice are changed. In short, economists study the incentives and consequences of particular actions.

A subsidy on hybrid electric vehicles (HEVs) would be a positive incentive that would encourage greater production and consumption of these vehicles. Honda's Insight is expected to go 1100 kilometres on a single tank of gas; the Toyota Prius is expected to go about 700 kilometres.

© Jose Gil/Shutterstock

In The **NEWS**

MORE MONEY FOR HEALTH CARE WON'T HELP

BY ANDREW COYNE

In . . . 2003–04, provincial and territorial governments across Canada spent roughly $80 billion on health care, according to figures compiled by the Canadian Institute for Health Information. Per capita, that works out to just under $2,500—the highest it has ever been.

In 1978–79, by way of comparison, government spending on health care totalled just $12.6 billion. Adjusting for differences in population and prices, that's about $1,450 per capita, in today's dollars. In other words, governments today are spending nearly twice as much real dollars on each citizen as they did a generation ago, just to provide basic health care.

That's not counting the growing cost of things for which Canadians are required to pay out of pocket, including the lengthening list of services that are no longer covered by medicare. These add another $40 billion or so to the national

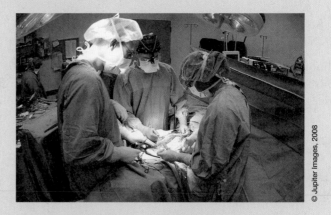

© Jupiter Images, 2008

tab, or roughly two and a half times as much as in 1979— again, that's per capita, after inflation.

And yet the one thing on which everyone agrees—and I mean everyone: doctors, nurses, Ottawa, the provinces,

IN THE NEWS *(continued)*

conservatives, liberals—is that the system is in desperate need of more money. Left-wingers want more public funds to be ploughed into it. Right-wingers want to open it up to user fees, parallel private systems, and the like. But both are united in the belief that there's nothing wrong with medicare that a little more cash (well, a lot more) couldn't solve.

We spend 10% of GDP on health care today, in return for which we wait six months or more for many surgeries. Thirty years ago, we spent just 7% of GDP on health, and waiting lists were unknown. Possibly the issue is not how much is spent, but how well. Perhaps, if resources were used more efficiently, we might find it possible to provide more services with shorter wait times—out of existing funds. Yet many analysts continue to insist there is very little in savings to be squeezed out of the system.

Just one question: How do they know? A few years ago, a Canadian Policy Research Networks study estimated it was possible to save as much as $7 billion, merely by getting the provinces to adopt existing "best practices" across the country: that is, without requiring any innovation or discovery, but simply on the basis of known methodologies, already in place in one part of the system or another. But that's a little like treating a patient with the help of the best medical minds, circa 1350: What is unknown vastly exceeds what is known.

The system is often and aptly described as a "black box," in which resources are allocated without the most elementary data on the costs and benefits of different procedures. The Kirby committee was startled to find, in interviews with hospital administrators across the country—people with three and four degrees, and years of managerial experience—that, in the blunt language of its report, "no one knows what anything costs."

How can this be? Quite simply, it had never occurred to anyone to ask. The system of funding is positively Soviet: Hospitals typically get so much for scalpels, so much for rubber gloves, and so forth. There's often no connection with how many patients they treat, or what procedures they perform. In the absence of such information, there is no real basis for competition among hospitals, and in the absence of competition, there is no incentive to collect it. But put a price on the services hospitals provide, and fund them

accordingly, as Kirby recommends, and suddenly a functioning market becomes possible: an "internal market," wholly within the publicly funded universe.

Doctors, on the other hand, are paid on a fee for service basis, and so could be said to operate under a rudimentary price system. But since they can always just pass the tab on to the government, they too have little incentive to economize: In fact, as countless studies have concluded, they have every incentive to load a patient up with services they don't need. That's why many reform models include shifting doctors to a "capitation" system of payment, allotting them a fixed annual budget depending on the number of patients they see. This has much the same practical effect as user fees—i.e., imposing budget discipline at a "micro" level—without raising the same issues of accessibility.

In an odd sense, medicare's weakness is its strength. Had we any reason to believe the system was operating at maximum efficiency, and still found waiting lists and other signs of strain, then it would indeed be time to think about injecting more cash, whether public or private. But since in fact there is every reason to think the system is massively inefficient, it should be possible to make quite significant improvements, without spending more money and without departing from the ideal of public funding.

SOURCE: Adapted from Andrew Coyne, "Tossing Money at Medicare Won't Help," *National Post*, September 8, 2004, p. A1. Material reprinted with the express permission of: "The National Post Company", a CanWest Partnership.

CONSIDER THIS:

If the health-care system is inefficient in its use of resources, then it could be possible to make improvements in the health-care system without spending more money. One way to improve efficiency is to change the incentives in the system. For example, by putting a price on the services, hospitals would have an incentive to economize on their use of resources. Similarly, by shifting doctors to a capitation system of payment, they would not have the incentive to load a patient up with services the patient does not need.

Section Check

1. People respond to incentives in predictable ways.
2. A negative incentive increases costs or reduces benefits, thus discouraging consumption or production.
3. A positive incentive decreases costs or increases benefits, thus encouraging consumption or production.

section

1.7

Specialization and Trade

- What is the relationship between opportunity cost and specialization?
- What are the advantages of specialization in production?

WHY DO PEOPLE SPECIALIZE?

As you look around, you can see that people specialize in what they produce. They tend to dedicate their resources to one primary activity, whether it be child-rearing, driving a bus, or making bagels. Why is this? The answer, short and simple, is opportunity costs. By concentrating their energies on only one, or a few, activities, individuals are **specializing.** This allows them to make the best use of (and thus gain the most benefit from) their limited resources. A person, a region, or a country can gain by specializing in the production of the good in which they have a comparative advantage. That is, if they can produce a good or service at a lower opportunity cost than others, we say that they have a **comparative advantage** in the production of that good or service.

specializing
concentrating in the production of one, or a few, goods

comparative advantage
producing a good or service at a lower opportunity cost than other producers

WE ALL SPECIALIZE

We all specialize to some extent and rely on others to produce most of the goods and services we want. The work that we choose to do reflects our specialization. For example, we may specialize in selling or fixing automobiles. The wages from that work can then be used to buy goods from a farmer who has chosen to specialize in the production of food. Likewise, the farmer can use the money earned from selling his produce to get his tractor fixed by someone who specializes in that activity.

Specialization is evident not only among individuals but among regions and countries as well. In fact, the story of the economic development of Canada involves specialization. Within Canada, the prairies with their wheat, the Maritime provinces of Eastern Canada with their fishing fleets, and British Columbia with its lumber are all examples of regional specialization.

ACTIVE LEARNING EXERCISE

COMPARATIVE ADVANTAGE

Q: Should a lawyer who types 100 words per minute hire an administrative assistant to type her legal documents, even though he can only type 50 words per minute? If the lawyer does the job, she can do it in five hours; if the administrative assistant does the job, it takes him ten hours. The lawyer makes $100 an hour, and the administrative assistant earns $10 an hour. Which one has the comparative advantage (the lowest opportunity cost) in typing documents?

A: If the lawyer types her own documents, it will cost $500 ($100 per hour × 5 hours). If she has the administrative assistant type her documents, it will cost $100 ($10 per hour × 10 hours). Clearly, then, the lawyer should hire the administrative assistant to type her documents because the administrative assistant has the comparative advantage (lowest opportunity cost) in this case, despite being half as good in absolute terms.

THE ADVANTAGES OF SPECIALIZATION

In a small business, employees may perform a wide variety of tasks—from hiring to word processing to marketing. As the size of the company increases, each employee can perform a more specialized job, with a consequent increase in output per worker. The primary advantages of specialization are that employees acquire greater skill from repetition, they avoid wasted time in shifting from one task to another, and they do the types of work for which they are best suited, and it promotes the use of specialized equipment for specialized tasks.

The advantages of specialization are seen throughout the workplace. For example, in larger firms, specialists conduct personnel relations and accounting is in the hands of full-time accountants instead of someone with half a dozen other tasks to perform. The owner of a small retail store selects the location for the store primarily through guesswork, placing it where she believes sales would be high or where an empty, low-rent building is available. In contrast, larger chains have store sites selected by experts who have experience in analyzing the factors that make different locations relatively more desirable, like traffic patterns, income levels, demographics, and so on.

SPECIALIZATION AND TRADE LEAD TO GREATER WEALTH AND PROSPERITY

Trade, or voluntary exchange, directly increases wealth by making both parties better off (or they wouldn't trade). It is the prospect of wealth-increasing exchange that leads to productive specialization. That is, trade increases wealth by allowing a person, a region, or a nation to specialize in those products that it produces at a lower opportunity cost and to trade for those products that others produce at a lower opportunity cost. For example, say Canada is better at producing wheat than Brazil, and Brazil is better at producing coffee than Canada. Canada and Brazil would each benefit if Canada produces wheat and trades some of it to Brazil for coffee. Coffee growers in Canada could grow coffee in expensive greenhouses, but it would result in higher coffee costs and prices, while leaving fewer resources available for employment in more productive jobs, such as wheat production. This is true for individuals, too. Imagine Tom had 10 kilograms of tea and Katherine had 10 kilograms of coffee. However, Tom preferred coffee to tea and Katherine preferred tea to coffee. So if Tom traded his tea to Katherine for her coffee, both parties would be better off. Trade simply reallocates existing goods, and voluntary exchange increases wealth by making both parties better off, or they would not agree to trade.

Section Check

1. We all specialize.
2. Specialization is important for individuals, businesses, regions, and nations.
3. Specialization and trade increase wealth.
4. The person, region, or country that can produce a good or service at a lower opportunity cost than other producers has a comparative advantage in the production of that good or service.

Market Prices Coordinate Economic Activity

- How does a market system allocate scarce resources?
- What are the important signals that market prices communicate?
- What are the effects of price controls and price supports?
- What are unintended consequences?
- What is a market failure?

HOW DOES THE MARKET SYSTEM WORK TO ALLOCATE RESOURCES?

In a world of scarcity, competition is inescapable, and one method of allocating resources among competing uses is the market system. The market system provides a way for millions of producers and consumers to allocate scarce resources. Buyers and sellers indicate their wants through their actions and inaction in the marketplace, and it is this collective "voice" that determines how resources are allocated. But how is this information communicated? Market prices serve as the language of the market system. By understanding what these market prices mean, you can get a better understanding of the vital function that the market system performs.

MARKET PRICES PROVIDE IMPORTANT INFORMATION

Market prices communicate important information to both buyers and sellers. These prices communicate information about the relative availability of products to buyers, and they provide sellers with critical information about the relative value that consumers place on those products. In effect, market prices provide a way for both buyers and sellers to communicate about the relative value of resources. This communication results in a shifting of resources from those uses that are less valued to those that are more valued. We will see how this works beginning in Chapter 3.

The basis of market economy is the voluntary exchange and the price system that guide people's choices and produces solutions to the questions of what goods to produce and how to produce those goods and distribute them.

Take something as simple as the production of a pencil. Where did the wood come from? Perhaps British Columbia or Quebec. The graphite may have come from the mines in Northern Ontario, and the rubber maybe from Malaysia. The paint, the glue, the metal piece that holds the eraser—who knows? The point is that market forces coordinated this activity among literally thousands of people, some of whom live in different countries and speak different languages. The market system brought these people together to make a pencil that sells for 25 cents at your bookstore. It all happened because the market system provided the incentive for people to pursue activities that benefit others. This same process produces millions of goods and services around the world from automobiles and computers to pencils and paper clips.

In countries that do not rely on the market system, there is no clear communication between buyers and sellers. In the former Soviet Union, where quality was virtually non-existent, there were shortages of quality goods and surpluses of low-quality goods. For example, there were thousands of tractors without spare parts and millions of pairs of shoes that were left on shelves because the sizes did not match those of the population.

In The **NEWS**

RISING FOOD PRICES CAUSING CONSUMERS TO CHANGE HABITS

BY ERIC BEAUCHESNE

OTTAWA—Canadians are not only cutting back on the use of their cars in the wake of surging gasoline prices but are also starting to change their food-buying habits in anticipation of higher food prices, according to new poll results. "Buffeted by continuing increases in gas and energy prices, Canadians are also preparing to change their eating habits and how they shop for food," stated the analysis of the Investors Group poll, released Tuesday. Many of those polled say they are buying more local produce, giving up exotic or out-of-season fruits and vegetables, eating less meat and having more meals at home rather than going to a restaurant.

The results of the survey earlier this month also suggest consumers' inflation fears are dovetailing with their concerns about the viability of non-renewable energy resources. "While concern about rising prices appears to be prompting lifestyle changes, a number of Canadians are also worried about the sustainability of non-renewable resource supplies," the analysis said, noting that 46 per cent fear the world's supply of such resources will be depleted within the next generation.

However, it appears that it took price increases, or in the case of food, the fear of higher prices, to prompt consumers to start acting on those environmental concerns, said Myron Knodel, tax and estate planning specialist with Investors Group, Canada's biggest mutual fund company. "The two, it

appears, are linked to a certain extent but I think the change in behaviour when it comes to spending habits currently . . . was the result of the increase in prices," he said in an interview.

"When prices went up that was an initial shock and people thought we've got to adjust our budgets . . . be more prudent in our spending, and along with that there is a greater awareness of the sustainability of our natural resources, and the two went hand in hand," he said. "But had the price pressures not occurred I do not know that their reaction or behaviour would have changed as much as it has did."

The survey indicated that the "most significant change in behaviour" is where prices have increased the most, at the pumps. For example, 83 per cent plan to buy a more fuel-efficient vehicle when they make their next car purchase.

SOURCE: Eric Beauchesne, "Rising food prices causing consumers to change habits; Higher fuel costs altering spending decisions," *Edmonton Journal*, June 18, 2008, p. E3. Material reprinted with the express permisson of: "CANWEST NEWS SERVICE," a CanWest Partnership.

CONSIDER THIS:

Rising gas prices have communicated important information to consumers about the relative availability of non-renewable resources such as oil. The resulting changes to consumer behaviour—in terms of new-car purchases, what type of food to buy, and where to buy it—are of interest to producers.

WHAT EFFECT DO PRICE CONTROLS HAVE ON THE MARKET SYSTEM?

Government policies called **price controls** sometimes force prices above or below what they would be in a market economy. Unfortunately, these controls often impose harm on the same people they are trying to help, in large part by short-circuiting the market's information transmission function. That is, price controls effectively strip the market price of its meaning for both buyers and sellers (which we will see in Chapters 3 and 4). A sales tax will also distort price signals, leading to a misallocation of resources (which we will see in Chapter 5).

price controls
government-mandated minimum or maximum prices

MARKET FAILURE

The market mechanism is a simple but effective and efficient general means of allocating resources among alternative uses. When the economy fails to allocate resources efficiently on its own, however, it is known as **market failure.** For example, a steel mill might put soot and other forms of "crud" into the air as a by-product of making steel. When it does this, it imposes costs on others not connected with using or producing steel from the steel mill. The soot may require homeowners to paint their homes more often, entailing a cost. And studies show that respiratory diseases are greater in areas with more severe air pollution, imposing costs and often shortening life itself. In addition,

market failure
when the economy fails to allocate resources efficiently on its own

the steel mill might discharge chemicals into a stream, thus killing wildlife and spoiling recreational activities for the local population. In this case, the steel factory does not bear the cost of its polluting actions and emits too much pollution. In other words, by transferring the pollution costs onto society, the firm has lowered its costs of production and is now producing more than the ideal output—this is inefficient because it is an over-allocation of resources.

Markets can also produce too little of a good—research, for example. The government might decide to subsidize promising scientific research that may benefit many people—like cancer research.

Whether the market economy has produced too little (underallocation) or too much (overallocation), the government can improve society's well-being by intervening. The case of market failure will be taken up in more detail in Chapter 6.

In addition, we cannot depend on the market economy to always communicate accurately. Some firms may have market power to distort prices in their favour. For example, the only regional cement company in the area has the ability to charge a higher price and provide a lower-quality product than if the company was in a highly competitive market. In this case, the lack of competition can lead to higher prices and reduced product quality. And without adequate information, unscrupulous producers may be able to misrepresent their products to the disadvantage of unwary consumers.

Does the Market Distribute Income Fairly?

Sometimes a painful trade-off exists between how much an economy can produce efficiently and how that output is distributed—the degree of equality. There is no guarantee that the market economy will provide everyone with adequate amounts of food, shelter, and transportation. That is, not only does the market determine what goods are going to be produced, and in what quantities, but it also determines the distribution of output among members of society. For example, in 2006, the richest 20 percent of Canadian households received 47 percent of the total national income, whereas the poorest 20 percent of Canadian households received only 4 percent of the total national income. Although one person may find it terribly unfair for some individuals to earn many times the amount that other individuals who work equally hard earn, another person may find it highly unfair to ask one group, the relatively rich, to pay a much higher proportion of their income in taxes than another group.

Section Check

1. Scarcity forces us to allocate our limited resources.
2. Market prices provide important information to buyers and sellers.
3. Price controls distort market signals.
4. A market failure is said to occur when the economy fails to allocate resources efficiently.

Summary

Section 1.1
- Economics is the study of the allocation of our limited resources to satisfy our unlimited wants.
- Scarcity refers to "the economic problem" we all face—our wants exceed our limited resources.

- Scarcity forces us to choose, and choices are costly because we must give up other opportunities that we value.
- Economics provides the tools to intelligently evaluate and decide on choices.

- The two branches of economics are microeconomics and macroeconomics: microeconomics focuses on smaller units within the economy—firms and households; macroeconomics deals with the aggregate, or total, economy.

Section 1.2

- Economic theories are statements about patterns of human behaviour.
- Economic theories are tested by using empirical analysis to examine the data and see if our hypothesis fits well with the facts.
- Common pitfalls to avoid when studying economics are: violating the *ceteris paribus* assumption, confusing causation and correlation, and the fallacy of composition.
- Positive analysis is testable and objective ("what is").
- Normative analysis is subjective ("what should or ought to be").

Section 1.3

- Scarcity refers to how we satisfy our unlimited wants with limited resources.
- Resources are defined as inputs—land, labour, capital, and entrepreneurship.
- Goods and services are those items (both tangible and intangible) that we value or desire.

Section 1.4

- Economics is the study of the choices we make among our many wants and desires.
- The opportunity cost of a decision refers to the value of the next-best foregone alternative.

Section 1.5

- Economists are usually interested in the effects of additional, or marginal, changes in a given situation.

- A rational person will generally pursue an activity if he or she perceives the marginal benefits to be greater than the marginal costs, or $E(MB) > E(MC)$—this is sometimes called the rule of rational choice.

Section 1.6

- Economists predict that people will change their behaviour in predictable ways when responding to changes in incentives.
- Positive incentives decrease costs or increase benefits, thus encouraging a particular activity or behaviour.
- Negative incentives increase costs or reduce benefits, thus discouraging a particular activity or behaviour.

Section 1.7

- Trade is generally mutually beneficial, whether it is between two individuals or two countries.
- A person, region, or country that can produce a good or service at a lower opportunity cost than other producers is said to have a comparative advantage in the production of that good or service.
- Trade allows individuals or countries to do what they do best—specialize.
- Specialization and trade increase wealth.

Section 1.8

- Through voluntary exchange and the price system, the market system provides a way for producers and consumers to allocate scarce resources.
- Price controls sometimes force prices above or below what they would be in a market economy.
- A market failure occurs when an economy fails to allocate resources efficiently on its own.

Key Terms and Concepts

For a complete glossary of chapter key terms, visit the textbook's Web site at http://www.sextonmicro2e.nelson.com.

economics 2
resources 2
the economic problem 2
macroeconomics 3
aggregate 3
microeconomics 3
theory 4
hypothesis 4
empirical analysis 4
ceteris paribus 5
correlation 5

causation 5
fallacy of composition 6
positive analysis 6
normative analysis 7
scarcity 9
labour 9
land 10
capital 10
human capital 10
entrepreneurship 10
goods 10

service 10
opportunity cost 11
marginal thinking 13
rule of rational choice 13
positive incentives 16
negative incentives 16
specializing 18
comparative advantage 18
price controls 21
market failure 21

Review Questions

1. Why should we use the *ceteris paribus* assumption in these statements?

   a. Car prices increased and people bought more cars as their incomes rose.

   b. The price of generic shampoo fell and people bought less of it as their income rose.

2. After reading this chapter, see if you can come up with a list of ten topics where you think the economic way of thinking would be helpful in your life.

3. Identify which of the following economic statements are positive and which are normative:

   a. A tax increase will increase unemployment.

   b. The government should reduce funding for social assistance programs.

   c. Tariffs on imported wine will lead to higher prices for domestic wine.

   d. A decrease in the capital gains tax rate will increase investment.

   e. Goods purchased on the Internet should be subject to provincial sales taxes.

   f. A reduction in interest rates will cause inflation.

4. The following statement represents which fallacy in thinking, and why: "I earn $12 per hour. If I am able to earn $12 per hour, everyone should be able to find work for at least that wage rate."

5. Which of the following goods are scarce?

   a. garbage

   b. salt water in the ocean

   c. clothes

   d. clean air in a big city

   e. dirty air in a big city

   f. a public library

6. List the opportunity costs of the following:

   a. going to university

   b. missing a lecture

   c. withdrawing and spending $100 from your savings account, which earns 5 percent interest annually

   d. going snowboarding on the weekend before final examinations

7. Which of the following are positive incentives? negative incentives? Why?

   a. a fine for not cleaning up after your dog defecates in the park

   b. a trip to Quebec City paid for by your parents or significant other for earning an A in your economics course

   c. a higher tax on cigarettes and alcohol

   d. a subsidy for installing solar panels on your house

8. Which region has a comparative advantage in the following goods?

   a. Wheat: Colombia or Canada

   b. Coffee: Colombia or Canada

   c. Lumber: Alberta or British Columbia

   d. Oil: Alberta or British Columbia

9. Why is it important that the country or region with the lower opportunity cost produce the good? How would you use the concept of comparative advantage to argue for reducing restrictions on trade between countries?

10. Imagine that you are trying to decide whether or not to cross a street without using the designated crosswalk at the traffic signal. What are the expected marginal benefits of crossing? the expected marginal costs? How would the following conditions change your benefit–cost equation?

    a. The street was busy.

    b. The street was empty and it was 3 A.M.

    c. You were in a huge hurry.

    d. There was a police officer 10 metres away.

    e. The closest crosswalk was 1 kilometre away.

    f. The closest crosswalk was 5 metres away.

Appendix

GRAPHS ARE AN IMPORTANT ECONOMIC TOOL

Sometimes the use of visual aids, such as graphs, greatly enhances our understanding of a theory. It is much the same as finding your way to a friend's house with the aid of a map rather than with detailed verbal or written instructions. Graphs are important tools for economists. They allow us to understand better the workings of the economy. To economists, a graph can be worth a thousand words. This text will use graphs throughout to enhance the understanding of important economic relationships. This appendix provides a guide on how to read and create your own graphs.

The most useful graph for our purposes is one that merely connects a vertical line (the *Y*-axis) with a horizontal line (the *X*-axis), as seen in Exhibit 1. The intersection of the two lines occurs at the origin, which is where the value of both variables is equal to zero. In Exhibit 1, the graph has four quadrants or "boxes." In this textbook we will be primarily concerned with the shaded box in the upper right-hand corner. This portion of the graph deals exclusively with positive numbers. Always keep in mind that moving to the right on the horizontal axis and up along the vertical axis each lead to higher values.

USING GRAPHS AND CHARTS

Exhibit 2 presents three common types of graphs. The **pie chart** in Exhibit 2(a) shows what college students earn. That is, each slice in the pie chart represents the percent of college students in a particular earnings category. Therefore, pie charts are used to show the relative size of various quantities that add up to a total of 100 percent.

Exhibit 2(b) is a **bar graph** that shows the sales of wireless phone service by province for a new company that has just entered the Canadian market. The height of the line represents sales in millions of dollars. Bar graphs are used to show a comparison of the sizes of quantities of similar items.

Exhibit 2(c) is a **time-series graph.** This type of graph shows changes in the value of a variable over time. This is a visual tool that allows us to observe important trends over a certain time period. In Exhibit 2(c) we see a graph that shows trends in the stock price of Fly-by-Chance Airlines for the period January to December 2008. The horizontal axis shows us the passage of time, and the vertical axis shows us the stock price in dollars per share.

USING GRAPHS TO SHOW THE RELATIONSHIP BETWEEN TWO VARIABLES

Although the graphs and chart in Exhibit 2 are important, they do not allow us to show the relationship between two vari-

Y-axis
the vertical axis on a graph

X-axis
the horizontal axis on a graph

pie chart
a circle subdivided into proportionate slices that represent various quantities that add up to 100 percent

bar graph
represents data using vertical bars rising from the horizontal axis

time-series graph
a type of line chart that plots data trends over time

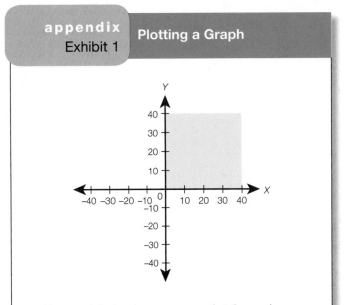

appendix Exhibit 1   Plotting a Graph

In the upper right-hand corner, we see that the graph includes a positive figure for the Y-axis and the X-axis. As we move to the right along the horizontal axis, the numerical values increase. As we move up along the vertical axis, the numerical values increase.

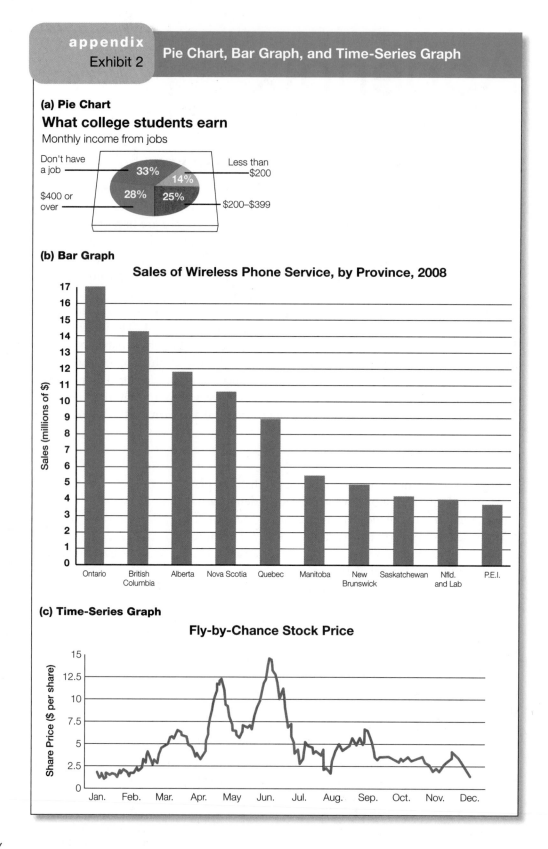

appendix
Exhibit 2

Pie Chart, Bar Graph, and Time-Series Graph

(a) Pie Chart

What college students earn

Monthly income from jobs

Don't have a job — 33%
Less than $200 — 14%
$400 or over — 28%
25% — $200–$399

(b) Bar Graph

Sales of Wireless Phone Service, by Province, 2008

Sales (millions of $)

Ontario, British Columbia, Alberta, Nova Scotia, Quebec, Manitoba, New Brunswick, Saskatchewan, Nfld. and Lab, P.E.I.

(c) Time-Series Graph

Fly-by-Chance Stock Price

Share Price ($ per share)

Jan. Feb. Mar. Apr. May Jun. Jul. Aug. Sep. Oct. Nov. Dec.

variable
something that is measured by a number, such as your height

positive relationship
when two variables change in the same direction

ables (a **variable** is something that is measured by a number, such as your height). To more closely examine the structure of and functions of graphs, let us consider the story of Katherine, an avid inline skater who has aspirations of winning the Z Games next year. To get there, however, she will have to put in many hours of practice. But how many hours? In search of information about the practice habits of other skaters, she logged onto the Internet, where she pulled up the results of a study conducted by ESPM 3 that indicated the score of each Z Games competitor and the amount of practice time per week spent by each skater. The results of this study (see Exhibit 3) indicated that skaters had to practise 10 hours per week to receive a score of 4.0, 20 hours per week to receive a score of 6.0, 30 hours per week to get a score of 8.0, and 40 hours per week to get a perfect score of 10. What does this information tell Katherine? By using a graph, she can more clearly understand the relationship between practice time and overall score.

A Positive Relationship

The study on scores and practice times revealed what is called a direct relationship, also called a positive relationship. A **positive relationship** means that the variables change in the same direction. That is, an increase in one variable (practice time) is accompanied by an increase in the other variable (overall score), or a decrease in one variable (practice time) is accompanied by a decrease in the other variable (overall score). In short, the variables change in the same direction.

A Negative Relationship

When two variables change in opposite directions, we say they are inversely related, or have a **negative relationship.** That is, when one variable rises, the other variable falls, or when one variable decreases, the other variable increases.

THE GRAPH OF A DEMAND CURVE

Let us now examine one of the most important graphs in all of economics—the demand curve. In Exhibit 4, we see Emily's individual demand curve for compact discs. It shows the price of CDs on the vertical axis and the quantity of CDs purchased per month on the horizontal axis. Every point in the space shown represents a price and quantity combination. The downward-sloping line, labelled demand curve, shows the different combinations of price and quantity purchased. Note that the higher you go up on the vertical (price) axis, the smaller the quantity purchased on the horizontal (quantity) axis, and the lower the price on the vertical axis, the greater the quantity purchased.

In Exhibit 4, we see that moving up the vertical price axis from the origin, the price of CDs increases from $5 to $25 in increments of $5. Moving out along the horizontal quantity axis, the quantity purchased increases from zero to five CDs per month. Point A represents a price of $25 and a quantity of one CD, point B represents a price of $20 and a quantity of two CDs, point C, $15 and a quantity of three CDs, and

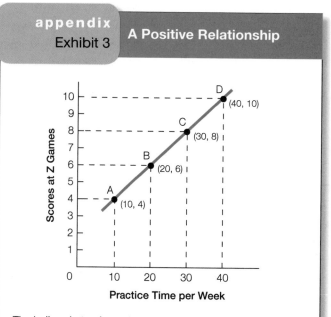

appendix Exhibit 3 — **A Positive Relationship**

The in-line skaters' practice times and scores in the competition are plotted on the graph. Each participant is represented by a point. The graph shows that those skaters who practised the most scored the highest. This is called a positive, or direct, relationship.

negative relationship
when two variables change in opposite directions

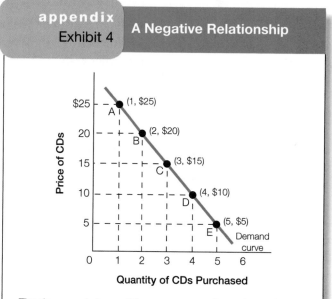

appendix Exhibit 4 — **A Negative Relationship**

The downward slope of the curve means that price and quantity purchased are inversely, or negatively, related: when one increases, the other decreases. That is, moving down along the demand curve from point A to point E, we see that as price falls, the quantity purchased increases. Moving up along the demand curve from point E to point A, we see that as the price increases, the quantity purchased falls.

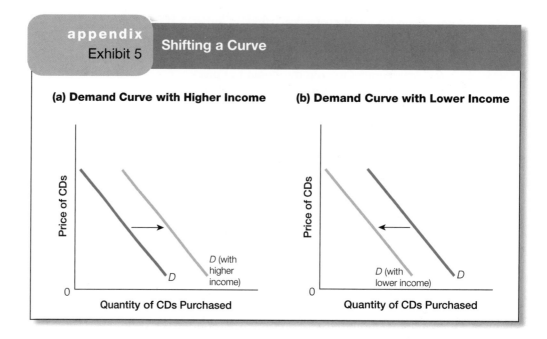

appendix
Exhibit 5   Shifting a Curve

(a) Demand Curve with Higher Income

Price of CDs

Quantity of CDs Purchased

D (with higher income)

D

(b) Demand Curve with Lower Income

Price of CDs

Quantity of CDs Purchased

D (with lower income)

D

so on. When we connect all the points, we have what economists call a curve. As you can see, curves are sometimes drawn as straight lines for ease of illustration. Moving down along the curve, we see that as the price falls, a greater quantity is demanded; moving up the curve to higher prices, a smaller quantity is demanded. That is, when CDs become less expensive, Emily buys more CDs. When CDs become more expensive, Emily buys fewer CDs, perhaps choosing to go to the movies or buy a pizza instead.

USING GRAPHS TO SHOW THE RELATIONSHIP BETWEEN THREE VARIABLES

Although only two variables are shown on the axes, graphs can be used to show the relationship between three variables. For example, say we add a third variable—income—to our earlier example. Our three variables are now income, price, and quantity purchased. If Emily's income rises, say she gets a raise at work, she is now able and willing to buy more CDs than before at each possible price. As a result, the whole demand curve shifts outward (rightward) compared to the old curve. That is, with the new income, she uses some of it to buy more CDs. This is seen in the graph in Exhibit 5(a). On the other hand, if her income falls, say she quits her job to go back to school, she now has less income to buy CDs. This causes the whole demand curve to shift inward (leftward) compared to the old curve. This is seen in the graph in Exhibit 5(b).

The Difference Between a Movement Along and a Shift in the Curve

It is important to remember the difference between a movement between one point and another along a curve and a shift in the whole curve. A change in one of the variables on the graph, like price or quantity purchased, will cause a movement along the curve, say from point A to point B, as shown in Exhibit 6. A change in one of the

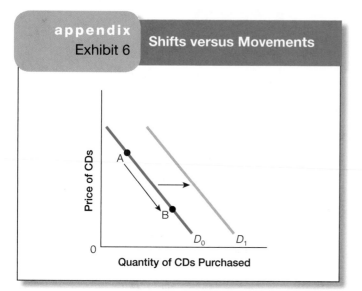

appendix
Exhibit 6   Shifts versus Movements

Price of CDs

A

B

D_0 D_1

Quantity of CDs Purchased

variables not shown (held constant in order to show only the relationship between price and quantity), like income in our example, will cause the whole curve to shift. The change from D_0 to D_1 in Exhibit 6 shows such a shift.

SLOPE

In economics, we sometimes refer to the steepness of the lines or curves on graphs as the **slope.** A slope can be either positive (upward sloping) or negative (downward sloping). A curve that is downward sloping represents an inverse, or negative, relationship between the two variables and slants downward from left to right, as seen in Exhibit 7(a). A curve that is upward sloping represents a direct, or positive, relationship between the two variables and slants upward from left to right, as seen in Exhibit 7(b). The numeric value of the slope shows the number of units of change of the *Y*-axis variable for each unit of change in the *X*-axis variable. Slope provides the direction (positive or negative) as well as the magnitude of the relationship between the two variables.

slope
the ratio of rise (change in the Y variable) over the run (change in the X variable)

Measuring the Slope of a Linear Curve

A straight-line curve is called a linear curve. The slope of a linear curve between two points measures the relative rates of change of two variables. Specifically, the slope of a linear curve can be defined as the ratio of the change in the *Y* value to the change in the *X* value. The slope can also be expressed as the ratio of the rise to the run, where the rise is the change in the *Y* variable (along the vertical axis) and the run is the change in the *X* variable (along the horizontal axis).

In Exhibit 8, we show two linear curves, one with a positive slope and one with a negative slope. In Exhibit 8(a), the slope of the positively sloped linear curve from point A to B is 1/2, because the rise is 1 (from 2 to 3) and the run is 2 (from 1 to 3). In Exhibit 8(b), the negatively sloped linear curve has a slope of −4, a rise of −8 (a fall of 8 from 10 to 2) and a run of 2 (from 2 to 4), which gives us a slope of −4 (−8/2). Note the appropriate signs on the slopes: The negatively sloped line carries a minus sign and the positively sloped line, a plus sign.

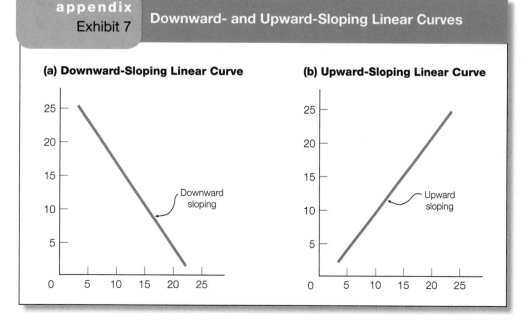

appendix Exhibit 7   **Downward- and Upward-Sloping Linear Curves**

(a) Downward-Sloping Linear Curve

Downward sloping

(b) Upward-Sloping Linear Curve

Upward sloping

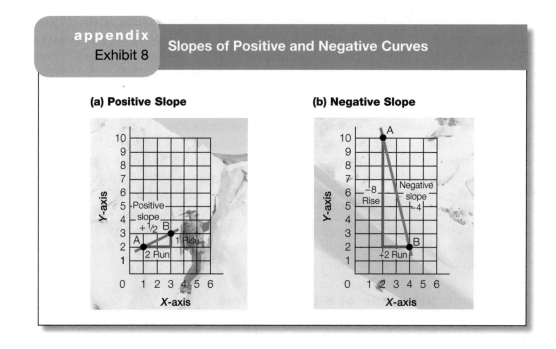

appendix Exhibit 8 **Slopes of Positive and Negative Curves**

Finding the Slope of a Nonlinear Curve

In Exhibit 9, we show the slope of a nonlinear curve. A nonlinear curve is a line that actually curves. Here the slope varies from point to point along the curve. However, we can find the slope of this curve at any given point by drawing a straight line tangent to that point on the curve. A tangency is when a straight line just touches the curve without actually crossing it. At point A, we see that the positively sloped line that is tangent to the curve has a slope of 1—the line rises one unit and runs one unit. At point B, the line is horizontal, so it has zero slope. At point C, we see a slope of −2 because the negatively sloped line has a rise of −2 units (a fall of two units) for every one unit run.

Remember, many students have problems with economics simply because they fail to understand graphs, so make sure that you understand this material before going on to Chapter 2.

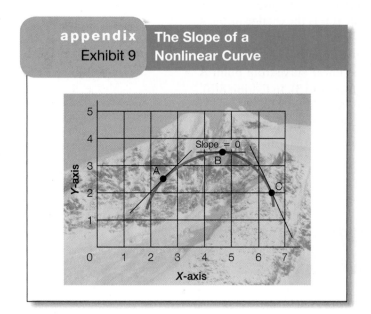

appendix Exhibit 9 **The Slope of a Nonlinear Curve**

Key Terms and Concepts

For a complete glossary of chapter key terms, visit the textbook's Web site at http://www.sextonmicro2e.nelson.com.

Y-axis 25	bar graph 25	positive relationship 26
X-axis 25	time-series graph 25	negative relationship 27
pie chart 25	variable 26	slope 29

Fill in the Blanks

Section 1.1

1. Economics is the study of the allocation of _____ resources to satisfy _____ wants for goods and services.

2. _____ is the problem that our wants exceed our limited resources.

3. Resources are _____ used to produce goods and services.

4. The economic problem is that _____ forces us to choose, and choices are costly because we must give up other opportunities that we _____.

5. Living in a world of scarcity means _____.

6. _____ deals with the aggregate (the forest), or total economy, whereas _____ deals with the smaller units (the trees) within the economy.

Section 1.2

7. Economic _____ are statements or propositions used to _____ and _____ patterns of human economic behaviour.

8. A _____ in economic theory is a testable prediction about how people will behave or react to a change in economic circumstances.

9. In order to isolate the effects of one variable on another, we use the _____ assumption.

10. When two events usually occur together, it is called _____.

11. The _____ is the incorrect view that what is true for an individual is always true for the group.

12. "A tax increase will lead to a lower rate of infiation" is a _____ economic statement.

Section 1.3

13. As long as human _____ exceed available _____, scarcity will exist.

14. The scarce resources that are used in the production of goods and services can be grouped into four categories: _____, _____, _____, and _____.

15. Capital includes human capital, the _____ people receive from _____.

16. Entrepreneurs are always looking for new ways to improve _____ or _____, driven by the lure of a positive incentive—_____.

17. Scarcity ultimately leads to _____ for the available goods and services.

18. Because we all have different _____, scarcity affects everyone differently.

Section 1.4

19. Economics is the study of the _____ we make among our many _____.

20. The highest or best forgone alternative resulting from a decision is called the _____.

Section 1.5

21. Most choices involve _____ of something to do rather than whether or not to do something.

22. Economists emphasize _____ thinking because the focus is on additional, or _____, choices, which involve the effects of _____ or _____ the current situation.

23. The rule of rational choice is that in trying to make themselves better off, people alter their behaviour if the _____ to them from doing so outweigh the _____ they will bear.

Section 1.6

24. If the benefits of some activity _____ and/or if the costs _____, economists expect the amount of that activity to rise. Likewise, if the benefits of some activity _____ and/or if the costs _____, economists expect the amount of that activity to fall.

25. _____ incentives either reduce costs or increase benefits, resulting in an increase in the activity or behaviour.

Section 1.7

26. People _____ by concentrating their energies on the activity to which they are best suited because individuals incur _____ opportunity costs as a result.

27. If a person, a region, or a country can produce a good or service at a lower opportunity cost than others can, we say that they have a _____ in the production of that good or service.

28. The primary advantages of specialization are that employees acquire greater _____ from repetition, they avoid _____ time in shifting from one task to another, and they do the types of work for which they are _____ suited.

Section 1.8

29. Market prices serve as the _____ of the market system. They communicate information about the _____ to buyers, and they provide sellers with critical information about the _____ that buyers place on those products. This communication results in a shifting of resources from those uses that are _____ valued to those that are _____ valued.

30. The basis of a market economy is _____ exchange and the _____ system that guides people's choices about questions of what goods to produce and how to produce those goods and distribute them.

31. _____ can lead the economy to fail to allocate resources efficiently, as in the cases of pollution and scientific research.

True or False

Section 1.1

1. Choices are costly because we must give up other opportunities that we value.

2. When our limited wants exceed our unlimited resources, we face scarcity.

3. If we valued leisure more highly, the opportunity cost of working would be lower.

4. Economics is a social science because it is concerned with reaching generalizations about human behaviour.

5. Microeconomics would deal with the analysis of a small individual firm, whereas macroeconomics would deal with very large global firms.

Section 1.2

6. Economic theories do not abstract from very many particular details of situations so they can better focus on every aspect of the behaviour to be explained.

7. Determining whether or not an economic hypothesis is acceptable is more difficult than in the natural or physical sciences in that, unlike a chemist in a chemistry lab, economists cannot control all the other variables that might influence human behaviour.

8. A positive statement must be both testable and true.

9. Normative analysis involves subjective, nontestable statements.

10. The majority of disagreements in economics stem from normative issues.

11. A hypothesis is a normative statement.

Section 1.3

12. In economics, labour includes more than physical effort, and land includes more than what people usually think of as land.

13. Entrepreneurship is the process of combining labour, land, and capital together to produce goods and services.

14. All goods and services can be subjected to economic analysis.

15. Even the wealthy individual who decides to donate all of her money to charity faces the constraints of scarcity.

16. Increases in production could enable us to eliminate scarcity.

17. If we had unlimited resources, we would not have to choose among our desires.

Section 1.4

18. Opportunity cost is the value of the best forgone alternative that was not chosen.

19. Scarcity implies that "there's no such thing as a free lunch."

Section 1.5

20. The actual result of changing behaviour following the rule of rational choice will always make people better off.

21. In terms of the rule of rational choice, zero levels of pollution, crime, and safety would be far too costly in terms of what we would have to give up to achieve them.

22. Most choices in economics are all or nothing.

23. Good economic thinking requires thinking about average amounts rather than marginal amounts.

24. The safety issue is generally not whether a product is safe, but rather how much safety consumers want.

Section 1.6

25. Positive incentives are those that either increase benefits or reduce costs, resulting in an increase in the level of the related activity or behaviour.

26. Negative incentives are those that either increase costs or reduce benefits, resulting in an increase in the level of the related activity or behaviour.

Section 1.7

27. People can gain by specializing in the production of the good in which they have a comparative advantage.

28. Without the ability to trade, people would not tend to specialize in those areas where they have a comparative advantage.

29. Voluntary trade directly increases wealth by making both parties better off, and it is the prospect of wealth-increasing exchange that leads to productive specialization.

Section 1.8

30. Government price controls can short-circuit the market's information transmission function.

31. When the economy produces too little or too much of something, the government can potentially improve society's well-being by intervening.

32. Not only does the market determine what goods are going to be produced and in what quantities, it also determines the distribution of output among members of society.

Multiple Choice

Section 1.1

1. Which of the following is true of resources?
  a. Their availability is unlimited.
  b. They are the inputs used to produce goods and services.
  c. Increasing the amount of resources available could eliminate scarcity.
  d. Both b and c.

2. What do economists mean when they state that a good is scarce?
  a. There is a shortage of the good at the current price.
  b. It is impossible to expand the availability of the good.
  c. People will want to buy more of the good regardless of price.
  d. Our wants exceed our limited resources.

3. Economics is concerned with
  a. the choices people must make because resources are scarce.
  b. human decision makers and the factors that influence their choices.
  c. the allocation of limited resources to satisfy virtually unlimited desires.
  d. all of the above.

4. Scarcity would cease to exist as an economic problem if
  a. we learned to cooperate and not compete with each other.
  b. there were new discoveries of an abundance of natural resources.
  c. output per worker increased.
  d. none of the above.

5. When we look at a particular segment of the economy, such as a given industry, we are studying
  a. macroeconomics.
  b. microeconomics.
  c. normative economics.
  d. positive economics.

6. Which of the following is most likely a topic of discussion in macroeconomics?
   a. an increase in the price of a pizza
   b. a decrease in the production of DVD players by a consumer electronics company
   c. an increase in the wage rate paid to automobile workers
   d. a decrease in the unemployment rate
   e. the entry of new firms into the software industry

Section 1.2

7. Economists use theories to
   a. abstract from the complexities of the world.
   b. understand economic behaviour.
   c. explain and help predict human behaviour.
   d. do all of the above.
   e. do none of the above.

8. The importance of the *ceteris paribus* assumption is that it
   a. allows one to separate normative economic issues from positive economic ones.
   b. allows one to generalize from the whole to the individual.
   c. allows one to analyze the relationship between two variables apart from the influence of other variables.
   d. allows one to hold all variables constant so the economy can be carefully observed in a suspended state.

9. Ten-year-old Tommy observes that people who play hockey are larger than average and tells his mom that he's going to play hockey because it will make him big and strong. Tommy is
   a. committing the fallacy of composition.
   b. violating the *ceteris paribus* assumption.
   c. mistaking correlation for causation.
   d. committing the fallacy of decomposition.

10. Which of the following correlations is likely to involve primarily one variable causing the other, rather than a third variable causing them both?
    a. The amount of time a team's third string plays in the game tends to be greater, the larger the team's margin of victory.
    b. Higher ice cream sales and higher crime rates both tend to increase at the same time.
    c. A lower price of a particular good and a higher quantity purchased tend to occur at the same time.
    d. The likelihood of rain tends to be greater after you have washed your car.

11. Which of the following is a statement of positive analysis?
    a. New tax laws are needed to help the poor.
    b. Teenage unemployment should be reduced.
    c. We should increase pension payments to the elderly.
    d. An increase in tax rates will reduce unemployment.
    e. It is only fair that firms protected from competition by government-granted monopolies pay higher corporate taxes.

12. "Mandating longer sentences for any criminal's third arrest will lead to a reduction in crime. That is the way it ought to be, as such people are a menace to society." This quotation
    a. contains positive statements only.
    b. contains normative statements only.
    c. contains both normative and positive statements.
    d. contains neither normative nor positive statements.

Section 1.3

13. Which of the following is part of the economic way of thinking?
    a. When an option becomes less costly, individuals will become more likely to choose it.
    b. Costs are incurred whenever scarce resources are used to produce goods or services.
    c. The value of a good is determined by its cost of production.
    d. Both a and b are part of the economic way of thinking.

14. An example of a capital resource is
    a. stock in a computer software company.
    b. the funds in a savings account at a bank.
    c. a bond issued by a company selling electric generators.
    d. a dump truck.

Section 1.4

15. Who would be most likely to drop out of university before graduation?
    a. an economics major who wishes to go to graduate school
    b. a math major with a B+ average
    c. a chemistry major who has just been reading about the terrific jobs available for those with chemistry degrees
    d. a star hockey player who has just received a multimillion-dollar contract offer

16. "If I hadn't been set up on this blind date tonight, I would have saved $50 and spent the evening watching TV." The opportunity cost of the date is
    a. $50.
    b. $50, plus the cost to you of giving up a night of TV.
    c. smaller, the more you enjoy the date.
    d. higher, the more you like that night's TV shows.
    e. described by both b and d.

17. Say you had an 8 A.M. economics class, but you would still come to campus at the same time even if you skipped your economics class. The cost of coming to the economics class would include:
    a. the value of the time it took to drive to campus.
    b. the cost of the gasoline it took to get to campus.
    c. the cost of insuring the car for that day.
    d. both a and b.
    e. none of the above.

18. Which of the following would be likely to raise your opportunity cost of attending a big hockey game this Saturday night?
    a. A friend calls you up and offers you free tickets to a concert by one of your favourite bands on Saturday night.
    b. Your employer offers you double your usual wage to work this Saturday night.
    c. Late Friday afternoon, your statistics professor makes a surprise announcement that there will be a major exam on Monday morning.
    d. All of the above.

19. Which of the following statements is true?
    a. The opportunity cost of a decision is always expressed in monetary terms.
    b. The opportunity cost of a decision is the value of the best forgone alternative.
    c. Some economic decisions have zero opportunity cost.
    d. The opportunity cost of postsecondary education is the same for all students at the same university but may differ among students at different universities.
    e. None of the above statements is true.

20. The opportunity cost of attending university is likely to include all except which of the following?
    a. the cost of required textbooks
    b. tuition fees
    c. the income you forgo in order to attend classes
    d. the cost of haircuts received during the school term
    e. the cost of paper, pencils, and laptop needed to take notes

Section 1.5

21. Ted has decided to buy a burger and fries at a restaurant but is considering whether or not to buy a drink as well. If the price of a burger is $2, fries are $1, drinks are $1, and a value meal with all three costs $3.40, the marginal cost to Ted of the drink is
    a. $1.
    b. $0.40.
    c. $1.40.
    d. $3.40.
    e. impossible to determine from the above information.

22. Which of the following demonstrates marginal thinking?
    a. deciding never to eat meat
    b. deciding to spend one more hour studying economics tonight because you think the improvement on your next test will be large enough to make it worthwhile to you
    c. deciding to go to a marketing class you usually skip because there is a guest lecturer you are really interested in hearing that day
    d. both b and c

23. If a driver who had no change and whose cellphone battery was dead got stranded near a pay phone and chose to buy a quarter from a passerby for a $5 bill,
    a. the passerby was made better off and the driver was made worse off by the transaction.
    b. both the passerby and the driver were made better off by the transaction.
    c. the transaction made the driver worse off by $4.75.
    d. both a and c are true.

24. The expected marginal benefit to you from purchasing a new sport-utility vehicle is $30 000. The price of the new sport-utility vehicle is $32 000.
    a. If you are acting rationally, you will borrow $2000 and purchase a new sport-utility vehicle.
    b. You will not purchase the new sport-utility vehicle at this time if you are acting rationally.
    c. If you do not purchase the new sport-utility vehicle, your net loss will be $2000.
    d. If you are acting rationally, you will not purchase a sport-utility vehicle until the marginal cost of doing so falls to $30 000.

25. Litres of milk at a local grocery store are priced at one for $2 or two for $3. The marginal cost of buying a second litre of milk equals
    a. $3.
    b. $2.
    c. $1.
    d. $0.

26. Which of the following statements is most consistent with the rule of rational choice?
    a. Environment Canada should strive to eliminate virtually all air and water pollution.
    b. When evaluating new prescription drugs, Health Canada should weigh each drug's potential health benefits against the potential health risks posed by known side effects.
    c. Police forces should be enlarged until virtually all crime is eliminated.
    d. Manufacturers of automobiles should seek to make cars safer, no matter the costs involved.

Section 1.6

27. Government subsidies designed to encourage automobile manufacturers to produce more "environmentally friendly" cars is an example of _____.
    a. a negative incentive
    b. a positive incentive
    c. inverse legislation
    d. a waste of time

28. The fines and penalties associated with breaking the law in Canada are an example of _____.
    a. a negative incentive
    b. a positive incentive
    c. inverse legislation
    d. a waste of time

Section 1.7

29. If a country wanted to maximize the value of its output, each job should be carried out by the person who
    a. has the highest opportunity cost.
    b. has a comparative advantage in that activity.
    c. can complete the particular job most rapidly.
    d. enjoys that job the least.

30. If resources and goods are free to move across provinces, and if Quebec producers choose to specialize in growing apples and Ontario producers choose to specialize in growing peaches, then we could reasonably conclude that
    a. Ontario has a comparative advantage in producing peaches.
    b. Quebec has a comparative advantage in producing peaches.
    c. the opportunity cost of growing peaches is lower in Ontario than in Quebec.
    d. the opportunity cost of growing apples is lower in Quebec than in Ontario.
    e. all of the above except b are true.

31. Which of the following is not true?
    a. Voluntary exchange is expected to be advantageous to both parties to the exchange.
    b. What one trader gains from a trade, the other must lose.
    c. If one party to a potential voluntary trade decides it does not advance his interests, he can veto the potential trade.
    d. The expectation of gain motivates people to engage in trade.

32. Kelly is a lawyer and also an excellent typist. She can type 120 words per minute, but she is pressed for time because she has all the legal work she can handle at $75 per hour. Kelly's friend Todd works as a waiter and would like some typing work (provided that he can make at least his wage as a waiter, which is $25 per hour). Todd can type only 60 words per minute.
   a. Kelly should do all the typing because she is faster.
   b. Todd should do the typing as long as his earnings are more than $25 and less than $37.50 per hour.
   c. Unless Todd can match Kelly's typing speed, he should remain a waiter.
   d. Todd should do the typing, and Kelly should pay him $20 per hour.
   e. Both a and c are correct.

Section 1.8

33. When the market mechanism fails to allocate resources efficiently, which of the following has happened?
   a. the natural functioning of the market
   b. positive incentive
   c. market failure
   d. all of the above

34. Who is primarily responsible for imposing price controls in a market economy?
   a. producers
   b. consumers
   c. the government
   d. all of the above

Problems

1. [Section 1.1]
   Are the following topics ones that would be covered in microeconomics or macroeconomics?
   a. the effects of an increase in the supply of lumber on the home-building industry
   b. changes in the national unemployment rate
   c. the effect of interest rates on the machine-tool industry
   d. the effect of interest rates on the demand for investment goods in society
   e. the way a firm maximizes profits

2. [Section 1.2]
   Are the following statements normative or positive, or do they contain both normative and positive statements?
   a. A higher income-tax rate would generate increased tax revenues. Those extra revenues should be used to give more government aid to the poor.
   b. The study of physics is more valuable than the study of sociology, but both should be studied by all college students.
   c. An increase in the price of wheat will decrease the amount of wheat purchased. However, it will increase the amount of wheat supplied to the market.
   d. A decrease in the price of butter will increase the amount of butter purchased, but that would be bad because it would increase Canadians' cholesterol levels.
   e. The birth rate is reduced as economies urbanize, but that also leads to an increased average age of developing countries' populations.

3. [Section 1.5]

Assume the total benefits to Mark from trips to a local amusement park during the year are given by the following schedule: 1 trip, $60; 2 trips, $115; 3 trips, $165; 4 trips, $200; 5 trips, $225; 6 or more trips, $240.

a. What is Mark's marginal benefit of the third trip? the fifth trip?

b. If the admission price to the amusement park were $45 per day, how many times would Mark be willing and able to go in a year? What if the price were $20 per day? Explain.

c. If the amusement park offered a year-long pass for $200 rather than a per-day admission, would Mark be willing to buy one? If so, how many times would he go? Explain.

4. [Section 1.5]

Assume the total cost of producing widgets was $4200 for 42 units; $4257 for 43 units; $4332 for 44 units; and $4420 for 45 units.

a. What is the marginal cost of producing the forty-third unit? the forty-fifth unit?

b. If the widget producer could sell however many he could produce at $60 per unit, how many would he choose to produce? If he could sell however many he could produce at $80 per unit? Explain.

Scarcity, Trade-Offs, and Economic Growth

The Three Economic Questions Every Society Faces

- What is to be produced?
- How are the goods to be produced?
- For whom are the goods produced?

SCARCITY AND THE ALLOCATION OF RESOURCES

Collectively, our wants far outstrip what can be produced from nature's scarce resources. So how should we allocate those scarce resources? Some methods of resource allocation might seem bad and counterproductive, like the "survival of the fittest" competition that exists on the floor of the jungle. Physical violence has been used since the beginning of time, as people, regions, and countries attacked one another to gain control over resources. One might argue that government should allocate scarce resources on the basis of equal shares or according to need. However, this approach poses problems because of diverse individual preferences, the problem of ascertaining needs, and the negative work and investment incentives involved. In reality, society is made up of many approaches to resource allocation. For now, we will focus on one form of allocating goods and services found in most countries—the market system.

Because of scarcity, certain economic questions must be answered, regardless of the level of affluence of the society or its political structure. We will consider three fundamental questions that inevitably must be faced: (1) What is to be produced? (2) How are the goods to be produced? (3) For whom are the goods produced? These questions are unavoidable in a world of scarcity.

WHAT IS TO BE PRODUCED?

How do individuals control production decisions in market-oriented economies? Questions arise such as "should we produce lots of cars and just a few school buildings, or relatively few cars and more school buildings?" The answer to these and other such questions is that people "vote" in economic affairs with their dollars (or pounds or yen). This concept is called **consumer sovereignty.** Consumer sovereignty explains how individual consumers in market economies determine what is to be produced.

consumer sovereignty
consumers vote with their dollars in a market economy; this explains what is produced

Televisions, DVD players, cellular telephones, pagers, camcorders, and computers, for example, became part of our lives because consumers "voted" hundreds of dollars apiece on these goods. As they bought more colour TVs, consumers "voted" fewer dollars on black-and-white TVs. Similarly, record albums gave way to tapes and CDs as consumers voted for these items with their dollars.

How Different Types of Economic Systems Answer the Question "What Is to Be Produced?"

Economies are organized in different ways to answer the question of what is to be produced. The dispute over the best way to answer this question has inflamed passions for centuries. Should central planning boards make the decisions, as in North Korea and Cuba? Sometimes these highly centralized economic systems are referred to as **command economies.** Under this type of regime, decisions about how many tractors or automobiles to produce are largely determined by a government official or committee associated with the central planning organization. That same group decides on the number and size of school buildings, refrigerators, shoes, and so on. Other countries—including Canada, the United States, much of Europe, and, increasingly, Asia and elsewhere—have largely adopted a decentralized decision-making process where literally millions of individual producers and

command economies
economies where the government uses central planning to coordinate most economic activities

In The **NEWS**

THE RISE OF THE CUV?

BY ERIC BEAUCHESNE

OTTAWA—Canada should benefit from the shift from gas-guzzling SUVs to more fuel-efficient CUVs, a trend that will continue to rob the Big Three North American automakers of market share, a new analysis of the troubled industry says.

Automakers are now scrambling to introduce new more fuel-efficient vehicles, including so-called crossover utility vehicles (CUVs), which make up the fastest-growing segment in the North American auto market, Scotiabank said in a report on the slump in market share by North American automakers.

That slump to about 50 per cent or less of the Canadian market last month, and just over 50 per cent of the U.S. market, is in part due to the growing share of the market being taken by CUVs from SUVs, it said. CUVs, such as Honda's CR-V, and Toyota's RAV4/EV, are smaller than SUVs, and look more like cars, but have more cargo space than cars.

The bad news for the Big Three North American automakers is that offshore producers, led by Honda, dominate the CUV market, with a near 60 per cent market share, it said. Honda alone has 19 per cent of the CUV market, compared with General Motors' 15 per cent, it said.

The report noted the slide in market share held by North American automakers has accelerated over the past three months as soaring gasoline prices intensified the shift from SUVs to CUVs.

SOURCE: Adapted from Eric Beauchesne, "Vehicle shift may benefit Canada," *Windsor Star,* Final Edition, November 29, 2005, p. D8. Materials reprinted with the express permission of: "CANWEST NEWS SERVICE", a CanWest Partnership.

CONSIDER THIS:
Consumers have voted and it looks like the gas-guzzling SUVs' days may be numbered. Crossover utility vehicles (CUVs) make up the fastest-growing segment of the North American auto market, a segment dominated by offshore producers. Will we eventually look at SUVs the same way we look at black-and-white TVs and record albums? Only time will tell.

consumers of goods and services determine what goods, and how many of them, will be produced. A country that uses such a decentralized decision-making process is often referred to as a **market economy.** Actually, no nation has a pure market economy. Most countries, including Canada, are said to have a **mixed economy.** In such economies, the government and the private sector together determine the allocation of resources.

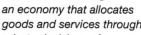

market economy
an economy that allocates goods and services through the private decisions of consumers, input suppliers, and firms

mixed economy
an economy where government and the private sector determine the allocation of resources

HOW ARE THE GOODS TO BE PRODUCED?

All economies, regardless of their political structure, must decide how to produce the goods and services that they want—because of scarcity. Goods and services can generally be produced in several ways. For example, a ditch can be dug by many workers using their hands, by a few workers with shovels, or by one person with a backhoe. Someone must decide which method is most appropriate. The larger the quantity of the good and the more elaborate the form of capital, the more labour that is saved and is thus made available for other uses. (Remember, goods like shovels or large earthmoving machines used to produce goods and services are called capital.) From this example, you might be tempted to conclude that it is desirable to use the biggest, most elaborate form of capital. But would you really want to plant your spring flowers with huge earthmoving machinery? That is, the most capital-intensive method of production may not always be the best. The best method is the least-cost method.

What Is the Best Form of Production?

The best or "optimal" form of production will usually vary from one economy to the next. For example, earthmoving machinery is used in digging large ditches in Canada, the United States, and Europe, whereas in developing countries, such as India, China, or Pakistan, shovels are often used. Similarly, when a person in Canada cuts the grass, he or she may use a power lawn mower, whereas in a developing country, a hand mower might be used or grass might not be cut at all. Why do these "optimal" forms of production vary so drastically? Compared to capital, labour is relatively cheap and plentiful in developing

ACTIVE LEARNING EXERCISE

MARKET SIGNALS

Q: Adam was a university graduate with a double major in economics and art. A few years ago, Adam decided that he wanted to pursue a vocation that utilized both of his talents. In response, he shut himself up in his studio and created a watercolour collection, "Graphs of Famous Recessions." With high hopes, Adam put his collection on display for buyers. After several years of displaying his econ art, however, the only one interested in the collection was his eight-year-old sister, who wanted the picture frames for her room. Recognizing that Adam was having trouble pursuing his chosen occupation, Adam's friend Karl told him that the market had failed. What do you think? Is Karl right?

A: No. Markets provide important signals, and the signal being sent in this situation is that Adam should look for some other means of support—something that society values. Remember the function of

consumer sovereignty in the marketplace. Clearly, consumers were not voting for Adam's art.

"We feel he's either going to be an artist or an economist."

labour intensive
production that uses a large amount of labour

capital intensive
production that uses a large amount of capital

countries but relatively scarce and expensive in Canada. In contrast, capital (machines and tools, mainly) is comparatively plentiful and cheap in Canada but scarcer and more costly in developing countries. That is, in developing countries, production would tend to be more **labour intensive,** or labour driven. In Canada, production would tend to be more **capital intensive,** or capital driven. Each nation tends to use the production processes that conserve its relatively scarce (and thus relatively more expensive) resources and use more of its relatively abundant resources.

FOR WHOM ARE THE GOODS PRODUCED?

In every society, some mechanism must exist to determine how goods and services are to be distributed among the population. Who gets what? Why do some people get to consume or use far more goods and services than others? This question of distribution is so important that wars and revolutions have been fought over it. Both the French and Russian Revolutions were concerned fundamentally with the distribution of goods and services. Even in societies where political questions are usually settled peacefully, the question of the distribution of income is an issue that always arouses strong emotional responses. As we shall see, in a market economy with private ownership and control of the means of production, the amount of goods and services one is able to obtain depends on one's income, which depends on the quantity and quality of the scarce resources the individual controls. For example, Tiger Woods makes a lot of money because he has unique and marketable skills as a golfer. This may or may not be viewed as "fair," an issue we shall look at in detail later in this book.

Avril Lavigne gets paid a lot of money because she controls a scarce resource: her talent and name recognition. As we will see in the next chapter, people's talents and other goods and services in limited supply relative to demand will command high prices.

Section Check

1. Every economy has to decide what to produce.
2. In a decentralized market economy, millions of buyers and sellers determine what and how much to produce.
3. In a mixed economy, the government and the private sector determine the allocation of resources.
4. The best form of production is the one that conserves the relatively scarce (more costly) resources and uses more of the abundant (less costly) resources.
5. When capital is relatively scarce and labour plentiful, production tends to be labour intensive.
6. When capital is relatively abundant and labour relatively scarce, production tends to be capital intensive.
7. In a market economy, the amount of goods and services one is able to obtain depends on one's income.
8. The amount of one's income depends on the quantity and the quality of the scarce resources that the individual controls.

section
2.2

The Circular Flow Model

- What are product markets?
- What are factor markets?
- What is the goods and services flow?
- What is the income flow?
- What is the circular flow model?

How do we explain how millions of people in an economy interact when it comes to buying, selling, producing, working, hiring, and so on? In a simple economy, there are two decision makers, the producers of goods and services, which we call firms, and households, the buyers of goods and services. Exchanges between these two decision makers take place in product markets and factor markets and involve flows of goods, services, and money.

PRODUCT MARKETS

Product markets are the markets for consumer goods and services. In the product market, households are buyers and firms are sellers. Households buy the goods and services that firms produce and sell.

product markets
the market where households are buyers and firms are sellers of goods and services

FACTOR MARKETS

Factor, or, **input markets** are the markets where households sell the use of their inputs (capital, land, labour, and entrepreneurship) to firms. In the factor markets, households are the sellers and the firms are the buyers.

factor (input) markets
the market where households sell the use of their inputs (capital, land, labour, and entrepreneurship) to firms

THE GOODS AND SERVICES FLOW

The **goods and services flow** represents the continuous flow of inputs and outputs in an economy. Households make inputs available to producers through the factor markets. These inputs are then turned into outputs which are then bought by households.

goods and services flow
the continuous flow of inputs and outputs in an economy

THE INCOME FLOW

The **income flow** represents the continuous flow of income and expenditure in an economy. Households receive money payments from firms as compensation for the labour, land, capital, and entrepreneurship needed to produce goods and services. These payments take the form of wages (salaries), rent, interest payments, and profits, respectively. The payments from households to firms are for the purchase of goods and services.

income flow
the continuous flow of income and expenditure in an economy

THE SIMPLE CIRCULAR FLOW MODEL

The simple **circular flow model of income and output** is illustrated in Exhibit 1. In the top half of the exhibit, the product market, households purchase goods and services that firms have produced. In the lower half of the exhibit, the factor (or input) market, households sell the inputs that firms use to produce goods and services. The income flow (going clockwise in Exhibit 1) describes how households receive income—money income—and use that income to buy goods and services—consumption spending. The goods and services flow (going counter-clockwise in Exhibit 1) details how households supply inputs—capital, land, labour, and entrepreneurship—to firms who use them in the production of outputs—goods and services.

circular flow model of income and output
an illustration of the continuous flow of goods, services, inputs, and payments between firms and households

Let's take a simple example to see how the circular flow model works. Suppose a teacher's supply of labour generates personal income in the form of wages (the factor market), which she can use to buy automobiles, vacations, food, and other goods (the product market). Suppose she buys an automobile (product market); the automobile dealer now has revenue to pay for his inputs (factor market)—wages to workers, purchase of new cars to replenish his inventory, rent for his building, and so on. So we see that in the simple circular flow model that income flows from firms to households (factor markets) and spending flows from households to firms (product markets). The simple circular

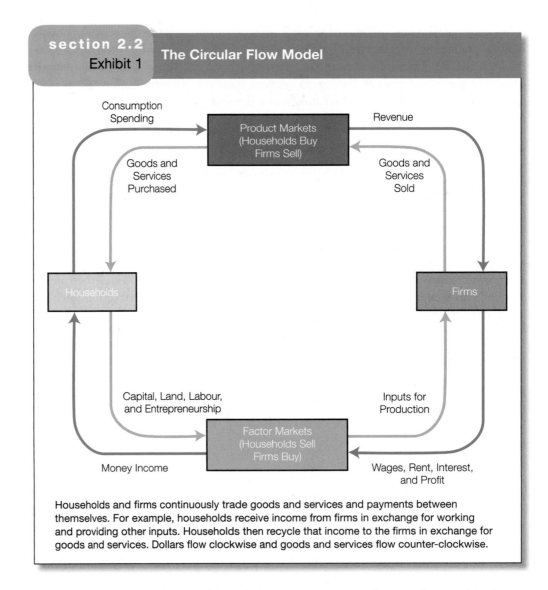

section 2.2
Exhibit 1   **The Circular Flow Model**

Consumption Spending

Revenue

Product Markets (Households Buy Firms Sell)

Goods and Services Purchased

Goods and Services Sold

Households

Firms

Capital, Land, Labour, and Entrepreneurship

Inputs for Production

Factor Markets (Households Sell Firms Buy)

Money Income

Wages, Rent, Interest, and Profit

Households and firms continuously trade goods and services and payments between themselves. For example, households receive income from firms in exchange for working and providing other inputs. Households then recycle that income to the firms in exchange for goods and services. Dollars flow clockwise and goods and services flow counter-clockwise.

flow model shows how households and firms interact in product markets and in factor markets and how product markets and factor markets are interrelated.

The circular flow model can become much more complex but here it is presented merely to introduce the major markets and players in the economy. For example, the model can be extended to show the role of government, financial, and foreign markets. Our simple model also does not show how firms and households send some of their income to the government for taxes or how households save some of their income for savings. Households are not the only buyers in the economy—firms, government, and foreigners buy some of the goods and services.

Section Check

1. In the product market, households are buyers and firms are sellers.
2. In the factor markets, households are the sellers and firms are the buyers.
3. Wages, rent, interest, and profits are the payments for the labour, land, capital, and entrepreneurship needed to produce goods and services. These transactions are carried out in factor, or input, markets.
4. The circular flow model illustrates the flow of goods, services, and payments among firms and households.

The Production Possibilities Curve

- What is a production possibilities curve?
- What is the law of increasing opportunity costs?
- What are unemployed resources?
- What are underemployed resources?
- What is efficiency?

THE PRODUCTION POSSIBILITIES CURVE

The economic concepts of scarcity, choice, and trade-offs can be shown with a simple graph called a production possibilities curve. The **production possibilities curve** represents the potential total output combinations of any two goods for an economy, given the inputs and technology available to the economy. That is, it illustrates an economy's potential for allocating its limited resources in producing various combinations of goods, in a given time period.

production possibilities curve
the potential total output combinations of any two goods for an economy

A Straight-Line Production Possibilities Curve— Grades in Economics and Accounting

What would the production possibilities curve look like if you were "producing" grades in two of your classes—say, economics and accounting? In Exhibit 1, we draw a hypothetical production possibilities curve for your expected grade in economics on the vertical axis and your expected grade in accounting on the horizontal axis. Assume, because of a part-time restaurant job, you choose to study ten hours a week and that you like both courses and are equally adept at studying for both courses.

We see in Exhibit 1 that the production possibilities curve is a straight line. For example, if all ten hours are spent studying economics, the expected grade in economics is 85 percent (an A) and the expected grade in accounting is 45 percent (an F). Moving down the production possibilities curve, we see that as you spend more of your time studying accounting, and less on economics, you can raise your expected grade in accounting but only at the expense of lowering your expected grade in economics. Specifically, moving down along the straight-line production possibilities curve, the trade-off is one letter-grade lower in economics for one higher letter-grade in accounting.

Of course, if you increased your study time it would be possible to expect higher grades in both courses. But that would be on a new production possibilities curve; along this production possibilities curve we are assuming that technology and the number of study hours are given. In the next section, the coverage is expanded to cover the more realistic case of a bowed production possibilities curve.

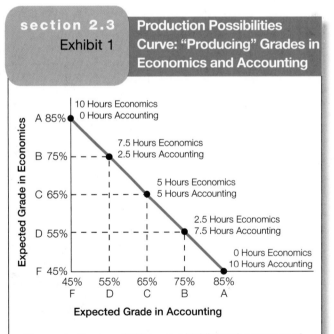

section 2.3 | **Production Possibilities**
Exhibit 1 | **Curve: "Producing" Grades in Economics and Accounting**

The production possibilities curve highlights the concept of trade-offs. Assuming you choose to study a total of ten hours a week, moving down the production possibilities curve shows that if you use your time to study accounting instead of economics you can raise your expected grade in accounting but only at the expense of lowering your expected grade in economics. With a straight-line production possibilities curve, the opportunity costs are constant.

The Bowed Production Possibilities Curve

To more clearly illustrate the production possibilities curve, imagine an economy that produces just two goods: food and shelter. The fact that we have many goods in the real world makes actual decision making more complicated, but it does not alter the basic principles being illustrated. Each point on the production possibilities curve shown in Exhibit 2 represents the potential amounts of food and shelter that can be produced in a given time period, given the quantity and quality of resources available in the economy for production.

Note in Exhibit 2 that if we devoted all of our resources to making shelters, we could produce 10 units of shelter, but no food (point A). If, on the other hand, we chose to devote all of our resources to food, we could produce 80 units of food, but no shelter (point E).

In reality, nations would rarely opt for production possibility A or E, preferring instead to produce a mixture of goods. For example, the economy in question might produce 9 units of shelter and 20 units of food (point B), or perhaps 7 units of shelter and 40 units of food (point C). Still other combinations along the curve, such as point D, are possible.

Off the Production Possibilities Curve

The economy cannot operate at point N (not attainable) during the given time period because there are presently not enough resources to produce that level of output. However, it is possible the economy can operate inside the production possibilities curve, at point I (inefficient). If the economy is operating at point I, or any other point inside the production possibilities curve, it is not at full capacity, and is operating inefficiently. In short, the economy is not using all of its scarce resources efficiently; as a result, actual output is less than potential output.

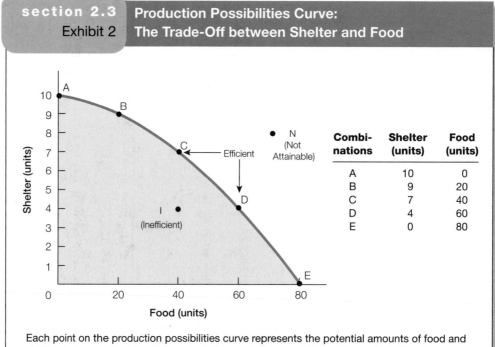

section 2.3
Exhibit 2

**Production Possibilities Curve:
The Trade-Off between Shelter and Food**

Combi-nations	Shelter (units)	Food (units)
A	10	0
B	9	20
C	7	40
D	4	60
E	0	80

Each point on the production possibilities curve represents the potential amounts of food and shelter that can be produced in a given time period, given the quantity and quality of resources available in the economy to use for production. All the points on the production possibility curve are efficient. Any points in the shaded area, like point I, are inefficient. Any point outside the production possibilites curve, like point N, is not attainable at the present time.

USING RESOURCES EFFICIENTLY

Most modern economies have resources that are idle, at least for some period of time—like during periods of high unemployment. If those resources were not idle, people would have more scarce goods and services available for their use. Unemployed resources create a serious problem. For example, consider an unemployed fisherman who is unable to find work at a "reasonable" wage, or those unemployed in depressed times when factories are already operating below capacity. Clearly, the resources of these individuals are not being used efficiently.

The fact that factories can operate below capacity suggests that it is not just labour resources that should be most effectively used. Rather, all resources entering into production must be used effectively. However, for several reasons, social concern focuses on labour. First, labour costs are the largest share of production costs. Also, unemployed or underemployed labourers (whose resources are not being used to their full potential) may have mouths to feed at home, whereas an unemployed machine does not (although the owner of the unemployed machine may).

INEFFICIENCY AND EFFICIENCY

Suppose for some reason there is widespread unemployment or resources are not being put to their best use. The economy would then be operating at a point, such as I, inside the production possibilities curve where the economy is operating inefficiently. At point I, 4 units of shelter and 40 units of food are being produced. By putting unemployed resources to work or by putting already employed resources to better use, we could expand the output of shelter by 3 units (moving to point C) without giving up any units of food. Alternatively, we could boost food output by 20 units (moving to point D) without reducing shelter output. We could even get more of both food and shelter moving to a point on the curve between C and D. Increasing or improving the utilization of resources, then, can lead to greater output of all goods. An efficient use of our resources means more of everything we want can be available for our use. Thus, **efficiency** requires society to use its resources to the fullest extent—getting the most from our scarce resources; that is, there are no wasted resources. If resources are being used efficiently, that is, at some point along a production possibilities curve, then more of one good or service requires the sacrifice of another good or service. Efficiency does not tell us which point along the production possibilites curve is *best,* but it does tell us that points inside the curve cannot be best because some resources are wasted.

efficiency
getting the most from society's scarce resources

THE MEASUREMENT OF OPPORTUNITY COST

When an economy is operating efficiently, the decision to increase the production of one good or service will carry with it a related opportunity cost. Within the framework of the production possibility model, the determination of opportunity cost is greatly simplified since the next best alternative is the only alternative—therefore, in our example, the opportunity cost of increasing the production of shelter would be measured in corresponding forgone units of food, and the opportunity cost of expanding food production would be measured in units of forgone shelter.

Note in Exhibit 2 if the economy is currently operating at point D (producing 4 units of shelter and 60 units of food) the decision to increase the amount of shelter it produces to 7 units will have an opportunity cost of 20 units of food—as this is the amount of food that the economy must give up to gain the additional units of shelter. In the diagram, this gain of shelter and related opportunity cost would involve the movement along the production possibilities curve from point D to point C.

THE LAW OF INCREASING OPPORTUNITY COSTS

Note that in Exhibits 2 and 3, the production possibilities curve is not a straight line like that in Exhibit 1. It is concave from below (that is, bowed outward from the origin). Looking at the figures, you can see that at very low food output, an increase in the amount of food produced will lead to only a small reduction in the units of shelter produced. For example, increasing food output from 0 to 20 (moving from point A to point B on the curve) requires the use of resources capable of producing 1 unit of shelter. This means that for the first 20 units of food, 1 unit of shelter must be given up. When food output is higher, however, more units of shelter must be given up when switching additional resources from the production of shelter to food. Moving from point D to point E, for example, an increase in food output of 20 (from 60 to 80) reduces the production of shelter from 4 to 0. At this point, then, the cost of those 20 additional units of food is 4 units of shelter, considerably more than the 1 unit of shelter required in the earlier scenario. This difference shows us that opportunity costs have not remained constant, but have risen, as more units of food and fewer units of shelter are produced. It is this increasing opportunity cost, then, that is represented by the bowed production possibilities curve.

What Is the Reason for the Law of Increasing Opportunity Cost?

increasing opportunity cost
the opportunity cost of producing additional units of a good rises as society produces more of that good

The basic reason for the **increasing opportunity cost** is that some resources and skills cannot be easily adapted from their current uses to alternative uses. For example, at low levels of food output, additional increases in food output can be obtained easily by switching relatively low-skilled carpenters from making shelter to producing food. However, to get even more food output, workers that are less well suited or appropriate for producing food (i.e., they are better adapted to making shelter) must be released from shelter making in order to increase food output. For example, a skilled carpenter may be an expert at making shelter but a very bad farmer, because he lacks the training and skills necessary in that occupation. So, using the skilled carpenter to farm results in a relatively greater opportunity cost than using the poor carpenter to farm. Hence, the production of additional units of food becomes increasingly costly as progressively even lower-skilled farmers (but good carpenters) convert to farming.

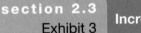

section 2.3
Exhibit 3   Increasing Opportunity Cost and the Production Possibilities Curve

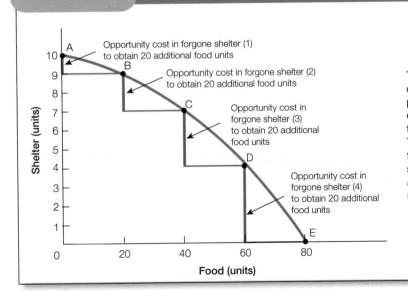

The production possibilities curve also illustrates the opportunity cost of producing more of a given product. For example, if we were to increase food output from 40 units to 60 units (moving from point C to point D), we must produce 3 fewer units of shelter. The opportunity cost of those 20 additional units of food is the 3 units of shelter we must forgo. We can see that moving down the curve from A to E, each additional 20 units of food costs society more and more shelter—the law of increasing opportunity cost.

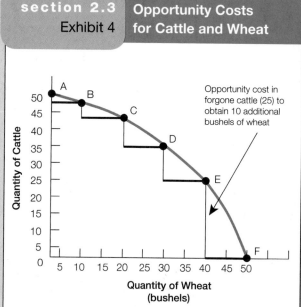

ACTIVE LEARNING EXERCISE

THE PRODUCTION POSSIBILITIES CURVE

Q: Imagine that you are the overseer on a small island that only produces two goods: cattle and wheat. About a quarter of the land is not fertile enough for growing wheat, so cattle graze on it. What would happen if you tried to produce more and more wheat, extending your planting even to the less fertile soil?

A: This is the law of increasing opportunity costs in action. As you planted more and more of your land in wheat, we would move into some of the rocky, less fertile land and, consequently, wheat yields on the additional land would fall. If we tried to plant the entire island with wheat, we would find that some of the rocky, less fertile land would yield virtually no extra wheat. It would, however, have been great for cattle grazing—a large loss. Thus, the opportunity cost of using that marginal land for wheat rather than cattle grazing would be very high. The law of increasing opportunity cost occurs because resources are not homogeneous (identical) and are not equally adaptable for producing cattle and wheat; some land is more suitable for cattle grazing, whereas some land is more suitable for wheat

growing. This is seen in Exhibit 4, where the vertical lines represent the opportunity cost of growing ten more bushels of wheat in terms of cattle production sacrificed. You can see that as wheat production increases, the opportunity costs in terms of lost cattle production rise.

section 2.3
Exhibit 4
Opportunity Costs for Cattle and Wheat

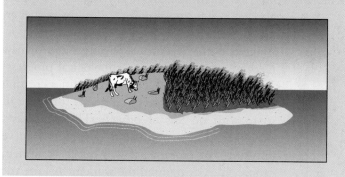

The opportunity cost of each ten bushels of wheat in terms of forgone cattle is measured by the vertical distances. As we move from A to F, the opportunity cost of wheat in terms of forgone cattle rises.

Section Check

1. The production possibilities curve represents the potential total output combinations of two goods available to a society given its resources and existing technology.
2. If the economy is operating within the production possibilities curve, the economy is operating inefficiently; this means that actual output is less than potential output.
3. Efficiency requires society to use its resources to the fullest extent—no wasted resources.
4. A bowed production possibilities curve means that the opportunity costs of producing additional units of a good rise as society produces more of that good (the law of increasing opportunity costs).

Economic Growth and the Production Possibilities Curve

■ How much should we sacrifice today to get more in the future?
■ How do we show economic growth on the production possibilities curve?

GENERATING ECONOMIC GROWTH

How have some nations been able to rapidly expand their output of goods and services over time, whereas others have been unable to increase their standards of living at all?

The economy can only grow with qualitative or quantitative changes in the factors of production—land, labour, capital, and entrepreneurship. Advancement in technology, improvements in labour productivity, or new sources of natural resources (such as previously undiscovered oil) could all lead to outward shifts of the production possibilities curve.

This idea can be clearly illustrated by using the production possibilities curve (Exhibit 1). In terms of the production possibilities curve, economic growth means an outward shift in the possible combinations of goods and services produced. With growth comes the possibility to have more of both goods than were previously available. Suppose we were producing at point C (7 units of shelter, 40 units of food) on our original production possibilities curve. Additional resources and/or new methods of using them (technological progress) can lead to new production possibilities creating the potential for more of all goods (or more of some with no less of others). These increases would push the production possibilities curve outward. For example, if you invest in human capital, such as training the workers making the shelter, it will increase the productivity of those workers. As a result, they will produce more units of shelter. This means, ultimately, that fewer resources will be used to make shelter, freeing them to be used for farming—resulting in more units of food. Notice that at point F (future) on the new curve, it is possible to produce 9 units of shelter and 70 units of food, more of both goods than was previously produced, at point C.

GROWTH DOESN'T ELIMINATE SCARCITY

With all of this discussion of growth, it is important to remember that growth, or increases in a society's output, does not make scarcity disappear. Even when output has grown more rapidly than the population so that people are made better off, they still face trade-offs: At any point

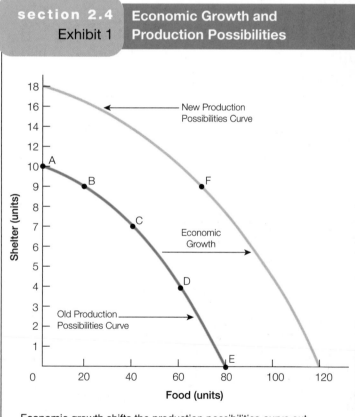

section 2.4
Exhibit 1
Economic Growth and Production Possibilities

Economic growth shifts the production possibilities curve outward, allowing increased output of both food and shelter (compare point F with point C).

along the production possibilities curve, in order to get more of one thing, you must give up something else. There are no free lunches on the production possibilities curve.

Capital Goods versus Consumption Goods

Economies that choose to invest more of their resources for the future will grow faster than those that don't. To generate economic growth, a society must produce fewer consumer goods—like pizza, DVD players, cellphones, cars, and so on—in the present and produce more capital goods. The society that devotes a larger share of its productive capacity to capital goods (machines, factories, tools, and education), rather than consumption goods (video games, pizza, and vacations), will experience greater economic growth. It must sacrifice some present consumption of consumer goods and services in order to experience growth in the future. Why? Investing in capital goods, like computers and other new technological equipment, as well as upgrading skills and knowledge, expands the ability to produce in the future. It shifts the economy's production possibilities outward, increasing the future production capacity of the economy. That is, the economy that invests more now (consumes less now) will be able to produce, and therefore consume, more in the future. In Exhibit 2, we see that Economy A invests more in capital goods than Economy B. Consequently, Economy A's production possibilities curve shifts out further than Economy B's over time.

SUMMING UP THE PRODUCTION POSSIBILITIES CURVE

The production possibilities curve shown in Exhibit 3 illustrates the choices faced by an economy that makes military goods and consumer goods. How are the economic concepts of scarcity, choice, opportunity costs, efficiency, and economic growth illustrated in this production possibilities curve framework? In Exhibit 3, we can show scarcity because resource combinations outside the initial production possibilities curve, like point D, are

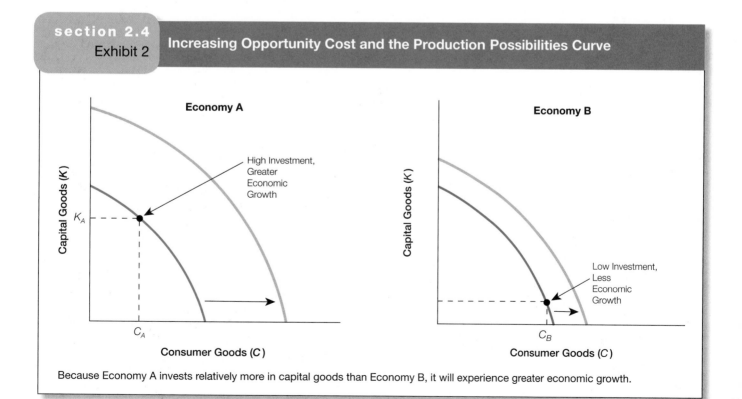

section 2.4
Exhibit 2   **Increasing Opportunity Cost and the Production Possibilities Curve**

Because Economy A invests relatively more in capital goods than Economy B, it will experience greater economic growth.

unattainable without economic growth. If the economy is operating efficiently, we are somewhere on that production possibilities curve, like point B or point C. However, if the economy is operating inefficiently, we are operating inside that production possibilities curve, like point A. We can also see in this graph that to get more military goods you must give up consumer goods—that is, there is an opportunity cost. Finally, we see that over time, with economic growth, the whole production possibilities curve can shift outward, making point D now attainable.

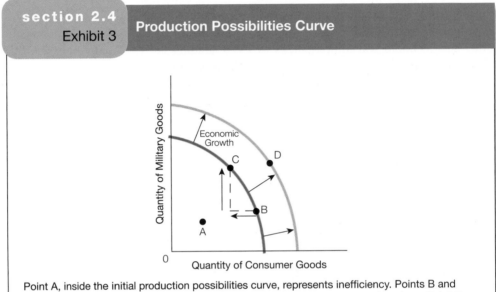

section 2.4
Exhibit 3   **Production Possibilities Curve**

Point A, inside the initial production possibilities curve, represents inefficiency. Points B and C, on the curve, are efficient points and represent two possible output combinations. Point D can only be attained with economic growth, illustrated by the outward shift in the production possibilities curve.

In The **NEWS**

TOURISM VERSUS ECOSYSTEMS

BY JON KRAKAUER

Canada's main transcontinental railway and transcontinental highway roll side-by-side down the length of Banff's main valley. On the busiest weekends, the road is clotted with cars, RVs, and tour buses, and a brown haze of exhaust fumes veils the celebrated vistas. Within the park lie three ski resorts and the town of Banff—home to 7000 permanent residents. On the typical summer day, the townies may see 25 000 tourists streaming through their streets.

One local businessman and town council member remarked, "Environmentalists love to talk gloom and doom—but all you have to do is drive five miles out of town and you're in the middle of miles and miles of nothing but nature. You get tired of looking at all these big bare mountains; what's wrong with putting a restaurant or a little chalet up there to make it nicer for the people who come here?"

One thing that is wrong with it, according to a biologist who has studied wildlife throughout the Rocky Mountains, is that the human presence in Banff is wreaking havoc on the area's fragile makeup. "I'd say the park is in very, very poor condition compared with what it was 10 years ago, 20 years ago, 30 years ago," declared the biologist. "There's been a major decline in most of our large predators—black bears, grizzlies, wolverines, lynx, cougars. Such species are one of our best indicators of overall ecological health, and the way things are going, most of these animals will not survive here."

IN THE NEWS (continued)

Can Banff currently have more tourism and a better environment? Society can choose high environmental quality but only at the cost of lower tourism or more tourism and commercialization at the expense of the ecosystem, but society must choose. It involves a trade-off, and in this case Canada must presently choose between tourism and ecosystems.

SOURCE: Adapted from Jon Krakauer, "Rocky Times in Banff," *National Geographic,* July 1995, pp. 46–69. By permission of John Ware Literary Agency.

CONSIDER THIS:
The principal point of this article is that there are trade-offs that require choice and those choices have costs. In order to totally preserve the ecosystem of Banff, it would mean far fewer tourists and commercial ventures. In this case, society must make a value judgment. If Banff is developed further, what will be the cost to future generations who will not be able to appreciate the visual splendours of this special "hamlet" nestled in the Canadian Rockies? On the other hand, how can you possibly accommodate the growing numbers of daily visitors without building additional restaurants, motels, and so on? Society must choose.

Section Check

1. Economies must decide how much current consumption they are willing to sacrifice for greater growth in the future.
2. Economic growth is represented by an outward shift of the production possibilities curve.
3. Economic growth increases the possibility of producing more of all goods.
4. Despite economic growth, scarcity inevitably remains a fact of life.

Summary

Section 2.1
- Every economy has to decide what goods to produce, how to produce the goods, and how to distribute the goods.
- In command economies, central planning (the government) is solely responsible for coordinating economic activities.
- In a mixed economy, the government and the private sector determine the allocation of resources.
- In a market economy, the amount of output one is able to obtain depends on one's income. The amount of one's income depends on the quantity and the quality of the scarce resources that the individual controls.
- The best form of production is the one that conserves the relatively scarce (more costly) resources and uses more of the abundant (less costly) resources.

- When capital is relatively scarce and labour plentiful, production tends to be labour intensive.
- When capital is relatively abundant and labour relatively scarce, production tends to be capital intensive.

Section 2.2
- The circular flow model illustrates the flow of goods, services, and payments among businesses and households.
- In the product market, households purchase goods and services that firms have produced.
- In the factor (or input) market, households sell the inputs that firms use to produce goods and services.
- The flow of money illustrates how households receive income (wages, rent, interest, and profit) from firms for

their inputs (labour, land, capital, and entrepreneurship) and use it to purchase goods and services.

■ The flow of goods and services illustrates the transition of inputs into outputs.

Section 2.3

■ The production possibilities curve represents the potential total output combinations of two goods available to a society.

■ Efficiency requires society to use its resources to the fullest extent—no wasted resources.

■ If the economy is operating within the production possibilities curve, the economy is operating inefficiently.

■ A bowed (or concave from the origin) production possibilities curve means that the opportunity costs of producing additional units of a good rise as society produces more of that good (the law of increasing opportunity costs).

Section 2.4

■ Economic growth is represented by an outward shift of the production possibilities curve.

Key Terms and Concepts

For a complete glossary of chapter key terms, visit the textbook's Web site at http://www.sextonmicro2e.nelson.com.

consumer sovereignty 42
command economies 42
market economy 43
mixed economy 43
labour intensive 44

capital intensive 44
product markets 45
factor (input) markets 45
goods and services flow 45
income flow 45

circular flow model of income and output 45
production possibilities curve 47
efficiency 49
increasing opportunity cost 50

Review Questions

1. What is the significance of the three basic economic questions?

2. How would the following events be shown using a production possibilities curve for shelter and food?

   a. The economy is experiencing double-digit unemployment.

   b. Economic growth is increasing at over 5 percent per year.

   c. Society decides it wants less shelter and more food.

   d. Society decides it wants more shelter and less food.

3. Using the table below, answer the following questions:

Combinations

	A	B	C	D	E
Guns	1	2	3	4	5
Butter	20	18	14	8	0

   a. What are the assumptions for a given production possibilities curve?

   b. What is the opportunity cost of one gun when moving from point B to point C? When moving from point D to point E?

   c. Do these combinations demonstrate constant or increasing opportunity costs?

4. Economy A produces more capital goods and fewer consumer goods than Economy B. Which economy will grow more rapidly? Draw two production possibilities curves, one for Economy A and one for Economy B. Demonstrate graphically how one economy can grow more rapidly than the other.

5. How does education add to a nation's capital stock?

6. How does a technological advance that increases the efficiency of shoe production affect the production possibilities curve between shoes and pizza? Is it possible to produce more shoes and pizza or just more shoes? Explain.

7. The leader of a political party running in an upcoming provincial government election promises to build new schools and new hospitals during the next four years without sacrificing any other goods and services. Explain using a production possibilities curve between schools and hospitals under what conditions the politician would be able to keep her promise.

8. In 2003, the United States waged war on Iraq. Illustrate a production possibilities curve showing Iraq's ability to produce tanks and consumer goods both pre-war and post-war.

Fill in the Blanks

Section 2.1

1. Because of scarcity, certain economic questions must be answered regardless of the level of affluence of the society or its political structure. Three fundamental questions that inevitably must be faced in a world of scarcity are (1) _____ is to be produced? (2) _____ are these goods to be produced? (3) _____ are the goods produced?

2. Market economies largely rely on a _____ decision-making process, where literally millions of individual producers and consumers of goods and services determine what will be produced.

3. Most countries, including Canada, have _____ economies, in which the government and private sector determine the allocation of resources.

4. The _____-cost method is the most appropriate method for producing a given product.

5. Methods of production used where capital is relatively scarce will be _____, and methods of production used where labour is relatively scarce will be _____.

Section 2.2

6. The markets where households are buyers and firms are sellers of goods and services are called _____ markets.

7. The markets where households sell the use of their _____ (capital, land, labour, and entrepreneurship) to _____ are called _____ or _____ markets.

8. The simple _____ model shows the continuous flow of goods, services, inputs, and payments through the _____ and _____ markets among households and _____.

Section 2.3

9. A _____ curve represents the potential total output combinations of any two goods for an economy.

10. On a production possibilities curve, we assume that the economy has a given quantity and quality of _____ and _____ available to use for production.

11. If an economy is operating inside its production possibilities curve, it is not at full capacity and is operating _____. Such an economy's actual output is less than _____ output.

12. By putting _____ resources to work or by putting already employed resources to _____ uses, we could expand output.

13. _____ requires society to use its resources to the fullest extent—getting the _____ we can out of our scarce resources.

14. If the production possibilities curve is _____ from below (that is, bowed outward from the origin), it reflects _____ opportunity costs of producing additional amounts of a good.

15. When easily adaptable resources are exhausted and resources and workers that are less well suited or appropriate must then be employed to increase output further, the _____ of production _____.

Section 2.4

16. To generate economic growth, a society must produce _____ consumer goods and _____ capital goods in the present.

17. Advancements in _____, improvements in _____, or new _____ could all lead to outward shifts of the production possibilities curve.

18. Increases in a society's output do not make _____ disappear. Even when output has grown more rapidly than the population so that people are made better off, they still face _____.

19. The production possibilities curve can be used to illustrate the economic concepts of _____ (resource combinations outside the production possibilities curve are unattainable), _____ (selecting among the alternative bundles available along the production possibilities curve), _____ (how much of one good you give up to get another unit of the second good as you move along the production possibilities curve), _____ (being on the production possibilities curve rather than inside it), and _____ (shifting the production possibilities curve outward).

True or False

Section 2.1

1. Consumer sovereignty describes how individual consumers in market economies determine what is to be produced.

2. Command economies rely on central planning, where decisions about what and how many are largely determined by a government official associated with the central planning organization.

3. All economies, regardless of political structure, must decide how, from several possible ways, to produce the goods and services that they want.

4. In any economy, it would always be less efficient to dig ditches by having many workers use their hands than to use workers with shovels or a backhoe.

5. Each nation tends to use the production processes that conserve its relatively scarce (and thus relatively more expensive) resources and use more of its relatively abundant resources.

6. In a market economy, with private ownership and control of the means of production, the amount of output one is able to obtain depends on the quantity and quality of the scarce resources that the individual controls.

Section 2.2

7. The market where households sell the use of their inputs to firms is called the product market.

8. The circular flow model illustrates the continuous flow of goods, services, inputs, and payments between firms and households.

Section 2.3

9. With a straight-line production possibilities curve, the opportunity cost of producing another unit of a good increases with its output.

10. The economy cannot produce beyond the levels indicated by the production possibilities curve during a given time period, but it is possible to operate inside the production possibilities curve.

11. Underutilized resources or those not being put to their best uses are illustrated by output combinations along the production possibilities curve.

12. We all have an interest in the efficient use of all of society's resources because there can be more of everything we care about available for our use as a result.

13. If resources are being used efficiently, at a point along a production possibilities curve, more of one good or service requires the sacrifice of another good or service as a cost.

14. The basic reason for increasing opportunity cost is that some resources and skills cannot be easily adapted from their current uses to alternative uses.

Section 2.4

15. Investing in capital goods will increase the future production capacity of an economy, so an economy that invests more now (consumes less now) will be able to produce, and therefore consume, more in the future.

16. An economy can grow despite a lack of qualitative and quantitative improvements in the factors of production.

17. Economic growth means a movement along an economy's production possibilities curve in the direction of producing more consumer goods.

18. From a point inside the production possibilities curve, in order to get more of one thing, an economy must give up something else.

Multiple Choice

Section 2.1

1. Which of the following is not a question that all societies must answer?
   a. How can scarcity be eliminated?
   b. What goods and services will be produced?
   c. Who will get the goods and services?
   d. How will the goods and services be produced?
   e. All of the above are questions that all societies must answer.

2. Economic disputes over the distribution of income are generally associated with which economic question?
   a. Who should produce the goods?
   b. What goods and services will be produced?
   c. Who will get the goods and services?
   d. How will the goods and services be produced?

3. Three economic questions must be determined in all societies. What are they?
   a. How much will be produced? When will it be produced? How much will it cost?
   b. What will the price of each good be? Who will produce each good? Who will consume each good?
   c. What is the opportunity cost of production? Does the society have a comparative advantage in production? Will consumers desire the goods being produced?
   d. What goods will be produced? How will goods be produced? For whom will the goods be produced?

4. The private ownership of property and the use of the market system to direct and coordinate economic activity are most characteristic of
   a. a command economy.
   b. a mixed economy.
   c. a market economy.
   d. a traditional economy.

5. The degree of government involvement in the economy is greatest in
   a. a command economy.
   b. a mixed economy.
   c. a market economy.
   d. a traditional economy.

6. When a command economy is utilized to resolve economic questions regarding the allocation of resources, then
   a. everyone will receive an equal share of the output produced.
   b. the preferences of individuals are of no importance.
   c. economic efficiency will be assured.
   d. the role of markets will be replaced by political decision making.

7. Which of the following is true?
   a. An advanced market economy would tend to use labour-intensive production methods.
   b. An economy in which labour is relatively scarce would tend to use capital-intensive production methods.
   c. An increase in the availability of labour relative to capital in an economy would tend to increase how labour intensive the production processes in that economy would be.
   d. All of the above are true.
   e. Both b and c are true.

Section 2.2

8. In a circular flow diagram,
   a. goods and services flow in a clockwise direction.
   b. goods and services flow in a counter-clockwise direction.
   c. product markets appear at the top of the diagram.
   d. factor markets appear at the left of the diagram.
   e. both b and c are true.

9. Which of the following is true?
   a. In the product markets, firms are buyers and households are sellers.
   b. In the factor markets, firms are sellers and households are buyers.
   c. Firms receive money payments from households for capital, land, labour, and entrepreneurship.
   d. All of the above are true.
   e. None of the above is true.

10. In the circular flow model,
   a. firms supply both products and resources.
   b. firms demand both products and resources.
   c. firms demand resources and supply products.
   d. firms supply resources and demand products.

Section 2.3

11. A point beyond the boundary of an economy's production possibilities curve is
   a. efficient.
   b. inefficient
   c. attainable.
   d. unattainable.
   e. both attainable and efficient.

Use the diagram below to answer questions 12 through 15.

12. Currently, it is not possible to produce at
   a. point A.
   b. point B.
   c. point E.
   d. point G.
   e. either point E or point G.

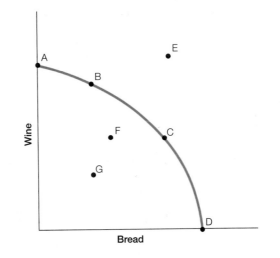

13. An economy is operating at full employment, and then workers in the bread industry are laid off. This change is portrayed in the movement from
   a. A to B.
   b. B to E.
   c. C to F.
   d. G to F.
   e. None of the above is correct.

14. Along the production possibilities curve, the most efficient point of production depicted is
   a. point B.
   b. point C.
   c. point D.
   d. point G.
   e. All points on the production possibilities curve are equally efficient.

15. The opportunity cost of one more unit of bread is greater at point _____ than at point _____.
   a. G; B
   b. C; A
   c. A; C
   d. None of the above. The opportunity cost of a good is constant everywhere along the production possibilities curve.

16. Which of the following is consistent with the implications of the production possibilities curve?
   a. If the resources in an economy are being used efficiently, scarcity will not be a problem.
   b. If the resources in an economy are being used efficiently, more of one good can be produced only if less of another good is produced.
   c. Producing more of any one good will require smaller and smaller sacrifices of other goods as more of that good is being produced in an economy.
   d. An economy will automatically attain that level of output at which all of its resources are fully employed.
   e. Both b and c are consistent with the implications of the production possibilities curve.

17. Which of the following is the most accurate statement about a production possibilities curve?
    a. An economy can produce at any point inside or outside its production possibilities curve.
    b. An economy can produce only on its production possibilities curve.
    c. An economy can produce at any point on or inside its production possibilities curve, but not outside the curve.
    d. An economy can produce at any point inside its production possibilities curve, but not on or outside the curve.

Section 2.4

18. Which of the following is most likely to shift the production possibilities curve outward?
    a. an increase in unemployment
    b. a decrease in the stock of physical or human capital
    c. a decrease in the labour force
    d. a technological advance

19. Which of the following is least likely to shift the production possibilities curve outward?
    a. a change in preferences away from one of the goods and toward the other
    b. an invention that reduces the amount of natural resources necessary for producing a good
    c. the discovery of new natural resources
    d. a reduction in people's preferences for leisure

20. Inefficiency is best illustrated by which of the following?
    a. forgoing civilian goods in order to produce more military goods
    b. limiting economic growth by reducing capital spending
    c. having high levels of unemployment of labour and other resources that could be productively employed
    d. producing outside the production possibilities frontier
    e. all of the above

21. Suppose Country A produces few consumption goods and many investment goods whereas Country B produces few investment goods and many consumption goods. Other things being equal, you would expect
    a. per-capita income to grow more rapidly in Country B.
    b. population to grow faster in Country B.
    c. the production possibilities curve for Country A to shift out more rapidly than that of Country B.
    d. that if both countries started with identical production possibilities curves, in 20 years, people in Country B would be able to produce more consumer goods than people in Country A.
    e. that both c and d are true.

22. A virulent disease spreads throughout the population of an economy, causing death and disability. This can be portrayed as
    a. a movement from a point on the production possibilities curve to a point inside the curve.
    b. a movement from a point on the production possibilities curve to the northeast.
    c. a movement along the production possibilities curve to the southeast.
    d. an outward shift of the production possibilities curve.
    e. an inward shift of the production possibilities curve.

23. Say that a technological change doubles an economy's ability to produce good X and triples the economy's ability to produce Y. As a result,

   a. the economy will tend to produce less X and more Y than before.
   b. the opportunity cost of producing units of Y in terms of X forgone will tend to fall.
   c. the production possibilities curve will shift out further along the *X*-axis than along the *Y*-axis.
   d. both b and c would be true.

Problems

1. [Section 2.2]

Identify where the appropriate entries go in the circular flow diagram below.

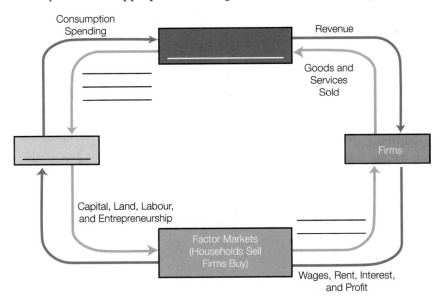

2. [Section 2.3]

Assume that the production possibilities for Alberta are the following combinations of kegs of beer and sides of beef.

Beer	Beef
55	0
54	1
52	2
49	3
45	4
40	5
34	6
27	7
19	8
10	9
0	10

a. Construct the production possibilities frontier for beer and beef on the grid below.

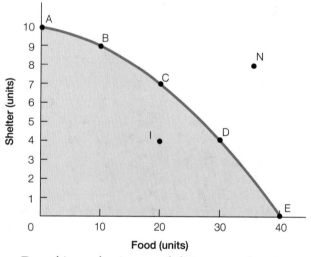

b. Given the information above, what is the opportunity cost of the fifty-fifth keg of beer in Alberta? of the sixth side of beef? of the ninth side of beef?

c. Suppose Alberta is currently producing 4 sides of beef and 45 kegs of beer. What is the opportunity cost of 5 more sides of beef in Alberta?

d. Would the combination of 40 kegs of beer and 4 sides of beef be efficient? Why or why not?

e. Is the combination of 9 kegs of beer and 10 sides of beef possible for Alberta? Why or why not?

3. [Section 2.4]

Given the following production possibilities curve:

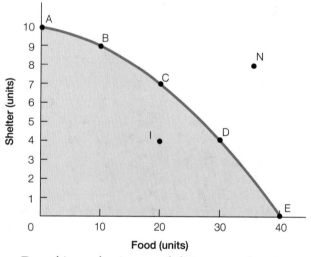

a. Does this production possibilities curve show increasing opportunity costs? Explain.

b. What is the opportunity cost of moving from point I to point D? Explain.

c. What is the opportunity cost of moving from point C to point B?

d. Which of points A–E is the most efficient? Explain.

e. Which of the identified production alternatives is currently impossible for this economy to achieve? What must happen in order for this production alternative to become attainable?

f. Which of the identified production alternatives is currently attainable but inefficient? What must happen in order for this production alternative to become efficient?

chapter 3

Supply and Demand

section
3.1

Markets

■ What is a market?
■ Why is it so difficult to define a market?

DEFINING A MARKET

Although we usually think of a market as a place where some sort of exchange occurs, a market is not really a place at all. A **market** is the process of buyers and sellers exchanging goods and services. This means that supermarkets, the Toronto Stock Exchange, drugstores, roadside stands, garage sales, Internet stores, and restaurants are all markets.

Every market is different. That is, the conditions under which the exchange between buyers and sellers takes place can vary. These differences make it difficult to precisely define a market. After all, an incredible variety of exchange arrangements exists in the real world—organized securities markets, wholesale auction markets, foreign exchange markets, real estate markets, labour markets, and so forth.

Goods being priced and traded in various ways at various locations by various kinds of buyers and sellers further compound the problem of defining a market. For some goods, such as housing, markets are numerous but limited to a geographic area. Homes in Niagara Falls, Ontario, for example (about 130 kilometres from downtown Toronto), do not compete directly with homes in Toronto. Why? Because people who work in Toronto will generally look for homes within commuting distance. Even within cities, there are separate markets for homes, differentiated by amenities such as bigger houses, newer houses, larger lots, and better schools.

In a similar manner, markets are numerous but geographically limited for a good such as cement. Because transportation costs are so high relative to the selling price, the

market
the process of buyers and sellers exchanging goods and services

good is not shipped any substantial distance, and buyers are usually in contact only with local producers. Price and output are thus determined in a number of small markets. In other markets, like those for gold or automobiles, markets are global. The important point is not what a market looks like, but what it does—it facilitates trade.

BUYERS AND SELLERS

The roles of buyers and sellers in markets are important. The buyers, as a group, determine the demand side of the market. Buyers include the consumers who purchase the goods and services and the firms that buy inputs—labour, capital, and raw materials. Sellers, as a group, determine the supply side of the market. Sellers include the firms that produce and sell goods and services, and the resource owners who sell their inputs to firms—workers who "sell" their labour and resource owners who sell raw materials and capital. It is the interaction of buyers and sellers that determines market prices and output—through the forces of supply and demand.

In this chapter, we focus on how supply and demand work in a **competitive market.** A competitive market is one in which there are a number of buyers and sellers offering similar products and no single buyer or seller can influence the market price; that is, buyers and sellers have very little market power. Because most markets contain a large degree of competitiveness, the lessons of supply and demand can be applied to many different types of problems.

competitive market
a market where the many buyers and sellers have very little market power—each buyer's and seller's effect on market price is negligible

---

Section Check

SECTION CHECK

1. Markets consist of buyers and sellers exchanging goods and services with one another.
2. Markets can be regional, national, or global.
3. Buyers determine the demand side of the market and sellers determine the supply side of the market.

---

section
3.2

Demand

- What is the law of demand?
- What is an individual demand curve?
- What is a market demand curve?
- What is a money price?
- What is a relative price?

THE LAW OF DEMAND

Some laws are made to protect us, such as "no speeding" or "no drinking and driving." Other times observed behaviour is so pervasive it is called a law—like the law of demand. According to the **law of demand,** the quantity of a good or service demanded varies inversely (negatively) with its price, *ceteris paribus.* More directly, the law of demand says that, other things being equal, when the price (P) of a good or service falls, the quantity

law of demand
the quantity of a good or service demanded varies inversely (negatively) with its price, ceteris paribus

demanded (Q_D) increases, and conversely, if the price of a good or service rises, the quantity demanded decreases.

$$P\uparrow \Rightarrow Q_D\downarrow \text{ and } P\downarrow \Rightarrow Q_D\uparrow$$

The law of demand puts the concept of basic human "needs," at least as an analytical tool, to rest. Needs are those things that you must have at any price. That is, there are no substitutes. There are usually plenty of substitutes available for any good, some better than others. The law of demand, with its inverse relationship between price and quantity demanded, implies that even so-called needs are more or less urgent depending on the circumstances (opportunity costs). Whenever you hear somebody say, "I need a new car," "I need a new CD player," or "I need new clothes," always be sure to ask: What does the person really mean? At what price does that person "need" the good?

WHY IS THERE A NEGATIVE RELATIONSHIP BETWEEN PRICE AND THE QUANTITY DEMANDED?

The law of demand describes a negative (inverse) relationship between price and quantity demanded. When price goes up, the quantity demanded goes down, and vice versa. But why is this so? The primary reason for this inverse relationship is the **substitution effect.** At higher prices, buyers increasingly substitute other goods for the good that now has a higher relative price. For example, if the price of orange juice increases, some consumers may substitute out of orange juice into other juices, such as apple or tomato juice, or perhaps water, milk, or coffee. This is what economists call the substitution effect of a price change. Of course, if the relative price of orange juice fell, then consumers would substitute out of other products and increase their quantity of orange juice demanded, because the lower relative price now makes it a more attractive purchase.

Another reason for the inverse relationship between price and quantity demanded is referred to as the **income effect.** In this explanation, higher prices make the buyer feel poorer, since they cannot buy the same quantity of goods as they did when prices were lower. As a result, quantity demanded decreases. When prices decline, this makes buyers feel richer, therefore causing quantity demanded to increase.

AN INDIVIDUAL DEMAND SCHEDULE

The **individual demand schedule** shows the relationship between the price of the good and the quantity demanded. For example, suppose Elizabeth enjoys eating apples. How many kilograms of apples would Elizabeth be willing and able to buy at various prices during the year? At a price of $3 a kilogram, Elizabeth buys 15 kilograms of apples over the course of a year. If the price is higher, at $4 per kilogram, she might buy only 10 kilograms; if it is lower, say $1 per kilogram, she might buy 25 kilograms of apples during the year. Elizabeth's demand for apples for the year is summarized in the demand schedule in Exhibit 1. Elizabeth might not be consciously aware of the amounts that she would purchase at prices other than the prevailing one, but that does not alter the fact that she has a schedule in the sense that she would have bought various other amounts had other prices prevailed. It must be emphasized that the schedule is a list of alternative possibilities. At any one time, only one of the prices will prevail, and thus a certain quantity will be purchased.

Need water? What if the price of water increases significantly? At the new higher price, consumers will still use almost as much water for essentials like drinking and cooking. However, they may no longer "need" to wash their cars as often, water their lawns daily, hose off their sidewalks, run the dishwasher so frequently, take long showers, or flush the toilet as often.

substitution effect
at higher prices, buyers increasingly substitute other goods for the good that now has a higher relative price

income effect
at higher prices, buyers feel poorer, causing a lowering of quantity demanded

individual demand schedule
a schedule that shows the relationship between price and quantity demanded

section 3.2 Exhibit 1	Elizabeth's Demand Schedule for Apples

Price (per kilogram)	Quantity Demanded (kilograms per year)
$5	5
4	10
3	15
2	20
1	25

AN INDIVIDUAL DEMAND CURVE

individual demand curve
a graphical representation that shows the inverse relationship between price and quantity demanded

By plotting the different prices and corresponding quantities demanded in Elizabeth's demand schedule in Exhibit 1 and then connecting them, we can create an **individual demand curve** for Elizabeth (Exhibit 2). From the curve, we can see that when the price is higher, the quantity demanded is lower, and when the price is lower, the quantity demanded is higher. The demand curve shows how the quantity demanded of the good changes as its price varies.

| **section 3.2** | **Elizabeth's Demand** |
| Exhibit 2 | **Curve for Apples** |

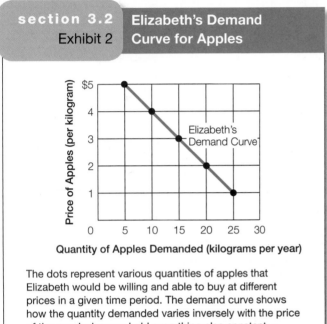

Quantity of Apples Demanded (kilograms per year)

The dots represent various quantities of apples that Elizabeth would be willing and able to buy at different prices in a given time period. The demand curve shows how the quantity demanded varies inversely with the price of the good when we hold everything else constant— *ceteris paribus*. Because of this inverse relationship between price and quantity demanded, the demand curve is downward sloping.

market demand curve
the horizontal summation of individual demand curves

WHAT IS A MARKET DEMAND CURVE?

Although we introduced this concept in terms of the individual, economists usually speak of the demand curve in terms of large groups of people—a whole nation, a community, or a trading area. As you know, every single individual has his or her demand curve for every product. The horizontal summation of the demand curves of many individuals is called the **market demand curve.**

Suppose the consumer group comprises Homer, Marge, and the rest of their small community, Springfield, and that the product is still apples. The effect of price on the quantity of apples demanded by Marge, Homer, and the rest of Springfield is given in the demand schedule and demand curves shown in Exhibit 3. At $4 per kilogram, Homer would be willing and able to buy 20 kilograms of apples per year, Marge would be willing and able to buy 10 kilograms, and the rest of Springfield would be willing and able to buy 2970 kilograms. At $3 per kilogram, Homer would be willing and able to buy 25 kilograms of apples per year, Marge would be willing and able to buy 15 kilograms, and the rest of Springfield would be willing and able to buy 4960 kilograms. The market demand curve is simply the (horizontal) sum of the quantities Homer, Marge, and the rest of Springfield demand at each price. That is, at $4, the quantity demanded in the market would be 3000 kilograms

What if this house had been on the market for a year at the same price and not sold? Although no one may want this house at the current asking price, a number of people may want it at a lower price—the law of demand.

of apples (20 + 10 + 2970 = 3000), and at $3, the quantity demanded in the market would be 5000 kilograms of apples (25 + 15 + 4960 = 5000).

In Exhibit 4, we offer a more complete set of prices and quantities from the market demand for apples during the year. Remember, the market demand curve shows the amounts that all the buyers in the market would be willing and able to buy at various prices. For example, if the price of apples is $2 per kilogram, consumers in the market

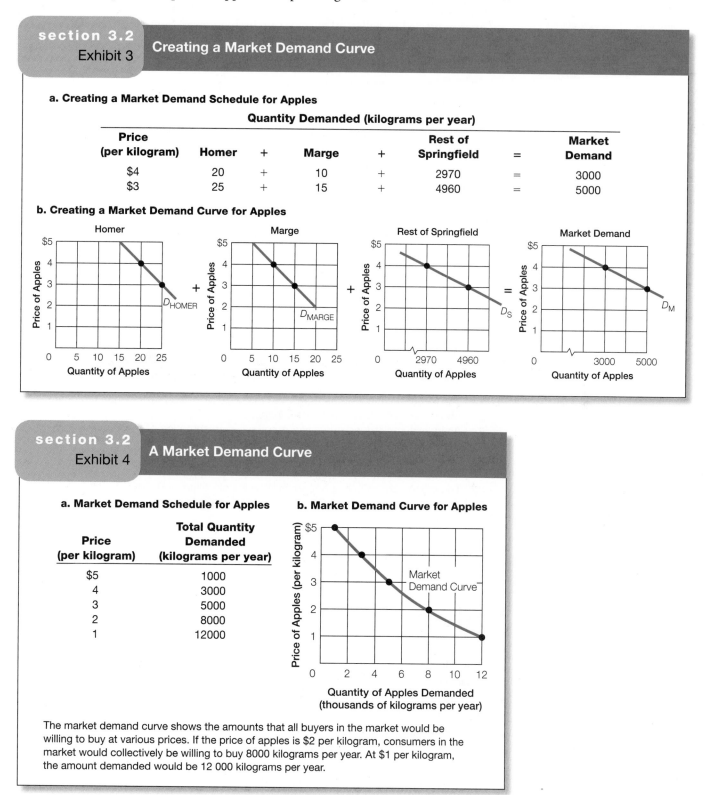

section 3.2
Exhibit 3   **Creating a Market Demand Curve**

a. Creating a Market Demand Schedule for Apples

Quantity Demanded (kilograms per year)

Price (per kilogram)	Homer	+	Marge	+	Rest of Springfield	=	Market Demand
$4	20	+	10	+	2970	=	3000
$3	25	+	15	+	4960	=	5000

b. Creating a Market Demand Curve for Apples

section 3.2
Exhibit 4   **A Market Demand Curve**

a. Market Demand Schedule for Apples

Price (per kilogram)	Total Quantity Demanded (kilograms per year)
$5	1000
4	3000
3	5000
2	8000
1	12000

b. Market Demand Curve for Apples

The market demand curve shows the amounts that all buyers in the market would be willing to buy at various prices. If the price of apples is $2 per kilogram, consumers in the market would collectively be willing to buy 8000 kilograms per year. At $1 per kilogram, the amount demanded would be 12 000 kilograms per year.

would collectively be willing and able to buy 8000 kilograms per year. At $1 per kilogram, the amount demanded would be 12 000 kilograms per year.

A MONEY PRICE

money price
the price that one pays in dollars and cents, sometimes called an absolute or nominal price

Over the past 50 years, few goods have fallen in **money price**—that is, the price that you would pay in dollars and cents. The money price is sometimes called the *absolute* or *nominal price*, expressed in dollars of current purchasing power. Some well-known examples of falling money prices include cellular telephones, DVD players, digital cameras, and home computers, but the evidence indicates that most prices have risen in money terms.

MONEY PRICES VERSUS RELATIVE PRICES

relative price
the price of one good relative to other goods

Money prices themselves are of little importance to most economic decisions in a world where virtually all prices are changing. It is **relative price,** the price of one good relative to other goods, that is crucial.

Suppose you were exploring the Canadian inflation rate of the 1980s and 1990s. You found that from 1980 to 2000, the price of new cars rose, but the quantities of cars demanded did not fall. Is this a flaw in the law of demand? No. Although car prices in dollars rose significantly over this period, so did just about everything else—including wages. The relative price of cars, the price of cars as compared to that of other goods, did not change much over this period. Thus, we would not expect this to cause a fall in the quantity demanded (holding other things constant, especially income). That is, because the relative price did not rise, we would not expect a fall in car sales.

Section Check

1. The law of demand states that when the price of a good falls (rises), the quantity demanded rises (falls), *ceteris paribus*.
2. An individual demand curve is a graphical representation of the relationship between the price and the quantity demanded.
3. The market demand curve shows the amount of a good that all the buyers in the market would be willing and able to buy at various prices.
4. The money price is what one pays in terms of dollars and cents.
5. The relative price is the price of one good relative to another.

---

section
3.3

Shifts in the Demand Curve

- What is the difference between a change in demand and a change in quantity demanded?
- What are the determinants of demand?
- What are substitutes and complements?
- What are normal and inferior goods?
- How does the number of buyers affect the demand curve?
- How do changes in taste affect the demand curve?
- How do changing expectations affect the demand curve?

A CHANGE IN DEMAND VERSUS A CHANGE IN QUANTITY DEMANDED

Economists think consumers are influenced by the prices of goods when they make their purchasing decisions. At lower prices, people prefer to buy more of a good than at higher prices, holding other factors constant. Why? Primarily, it is because many goods are substitutes for one another. For example, an increase in the price of apples might tempt some buyers to switch from buying apples to buying oranges or peaches.

Understanding this relationship between price and quantity demanded is so important that economists make a clear distinction between it and the various other factors that can influence consumer behaviour. A change in a good's price is said to lead to a **change in quantity demanded.** That is, it "moves you along" a given demand curve. The demand curve is drawn under the assumption that all other things are held constant, except the price of the good. However, economists know that price is not the only thing that affects the quantity of a good that people buy. The other factors that influence the demand curve are called *determinants of demand* and a change in these other factors *shifts the entire demand curve.* These determinants of demand are called demand shifters and they lead to a **change in demand.**

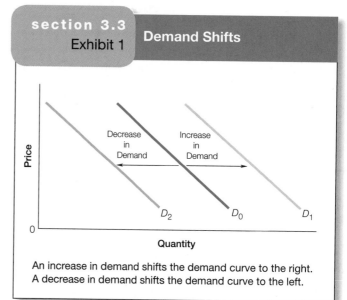

Demand Shifts

An increase in demand shifts the demand curve to the right. A decrease in demand shifts the demand curve to the left.

change in quantity demanded
a change in a good's price leads to a change in quantity demanded, a move along a given demand curve

change in demand
the prices of related goods, income, number of buyers, tastes, and expectations can change the demand for a good. That is, a change in one of these factors shifts the entire demand curve

SHIFTS IN DEMAND

An increase in demand shifts the demand curve to the right; a decrease in demand shifts the demand curve to the left, as seen in Exhibit 1. Some of the possible demand shifters are the prices of related goods, income, number of buyers, tastes, and expectations. We will now look more closely at each of these variables.

THE PRICES OF RELATED GOODS

In deciding how much of a good or service to buy, consumers are influenced by the price of that good or service, a relationship summarized in the law of demand. However, consumers are also influenced by the prices of *related* goods and services—substitutes and complements.

Substitutes

Suppose you go into a store to buy a couple of six packs of Coca-Cola and you see that Pepsi is on sale for half its usual price. Is it possible that you might decide to buy Pepsi instead of Coca-Cola? Economists argue that this is the case, and empirical tests have confirmed that people are responsive to both the price of the good in question and the prices of related goods. In this example, Pepsi and Coca-Cola are said to be substitutes. Two goods are **substitutes** if an increase (a decrease) in the price of one good causes an increase (a decrease) in the demand for another good, a direct (or positive) relationship. Because personal tastes differ, what are substitutes for one person may not be so for another person. Furthermore, some substitutes are better than others. For most people, good substitutes include butter and margarine, movie tickets and video rentals, jackets and sweaters, and peas and carrots.

substitute
an increase (a decrease) in the price of one good causes the demand curve for another good to shift to the right (left)

Complements

If an increase (a decrease) in the price of one good causes a decrease (an increase) in the demand of another good (an inverse or negative relationship), the two goods are called **complements.** Complements are goods that "go together," often consumed and used simultaneously, such as skis and bindings, hot dogs and buns, DVDs and DVD players, or printers and ink cartridges. For example, if the price of motorcycles rises and it causes the demand for motorcycle helmets to fall (shift to the left), the two goods are complements. Or if a decrease in the price of DVD players leads to an increase in the demand (a rightward shift) for DVDs, then DVD players and DVDs are complements.

complement

an increase (a decrease) in the price of one good shifts the demand curve for another good to the left (right)

Substitutes	Complements
$P_{\text{GOOD A}} \uparrow \Rightarrow \uparrow D_{\text{GOOD B}}$	$P_{\text{GOOD A}} \uparrow \Rightarrow \downarrow D_{\text{GOOD B}}$
$P_{\text{GOOD A}} \downarrow \Rightarrow \downarrow D_{\text{GOOD B}}$	$P_{\text{GOOD A}} \downarrow \Rightarrow \uparrow D_{\text{GOOD B}}$

INCOME

Economists have observed that generally the consumption of goods and services is positively related to the income available to consumers. Empirical studies support the notion that as individuals receive more income they tend to increase their purchases of

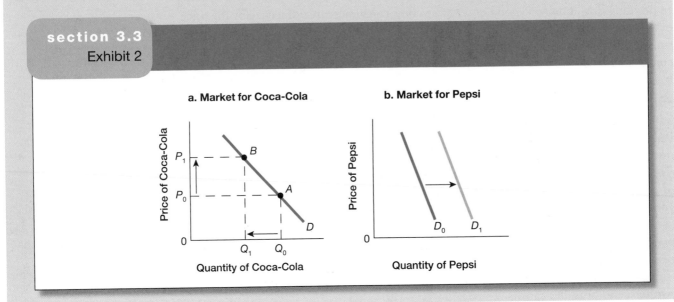

ACTIVE LEARNING EXERCISE

SUBSTITUTE GOODS

Q: Can you describe the change we would expect to see in the demand curve for Pepsi if the relative price for Coca-Cola increased significantly?

A: If the price of one good increases and, as a result, an individual buys more of another good, the two related goods are substitutes. That is, buying more of one reduces purchases of the other. In Exhibit 2(a),

we see that as the price of Coca-Cola increased—a movement up along your demand curve for it—you increased your demand for Pepsi, resulting in a shift in the demand for Pepsi (Exhibit 2(b)). If you hated a particular brand of soft drink, however, it might not matter if someone was giving it away, but that is highly unlikely. The substitution effect varies among individuals, but in the aggregate we can recognize substitutes fairly well.

section 3.3
Exhibit 2

a. Market for Coca-Cola

Price of Coca-Cola

P_1 ⋯⋯ B
P_0 ⋯⋯⋯ A
                    D
0   Q_1 Q_0
Quantity of Coca-Cola

b. Market for Pepsi

Price of Pepsi

              D_0 D_1
0
Quantity of Pepsi

ACTIVE LEARNING EXERCISE

COMPLEMENTARY GOODS

Q: As he looked over the racquets hanging on the wall of the local sports shop, an aspiring young tennis player, Clay Kort, noticed that the price of the racquets was much higher (due to cost increases) than last month. Clay predicted that this increase in the relative price of tennis racquets would probably lead to a reduced demand for tennis balls. Do you agree with Clay?

A: Yes, Clay has correctly indentified tennis racquets and tennis balls as possessing a strong complementary relationship. That is, tennis racquets and

tennis balls "go together." In Exhibit 3(a), we see that as the price of tennis racquets increases, the quantity demanded of tennis racquets falls (a movement in demand). And with fewer tennis racquets being purchased, we would expect people to decrease their demand (a leftward shift) for tennis balls (Exhibit 3(b)). There are many other examples of complements in athletic equipment: skis and bindings, golf clubs and golf balls, hockey sticks and hockey pucks, and so on.

section 3.3
Exhibit 3

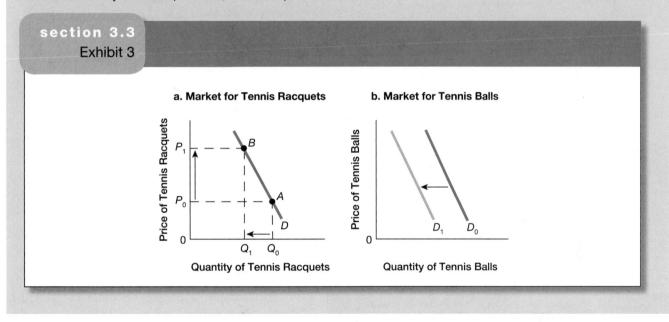

a. Market for Tennis Racquets

b. Market for Tennis Balls

most goods and services. Other things held equal, rising income usually leads to an increase in the demand for goods (a rightward shift of the demand curve), and decreasing income usually leads to a decrease in the demand for goods (a leftward shift of the demand curve).

Normal and Inferior Goods

If demand for a good increases when incomes rise and decreases when incomes fall, the good is called a **normal good.** Most goods are normal goods. Consumers will typically buy more CDs, clothes, pizzas, and trips to the movies as their incomes rise. However, if demand for a good decreases when incomes rise and increases when incomes fall, the good is called an **inferior good.** For example, for most people inferior goods might include do-it-yourself haircuts, used cars, thrift-shop clothing, macaroni and cheese, and so on. The term *inferior* in this sense does not refer to the quality of the good in question but shows that when income changes, demand changes in the opposite direction (inversely).

normal good
if income increases, the demand for a good increases; if income decreases, the demand for a good decreases

inferior good
if income increases, the demand for a good decreases; if income decreases, the demand for a good increases

ACTIVE LEARNING EXERCISE

NORMAL AND INFERIOR GOODS

Q: Chester owns a furniture shop. If there was a recent boom in the economy (higher average income per person and fewer people unemployed), can Chester expect to sell more furniture?

A: Yes, furniture is generally considered a normal good, so a rise in income will increase the demand for furniture (Exhibit 4(a)). However, if Chester sells unfin-

ished, used, or lower-quality furniture, the demand for his products may fall, as higher incomes allow customers to buy furniture that is finished, new, or of higher quality. Chester's furniture would then be an inferior good (Exhibit 4(b)).

section 3.3
Exhibit 4

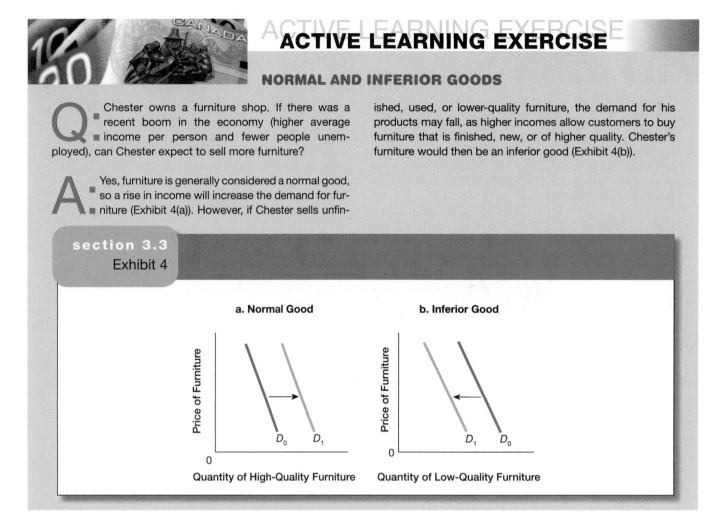

a. Normal Good

Price of Furniture

D_0 D_1

0

Quantity of High-Quality Furniture

b. Inferior Good

Price of Furniture

D_1 D_0

0

Quantity of Low-Quality Furniture

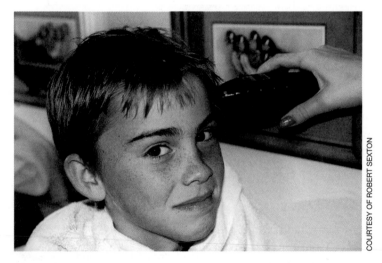

COURTESY OF ROBERT SEXTON

For most people, do-it-yourself haircuts are an inferior good. That is, an increase in income will lead to a reduction in do-it-yourself haircuts.

For example, if people's incomes rise and they increase their demand for movie tickets, we say that movie tickets are a normal good. But if people's incomes fall and they increase their demand for bus rides, we say bus rides are an inferior good. Whether goods are normal or inferior, the point here is that income influences demand—usually positively, but sometimes negatively.

Normal Good	**Inferior Good**
Income ↑ ⇒ Demand ↑	Income ↑ ⇒ Demand ↓
Income ↓ ⇒ Demand ↓	Income ↓ ⇒ Demand ↑

NUMBER OF BUYERS

The demand for a good or service will vary with the size of the potential consumer population. The demand for wheat, for example, rises as population increases because the added population wants to consume wheat products, like bread or cereal. Marketing experts, who closely follow the patterns of consumer behaviour with regards to a particular good or service, are usually vitally concerned with the "demographics" of the product—the vital statistics of the potential consumer population, including size, income, and age characteristics. For example, market researchers for baby-food companies keep a close watch on the birth rate.

TASTES

The demand for a good or service may increase or decrease suddenly with changes in fashions or fads. Taste changes may be triggered by advertising or promotion, by a news story, by the behaviour of some popular public figure, and so on. Taste changes are particularly noticeable in apparel. Skirt lengths, coat lapels, shoe styles, and tie sizes change frequently.

Changes in preferences naturally lead to shifts in demand. Much of the predictive power of economic theory, however, stems from the assumption that tastes are relatively stable, at least over a substantial period of time. Tastes *do* change, though. A person may grow tired of one type of recreation or food and try another type. Changes in occupation, number of dependants, state of health, and age also tend to alter preferences. The birth of a baby may cause a family to spend less on recreation and more on food and clothing. Illness increases the demand for medicine and lessens purchases of other goods. A cold winter increases the demand for natural gas. Changes in customs and traditions also affect preferences, and the development of new products draws consumer preferences away from other goods. Compact discs have replaced record albums, just as in-line skates have replaced traditional roller skates.

EXPECTATIONS

Sometimes the demand for a good or service in a given time period will dramatically increase or decrease because consumers expect the good to change in price or availability at some future date. For example, in the summer of 1997, many buyers expected coffee harvests to be lower because of El Niño. As a result of their expectations of higher future coffee prices, buyers increased their current demand for coffee. That is, the current demand for coffee shifted to the right. Other examples, such as waiting to buy a home computer because price reductions may be even greater in the future, are also common. Or, if you expect to earn additional income next month, you may be more willing to dip into your current savings to buy something this month.

CHANGES IN DEMAND VERSUS CHANGES IN QUANTITY DEMANDED REVISITED

Economists put particular emphasis on the impact on consumer behaviour of a change in the price of a good. We are interested in distinguishing between consumer behaviour related to the price of a good itself (movement *along* a demand curve) from behaviour related to other factors changing (shifts of the demand curve).

As indicated earlier, if the price of a good changes, we say that this leads to a *"change in quantity demanded."* If one of the other factors (determinants) influencing consumer behaviour changes, we say there is a *"change in demand."* The effects of some of the determinants that cause a change in demand (shifters) are reviewed in Exhibit 5.

section 3.3
Exhibit 5

section 3.3
Exhibit 5   **Possible Demand Shifters**

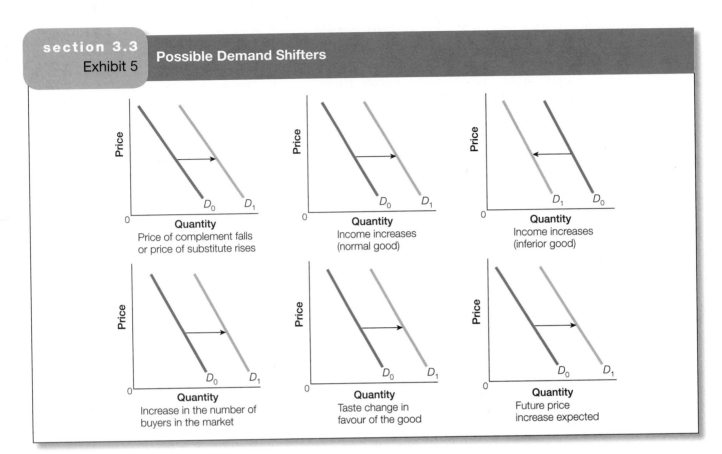

Price of complement falls
or price of substitute rises

Income increases
(normal good)

Income increases
(inferior good)

Increase in the number of
buyers in the market

Taste change in
favour of the good

Future price
increase expected

In The **NEWS**

CHINA AND INDIA ARE GROWTH DRIVERS FOR GLOBAL AUTO INDUSTRY

BY ERIC BEAUCHESNE

Developing countries will provide the growth markets for global auto sales, a Canadian financial institution says.

Global auto sales, which hit a record [in 2004], will edge ahead [in 2005] as sales growth in developing markets, especially China and India, offset stagnant sales in industrial markets such as North America, Europe and Japan, Scotiabank predicted in a year-end auto report.

Sales worldwide rose three per cent to an estimated all-time high 45.5 million vehicles [in 2004], thanks to a synchronized global economic recovery and despite record oil prices, it said. And sales will rise a more moderate two per cent in 2005 to nearly 46.2 million.

Vehicle sales in China rose by an estimated 15 per cent [in 2004] to about 2.3 million, surpassing both Italy and France to become the fourth-largest car market in the world.

While sales growth slowed from a 71 per cent explosion in 2003, it was still a strong increase, noted Scotiabank economist and auto industry analyst Carl Gomes. Higher incomes and falling car prices are more than offsetting rising interest rates aimed at dampening inflation there.

By the end of the decade China is expected to be the world's second-largest car market—surpassing both Germany

and Japan—with sales only behind the United States, he said. India's market is only half that of China, but [in 2004] surpassed China as the fastest growing market in the world.

"These two nations are now the major growth drivers for the global auto industry," Gomes said. "India has the world's second-largest population with 1.05 billion people—and its population growth is outpacing China's."

Just to keep pace with the growth in the population, sales in India must rise by 20 per cent a year, he noted. That doesn't include the sales growth that will come from an expected increase in vehicle ownership rates in India from only 10 per 1000 population, which compares with 19 per 1000 in China and 600 in Canada.

SOURCE: Adapted from Eric Beauchesne, "Developing countries will power auto sales: study: china is driving force," *Calgary Herald*, December 31, 2004, p. E3. Material reprinted with the express permission of: "CAN-WEST NEWS SERVICE", a CanWest Partnership.

CONSIDER THIS:

The global demand for automobiles will increase because of rising demand in two important markets: China and India. Rising incomes and rising populations are the major factors increasing demand in the two markets.

ACTIVE LEARNING EXERCISE

CHANGES IN DEMAND VERSUS CHANGES IN QUANTITY DEMANDED

Q: How would you use a graph to demonstrate the two following scenarios? (1) Someone buys more CDs because the price of CDs has fallen; and (2) a student buys more CDs because she just got a 20 percent raise at work, giving her additional income.

A: In Exhibit 6, the movement from A to B is called an *increase in quantity demanded,* and the movement from B to A is called a *decrease in quantity demanded*. Economists use the phrase "increase or decrease in quantity demanded" to describe movements along a given demand curve. However, the change from A to C is called an *increase in demand,* and the change from C to A is called a *decrease in demand*. The phrase "increase or decrease in demand" is reserved for a shift in the whole curve. So if an individual buys more CDs because the price fell, we say there was an increase in quantity demanded. However, if she buys more CDs even at the current price, say $10, we say there is an increase in demand. In this case, the increase in income was responsible for the increase in demand, as she chose to spend some of her new income on CDs.

section 3.3
Exhibit 6

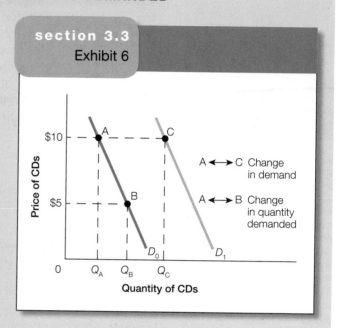

Section Check

1. A change in the quantity demanded describes a movement along a given demand curve in response to a change in the price of the good.
2. A change in demand shifts the entire demand curve. An increase in demand shifts the demand curve to the right; a decrease shifts it to the left.
3. A change in the price of a substitute shifts the demand curve for the good in question. The relationship is direct.
4. A change in the price of a complement shifts the demand curve for the good in question. The relationship is inverse.
5. Changes in income cause demand curve shifts. For normal goods the relationship is direct; for inferior goods it is inverse.
6. The position of the demand curve will vary according to the number of consumers in the market.
7. Taste changes will shift the demand curve.
8. Changes in expected future prices and income can shift the current demand curve.

Supply

section

3.4

- What is the law of supply?
- What is an individual supply curve?
- What is a market supply curve?

law of supply

the higher (lower) the price of the good, the greater (smaller) the quantity supplied

In order to get more oil, drillers must sometimes drill deeper or go into unexplored areas, and they still may come up with a dry hole. If it costs more to increase oil production, then oil prices would have to rise in order for producers to increase their output.

individual supply curve

a graphical representation that shows the positive relationship between the price and the quantity supplied

THE LAW OF SUPPLY

In a market, the answer to the fundamental question "What do we produce, and in what quantities?" depends on the interaction of both buyers and sellers. Demand is only half the story. The willingness and ability of suppliers to provide goods are equally important factors that must be weighed by decision makers in all societies. As in the case of demand, factors other than the price of the good are also important to suppliers, such as the cost of inputs or advances in technology. As with demand, the price of the good is an important factor. Although behaviour will vary among individual suppliers, economists expect, other things being equal, that the quantity supplied will vary directly with the price of the good, a relationship called the **law of supply.** According to the law of supply, the higher the price of the good (P), the greater the quantity supplied (Q_S), and the lower the price of the good, the smaller the quantity supplied.

$$P \uparrow \Rightarrow Q_S \uparrow \text{ and } P \downarrow \Rightarrow Q_S \downarrow$$

The relationship described by the law of supply is a direct, or positive, relationship, because the variables move in the same direction.

A POSITIVE RELATIONSHIP BETWEEN PRICE AND QUANTITY SUPPLIED

Firms supplying goods and services want to increase their profits, and the higher the price per unit, the greater the profitability generated by supplying more of that good. For example, if you were an apple grower, wouldn't you much rather be paid $5 a kilogram than $1 a kilogram?

There is another reason that supply curves are upward sloping. The law of increasing opportunity costs demonstrated that when we hold technology and input prices constant, producing additional units of a good will require increased opportunity costs. That is, when we produce more of anything, we use the most efficient resources first (those with the lowest opportunity cost) and then draw on less efficient resources (those with higher opportunity cost) as more of the good is produced. So if costs are rising for producers as they produce more units, they must receive a higher price to compensate them for their higher costs. In short, increasing production costs mean that suppliers will require higher prices to induce them to increase their output.

AN INDIVIDUAL SUPPLY CURVE

To illustrate the concept of an **individual supply curve,** consider the amount of apples that an individual supplier, John Macintosh, is willing and able to supply in one year. The law of supply can be illustrated, like the law of demand, by a table or graph. John's supply schedule for apples is shown in Exhibit 1(a). The price–quantity supplied combinations were then plotted and joined to create the individual supply curve shown in Exhibit 1(b). Note that the individual supply curve is upward sloping as you move from left to right. At higher prices, it will be more attractive to increase production. Existing firms, or growers, will produce more at higher prices than at lower prices.

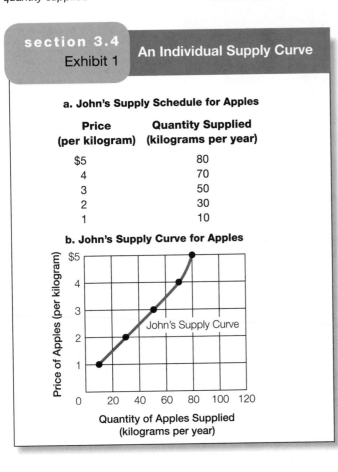

section 3.4
Exhibit 1

An Individual Supply Curve

a. John's Supply Schedule for Apples

Price (per kilogram)	Quantity Supplied (kilograms per year)
$5	80
4	70
3	50
2	30
1	10

b. John's Supply Curve for Apples

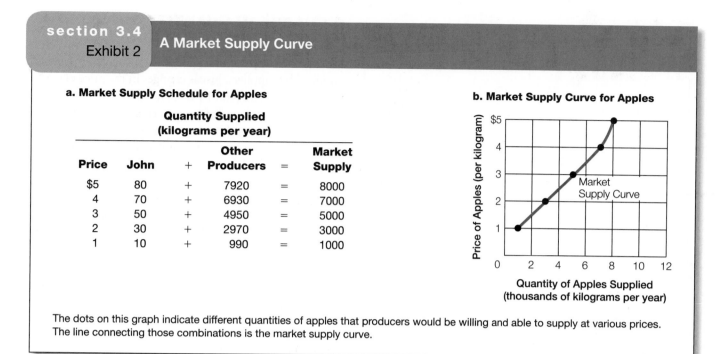

section 3.4
Exhibit 2   **A Market Supply Curve**

a. Market Supply Schedule for Apples

Price	John	+	Other Producers	=	Market Supply
			Quantity Supplied (kilograms per year)		
$5	80	+	7920	=	8000
4	70	+	6930	=	7000
3	50	+	4950	=	5000
2	30	+	2970	=	3000
1	10	+	990	=	1000

b. Market Supply Curve for Apples

The dots on this graph indicate different quantities of apples that producers would be willing and able to supply at various prices. The line connecting those combinations is the market supply curve.

THE MARKET SUPPLY CURVE

The **market supply curve** may be thought of as the horizontal summation of the supply curves for individual firms. The market supply schedule, which reflects the total quantity supplied at each price by all of the apple producers, is shown in Exhibit 2(a). Exhibit 2(b) illustrates the resulting market supply curve for this group of apple producers.

market supply curve
a graphical representation of the amount of goods and services that suppliers are willing and able to supply at various prices

Section Check

1. The law of supply states that the higher (lower) the price of the good, the greater (smaller) the quantity supplied.
2. There is a positive relationship between price and quantity supplied because profit opportunities are greater at higher prices and because the higher production costs of increased output mean that suppliers will require higher prices.
3. The market supply curve is a graphical representation of the amount of goods and services that suppliers are willing and able to supply at various prices.

section
3.5

Shifts in the Supply Curve

- What is the difference between a change in supply and a change in quantity supplied?
- How does the number of suppliers affect the supply curve?
- How does technology affect the supply curve?
- How do taxes affect the supply curve?

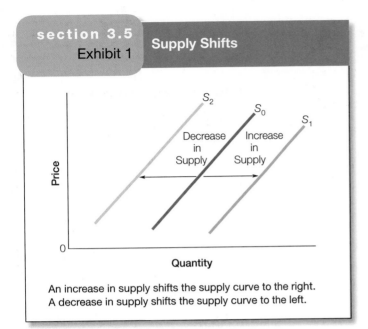

section 3.5
Exhibit 1   **Supply Shifts**

An increase in supply shifts the supply curve to the right.
A decrease in supply shifts the supply curve to the left.

section 3.5
Exhibit 2   **Substitutions in Production**

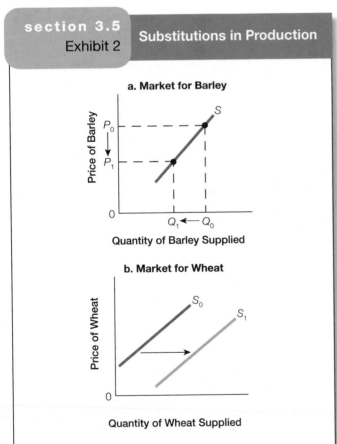

If land can be used for either barley or wheat, a decrease in
the price of barley (a movement along the supply curve)
may cause some farmers to shift out of the production of
barley and into wheat—shifting the wheat supply curve to
the right.

A CHANGE IN QUANTITY SUPPLIED VERSUS A CHANGE IN SUPPLY

Changes in the price of a good lead to changes in quantity supplied by suppliers, just as changes in the price of a good lead to changes in quantity demanded by buyers. Similarly, a change in supply, whether an increase or a decrease, will occur for reasons other than changes in the price of the product itself, just as changes in demand are due to factors (determinants) other than the price of the good. In other words, a change in the price of the good in question is shown as a movement along a given supply curve, leading to a change in quantity supplied. A change in any other factor that can affect supplier behaviour (input prices, the prices of related products, expectations, number of suppliers, technology, regulation, taxes and subsidies, and weather) results in *a shift in the entire supply curve*, leading to a change in supply.

SHIFTS IN SUPPLY

An increase in supply shifts the supply curve to the right; a decrease in supply shifts the supply curve to the left, as seen in Exhibit 1. We will now look at some of the possible determinants of supply—factors that determine the position of the supply curve—in greater depth.

INPUT PRICES

Suppliers are strongly influenced by the costs of inputs used in the production process, such as steel used for automobiles or microchips used in computers. For example, higher labour, materials, energy, or other input costs increase the costs of production, causing the supply curve to shift to the left at each and every price. If input prices fall, this will lower the costs of production, causing the supply curve to shift to the right—more will be supplied at each and every price.

THE PRICES OF RELATED PRODUCTS

Suppose you own your own farm, on which you plant wheat and barley. Then, the price of barley falls and farmers reduce the quantity supplied of barley, as seen in Exhibit 2(a). What effect would the lower price of barley have on your wheat production? Easy—it would increase the supply of wheat. You would want to produce relatively less of the crop that had fallen in price (barley) and relatively more of the now more attractive other crop (wheat). Wheat and barley are *substitutes in production* because both goods can be produced using the same resources. This example demonstrates why the price of related products is important as a supply shifter as well as a demand shifter. Producers tend to substitute the production of more profitable products for that of less profitable products. This is desirable from society's perspective as well because more profitable products tend to be those considered more valuable by society, whereas less profitable products are usually considered less valuable. Hence, the lower price in the barley market has caused an increase in supply (a rightward shift) in the wheat market, as seen in Exhibit 2(b).

EXPECTATIONS

Another factor shifting supply is suppliers' expectations. If producers expect a higher price in the future, they will supply less now than they otherwise would have, preferring to wait and sell when their goods will be more valuable. For example, if an oil producer expected the future price of oil to be higher next year, he might decide to store some of his current production of oil for next year when the price would be higher. Similarly, if producers expect now that the price will be lower later, they will supply more now.

NUMBER OF SUPPLIERS

We are normally interested in market demands and supplies (because together they determine prices and quantities) rather than in the behaviour of individual consumers and firms. As we discussed earlier, the supply curves of individual suppliers can be summed horizontally to create a market supply curve. An increase in the number of suppliers leads to an increase in supply, denoted by a rightward shift in the supply curve. An exodus of suppliers has the opposite impact, a decrease in supply, which is indicated by a leftward shift in the supply curve.

TECHNOLOGY

Most of us think of prices as constantly rising, given the existence of inflation, but, in fact, decreases in costs often occur because of technological progress, and such advances can lower prices. Human creativity works to find new ways to produce goods and services using fewer or less costly inputs of labour, natural resources, or capital. In recent years, despite generally rising prices, the prices of electronic equipment such as computers, cellular telephones, and DVD players have fallen dramatically. At any given price this year, suppliers are willing to provide many more (of a given quality of) computers than in the 1970s, simply because technology has dramatically reduced the cost of providing them. Graphically, the increase in supply is indicated by a shift to the right in the supply curve.

REGULATION

Supply may also change because of changes in the legal and regulatory environment in which firms operate. Government regulations can influence the costs of production to the firm, leading to cost-induced supply changes similar to those just discussed. For example, if new safety or anti-pollution requirements increase labour and capital costs, the increased cost will result, other things equal, in a decrease in supply, shifting the supply curve to the left, or up. An increase in a government-imposed minimum wage may have a similar effect by raising labour costs and decreasing supply in markets that employ many low-wage workers. However, deregulation—the process by which governments reduce or outright eliminate restrictions on individuals or businesses—can shift the supply curve to the right.

TAXES AND SUBSIDIES

Certain types of taxes can also increase the costs of production borne by the supplier, causing the supply curve to shift to the left at each price. The opposite of a tax (a subsidy) can lower the firm's costs and shift the supply curve to the right. For example, the government sometimes provides farmers with subsidies to encourage the production of certain agricultural products.

WEATHER

In addition, weather can certainly affect the supply of certain commodities, particularly agricultural products and transportation services. A drought or freezing temperatures will almost certainly cause the supply curves for many crops to shift to the left, whereas exceptionally good weather can shift a supply curve to the right.

CHANGE IN SUPPLY VERSUS CHANGE IN QUANTITY SUPPLIED—REVISITED

If the price of a good changes, we say this leads to a change in the quantity supplied. If one of the other factors influences sellers' behaviour, we say this leads to a change in supply. For example, if production costs rise because of a wage increase or higher fuel costs, other things remaining constant, we would expect a decrease in supply—that is, a leftward shift in the supply curve. Alternatively, if some variable, like lower input prices, causes the costs of production to fall, the supply curve will shift to the right. Exhibit 3 illustrates the effect of some of the determinants that cause shifts in the supply curve.

section 3.5
Exhibit 3   **Possible Supply Shifts**

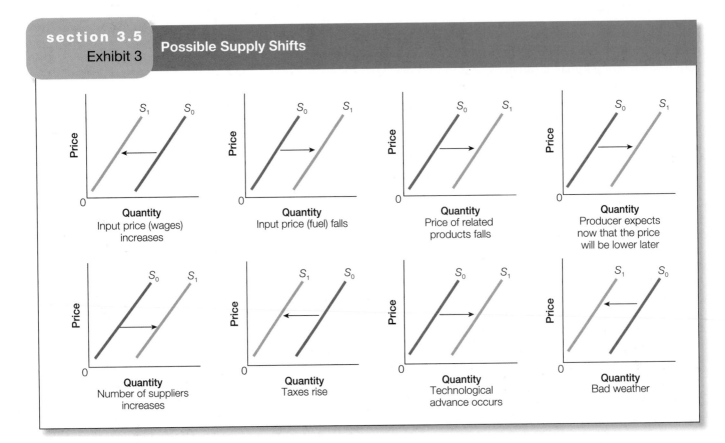

In The **NEWS**

ALBERTA FARMERS PLANT RECORD CANOLA; AGRICULTURE BOOM CREATES BUOYANT MOOD

BY GINA TEEL

Fat prices for canola motivated Alberta farmers to plant a record number of hectares of the cash crop this year, seeing the province notch the biggest percentage increase on the canola-loving Prairies, in terms of new acreage devoted to the popular oilseed.

Provincially, the area seeded to canola is expected to reach 2.1 million hectares, or 263,000 more hectares than in 2007, and well above the five-year average of 1.7 million hectares, Statistics Canada said Tuesday in its latest principal field crop report.

Prairie-wide, it's estimated a whopping 405,000 more hectares were seeded to canola this year, to 6.3 million hectares.

David Burroughs, an analyst with Statistics Canada, said the seeding estimates suggest a similar story is afoot across the board.

"If you're asking about canola, the prices there were pretty darn good, and it just seems there isn't anything you can plant this year that you can't make money on," he said.

The 405,000-hectare increase in canola is equal to 650,000 tonnes of production—assuming normal weather from here to harvest, he said.

Prairie farmers have made room for the canola by ripping up fallow hectares, he said—land most industry observers thought would be going into barley and oats. Seeded hectares of both those crops are down in Alberta this year.

SOURCE: Adapted from Gina Teel, "Alberta farmers plant record canola; Agriculture boom creates buoyant mood," *Calgary Herald*, June 25, 2008, p. D1. Material reprinted with the express permission of: "Calgary Herald Group Inc.", a CanWest Partnership.

CONSIDER THIS:

Why did Alberta farmers choose to plant more canola in 2008 as compared to previous years? The answer is simple: price. Since Alberta farmers can use their land to plant any number of crops (canola, wheat, barley, oats), the increase in the price of canola (a movement along the supply curve) has caused some farmers to shift out of the production of these other crops and into canola—shifting the supply curves for the other crops to the left.

ACTIVE LEARNING EXERCISE

CHANGE IN SUPPLY VERSUS CHANGE IN QUANTITY SUPPLIED

Q: How would you graph the following two scenarios: (1) the price of wheat has risen; and (2) good weather has caused an unusually abundant wheat harvest?

A: In the first scenario, there is an increase in the price of wheat, so there is a change in quantity supplied (i.e., a movement along the supply curve). In the second scenario, the good weather causes the supply curve for wheat to shift to the right. This is called a change in supply (not quantity supplied). A shift in the whole supply curve is caused by one of the other variables, not by a change in the price of the good in question.

As shown in Exhibit 4, the movement from A to B is called an increase in quantity supplied, and the movement from B to A is called a decrease in quantity supplied. However, the change from B to C is called an increase in supply and the movement from C to B is called a decrease in supply.

section 3.5
Exhibit 4

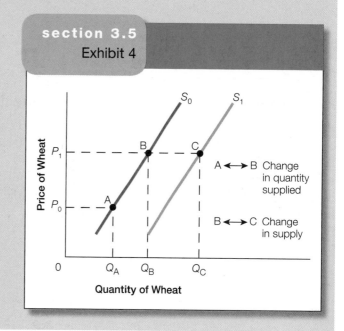

Section Check

1. A movement along a given supply curve is caused by a change in the price of the good in question. As we move along the supply curve, we say there is a change in the quantity supplied.
2. A shift of the entire supply curve is called a change in supply.
3. An increase in supply shifts the supply curve to the right; a decrease shifts it to the left.
4. Input prices, the prices of related products, expectations, the number of suppliers, technology, regulation, taxes and subsidies, and weather can all lead to changes in supply.
5. The supply of a good increases (decreases) if the price of one of its substitutes in production falls (rises).

Summary

Section 3.1
- A market is the process of buyers and sellers exchanging goods and services.

Section 3.2
- The law of demand states that when the price of a good falls (rises), the quantity demanded rises (falls), *ceteris paribus*.

Section 3.3
- A change in the price of the good leads to a change in quantity demanded (this is referred to as a *movement* along a demand curve).
- A change in the price of related goods (substitutes and complements), income, number of buyers, tastes, and expectations can lead to a change in demand (this is referred to as a *shift* of the demand curve).

Section 3.4
- The law of supply states that the higher (lower) the price of the good, the greater (smaller) the quantity supplied, *ceteris paribus*.

Section 3.5
- A change in the price of the good leads to a change in the quantity supplied (this is referred to as a *movement* along a supply curve).
- Input prices, the prices of related products, expectations, the number of suppliers, technology, regulation, taxes and subsidies, and weather can all lead to a change in supply (this is referred to as a *shift* of the supply curve).

Key Terms and Concepts

For a complete glossary of chapter key terms, visit the textbook's Web site at http://www.sextonmicro2e.nelson.com.

market 65
competitive market 66
law of demand 66
substitution effect 67
income effect 67
individual demand schedule 67
individual demand curve 68

market demand curve 68
money price 70
relative price 70
change in quantity demanded 71
change in demand 71
substitute 71

complements 72
normal good 73
inferior good 73
law of supply 78
individual supply curve 78
market supply curve 79

Review Questions

1. Using the demand curve, show the effect of the following events on the market for beef:
   a. Consumer income increases.
   b. The price of beef increases.
   c. There is an outbreak of mad cow disease.
   d. The price of chicken (a substitute) increases.
   e. The price of barbecue grills (a complement) increases.

2. Draw demand curves for the following goods. If the price of the first good listed rises, what will happen to the demand for the second good and why?
   a. hamburger and ketchup
   b. Coca-Cola and Pepsi
   c. camera and film
   d. golf clubs and golf balls

3. Show the impact of each of the following events on the demand for or the supply of oil.
   a. OPEC becomes more effective in limiting the supply of oil.
   b. OPEC becomes less effective in limiting the supply of oil.
   c. The price for natural gas (a substitute for heating oil) rises.
   d. New oil discoveries occur in Alberta.
   e. Electric and hybrid cars become subsidized and their prices fall.

4. Which of the following will cause an increase in the quantity of cell phones demanded? in the demand for cellphones?
   a. The price of cellphones falls.
   b. Your income increases.
   c. The price of cellphone service (a complement) increases.
   d. The price of pagers (a substitute) falls.

5. Which curve (supply or demand) would shift and in which direction in the following cases?
   a. an increase in income and a decreasing price of a complement, for a normal good
   b. a technological advance and lower input prices
   c. a decrease in the price of a substitute and a decrease in income, for an inferior good
   d. producers' expectations that prices will soon fall, and increasingly costly government regulations

6. If the price of ice cream increased,
   a. what would be the effect on the demand for ice cream?
   b. what would be the effect on the demand for frozen yogurt?

7. If the price of corn rose,
   a. what would be the effect on the supply of corn?
   b. what would be the effect on the supply of wheat?

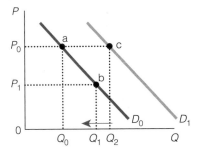

8. Using the graph above, answer the following questions:
   a. What is the shift from D_0 to D_1 called?
   b. What is the movement from b to a called?

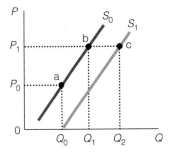

9. Using the graph above, answer the following questions:
   a. What is the shift from S_0 to S_1 called?
   b. What is the movement from a to b called?
   c. What is the movement from b to a called?
   d. What is the shift from S_1 to S_0 called?

Fill in the Blanks

Section 3.1

1. A _____ is the process of buyers and sellers _____ goods and services.

2. The important point about a market is what it does—it facilitates _____.

3. _____, as a group, determine the demand side of the market. _____, as a group, determine the supply side of the market.

4. A _____ market consists of many buyers and sellers where no single buyer or seller can influence the market price.

Section 3.2

5. According to the law of demand, other things being equal, when the price of a good or service falls, the _____ increases.

6. The primary reason for the inverse relationship between price and quantity demanded in the law of demand is the _____ effect.

7. An _____ reveals the different amounts of a particular good a person would be willing and able to buy at various possible prices in a particular time interval, other things being equal.

8. The _____ for a product is the horizontal summation of the demand curves of the individuals in the market.

9. The _____ price of a good is the price you would pay for it in dollars and cents, expressed in dollars of current purchasing power. The _____ price of a good is its price in terms of other goods.

Section 3.3

10. A change in _____ leads to a change in quantity demanded, illustrated by _____ a demand curve.

11. A change in demand is caused by changes in any of the other factors (besides the good's price) that would affect how much of the good is purchased: the _____, _____, the _____ of buyers, _____, and _____.

12. An increase in demand is represented by a _____ shift in the demand curve; a decrease in demand is represented by a _____ shift in the demand curve.

13. Two goods are called _____ if an increase in the price of one causes an increase in the demand for the other.

14. For normal goods an increase in income leads to a(n) _____ in demand, and a decrease in income leads to a(n) _____ in demand, other things being equal.

15. An increase in the expected future price of a good or an expected future income increase may _____ current demand.

Section 3.4

16. According to the law of supply, the higher the price of the good, the greater the _____, and the lower the price of the good, the smaller the _____.

17. The quantity supplied is positively related to the price because firms supplying goods and services want to increase their _____, and because increasing _____ costs mean that the suppliers will require prices to induce them to increase their output.

18. An individual supply curve is a graphical representation that shows the _____ relationship between the price and the quantity supplied.

19. The market supply curve is a graphical representation of the amount of goods and services that suppliers are _____ and _____ to supply at various prices.

Section 3.5

20. Possible supply determinants (factors that determine the position of the supply curve) are _____ prices; _____; _____ of suppliers; and _____, _____, _____, and _____.

21. If input prices fall, this will _____ the costs of production, causing the supply curve to shift to the _____.

22. The supply of a good _____ if the price of one of its substitutes in production falls.

23. The supply of a good _____ if the price of one of its substitutes in production increases.

True or False

Section 3.1

1. The differences in the conditions under which the exchange between buyers and sellers occurs make it difficult to precisely define a market.

2. All markets are effectively global in scope.

Section 3.2

3. The law of demand puts the concept of basic human "needs" to rest as an analytical tool because there are usually plenty of substitutes available for any good.

4. There is an inverse or negative relationship between price and quantity demanded.

5. The market demand curve is the vertical summation of individual demand curves.

6. A relative price is the price of one good relative to the price of other goods.

Section 3.3

7. A change in a good's price does not change its demand.

8. A change in demand is illustrated by a shift in the entire demand curve.

9. Because personal tastes differ, what are substitutes for one person may not be substitutes for another person.

10. Two goods are complements if an increase in the price of one causes an increase in the demand for the other.

11. Those goods for which falling income leads to decreased demand are called inferior goods.

12. Either an increase in the number of buyers or an increase in tastes or preferences for a good or service will increase the market demand for a good or service.

13. A decrease in the price of ice cream would cause an increase in the demand for frozen yogurt, a substitute.

Section 3.4

14. The law of supply states that, other things being equal, the quantity supplied will vary directly (a positive relationship) with the price of the good.

15. The market supply curve for a product is the vertical summation of the supply curves for individual firms.

Section 3.5

16. A change in the price of a good leads to a change in the quantity supplied, but not a change in its supply.

17. An increase in supply leads to a movement up along the supply curve.

18. A decrease in supply shifts the supply curve to the left.

19. Just as demanders will demand more now if the price of a good is expected to rise in the near future, sellers will supply more now if the price of a good is expected to rise in the near future.

20. Both technological progress and cost-increasing regulations will increase supply.

Multiple Choice

Section 3.1

1. Which of the following is a market?
    a. a garage sale
    b. a restaurant
    c. the Toronto Stock Exchange
    d. an eBay auction
    e. all of the above

2. In a competitive market,
    a. there are a number of buyers and sellers.
    b. sellers, but not buyers, have significant control over the market price.
    c. no single buyer or seller can appreciably affect the market price.
    d. both a and c are true.

Section 3.2

3. If the demand for milk is downward sloping, then an increase in the price of milk will result in a(n)
    a. increase in the demand for milk.
    b. decrease in the demand for milk.
    c. increase in the quantity of milk demanded.
    d. decrease in the quantity of milk demanded.
    e. decrease in the supply of milk.

4. If the dollar price of Good A rises by 15 percent while the prices of other goods rise an average of 25 percent, then Good A's nominal price has _____ and its relative price has _____.
    a. risen, risen
    b. risen, fallen
    c. fallen, risen
    d. fallen, fallen

Section 3.3

5. Which of the following would not cause a change in the demand for cheese?
  a. an increase in the price of crackers, which are consumed with cheese
  b. an increase in the income of cheese consumers
  c. an increase in the population of cheese lovers
  d. an increase in the price of cheese
  e. none of the above

6. *Ceteris paribus,* an increase in the price of DVD players would tend to
  a. decrease the demand for DVD players.
  b. increase the price of televisions, a complement to DVD players.
  c. increase the demand for DVD players.
  d. increase the demand for VCRs, a substitute for DVD players.
  e. decrease the quantity of DVD players supplied.

7. CBC Newsworld announces that bad weather in Central America has greatly reduced the number of cocoa-bean plants and as a result, the price of chocolate is expected to rise soon. As a result,
  a. the current market demand for chocolate will decrease.
  b. the current market demand for chocolate will increase.
  c. the current quantity demanded for chocolate will decrease.
  d. there is no change in the current market for chocolate, but there will be after the current crop of cocoa-bean plants is processed into chocolate.

8. Whenever the price of Good A increases, the demand for Good B increases as well. Goods A and B appear to be
  a. complements.
  b. substitutes.
  c. inferior goods.
  d. normal goods.
  e. inverse goods.

Section 3.4

9. An upward-sloping supply curve shows that
  a. buyers are willing to pay more for particularly scarce products.
  b. suppliers expand production as the product price falls.
  c. suppliers are willing to increase production of their goods if they receive higher prices for them.
  d. buyers are willing to buy more as the product price falls.
  e. buyers are not affected either directly or indirectly by the sellers' costs of production.

10. Along a supply curve,
  a. supply changes as price changes.
  b. quantity supplied changes as price changes.
  c. supply changes as technology changes.
  d. quantity supplied changes as technology changes.

Section 3.5

11. All of the following factors will affect the supply of shoes except one. Which will not affect the supply of shoes?
  a. higher wages for shoe-factory workers
  b. higher prices for leather

c. a technological improvement that reduces waste of leather and other raw materials in shoe production

d. an increase in consumer income

12. Which of the following is not a determinant of supply?
   a. input prices
   b. technology
   c. tastes
   d. expectations
   e. the prices of related products

13. If a farmer were choosing between growing wheat on his own land and growing soybeans on his own land,
   a. an increase in the price of soybeans would increase his supply of soybeans.
   b. an increase in the price of soybeans would increase his supply of wheat.
   c. an increase in the price of soybeans would decrease his supply of soybeans.
   d. an increase in the price of soybeans would decrease his supply of wheat.
   e. an increase in the price of soybeans would not change his supply of either wheat or soybeans.

14. Antonio's makes the greatest pizza and delivers it hot to all the dorms around the campus. Last week Antonio's supplier of pepperoni informed him of a 25 percent increase in price. Which variable determining the position on the supply curve has changed, and what effect does it have on supply?
   a. future expectations; supply decreases
   b. future expectations; supply increases
   c. input prices; supply decreases
   d. input prices; supply increases
   e. technology; supply increases

Problems

1. [Section 3.2]
   Assume the following demand schedule information:

Ben		Bill		Bob	
P	Q_D	P	Q_D	P	Q_D
$5	1	$5	2	$5	3
4	2	4	4	4	6
3	3	3	6	3	9
2	4	2	8	2	12
1	5	1	10	1	15

a. Show the market demand schedule if Ben and Bob are the only demanders.

P	Q_D
$5	
4	
3	
2	
1	

b. Show the market demand schedule if Bill joins Ben and Bob in the market.

P	Q_D
$5	
4	
3	
2	
1	

c. Show the market demand schedule if Ben now leaves the market, and only Bill and Bob remain.

P	Q_D
$5	
4	
3	
2	
1	

2. [Section 3.3]

Graph and explain the effect of an increase in the price of ice cream in the frozen yogurt market.

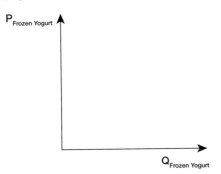

3. [Section 3.3]

Show and describe what would happen to the market demand curve for a good in each of the following cases:

a. An increase in the price of a substitute and a decrease in the price of a complement.

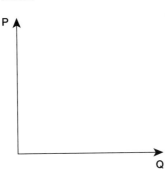

b. A decrease in the price of a substitute and an increase in the price of a complement.

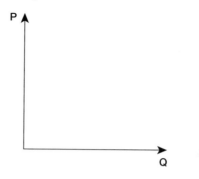

c. An increase in the number of buyers and an increase in income, for a normal good.

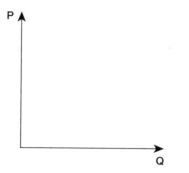

d. A decrease in the number of buyers and an increase in income, for an inferior good.

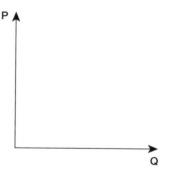

e. A decrease in expected future prices and a shift in tastes away from the good.

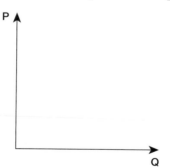

4. [Section 3.4]

Assume the following supply schedule information:

Stan		Steve		Stu	
P	Q$_S$	P	Q$_S$	P	Q$_S$
$5	10	$5	15	$5	5
4	8	4	12	4	4
3	6	3	9	3	3
2	4	2	6	2	2
1	2	1	3	1	1

a. Show the market supply schedule if Stan and Steve are the only suppliers.

P	Q$_S$
$5	
4	
3	
2	
1	

b. Show the market supply schedule if Stu joins Stan and Steve in the market.

P	Q$_S$
$5	
4	
3	
2	
1	

c. Show the market supply schedule if Stan now leaves the market, and only Steve and Stu remain.

P	Q$_S$
$5	
4	
3	
2	
1	

5. [Section 3.5]

Graph and explain the effect of a decrease in the price of corn on the soybean market, assuming corn and soybeans can be grown on the same land.

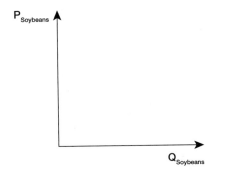

$P_{Soybeans}$

$Q_{Soybeans}$

6. [Section 3.5]

Show and describe what would happen to the market supply curve for a good in each of the following cases:

a. An increase in the number of suppliers and an increase in subsidies.

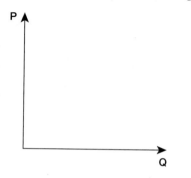

b. An decrease in the number of suppliers and an increase in taxes.

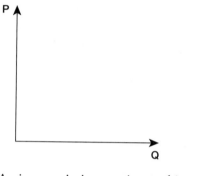

c. An increase in input prices and increasing costs of regulation.

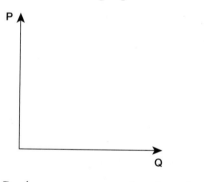

d. Producers expect now that the price will be lower later.

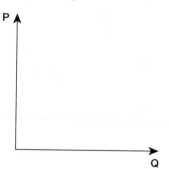

Bringing Supply and Demand Together

Market Equilibrium Price and Quantity

- What is the equilibrium price?
- What is the equilibrium quantity?
- What is a shortage?
- What is a surplus?

In the last chapter, we learned about demand and supply separately. Bearing in mind our discussion of the "fuzzy" nature of many real-world markets, we now bring the market supply and market demand together.

EQUILIBRIUM PRICE AND QUANTITY

The price at the intersection of the market demand curve and the market supply curve is called the **equilibrium price** and the quantity is called the **equilibrium quantity.** At the equilibrium price, the amount that buyers are willing and able to buy is exactly equal to the amount that sellers are willing and able to produce. If the market price is above or below the equilibrium price, there will be shortages or surpluses. However, the actions of many buyers and sellers will move the price back to the equilibrium level. Let us see how this happens.

equilibrium price
the price at the intersection of the market supply and demand curves; at this price the quantity demanded equals the quantity supplied

equilibrium quantity
the quantity at the intersection of the market supply and demand curves; at the equilibrium quantity, the quantity demanded equals the quantity supplied

SHORTAGES AND SURPLUSES

surplus
a situation where quantity supplied exceeds quantity demanded

shortage
a situation where quantity demanded exceeds quantity supplied

The equilibrium market solution is best understood with the help of a simple graph. Let's return to the apple example we used in our earlier discussions of supply and demand in Chapter 3. Exhibit 1 combines the market demand curve for apples with the market supply curve. At $3 per kilogram, buyers are willing to buy 5000 kilograms of apples and sellers are willing to supply 5000 kilograms of apples. Neither may be "happy" about the price, because the buyers would like a lower price and the sellers would like a higher price. But both buyers and sellers are able to carry out their purchase and sales plans at that $3 price. However, at any other price, either suppliers or demanders would be unable to trade as much as they would like.

As you can see in Exhibit 1, at $4 per kilogram, the quantity of apples demanded would be 3000 kilograms, but the quantity supplied would be 7000 kilograms. At that price, a **surplus,** or excess quantity supplied, would exist. That is, at this price, growers would be willing to sell more apples than demanders would be willing to buy. To cut growing inventories, frustrated suppliers would cut their price and cut back on production. And as price falls, consumers would buy more, ultimately eliminating the unsold surplus and returning the market to the equilibrium.

What would happen if the price of apples were cut to $1 per kilogram? The yearly quantity demanded of 12 000 kilograms would be greater than the 1000 kilograms that producers would be willing to supply at that low price. So, at $1 per kilogram, a **shortage,** or excess quantity demanded, would exist. Because of the apple shortage, frustrated buyers would be forced to compete for the existing supply, bidding up the price. The rising price would have two effects: (1) producers would be willing to increase the quantity supplied; and (2) the higher price would decrease the quantity demanded. Together, these two effects would ultimately eliminate the shortage, returning the market to the equilibrium.

LEARNING THE FIRST LESSON OF SUPPLY *and* DEMAND...

section 4.1
Exhibit 1

A Hypothetical Market Supply and Demand Schedule for Apples

Price	Quantity Supplied	Quantity Demanded	Difference	State of Market
$5	8 000	1 000	7 000	Surplus
4	7 000	3 000	4 000	Surplus
3	5 000	5 000	0	Equilibrium
2	3 000	8 000	−5 000	Shortage
1	1 000	12 000	−11 000	Shortage

The equilibrium is $3 per kilogram and 5000 kilograms of apples, where quantity demanded and quantity supplied are equal. At higher prices, quantity supplied exceeds quantity demanded, resulting in a surplus. Below $3, quantity demanded exceeds quantity supplied, leading to a shortage.

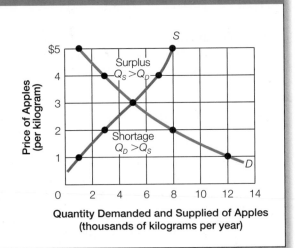

Quantity Demanded and Supplied of Apples
(thousands of kilograms per year)

ACTIVE LEARNING EXERCISE

SHORTAGES

Q: Imagine that you own a butcher shop. Recently, you have noticed that at about noon, you run out of your daily supply of chicken. Puzzling over your predicament, you hypothesize that you are charging less than the equilibrium price for your chicken. Should you raise the price of your chicken? Explain using a simple graph.

A: If the price you are charging is below the equilibrium price (P_E), you can draw a horizontal line from that price straight across Exhibit 2 and see where it intersects the supply and demand curves. The point where this horizontal line intersects the demand curve indicates how much chicken consumers are willing to buy at that below-equilibrium price (P_{BE}). Likewise, the intersection of this horizontal line with the supply curve indicates how much chicken producers are willing to supply at P_{BE}. From this, it is clear that a shortage (or excess quantity demanded) exists, because consumers want more chicken (Q_D) than producers are willing to supply (Q_S) at this relatively low price. This excess quantity demanded results in competition among buyers, which will push prices up and reduce or eliminate the shortage. That is, it would make sense to raise your price on the chicken. As price moves upward toward the equilibrium price, consumers are willing to purchase less (some will

substitute fish, steak, and ground round), and producers will have an incentive to supply more chicken.

section 4.1
Exhibit 2

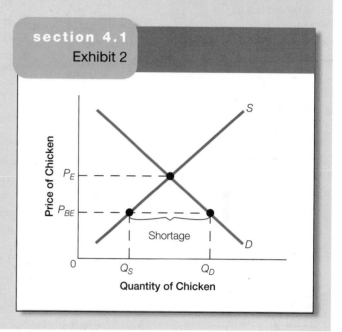

Section Check

1. The intersection of the supply and demand curve shows the equilibrium price and equilibrium quantity in a market.
2. A surplus is a situation where quantity supplied exceeds quantity demanded.
3. A shortage is a situation where quantity demanded exceeds quantity supplied.
4. Shortages and surpluses set in motion actions by many buyers and sellers that will move the market toward the equilibrium price and quantity unless otherwise prevented.

Changes in Equilibrium Price and Quantity

section

4.2

- What happens to equilibrium price and quantity when the demand curve shifts?
- What happens to equilibrium price and quantity when the supply curve shifts?
- What happens when both supply and demand shift in the same time period?
- What is an indeterminate solution?

When one of the many determinants of demand or supply changes, the demand and supply curves will shift, leading to changes in the equilibrium price and equilibrium quantity. When analyzing a change in demand or supply, it is important to answer three key questions to help ensure that the analysis is complete:

1. Which side of the market is being affected by the event in question, demand or supply?
2. Is the event in question a "shift" or a "movement"?
3. Is the event in question having an expansionary or contractionary impact on the market?

We first consider a change in demand.

A CHANGE IN DEMAND

A shift in the demand curve—caused by a change in the price of a related good (substitutes or complements), income, the number of buyers, tastes, or expectations—results in a change in both equilibrium price and equilibrium quantity. But how and why does this happen? This result can be most clearly explained through the use of an example. What happens in the gasoline market during the summer months when people typically do more travelling?

1. This event has a demand side effect, since we are looking at the impact of consumer behaviour.
2. The event is a shift, since it does not directly involve a change in the price of gasoline.
3. The event is expansionary, since we are looking at how consumers buy more gasoline in the summer months than in the winter months.

Therefore, the demand for gasoline increases during the summer. The greater demand for gasoline during the summer sends prices upward, *ceteris paribus*. As shown in Exhibit 1, the rightward shift of the demand curve results in an increase in both equilibrium price and quantity.

A CHANGE IN SUPPLY

Like a shift in demand, a shift in the supply curve will also influence both equilibrium price and equilibrium quantity, assuming that demand for the product has not changed. Let's look at another example: Why are strawberries less expensive in summer than in winter (assuming that consumers' tastes and preferences are fairly constant throughout the year)?

1. This event has a supply side effect, since the behaviour of consumers is assumed to be constant.
2. The event is a shift, since it does not directly involve a change in the price of strawberries.
3. The event is expansionary, since producers can make more fresh strawberries available in the summer, when they are in season, than in the winter.

Therefore, as shown in Exhibit 2, this increase in supply shifts the supply curve to the right, resulting in a lower equilibrium price (from P_{WINTER} to P_{SUMMER}) and a greater equilibrium quantity (from Q_{WINTER} to Q_{SUMMER}).

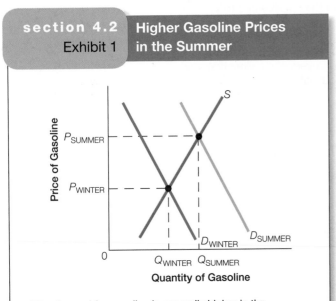

section 4.2   Higher Gasoline Prices
Exhibit 1   in the Summer

The demand for gasoline is generally higher in the summer than in the winter. The increase in demand during the summer, coupled with a fixed supply, means a higher price and a greater quantity.

section 4.2
Exhibit 2   **Lower Strawberry Prices in the Summer**

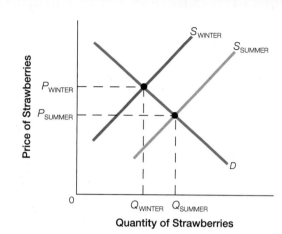

In the summer the supply of fresh strawberries is greater and this leads to a lower equilibrium price and a greater equilibrium quantity, *ceteris paribus.* In the winter, the supply of fresh strawberries is lower and this leads to a higher equilibrium price and a lower equilibrium quantity, *ceteris paribus.*

ACTIVE LEARNING EXERCISE

CHANGE IN DEMAND

Q: In ski resorts like Whistler, BC, hotel prices are higher in January and February (in-season when there are more skiers) than in November (off-season when there are fewer skiers). Why is this the case?

A: In the (likely) event that supply is not altered significantly, demand is chiefly responsible for the higher prices in the prime skiing months. In Exhibit 3, we see that the demand is higher in-season (February) than off-season (November).

section 4.2
Exhibit 3

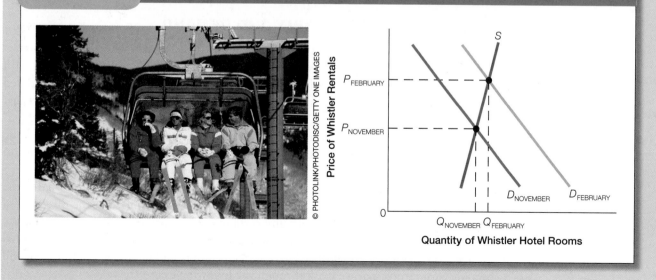

In The NEWS

MAD COW CRISIS HITS CANADIAN CATTLE INDUSTRY

BY JUDY MONCHUK

Nicki Murray's world turned upside down [in May 2003] when mad cow disease was detected in an Alberta animal. Suddenly, the cattle that had provided a livelihood and a history to her family weren't wanted anywhere in the world.

Adversity may be part of farm life, but nothing prepared rural families for the unprecedented economic crisis, which has no end in sight.

For almost 10 months, Murray has ridden an emotional roller coaster trying to keep life as normal as possible for her five young sons.

"It's like we're waiting in limbo, you can't dream of anything," said Murray of Picture Butte, Alta. She can look out her front door and see the feedlot operation her husband Shawn has struggled to keep going—and knows her neighbours are facing the same thing.

"There's no vision as to where you're going to be in a month or a year," said Murray, whose husband's grandfather began raising cattle in 1905. "And that's emotionally draining."

It's here in an area known as Feedlot Alley that the mad cow crisis has hit particularly hard. In this southern Alberta expanse of rolling valley, 650,000 cattle are fattened for slaughter, most in family-run operations that hold anywhere from 3,000 to upwards of 15,000 head of cattle.

Cattle prices collapsed in the wake of the detection of bovine spongiform encephalopathy (BSE) in a northern Alberta breeder cow. For months there were no international markets for Canadian beef: a huge blow to an industry which exports up to 60 per cent of its product, much of it to the United States.

The feedlot industry has taken the hardest hit. Many producers have seen equity built up over a lifetime of work evaporate by 75 per cent. As bills pile up, the bankers have begun knocking.

Businesses that rely on the beef industry have also been hurt. Farm machinery sales are down. Restaurants sit empty. Truckers who used to haul live cattle to the U.S. have found other ways to survive.

The Murrays have tried to shelter their boys from much of the stress, but that doesn't always work. Their eldest son sees the toll. "Dad's more depressed, he's not smiling as much," said 14-year-old Taner. "He's usually talking to Mom because Mom helps him get through it."

Taner expects his family will get through the crisis, although that seems a long way off. But when Taner looks at his future, he sees it away from cattle farming.

That's not a surprise to his mother.

"My youngest boys seem to have more love for the land and love for animals," said Murray. "Taner has always said he wouldn't farm, but I'm sure this wouldn't convince him of anything different."

SOURCE: Adapted from Judy Monchuk, "Farm Life in Limbo," *Star-Phoenix* (Saskatoon), March 30, 2004, p. B8. © The Canadian Press. Reprinted with permission from *The Canadian Press.*

CONSIDER THIS:

Alberta and Saskatchewan produce 80 percent of Canada's finished cattle, animals used for prime cuts and export. The mad cow crisis in 2003 caused a massive decrease in the demand for Canadian cattle, resulting in a collapse in cattle prices.

CHANGES IN BOTH SUPPLY AND DEMAND

We have discussed that as part of the continual adjustment process that occurs in the marketplace, supply and demand can each shift in response to many different factors, with the market then adjusting toward the new equilibrium. We have, so far, only considered what happens when just one such change occurs at a time. In these cases, we learned that the results of these adjustments in supply and demand on the equilibrium price and quantity are predictable. However, very often supply and demand will both shift in the same time period. Can we predict what will happen to equilibrium prices and equilibrium quantities in these situations?

As you will see, when supply and demand move at the same time, we can predict the change in one variable (price or quantity), but we are unable to predict the direction of the effect on the other variable with any certainty. This change in the second variable, then, is said to be indeterminate because it cannot be determined without additional information about the size of the relative shifts in supply and demand. This concept will become clearer to you as we work through the following example.

section 4.2
Exhibit 4 **Shifts in Supply and Demand**

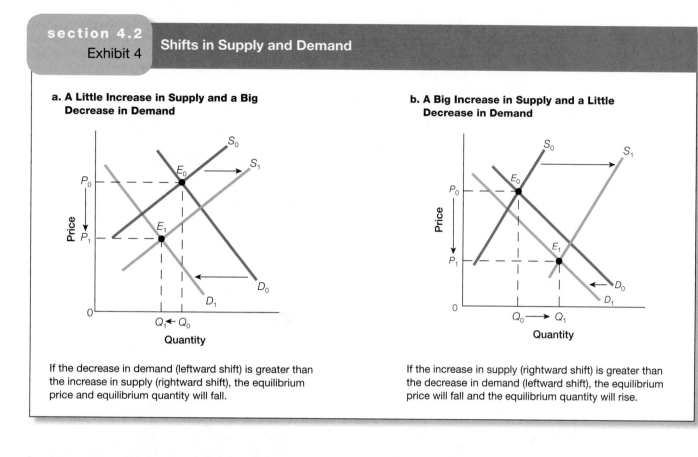

a. A Little Increase in Supply and a Big Decrease in Demand

b. A Big Increase in Supply and a Little Decrease in Demand

If the decrease in demand (leftward shift) is greater than the increase in supply (rightward shift), the equilibrium price and equilibrium quantity will fall.

If the increase in supply (rightward shift) is greater than the decrease in demand (leftward shift), the equilibrium price will fall and the equilibrium quantity will rise.

An Increase in Supply and a Decrease in Demand

When considering this scenario, it might help you to break it down into its individual parts. As you learned in the last section, an increase in supply (a rightward shift in the supply curve) results in a decrease in the equilibrium price and an increase in the equilibrium quantity. A decrease in demand (a leftward movement of the demand curve), on the other hand, results in a decrease in both the equilibrium price and the equilibrium quantity. These shifts are shown in Exhibit 4(a). Taken together, then, these changes will clearly result in a decrease in the equilibrium price because both the increase in supply and the decrease in demand work to push this price down. This drop in equilibrium price (from P_0 to P_1) is shown in the movement from E_0 to E_1.

The effect of these changes on equilibrium price is clear, but how does the equilibrium quantity change? The impact on equilibrium quantity is indeterminate because the increase in supply increases the equilibrium quantity and the decrease in demand decreases it. In this scenario, the change in the equilibrium quantity will vary depending on the relative changes in supply and demand. If, as shown in Exhibit 4(a), the decrease in demand is greater than the increase in supply, the equilibrium quantity will decrease. If, however, as shown in Exhibit 4(b), the increase in supply is greater than the decrease in demand, the equilibrium quantity will increase.

THE COMBINATIONS OF SUPPLY AND DEMAND SHIFTS

The eight possible changes in demand and/or supply are presented in Exhibit 5, along with the resulting changes in equilibrium quantity and equilibrium price. Although you could memorize the impact of the various possible changes in demand and supply, it would be more profitable to draw a graph, such as shown in Exhibit 6, whenever a situation of changing demand and/or supply arises. Remember that an increase in either demand or supply means a rightward shift in the curve, whereas a decrease in either demand or supply means a leftward shift. Also, when both demand and supply change, one of the two equilibrium values, price or quantity, will change in an indeterminate manner (can increase, decrease, or stay the same) depending on the relative magnitude of the changes in supply and demand.

section 4.2
Exhibit 5   **The Effect of Changing Demand and/or Supply**

If Demand	and Supply	then Equilibrium Quantity	and Equilibrium Price
1. Increases	Stays unchanged	Increases	Increases
2. Decreases	Stays unchanged	Decreases	Decreases
3. Stays unchanged	Increases	Increases	Decreases
4. Stays unchanged	Decreases	Decreases	Increases
5. Increases	Increases	Increases	Indeterminate*
6. Decreases	Decreases	Decreases	Indeterminate*
7. Increases	Decreases	Indeterminate*	Increases
8. Decreases	Increases	Indeterminate*	Decreases

*May increase, decrease, or remain the same, depending on the size of the change in demand relative to the change in supply.

section 4.2
Exhibit 6   **The Combinations of Supply and Demand Shifts**

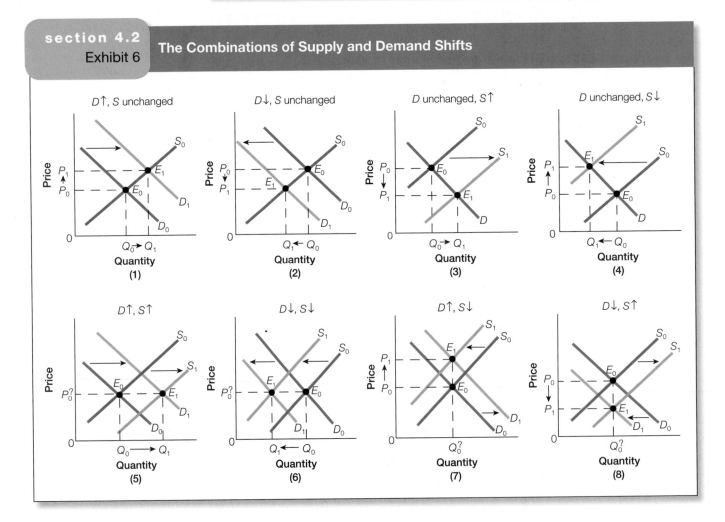

NEL

SECTION CHECK

Section Check

1. Changes in demand will cause a change in the equilibrium price and quantity, *ceteris paribus.*
2. Changes in supply will cause a change in the equilibrium price and quantity, *ceteris paribus.*
3. Supply and demand curves can shift simultaneously in response to changes in both supply and demand determinants.
4. When there are simultaneous shifts in both supply and demand curves, we will be able to determine one, but not both, of the variables. Either the equilibrium price or the equilibrium quantity will be indeterminate without more information.

Price Controls

- What are price controls?
- What are price ceilings?
- What are price floors?

PRICE CONTROLS

Although nonequilibrium prices can occur naturally, reflecting uncertainty, they seldom last for long. Governments, however, may impose nonequilibrium prices for significant time periods. Price controls involve the use of the power of the government to establish prices different from the equilibrium prices that would otherwise prevail. The motivations for price controls vary with the market under consideration. For example, a **price ceiling,** a legal maximum price, is often set for goods deemed important to low-income households, like housing. Or a **price floor,** a legal minimum price, may be set on wages because wages are the primary source of income for most people.

Price controls are not always implemented by the federal government. Provincial governments can and do impose local price controls. One fairly well-known example is rent controls, which limit how much landlords can charge for rental housing.

price ceiling
a legally established maximum price

price floor
a legally established minimum price

PRICE CEILINGS: RENT CONTROL

Rent controls have been imposed in some provinces. Although the rules may vary, generally the price (or rent) of an apartment remains fixed over the tenure of an occupant, except for allowable annual increases tied to the cost of living or some other price index. When an occupant moves out, the owners can usually, but not always, raise the rent to a near-market level for the next occupant. The controlled rents for existing occupants, however, are generally well below market rental rates.

Results of Rent Controls

Rent controls distort market signals and lead to shortages. In addition, they often do not even help the intended recipients—low-income households. Most people living in rent-controlled apartments have a good deal, one that they would lose by moving as their family circumstances or income changes. Tenants thus are reluctant to give up their governmentally granted right to a below-market-rent apartment. In addition, because the rents received by landlords are constrained and below market levels, the rate of return (roughly, the profit) on housing investments falls compared to that on other forms of real estate not subject to rent controls, like office rents or mortgage payments on condominiums. Hence, the incentive to construct new housing is reduced. Where rent controls are truly effective, there is generally little new construction going on and a shortage of apartments that persists and grows over time.

Also, when landlords are limited in what rent they can charge, there is little incentive to improve or upgrade apartments, such as by putting in new kitchen appliances or new carpeting, in order to get more rent. In fact, there is some incentive to avoid routine maintenance, thereby lowering the cost of apartment ownership to a figure approximating the controlled rental price, although the quality of the housing stock will deteriorate over time.

Another impact of rent control is that it promotes housing discrimination. Where rent controls do not exist, a prejudiced landlord might willingly rent to someone he believes is undesirable simply because the undesirable family is the only one willing to pay the requested rent (and the landlord is not willing to lower the rent substantially to get a desirable family, since this could translate into the loss of thousands of dollars in income). With rent controls, many families are likely to want to rent the controlled apartment, some desirable and some undesirable as seen by the landlord, simply because the rent is at a below-equilibrium price. The landlord can indulge in his "taste" for discrimination without any additional financial loss beyond that required by the controls.

Consequently, he will be more likely to choose to rent to a desirable family, perhaps a family without children or pets, rather than an undesirable one, perhaps one with lower income and so a greater risk of nonpayment.

Exhibit 1 shows the impact of rent control. If the price ceiling is set below the market price, the quantity demanded will increase to Q_D from Q^* and the quantity supplied will fall to Q_S from Q^*. The rent control policy will therefore create a shortage, the difference between Q_S and Q_D.

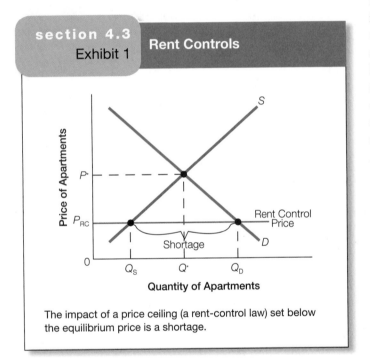

section 4.3
Exhibit 1   **Rent Controls**

The impact of a price ceiling (a rent-control law) set below the equilibrium price is a shortage.

PRICE FLOORS: THE MINIMUM WAGE

The argument for a minimum wage is simple: Existing wages for workers in some types of labour markets do not allow for a very high standard of living, and a minimum wage allows those workers to live better than before. Provincial government legislation makes it illegal to pay most workers an amount below the current legislated minimum wage.

Let us examine graphically the impact of a minimum wage on low-skilled workers. In Exhibit 2, suppose the government sets the minimum wage, W_{MIN}, above the market equilibrium wage, W_E. In Exhibit 2, we see that the price floor is binding; that is, there is a surplus of low-skilled workers at W_{MIN} because the quantity of labour supplied is greater than the quantity of labour demanded. The reason for the surplus of low-skilled workers (unemployment) at W_{MIN} is that more people are willing to work than employers are willing and able to hire.

Notice that not everyone loses from a minimum wage. Those workers who continue to hold jobs now have higher incomes (those workers between 0 and Q_D in Exhibit 2). However, many low-skilled workers suffer from a minimum wage—they either lose their jobs or are unable to get them in the first place (those between Q_D and Q_S in Exhibit 2). Although studies disagree somewhat on the precise magnitudes, they largely agree that minimum-wage laws do create some unemployment, and that the unemployment is concentrated among teenagers—the least-experienced and least-skilled members of the labour force.

Most Canadian workers are not affected by the minimum wage because in the market for their skills, they earn wages that exceed the minimum wage. For example, a minimum wage will not affect the unemployment rate for accountants. In Exhibit 3, we see the labour market for skilled and experienced workers. In this market the minimum wage (the price floor) is not binding because these workers are earning wages that far exceed the minimum wage—W_E is much higher than W_{MIN}.

The above analysis does not "prove" minimum-wage laws are "bad" and should be abolished. To begin with, there is the empirical question of how much unemployment is caused by minimum wages. Secondly, some might believe that the cost of unemployment resulting from a minimum wage is a reasonable price to pay for assuring that those with jobs get a "decent" wage. The analysis does point out, however, that there is a cost to having a minimum wage, and the burden of the minimum wage falls not only on low-skilled workers and employers but also on consumers of products made more costly by the minimum wage.

What do you think would happen to the number of low-skilled workers getting jobs if we raised the minimum wage to $20 an hour?

UNINTENDED CONSEQUENCES

When markets are altered for policy reasons it is wise to remember that the actual results of actions are not always as initially intended or result in **unintended consequences.** As economists, we must always look for the secondary effects of an action that may occur along with the initial effects. For example, the government is often well intentioned when

unintended consequences
the secondary effects of an action that may occur after the initial effects

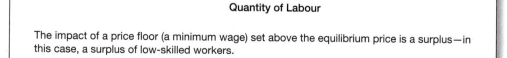

section 4.3
Exhibit 2

The Unemployment Effects of a Minimum Wage on Low-Skilled Workers

[Graph: Wage (price of labour) on vertical axis, Quantity of Labour on horizontal axis. Shows demand curve D_{LABOUR} (downward sloping) and supply curve S_{LABOUR} (upward sloping) intersecting at equilibrium point (Q_E, W_E). A horizontal line at W_{MIN} (labelled MINIMUM WAGE) lies above W_E. At the minimum wage, quantity demanded is Q_D and quantity supplied is Q_S. The gap between Q_D and Q_S at W_{MIN} is labelled "Unemployed (labour surplus)".]

The impact of a price floor (a minimum wage) set above the equilibrium price is a surplus—in this case, a surplus of low-skilled workers.

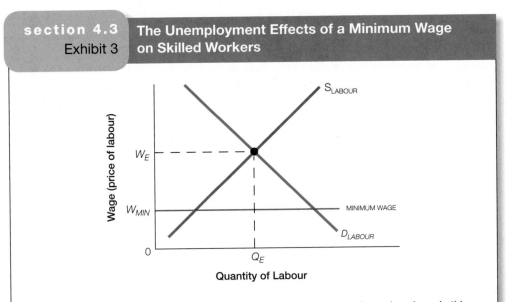

section 4.3
Exhibit 3

The Unemployment Effects of a Minimum Wage on Skilled Workers

There is no impact of a price floor on the market for skilled and experienced workers. In this market, the price floor (the minimum wage) is not binding.

In The **NEWS**

MINIMUM-WAGE WORKERS TEND TO BE TEENS OR YOUNG ADULTS

Minimum-wage workers in 2003 tended to be teens or young adults with lower levels of education in service-sector jobs, employed part time with short job tenure, says Statistics Canada.

They represented about four per cent of paid workers, down from 5.7 per cent in 1997, and across the country they totalled 547,000 people.

"Some were working to finance their education or support their families, while others were older workers looking to supplement their pension," the agency said....

Women accounted for almost two-thirds of minimum-wage workers in 2003. One in 20 women was a minimum-wage worker, compared with one in 35 men.

Individuals aged 24 and under were eight times as likely to be minimum-wage workers as those over 24.

And "nearly half of minimum-wage workers were aged 15 to 19, with more than three-quarters of these attending school either full or part time. Another 15 per cent were between 20 and 24, four out of 10 of whom were students."

About 41 per cent of all minimum-wage workers did not have a high-school diploma, compared with 15 per cent of all employees.

"This would explain the high rates of minimum-wage work among young people, many of whom have not yet completed their studies."

Most of them worked in accommodation and food services or retail trade.

However, some 27,000 heads of family with no spouse worked for minimum wage or less.

SOURCE: "Minimum-Wage Earners Tend to Be Young, Says Statistics Canada Study," *The Province* (Vancouver), March 28, 2004, p. A61. © The Canadian Press. Reprinted with permission from *The Canadian Press.*

CONSIDER THIS:

Nearly half of minimum-wage workers were aged 15 to 19, with the majority of these attending school either full- or part-time. However, some 27 000 heads of family with no spouse worked for minimum wage.

it adopts price controls to help low-skilled workers, or tenants in search of affordable housing; however, such policies can also cause unintended consequences, which may completely undermine the intended effects. For example, rent controls may have an immediate effect of lowering rents, but secondary effects may well include very low vacancy rates, discrimination against low-income and large families, and deterioration of the quality of rental units. Similarly, a sizeable increase in the minimum-wage rate may help many low-skilled workers or apprentices, but will result in higher unemployment and/or a reduction in fringe benefits, such as vacations and discounts to employees. Society has to make tough decisions, and if the government subsidizes some program or groups of people in one area, then something must always be given up somewhere else. The "law of scarcity" cannot be repealed!

Section Check

1. Price controls involve government mandates to keep prices above or below the market-determined equilibrium price.
2. Price ceilings are government-imposed maximum prices.
3. If price ceilings are set below the equilibrium price, shortages will result.
4. Price floors are government-imposed minimum prices.
5. If price floors are set above the equilibrium price, surpluses will result.
6. The law of unintended consequences states that the results of certain actions may not always be as clear as they initially appear.

Summary

Section 4.1

- The intersection of the supply and demand curves determines the equilibrium price and equilibrium quantity in a market.
- At the equilibrium price, quantity supplied equals quantity demanded.
- When the market price is above the equilibrium price, there will be a surplus, which causes the market price to fall.
- When the market price is below the equilibrium price, there will be a shortage, which causes the market price to rise.

Section 4.2

- Changes in demand and supply will cause a change in the equilibrium price and/or quantity.

Section 4.3

- A price ceiling, like rent control, is a legal maximum price.
- If a price ceiling is set below the equilibrium price (therefore binding), it will lead to a shortage.
- A price floor, like a minimum wage, is a legal minimum price.
- If a price floor is set above the equilibrium price (therefore binding), it will lead to a surplus.

Key Terms and Concepts

For a complete glossary of chapter key terms, visit the textbook's Web site at http://www.sextonmicro2e.nelson.com.

equilibrium price 95
equilibrium quantity 95
surplus 96
shortage 96

price ceiling 103
price floor 103
unintended consequences 105

Review Questions

1. Using supply and demand curves, show the effect of each of the following events on the market for wheat.

   a. Saskatchewan suffers a drought.

   b. The price of corn decreases (assume that many farmers can grow either corn or wheat).

   c. The prairie provinces have great weather.

   d. The price of fertilizer declines.

   e. More farmers start growing wheat.

2. If a price is above the equilibrium price, explain the forces that bring the market back to the equilibrium price and quantity. If a price is below the equilibrium price, explain the forces that bring the market back to the equilibrium price and quantity.

3. The market for hockey tickets at your university arena, which seats 2000, is the following:

Price	Q_D	Q_S
$2	4000	2000
$4	2000	2000
$6	1000	2000
$8	500	2000

   a. What is the equilibrium price?

   b. What is unusual about the supply curve?

   c. At what price would there be a shortage?

   d. At what price is there a surplus?

   e. Suppose that the addition of new students (all big hockey fans) next year will add 1000 to the quantity demanded at each price. What will this do to next year's demand curve? What is the new equilibrium price?

4. What would be the impact of a rental price ceiling set above the equilibrium rental price for apartments? below the equilibrium rental price?

5. What would be the impact of a price floor set above the equilibrium price for dairy products? Below the equilibrium price?

6. Why do both price floors and price ceilings reduce the quantity of goods traded in those markets?

7. Why do 10 a.m. classes fill up before 8 a.m. classes during class registration? Use the supply and demand curves to help explain your answers.

8. What would happen to the equilibrium price and equilibrium quantity in the following cases?

   a. an increase in income for a normal good and a decrease in the price of an input

   b. a technological advance and a decrease in the number of buyers

   c. an increase in the price of a substitute and an increase in the number of suppliers

   d. producers' expectations that prices will soon fall and a reduction in consumer tastes for the good

Fill in the Blanks

Section 4.1

1. The price at the intersection of the market demand curve and the market supply curve is called the _____ price, and the quantity is called the _____ quantity.

2. A situation where quantity supplied is greater than quantity demanded is called a _____.

3. A situation where quantity demanded is greater than quantity supplied is called a _____.

4. At a price greater than the equilibrium price, a _____, or excess quantity supplied, would exist. Sellers would be willing to sell _____ than demanders would be willing to buy. Frustrated suppliers would _____ their price and consumers would buy _____, returning the market to equilibrium.

Section 4.2

5. An increase in demand results in a _____ equilibrium price and a _____ equilibrium quantity.

6. A decrease in supply results in a _____ equilibrium price and a _____ equilibrium quantity.

7. If demand decreases and supply increases, but the decrease in demand is greater than the increase in supply, the equilibrium quantity will _____.

8. If supply decreases and demand increases, the equilibrium price will _____ and the equilibrium quantity will _____.

Section 4.3

9. A price _____ is a legally established maximum price; a price _____ is a legally established minimum price.

10. Rent controls distort market signals and lead to _____ of rent-controlled apartments.

11. The quality of rent-controlled apartments would tend to _____ over time.

12. An increase in the minimum wage would tend to create _____ unemployment for low-skilled workers.

13. The secondary effects of an action that may occur after the initial effects are called _____.

True or False

Section 4.1

1. If the quantity demanded does not equal quantity supplied, a shortage will always occur.

2. At the equilibrium price the quantity demanded equals the quantity supplied.

Section 4.2

3. A decrease in demand results in a lower equilibrium price and a higher equilibrium quantity.

4. An increase in supply results in a lower equilibrium price and a higher equilibrium quantity.

5. An increase in supply, combined with a decrease in demand, will decrease the equilibrium price but result in an indeterminate change in the equilibrium quantity.

6. If supply increases and demand decreases, but the increase in supply is greater than the decrease in demand, the equilibrium quantity will decrease.

7. An increase in both demand and supply increases the equilibrium quantity.

Section 4.3

8. Neither a price ceiling at the equilibrium price nor a price floor at the equilibrium price would have any effect on the market price or quantity exchanged.

9. A price ceiling decreases the quantity of a good exchanged, but a price floor increases the quantity of a good exchanged.

10. A minimum wage (price floor) is likely to be binding in the market for experienced and skilled workers.

Multiple Choice

Section 4.1

1. Which of the following is true at market equilibrium?
   a. quantity supplied exceeds quantity demanded
   b. quantity supplied is less than quantity demanded
   c. quantity supplied is equal to quantity demanded
   d. all of the above

2. A market will experience a _____ in a situation where quantity supplied exceeds quantity demanded, and a _____ in a situation where quantity demanded exceeds quantity supplied.
   a. shortage; shortage
   b. surplus; surplus
   c. shortage; surplus
   d. surplus; shortage

3. The price of a good will tend to rise when
   a. a temporary shortage at the current price occurs (assuming no price controls are imposed).
   b. a temporary surplus at the current price occurs (assuming no price controls are imposed).
   c. demand decreases.
   d. supply increases.

Section 4.2

4. If incomes are rising, in the market for an inferior good,
   a. its price will rise, and the quantity exchanged will rise.
   b. its price will rise, and the quantity exchanged will fall.
   c. its price will fall, and the quantity exchanged will rise.
   d. its price will fall, and the quantity exchanged will fall.

5. If many cooks view butter and margarine to be substitutes, and the price of butter rises, then in the market for margarine
   a. the equilibrium price will rise, whereas the change to equilibrium quantity is indeterminate.
   b. the equilibrium price will rise, and the equilibrium quantity will decrease.
   c. both the equilibrium price and quantity will rise.
   d. the equilibrium price will fall, and the equilibrium quantity will fall.
   e. the equilibrium price will fall, and the equilibrium quantity will increase.

6. If you observed that the market price of a good rose while the quantity exchanged fell, which of the following could have caused the change?
   a. an increase in supply
   b. a decrease in supply
   c. an increase in demand
   d. a decrease in demand
   e. none of the above

7. If both supply and demand decreased, but supply decreased more than demand, the result would be
   a. a higher price and a lower equilibrium quantity.
   b. a lower price and a lower equilibrium quantity.
   c. no change in the price and a lower equilibrium quantity.
   d. a higher price and a greater equilibrium quantity.
   e. a lower price and a greater equilibrium quantity.

8. If you observed the price of a good decreasing and the quantity exchanged increasing, it would be most likely caused by
   a. an increase in demand.
   b. a decrease in demand.
   c. an increase in supply.
   d. a decrease in supply.

9. If you observed the price of a good decreasing and the quantity exchanged decreasing, it would be most likely caused by
   a. an increase in demand.
   b. a decrease in demand.
   c. an increase in supply.
   d. a decrease in supply.

10. If, in a given market, the price of inputs increases and income increases (assuming it is a normal good), then
   a. price would increase but the change in quantity exchanged would be indeterminate.
   b. price would decrease but the change in quantity exchanged would be indeterminate.
   c. quantity exchanged would increase but the change in price would be indeterminate.
   d. quantity exchanged would decrease but the change in price would be indeterminate.

Section 4.3

11. If the equilibrium price of widgets is $22, and then a price floor of $20 is imposed by the government, as a result,
    a. there will be no effect on the widget market.
    b. there will be a shortage of widgets.
    c. there will be a surplus of widgets.
    d. the price of widgets will decrease.

12. Which of the following is true?
    a. A price ceiling reduces the quantity exchanged in the market, but a price floor increases the quantity exchanged in the market.
    b. A price ceiling increases the quantity exchanged in the market, but a price floor decreases the quantity exchanged in the market.
    c. Both price floors and price ceilings reduce the quantity exchanged in the market.
    d. Both price floors and price ceilings increase the quantity exchanged in the market.

13. Which of the following will most likely occur with a 20 percent increase in the minimum wage?
    a. higher unemployment rates among the experienced and skilled workers
    b. higher unemployment rates among the young and low-skilled workers
    c. lower unemployment rates for the young and low-skilled workers
    d. the price floor (minimum wage) will be binding in the young and low-skilled labour market but not in the experienced and skilled labour market
    e. both b and d

14. If a price floor was set at the current equilibrium price, which of the following would cause a surplus as a result?
    a. an increase in demand
    b. a decrease in demand
    c. an increase in supply
    d. a decrease in supply
    e. either b or c

15. A current shortage is due to a price ceiling. If the price ceiling is removed,
    a. price would increase, quantity supplied would increase, and quantity demanded would decrease.
    b. price would increase, quantity supplied would decrease, and quantity demanded would increase.
    c. price would decrease, quantity supplied would increase, and quantity demanded would decrease.
    d. price would decrease, quantity supplied would decrease, and quantity demanded would increase.

16. A current surplus is due to a price floor. If the floor is removed,
    a. price would increase, quantity demanded would increase, and quantity supplied would decrease.
    b. price would increase, quantity demanded would decrease, and quantity supplied would increase.
    c. price would decrease, quantity demanded would increase, and quantity supplied would decrease.
    d. price would decrease, quantity demanded would decrease, and quantity supplied would increase.

Problems

1. **[Sections 4.1 and 4.2]**

   Assume the following information for the demand and supply schedules for Good Z.

Demand		Supply	
Price	Quantity Demanded	Price	Quantity Supplied
$10	10	$1	10
9	20	2	15
8	30	3	20
7	40	4	25
6	50	5	30
5	60	6	35
4	70	7	40
3	80	8	45
2	90	9	50
1	100	10	55

   a. Draw the corresponding supply and demand curves.
   b. What is the equilibrium price and quantity traded?
   c. If the price were $9, would there be a shortage or a surplus? How large?
   d. If the price were $3, would there be a shortage or a surplus? How large?
   e. If the demand for Z increased by 15 units at every price, what would the new equilibrium price and quantity traded be?
   f. Given the original demand for Z, if the supply of Z were increased by 15 units at every price, what would the new equilibrium price and quantity traded be?

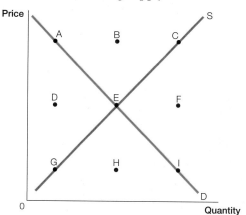

2. **[Sections 4.2 and 4.3]**

   Refer to the following supply and demand curve diagram.

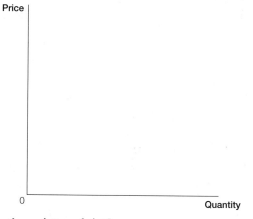

a. Starting from an initial equilibrium at E, what shift or shifts in supply and/or demand could move the equilibrium price and quantity to each of points A through I?

b. Starting from an initial equilibrium at E, what would happen if there were both an increase in the price of an input and an increase in income, if it is a normal good?

c. Starting from an initial equilibrium at E, what would happen if there were both an increase in the price of an input and an advance in technology?

d. If a price floor is imposed above the equilibrium price, which of A through I would tend to be the quantity supplied, and which would tend to be the quantity demanded? Which would be the new quantity exchanged?

e. If a price ceiling is imposed below the equilibrium price, which of A through I would tend to be the quantity supplied, and which would tend to be the quantity demanded? Which would be the new quantity exchanged?

3. **[Section 4.3]**
   Draw a supply and demand curve diagram with a price floor above the equilibrium price, and indicate the quantity supplied and quantity demanded at that price and the resulting surplus.

   a. What happens to the quantity supplied, the quantity demanded, and the surplus if the price floor is raised? if it is lowered?

   b. What happens to the quantity supplied, the quantity demanded, and the surplus if, for a given price floor, the demand curve shifts to the right?

   c. What happens to the quantity supplied, the quantity demanded, and the surplus if, for a given price floor, the supply curve shifts to the right?

4. **[Section 4.3]**
   Draw a supply and demand curve diagram with a price ceiling below the equilibrium price, and indicate the quantity supplied and quantity demanded at that price, and the resulting shortage.

   a. What happens to the quantity supplied, the quantity demanded, and the shortage if the price ceiling is raised? if it is lowered?

   b. What happens to the quantity supplied, the quantity demanded, and the shortage if, for a given price ceiling, the demand curve shifts to the right?

   c. What happens to the quantity supplied, the quantity demanded, and the shortage if, for a given price ceiling, the supply curve shifts to the right?

chapter

5

Elasticity

Price Elasticity of Demand

- What are price elasticities of demand?
- How do we measure consumers' responses to price changes?
- What determines the price elasticity of demand?
- How do we use the "midpoint method" in calculating price elasticities of demand?

WHAT IS THE PRICE ELASTICITY OF DEMAND?

In learning and applying the law of demand, we have established the basic fact that quantity demanded changes inversely with changes in price, *ceteris paribus*. But how much does quantity demanded change? The extent to which a change in price impacts quantity demanded may vary considerably from product to product and over the various price ranges for the same product. The **price elasticity of demand** measures the responsiveness of quantity demanded to a change in price. More specifically, price elasticity is defined as the percentage change in quantity demanded divided by the percentage change in price:

$$\text{Price elasticity of demand } (E_D) = \frac{\text{Percentage change in quantity demanded}}{\text{Percentage change in price}}$$

price elasticity of demand
a measure of the responsiveness of quantity demanded to a change in price

Note that, following the law of demand, there is an inverse relationship between price and quantity demanded. For this reason, price elasticity of demand is, in theory, always negative. In practice, however, this quantity is always expressed in absolute value terms, as a positive number, for simplicity.

IS THE DEMAND CURVE ELASTIC OR INELASTIC?

It is important to understand the basic intuition behind elasticities. This can be best understood by initially focusing on the percentage changes in quantity demanded and price.

Think of elasticity as an elastic rubber band. If the quantity demanded is very responsive to even a small change in price, we call it elastic. On the other hand, if even a huge change in price results in only a small change in quantity demanded, then the demand is said to be *inelastic*. For example, if a 10 percent increase in the price leads to a 50 percent reduction in the quantity demanded, we say that demand is *elastic* because the quantity demanded is very sensitive to the price change.

$$E_D = \frac{\%\Delta\ Q_D}{\%\Delta\ P} = \frac{50 \text{ percent}}{10 \text{ percent}} = 5$$

elastic demand segment
a portion of the demand curve where the percentage change of quantity demanded is greater than the percentage change in price ($E_D > 1$)

Demand is elastic in this case because a 10 percent change in price led to a larger (50 percent) change in quantity demanded.

Alternatively, if a 10 percent increase in the price leads to a 1 percent reduction in quantity demanded, we say that demand is *inelastic* because the quantity demanded did not respond much to the price reduction.

$$E_D = \frac{\%\Delta\ Q_D}{\%\Delta\ P} = \frac{1 \text{ percent}}{10 \text{ percent}} = 0.10$$

Demand is inelastic in this case because a 10 percent change in price led to a smaller (1 percent) change in quantity demanded.

THE RANGES OF ELASTICITY

Economists refer to a variety of demand curves based on the magnitude of their elasticity. A demand curve or a portion of a demand curve can be elastic, or inelastic, or unit elastic. A demand curve is:

Elastic ($E_D > 1$) if Percentage change in Q_D > Percentage change in P

Inelastic ($E_D < 1$) if Percentage change in Q_D < Percentage change in P

Unit elastic ($E_D = 1$) if Percentage change in Q_D = Percentage change in P

If bus fares increase, will ridership fall a little or a lot? It all depends on the price elasticity of demand. If the price elasticity of demand is elastic, a $0.50 price increase will lead to a relatively large reduction in bus travel as riders find viable substitutes. If the price elasticity of demand is inelastic, a $0.50 price increase will lead to a relatively small reduction in bus ridership as riders are not able to find good alternatives to bus transportation.

Elastic Demand Segments

Elastic demand segments are those with an elasticity that is numerically *greater* than one ($E_D > 1$). In this case, a given percentage increase in price, say 10 percent, leads to a larger percentage change in quantity demanded, say 20 percent, as seen in Exhibit 1(a). If the curve were perfectly elastic, a small percentage increase in price would cause the quantity demanded to fall dramatically to zero. For example, say there were two side-by-side roadside fruit stands selling the same quality of apples. If one stand had lower prices, then the higher-priced fruit stand would soon be selling no apples. In Exhibit 1(b), a perfectly elastic demand curve (horizontal) is illustrated. Economists define the elasticity of demand in this case as infinity, because the quantity demanded is infinitely responsive to even a very small percentage change in price.

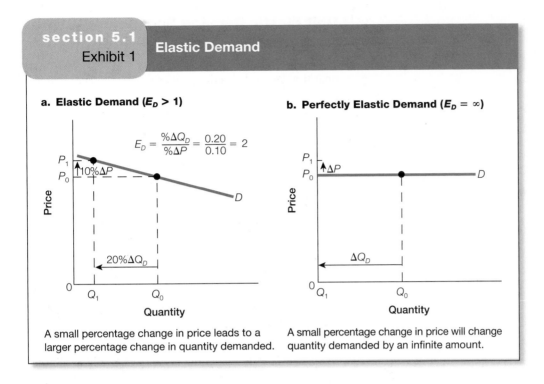

section 5.1 Exhibit 1 — **Elastic Demand**

a. Elastic Demand ($E_D > 1$)

$$E_D = \frac{\%\Delta Q_D}{\%\Delta P} = \frac{0.20}{0.10} = 2$$

10%ΔP

20%ΔQ_D

A small percentage change in price leads to a larger percentage change in quantity demanded.

b. Perfectly Elastic Demand ($E_D = \infty$)

ΔP

ΔQ_D

A small percentage change in price will change quantity demanded by an infinite amount.

Inelastic Demand Segments

Inelastic demand segments are those with elasticity *less* than one ($E_D < 1$). In this case, a given percentage (for example, 10 percent) change in price is accompanied with a smaller (for example, 5 percent) reduction in quantity demanded, as seen in Exhibit 2(a). If the demand curve is perfectly inelastic, the quantity demanded is the same regardless of the price, as illustrated in Exhibit 2(b).

inelastic demand segment
a portion of the demand curve where the percentage change in quantity demanded is less than the percentage change in price ($E_D < 1$)

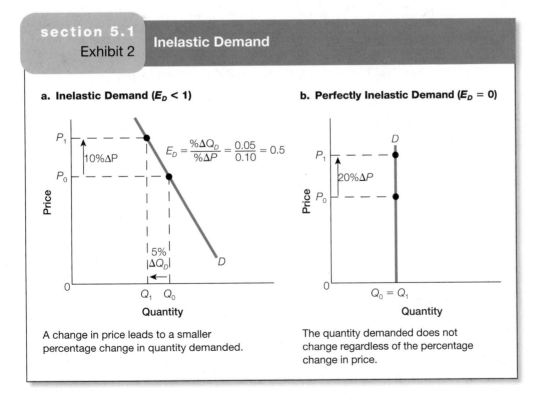

section 5.1 Exhibit 2 — **Inelastic Demand**

a. Inelastic Demand ($E_D < 1$)

10%ΔP

$$E_D = \frac{\%\Delta Q_D}{\%\Delta P} = \frac{0.05}{0.10} = 0.5$$

5% $|\Delta Q_D|$

A change in price leads to a smaller percentage change in quantity demanded.

b. Perfectly Inelastic Demand ($E_D = 0$)

20%ΔP

$Q_0 = Q_1$

The quantity demanded does not change regardless of the percentage change in price.

Unit Elastic Demand

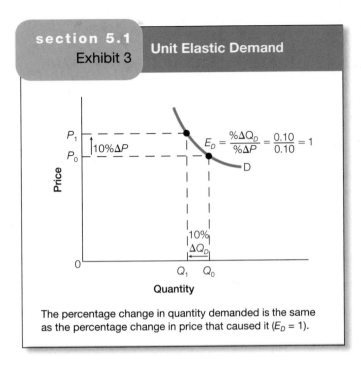

$$E_D = \frac{\%\Delta Q_D}{\%\Delta P} = \frac{0.10}{0.10} = 1$$

The percentage change in quantity demanded is the same as the percentage change in price that caused it ($E_D = 1$).

unit elastic demand
demand with a price elasticity of 1; the percentage change in quantity demanded is equal to the percentage change in price

Unit Elastic Demand Segments

Goods for which E_D equals one ($E_D = 1$) are said to be **unit elastic demand.** In this case, the percentage change in quantity demanded is the same as the percentage change in price that caused it. For example, a 10 percent increase in price will lead to a 10 percent reduction in quantity demanded. This is illustrated in Exhibit 3.

THE DETERMINANTS OF THE PRICE ELASTICITY OF DEMAND

As you have learned, the elasticity of demand for a specific good refers to movements along its demand curve as its price changes. A lower price will increase quantity demanded, and a higher price will reduce quantity demanded. But what factors will influence the magnitude of the change in quantity demanded in response to a price change? That is, what will make the demand curve relatively more elastic (where Q_D is responsive to price changes), and what will make the demand curve relatively less elastic (where Q_D is less responsive to price changes)?

For the most part, the price elasticity of demand depends on the following factors: (1) the availability of close substitutes, (2) the proportion of income spent on the good, and (3) the amount of time that has elapsed since the price change.

Availability of Close Substitutes

Goods *with* close substitutes tend to have more elastic demands. Why? Because if the price of such a good increases, consumers can easily switch to other now relatively lower-priced substitutes. There are many examples, such as butter and margarine, one brand of root beer as opposed to another, or different brands of gasoline, where the ease of substitution will make demand quite elastic for most individuals. Goods *without* close substitutes, such as insulin for diabetics, cigarettes for chain smokers, or heroin for addicts tend to have inelastic demands.

The degree of substitutability may also depend on whether the good is a necessity or a luxury. Goods that are necessities, like food, cannot be easily substituted for and thus tend to have lower elasticities than luxury items, like jewellery.

Narrowly Defined Goods

When the demand for a good is broadly defined, it tends to be less elastic than when it is narrowly defined. For example, the elasticity of demand for food, a very broad category, tends to be inelastic because there are very few substitutes for food. But for a certain type of food, like pizza, a narrowly defined good, it is much easier to find a substitute—perhaps tacos, burgers, salads, or french fries. That is, the demand for a particular type of food is more elastic because there are more and better substitutes than for food as an entire category.

Proportion of Income Spent on the Good

The smaller the proportion of income spent on a good, the lower its elasticity of demand. If the amount spent on a good relative to income is small, then the impact of a change in its price on one's budget will also be small. As a result, consumers will respond less to price changes for these goods than for similar percentage changes in large-ticket items, where a price change could have a potentially large impact on the consumer's budget. For example, a 50 percent increase in the price of salt will have a much smaller impact on consumers' behaviour than a similar percentage increase in the price of a new automobile. Similarly, a 50 percent increase in the cost of university tuition will have a greater impact on students' (and sometimes parents') budgets than a 50 percent increase in beer prices.

Time

For many goods, the more time that people have to adapt to a new price change, the greater the elasticity of demand. Immediately after a price change, consumers may be unable to locate very good alternatives or easily change their consumption patterns. But the more time that passes, the more time consumers have to find or develop suitable substitutes and to plan and implement changes in their patterns of consumption. For example, drivers may not respond immediately to an increase in gas prices, perhaps believing it to be temporary. However, if the price persists over a longer period, we would expect people to drive less, buy more fuel-efficient cars, move closer to work, carpool, take the bus, or even bike to work. Hence, for many goods, especially non-durable goods (goods that do *not* last a long time), the short-run demand curve is generally less elastic than the long-run demand curve, as illustrated by Exhibit 4.

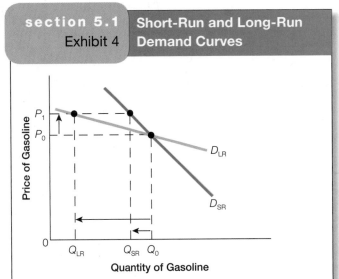

section 5.1
Exhibit 4
Short-Run and Long-Run Demand Curves

For many goods, like gasoline, price is much more elastic in the long run than the short run because buyers take time to change their consumption patterns. In the short run, the increase in price from P_0 to P_1 has only a small effect on the quantity demanded for gasoline. In the long run, the effect of the price increase will be much larger.

In The **NEWS**

SMOKING: PRICE MATTERS, WARNINGS DON'T WORK

BY WILLIAM WATSON

A new study on the effects of health warnings on cigarette packages was done by two Concordia University economists, Ian Irvine and Nikolay Gospodinov. Using data from Health Canada's Canadian Tobacco Use Monitoring Survey, they looked at what happened to smoking rates between July 2000 and June 2001. They chose those 12 months because, in January 2001, the federal government began to require cigarette packages to carry those really gruesome health warnings showing damaged hearts and cancerous lungs. Later that year 14% of smokers told an Environics survey that the new messages had been a major factor in their latest attempt to quit.

Maybe so, but the Concordia economists found that between 2000 and 2001 there was in fact no discernible reduction in smoking that could not be attributed to other influences. Smoking did decline but smoking has been declining at about 3% per year for two decades, and other factors, most notably a big tax-prompted increase in the price of cigarettes in early 2001, were probably responsible.

Some anti-tobacco activists argue this isn't a valid test since the warnings' effect likely wouldn't be immediate but instead would build up over time. The economists respond that smokers are in a "constant state of quit contemplation," so dramatic ads should have shocked them into taking action about their addiction.

In terms of how much smokers smoked, the statistical correlations do suggest the warnings may have induced a reduction of two cigarettes per smoker per week, but the correlation is weak and the possibility that there was no effect at all can't be rejected at normal levels of "statistical confidence." None of this means public health campaigns are bad, but it does suggest all the fuss about cigarette labeling may be just so much, well, blown smoke.

SOURCE: Adapted from William Watson, "Economists Worth Listening To," *National Post*, October 21, 2004, p. A18. Reprinted with permission from the author.

(continued)

IN THE NEWS (continued)

CONSIDER THIS:
The big increase in the price of cigarettes in early 2001 (due to a tax increase on cigarettes) was responsible for some of the decline in smoking. Health warnings, on the other hand, had little impact on reducing smoking. Some other studies have shown that a 10 percent increase in the price of cigarettes will lead to a 7 percent reduction in smoking. In this price range, demand is inelastic at −0.7.

Calculating Elasticity Using the Midpoint Method: A More Detailed Approach

Now that we have looked at the basic theory of elasticities by focusing on the percentage changes in quantity demanded and price, suppose we wanted to perform the same calculation using points from a demand curve. What we would soon realize is that the direction of the calculation has an impact on our answer! To help understand this potential problem, consider the following example:

Point	Price	Quantity
A	$2	100
B	$4	40

When going from point A to point B, the percentage increase in price is 100 percent, and the percentage decline in quantity is 60 percent, giving us a price elasticity of demand coefficient of 0.6 (60/100). However, when we go from point B to point A, the percentage decrease in price is 50 percent, and the percentage increase in quantity is 150 percent, giving us a price elasticity of demand coefficient of 3 (150/50).

The reason for the different answers in the above case was due to the traditional method for calculating percentage. According to the traditional approach, the change in the given values is divided by the initial value in determining percentage change. However, since this initial value can be different depending on whether you are starting from point A or from point B, you can, and often do, get different answers. To solve this problem, a technique known as the *midpoint method* is used in place of the traditional approach. The midpoint method uses a midpoint (or average) of the initial and final values in calculating percentage change as opposed to an initial value. And since this midpoint value is the same regardless of the direction of the calculation, we always get the same answer. Consider the same example again, now using the midpoint method.

Point	Price	Quantity
A	$2	100
B	$4	40
Midpoint	*$3*	*70*

According to the midpoint method, when going from point A to point B, the percentage increase in price is 67 percent ($2/$3), and the percentage decline in quantity is 86 percent (60/70), giving us a price elasticity of demand coefficient of 1.3 (86/67). Conveniently, when we go from point B to point A, the percentage decrease in price is 67 percent, and the percentage increase in quantity is 86 percent, giving us a price elasticity of demand coefficient of 1.3 (86/67). Problem solved!

Price elasticity of demand between two points (Q_A, P_A) and (Q_B, P_B), can then be expressed in terms of the midpoint method with the following formula:

$$E_D = \frac{\%\Delta\ Q_D}{\%\Delta\ P} = \frac{(Q_A - Q_B)/[(Q_A + Q_B)/2]}{(P_A - P_B)/[(P_A + P_B)/2]}$$

Section Check

1. Price elasticity of demand measures the percentage change in quantity demanded divided by the percentage change in price.
2. If the demand for a good is price elastic in the relevant range, quantity demanded is very responsive to a price change. If the demand for a good is relatively price inelastic, quantity demanded is not very responsive to a price change.
3. The price elasticity of demand depends on: (1) the availability of close substitutes, (2) the proportion of income spent on the good, and (3) the amount of time that buyers have to respond to a price change.
4. The "midpoint method" for calculating percentage change involves using the average of the changing values, thereby eliminating the direction bias found in the traditional approach.

---

section

5.2

Total Revenue and Price Elasticity of Demand

- What is total revenue?
- What is the relationship between total revenue and the price elasticity of demand?
- Does the price elasticity of demand vary along a linear demand curve?

HOW DOES THE PRICE ELASTICITY OF DEMAND IMPACT TOTAL REVENUE?

The price elasticity of demand for a good also has implications for total revenue. Total revenue (TR) is simply the price of the good (P) times the quantity of the good sold (Q): $TR = P \times Q$. In Exhibit 1, we see that when the demand is price elastic ($E_D > 1$), total revenues will rise as the price declines because the percentage increase in the quantity demanded is greater than the percent reduction in price. For example, if the price of a good is cut in half (say from $10 to $5) and the quantity demanded more than doubles (say from 40 to 100), total revenue will rise from $400 ($10 × 40 = $400) to $500 ($5 × 100 = $500). Equivalently, if the price rises from $5 to $10 and the quantity demanded falls from 100 to 40 units, then total revenue falls from $500 to $400. As this example illustrates, if the demand curve is relatively elastic, total revenue varies inversely with a price change.

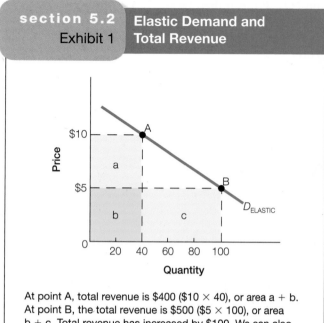

section 5.2 — Exhibit 1 — Elastic Demand and Total Revenue

At point A, total revenue is $400 ($10 × 40), or area a + b. At point B, the total revenue is $500 ($5 × 100), or area b + c. Total revenue has increased by $100. We can also see in the graph that total revenue has increased because the area b + c is greater than area a + b, or c > a.

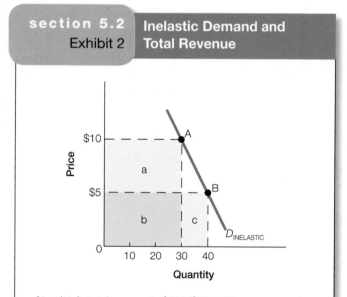

section 5.2 — Exhibit 2 — Inelastic Demand and Total Revenue

At point A, total revenue is $300 ($10 × 30), or area a + b. At point B, the total revenue is $200 ($5 × 40), or area b + c. Total revenue has fallen by $100. We can also see in the graph that total revenue has decreased because area a + b is greater than area b + c, or a > c.

You can see from the following what happens to total revenue when demand is price elastic. (Note: The sizes of the price and quantity arrows represent the sizes of the percentage changes.)

When Demand Is Price Elastic

$$\downarrow TR = \uparrow P \times \downarrow Q$$

or

$$\uparrow TR = \downarrow P \times \uparrow Q$$

On the other hand, if demand for a good is relatively inelastic ($E_D < 1$), the total revenue will be lower at lower prices than at higher prices because a given price reduction will be accompanied by a proportionately smaller increase in quantity demanded. For example, as seen in Exhibit 2, if the price of a good is cut, say from $10 to $5, and the quantity demanded less than doubles—say it increases from 30 to 40—total revenue will fall from $300 ($10 × 30 = $300) to $200 ($5 × 40 = $200). Equivalently, if the price increases from $5 to $10 and the quantity demanded falls from 40 to 30, total revenue will increase from $200 to $300. To summarize, then, if the demand curve is inelastic, total revenue will vary directly with a price change.

When Demand Is Price Inelastic

$$\uparrow TR = \uparrow P \times \downarrow Q$$

or

$$\downarrow TR = \downarrow P \times \uparrow Q$$

In this case, the net effect on total revenue is reversed but easy to see. (Again, the size of the price and quantity arrows represents the size of the percentage changes.)

PRICE ELASTICITY CHANGES ALONG A LINEAR DEMAND CURVE

As we have already shown earlier in the chapter, the slopes of demand curves can be used to estimate their *relative* elasticities of demand: The steeper one demand curve is relative to another, the more inelastic it is relative to the other. However, beyond the extreme cases of perfectly elastic and perfectly inelastic curves, great care must be taken when trying to estimate the degree of elasticity of one demand curve from its slope. In fact, as we shall see, a straight-line demand curve with a constant slope will change elasticity continuously as you move up or down it.

We can easily demonstrate that the elasticity of demand varies along a linear demand curve by using what we already know about the interrelationship between price and total

ACTIVE LEARNING EXERCISE

ELASTICITIES AND TOTAL REVENUE

Q: Is a poor (great) wheat harvest bad (good) for all farmers? (Hint: Assume that demand for wheat is inelastic—the demand for food is generally inelastic.)

A: Without a simultaneous reduction in demand, a reduction in supply results in higher prices. With that, if demand for the wheat is inelastic over the pertinent portion of the demand curve, the price increase will cause farmers' total revenues to rise. As shown in Exhibit 3(a), if demand for the crop is inelastic, an increase in price would cause farmers to lose the revenue indicated by area c. They would, however, experience an increase in revenue equal to area a, resulting in an overall increase in total revenue equal to area a − c. Clearly, if some farmers lose their entire crop because of, say, bad weather, they are worse off; but *collectively* farmers can profit from events that

reduce crop size—and they do, because the demand for most agricultural products is inelastic. Interestingly, if all farmers were hurt equally, say, losing one-third of their crop, each farmer would be better off. Of course, consumers would be worse off because the price of agricultural products would be higher. Alternatively, what if phenomenal weather has led to record wheat harvests or a technological advance has led to more productive wheat farmers? Either event would increase the supply from S_0 to S_1 in Exhibit 3(b). The increase in supply leads to a lower price, from P_0 to P_1. Because the demand for wheat is inelastic, the quantity sold of wheat rises less than proportionately to the fall in the price. That is, in percentage terms the price falls more than the quantity demanded rises. Each farmer is selling a few more bushels of wheat, but the price of each bushel has fallen even more, so collectively wheat farmers will experience a decline in total revenue despite the good news.

section 5.2
Exhibit 3

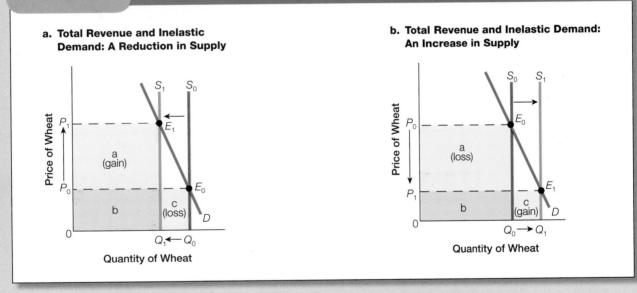

a. Total Revenue and Inelastic Demand: A Reduction in Supply

b. Total Revenue and Inelastic Demand: An Increase in Supply

revenue. Exhibit 4 shows a linear (constant slope) demand curve. In Exhibit 4(a), we see that when the price falls on the upper half of the demand curve from P_0 to P_1, and quantity demanded increases from Q_0 to Q_1, total revenue increases. That is, the new area of total revenue (area b + c) is larger than the old area of total revenue (area a + b). It is also true that if price increased in this region (from P_1 to P_0), total revenue would fall, because b + c is greater than a + b. In this region of the demand curve, then, there is a negative relationship between price and total revenue. As we discussed earlier, this is a characteristic of an elastic demand curve ($E_D > 1$).

Exhibit 4(b) illustrates what happens to total revenue on the lower half of the same demand curve. When the price falls from P_2 to P_3 and the quantity demanded increases from Q_2 to Q_3, total revenue actually decreases because the new area of total revenue (area e + f) is less than the old area of total revenue (area d + e). Likewise, it is clear that an increase in price from P_3 to P_2 would increase total revenue. In this case, there is a positive relationship between price and total revenue, which, as we discussed, is characteristic of an inelastic demand curve ($E_D < 1$). Together, parts (a) and (b) of Exhibit 4 illustrate that, although the slope remains constant, the elasticity of a linear demand curve changes along the length of the curve—from relatively elastic at higher price ranges to relatively inelastic at lower price ranges.

section 5.2
Exhibit 4   **Price Elasticity Along a Linear Demand Curve**

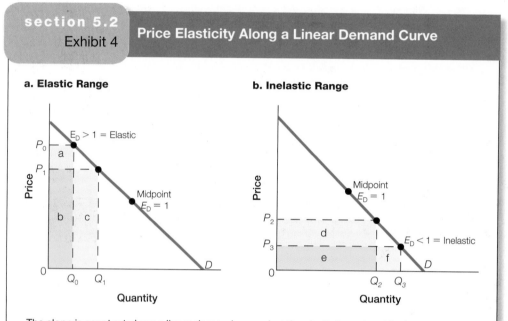

The slope is constant along a linear demand curve, but the elasticity varies. Moving down along the demand curve, the elasticity is elastic at higher prices and inelastic at lower prices. It is unit elastic at its midpoint, the boundary between the inelastic and elastic ranges.

Section Check

1. Total revenue is the price of the good times the quantity sold ($TR = P \times Q$).
2. If demand is price elastic ($E_D > 1$), total revenue will vary inversely with a change in price.
3. If demand is price inelastic ($E_D < 1$), total revenue will vary in the same direction as a change in price.
4. A linear demand curve is more price elastic at higher price ranges and more price inelastic at lower price ranges, and it is unit elastic at the midpoint: $E_D = 1$.

section
5.3   # Other Demand Elasticities

- What is the cross-price elasticity of demand?
- What is the income elasticity of demand?

WHAT IS THE CROSS-PRICE ELASTICITY OF DEMAND?

Price elasticities of demand are not the only elasticity calculation economists use to better understand buyer behaviour. Sometimes the quantity of the good demanded is affected by the price of a related good (substitutes and complements). For example, if the price of potato chips falls, what is the impact, if any, on the quantity of soda (a complement) demanded? Or if the price of soda increases, to what degree will iced tea (a substitute) sales be affected? The cross-price elasticity of demand measures both the direction and magnitude of the impact that a price change for one good will have on the quantity demanded of another related good. Specifically, the **cross-price elasticity of demand** is defined as the percentage change in the quantity demanded of one good (good A) divided by the percentage change in price of another good (good B), or,

Cross-price elasticity of demand $(E_{AB}) = \dfrac{\text{Percentage change in quantity demanded of A}}{\text{Percentage change in the price of B}}$

The cross-price elasticity of demand indicates not only the degree of the connection between the two variables but also whether the goods in question are substitutes or complements to one another.

cross-price elasticity of demand
a measure of the impact that a price change of one good will have on the quantity demanded of another good at a given price

Calculating the Cross-Price Elasticity of Demand

Let's calculate the cross-price elasticity of demand between soda and iced tea, where a 10 percent increase in the price of soda results in a 20 percent increase in the quantity of iced tea demanded. In this case, the cross-price elasticity of demand would be +2 (+20 percent ÷ +10 percent = +2). Consumers responded to the soda price increase by buying less soda (moving along the demand curve for soda) and increasing the quantity demanded of iced tea at every price (shifting the demand curve for iced tea). In general, if the cross-price elasticity is positive, we can conclude that the two goods are substitutes because the price of one good and the demand for the other move in the same direction.

As another example, let's calculate the cross-price elasticity of demand between potato chips and soda, where a 10 percent decrease in the price of potato chips results in a 30 percent increase in the quantity of soda demanded. In this case, the cross-price elasticity of demand is −3 (+30 percent ÷ −10 percent = −3). The quantity demanded of potato chips increases as a result of the price decrease, and consumers then purchase additional soda to wash down those extra bags of salty chips. Potato chips and soda, then, are complements. In general, if the cross-price elasticity is negative, we can conclude that the two goods are complements because the price of one good and the demand for the other move in opposite directions.

WHAT IS THE INCOME ELASTICITY OF DEMAND?

Even though the most widely employed demand relationship is that between price and quantity demanded, it is also sometimes useful to relate quantity demanded to income. The income elasticity of demand is a measure of the relationship between a relative change in income and the consequent relative change in quantity demanded, *ceteris paribus*. The income elasticity of demand coefficient not only expresses the degree of the connection between the two variables, but it also indicates whether the good in question is normal or inferior. Specifically, the **income elasticity of demand** is defined as the percentage change in the quantity demanded at a given price divided by the percentage change in income, or

Income elasticity of demand $(E_I) = \dfrac{\text{Percentage change in quantity demanded}}{\text{Percentage change in income}}$

income elasticity of demand
a measure of the responsiveness of the quantity demanded of a good to a change in income

Calculating the Income Elasticity of Demand

Let's calculate the income elasticity of demand for lobster, where a 10 percent increase in income results in a 15 percent increase in the quantity of lobster demanded at a given price. In this case, the income elasticity of demand is $+1.5$ ($+15$ percent $\div$ $+10$ percent $= +1.5$). Lobster, then, is a normal good because an increase income results in an increase in demand. In general, if the income elasticity is positive, then the good in question is a normal good because income and demand move in the same direction.

In comparison, let's calculate the income elasticity of demand for beans, where a 10 percent increase in income results in a 15 percent decrease in the demand for beans at each price. In this case, the income elasticity of demand is -1.5 (-15 percent $\div$ $+10$ percent $= -1.5$). In this example, then, beans are an inferior good because an increase in income results in a decrease in the purchase of beans at a given price. If the income elasticity is negative, then the good in question is an inferior good because the change in income and the change in demand move in opposite directions.

Section Check

SECTION CHECK

1. The cross-price elasticity of demand is the percentage change in the quantity demanded of one good divided by the percentage change in the price of another related good.
2. If the sign on the cross-price elasticity of demand is positive, the two goods are substitutes; if it is negative, the two goods are complements.
3. The income elasticity of demand is the percentage change in quantity demanded divided by the percentage change in income.
4. If the income elasticity of demand is positive, then the good is a normal good; if it is negative, the good is an inferior good.

section

5.4   Price Elasticity of Supply

■ What is the price elasticity of supply?
■ How does time affect the supply elasticity?

WHAT IS THE PRICE ELASTICITY OF SUPPLY?

According to the law of supply, there is a positive relationship between price and quantity supplied, *ceteris paribus*. But by how much does quantity supplied change as price changes? It is often helpful to know the degree to which a change in price changes the quantity supplied. The **price elasticity of supply** measures how responsive the quantity sellers are willing and able to sell is to changes in the price. In other words, it measures the relative change in the quantity supplied that results from a change in price. Specifically, the price elasticity of supply (E_S) is defined as the percentage change in the quantity supplied divided by the percentage change in price, or

price elasticity of supply
the measure of the sensitivity of the quantity supplied to changes in price of a good

$$(E_S) = \frac{\text{Percentage change in quantity supplied}}{\text{Percentage change in price}}$$

Calculating the Price Elasticity of Supply

The price elasticity of supply is calculated in much the same manner as the price elasticity of demand. Consider, for example, the case in which it is determined that a 10 percent increase in the price of carrots results in a 25 percent increase in the quantity of carrots supplied after, say, a few harvest seasons. In this case, the price elasticity is +2.5 (+25 percent ÷ +10 percent = +2.5). This coefficient indicates that each 1 percent increase in the price of carrots induces a 2.5 percent increase in the quantity of carrots supplied.

The Ranges of the Price Elasticity of Supply

Economists delineate several ranges of the price elasticity of supply. As with the elasticity of demand, these ranges centre on whether the elasticity coefficient is greater than or less than one. Goods with a supply elasticity that is greater than one ($E_S > 1$) are said to be relatively elastic in supply. With that, a 1 percent change in price will result in a greater than 1 percent change in quantity supplied. In our earlier example, carrots were elastic in supply, because a 1 percent price increase resulted in a 2.5 percent increase in quantity supplied. An example of an elastic supply curve is shown in Exhibit 1(a).

© PHOTODISC/GETTY ONE IMAGES

Goods with a supply elasticity that is less than one ($E_S < 1$) are said to be inelastic in supply. This means that a 1 percent change in the price of these goods will induce a proportionately smaller change in the quantity supplied. This situation is shown in the supply curve in Exhibit 1(b).

Finally, there are two extreme cases of price elasticity of supply: perfectly inelastic supply and perfectly elastic supply. In a condition of perfectly inelastic supply, an increase in price will not change the quantity supplied. For example, in a sports arena in the short run (that is, in a period too brief to adjust the structure), the number of seats available will be almost fixed, say at 20 000 seats. Additional portable seats might be available, but for the most part, even if there is a higher price, there will only be 20 000 seats available. We say that the elasticity of supply is zero, which describes a perfectly inelastic supply curve. Famous paintings, like Van Gogh's *Starry Night*, provide another example; there is only one original in existence and, therefore, only one can be supplied, regardless of price. An example of this condition is shown in Exhibit 1(c).

At the other extreme is a perfectly elastic supply curve, where the elasticity equals infinity, as seen in Exhibit 1(d). In a condition of perfectly elastic supply, nothing will be supplied at any price up to a certain level, but at some higher price, sellers would be willing to supply whatever quantity buyers wished to buy. In this case, if the price is below the market price at P_0, the quantity supplied will fall to zero. But at P_1, sellers will sell all that buyers wish to buy. However, most cases fall somewhere between the two extremes of perfectly elastic and perfectly inelastic.

Immediately after harvest season is over, the supply of pumpkins is inelastic. That is, even if the price for pumpkins rises, say 10 percent, the amount of pumpkins produced will be very small until the next harvest season. Some pumpkins may be grown in greenhouses (at a much higher price to consumers), but most farmers will wait until the next growing season.

How Does Time Impact Supply Elasticities?

Time is usually critical in supply elasticities (as well as in demand elasticities) because it is more costly for producers to bring forth and release resources in a shorter period of

section 5.4
Exhibit 1
The Price Elasticity of Supply

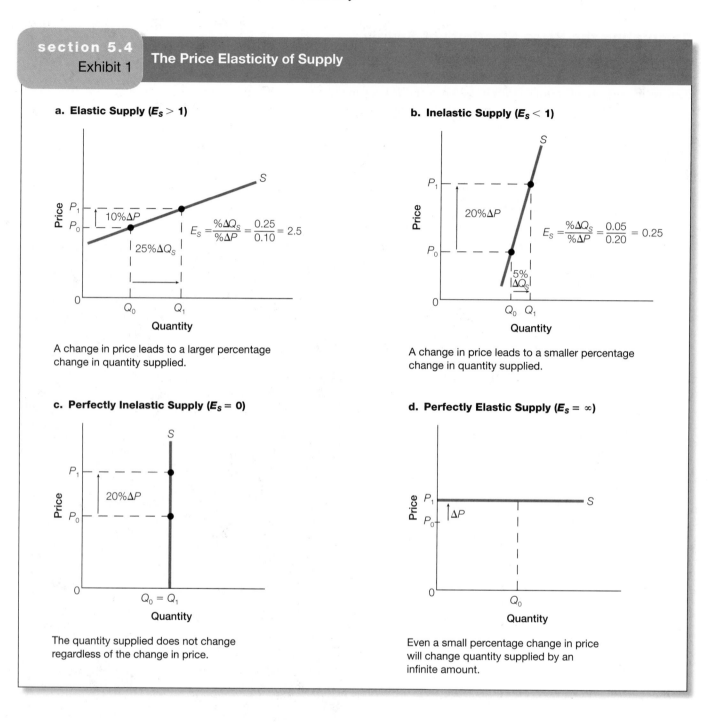

a. Elastic Supply ($E_s > 1$)

$$E_s = \frac{\%\Delta Q_S}{\%\Delta P} = \frac{0.25}{0.10} = 2.5$$

A change in price leads to a larger percentage change in quantity supplied.

b. Inelastic Supply ($E_s < 1$)

$$E_s = \frac{\%\Delta Q_S}{\%\Delta P} = \frac{0.05}{0.20} = 0.25$$

A change in price leads to a smaller percentage change in quantity supplied.

c. Perfectly Inelastic Supply ($E_s = 0$)

The quantity supplied does not change regardless of the change in price.

d. Perfectly Elastic Supply ($E_s = \infty$)

Even a small percentage change in price will change quantity supplied by an infinite amount.

time. For example, the higher wheat prices may cause farmers to grow more wheat, but big changes cannot occur until the next growing season. That is, immediately after harvest season, the supply of wheat is relatively inelastic, but over a longer period that extends over the next growing period, the supply curve becomes much more elastic. Hence, supply tends to be more elastic in the long run than the short run, as shown in Exhibit 2.

Another example of a good whose supply is highly inelastic in the short run is rental units in most urban areas without rent controls. There is generally only a fixed amount of rental units available in the short run. Thus, in the short run, an increase in demand will only lead to higher prices (rents). However, in the long run, these same higher prices (rents) provide an incentive to renovate and build new rental units.

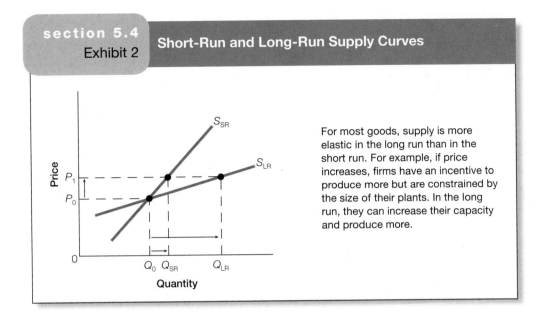

section 5.4
Exhibit 2
Short-Run and Long-Run Supply Curves

For most goods, supply is more elastic in the long run than in the short run. For example, if price increases, firms have an incentive to produce more but are constrained by the size of their plants. In the long run, they can increase their capacity and produce more.

In the short run, firms can increase output by using their existing facilities to a greater capacity, paying workers to work overtime and hiring additional workers. However, firms will be able to increase output much more in the long run when they can build new factories. In addition, some new firms can enter in the long run. In other words, the quantity supplied will be much more elastic in the long run than in the short run.

Section Check

1. The price elasticity of supply measures the relative change in the quantity supplied that results from a change in price.
2. If the supply price elasticity is greater than one, it is elastic; if it is less than one, it is inelastic.
3. Supply tends to be more elastic in the long run than the short run.

Elasticity and Taxes

■ What is tax incidence?
■ How does the relative elasticity of supply and demand determine the tax burden?

WHAT IS TAX INCIDENCE?

To varying degrees, all levels of government (federal, provincial, and municipal) use taxes to generate needed revenue. Although the legislation that accompanies a tax designates who is required to pay the particular tax, for example, the GST being a consumption-based tax is paid by consumers, the ultimate impact of the tax—also known as the tax burden—is less certain. In economics, the term **tax incidence** refers to the analysis of the effect of a particular tax on the distribution of economic welfare. In other words, tax incidence looks at the ultimate burden of a tax.

tax incidence
the analysis of the effect of a particular tax on the distribution of economic welfare

COMBINING SUPPLY AND DEMAND ELASTICITIES

The relative elasticity of supply and demand determines the distribution of the tax burden for a good. As we shall see, if demand has a lower elasticity than supply in the relevant tax region, the largest portion of the tax is paid by the consumer. However, if demand is relatively more elastic than supply in the relevant tax region, the largest portion of the tax is paid by the producer.

In Exhibit 1, the pre-tax equilibrium price is $1 and the pre-tax equilibrium quantity is Q_{BT}—the quantity before tax. If the government imposes a $0.50 tax on the seller, the supply curve shifts vertically by the amount of the tax (just as if an input price rose by $0.50).

In the case where demand is relatively less elastic than supply in the relevant region, almost the whole tax is passed on to the consumer, *ceteris paribus*. For example, in Exhibit 1(a), sellers are very responsive to changes in the price of the good (explaining the relatively flat supply curve), whereas consumers are relatively less responsive (explaining the relatively steep demand curve). In response to the tax, the price paid by consumers rises substantially, indicating that consumers bear most of the burden of the tax. With a post-tax equilibrium price of $1.40, consumers end up paying 40 cents more per unit compared to the per-tax equilibrium price. The price received by producers, however, does not fall by very much, indicating that sellers bear only a small burden of the tax. At 90 cents per unit ($1.40 − $0.50 = $0.90), the producer burden amounts to only 10 cents.

In Exhibit 1(b), demand is relatively more elastic than the supply in the relevant region. Here, we see that the greater burden of the same 50-cent tax falls on the producer, *ceteris paribus*. In response to the tax, the price paid by consumers does not rise very much, but the price received by producers falls substantially. With a post-tax equilibrium price of $1.10, the producer will only receive 60 cents per unit ($1.10 − $0.50 = $0.60), resulting in a 40 cent per-unit tax burden. Consumers, on the other hand, end up paying 10 cents more per unit compared to the pre-tax equilibrium price.

In general, then, the tax burden falls on the side of the market that is less elastic. Note that who actually pays the tax at the time of the purchase has nothing to do with who incurs the ultimate burden of the taxation—that depends on the relative elasticity.

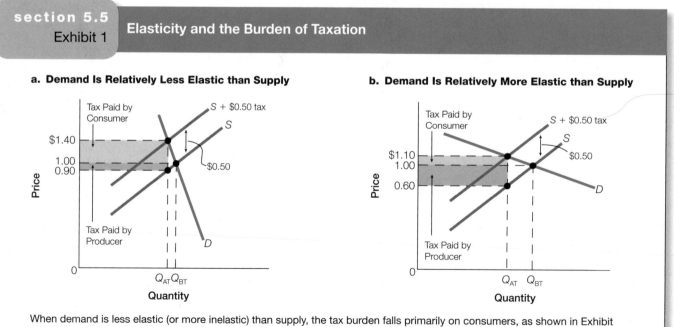

section 5.5
Exhibit 1

Elasticity and the Burden of Taxation

When demand is less elastic (or more inelastic) than supply, the tax burden falls primarily on consumers, as shown in Exhibit 1(a). When demand is more elastic than supply, as shown in Exhibit 1(b), the tax burden falls primarily on producers.

In The **NEWS**

DRUGS ACROSS THE BORDER

BY JOHN WARD ANDERSON AND WILLIAM BRANIGIN

"They are just limited by their imagination," said a U.S. official who closely monitors Mexican trafficking groups. "Money is no obstacle at all." Trafficking schemes run the gamut from the mundane to the Byzantine. In recent years, drug mafias have bought 727-style planes and built a fleet of two-man submarines to move drugs into the United States. They have secreted loads in propane tanks and containers of hazardous materials, in small cans of tuna fish and five-gallon drums of jalapeño peppers. One trafficking group fashioned a special mold that was successfully used to ship cocaine from Mexico through the United States and into Canada completely sealed inside the walls of porcelain toilets.

The groups are using satellite-linked navigation and positioning aids to coordinate airplane drops to boats waiting in the Caribbean and to trucks in the Arizona and Texas deserts. They are using small planes equipped with ordinary car radar detectors to probe radar coverage along the border, then slipping other drug-laden aircraft through the gaps before U.S. officials can react. They are racing hauls of drugs up the coast in 22-foot-long powerboats with massive engines, digging holes in the Gulf beaches of Texas and burying their loads like hidden treasure for pickup at a later date.

Among the more ambitious drug-smuggling methods in recent years was the construction of tunnels under the border at Douglas, Arizona, and Otay Mesa, California, used to smuggle tons of cocaine into the United States until they were shut down following a tip from an informant.

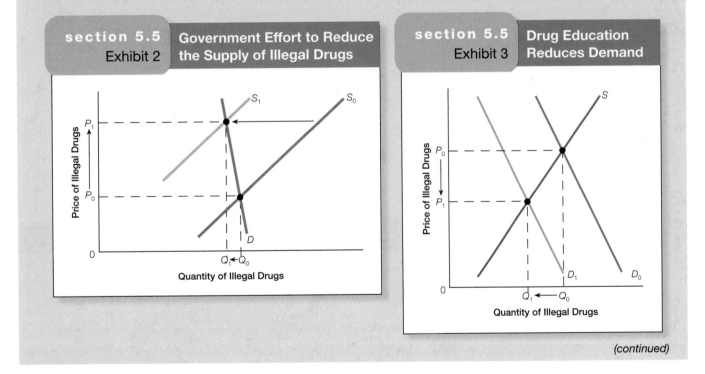

section 5.5 Exhibit 2 — Government Effort to Reduce the Supply of Illegal Drugs

section 5.5 Exhibit 3 — Drug Education Reduces Demand

(continued)

IN THE NEWS *(continued)*

CONSIDER THIS:

The United States spends billions of dollars a year to halt the importation of illegal drugs across the border. Although these efforts are clearly targeted at suppliers, who really pays the higher enforcement and evasion costs? The government crackdown has increased the probability of apprehension and conviction for drug smugglers. That increase in risk for suppliers increases their cost of doing business—raising the cost of importing and distributing illegal drugs. This would shift the supply curve for illegal drugs to the left, from S_0 to S_1, as seen in Exhibit 2. For most drug users—addicts, in particular—the price of drugs like cocaine and heroin lies in the highly inelastic region of the demand curve. Because the demand for drugs is relatively inelastic in this region, the seller would be able to shift most of this cost onto the consumer (think of it like the tax shift just discussed). That is, enforcement efforts increase the price of illegal drugs, but only a small reduction in quantity demanded results from this price increase. Increased enforcement efforts may have unintended consequences due to the fact that buyers bear the majority of the burden of this price increase. Tighter smuggling controls may, in fact, result in higher levels of burglary, muggings, and white-collar crime, as more cash-strapped buyers search for alternative ways of funding their increasingly expensive habit. In addition, with the huge financial rewards in the drug trade,

tougher enforcement and higher illegal-drug prices could lead to even greater corruption in law enforcement and the judicial system.

This is not to say that we should abandon our efforts against illegal drugs. Illegal drugs can impose huge personal and social costs—billions of dollars' of lost productivity and immeasurable personal tragedy. However, solely targeting the supply side can have unintended consequences. Policymakers may get their best results by focusing on a reduction in demand—changing user preferences. For example, if drug education leads to a reduction in the demand for drugs, the demand curve will shift to the left—reducing the price and the quantity of illegal drugs exchanged, as seen in Exhibit 3. The remaining drug users, at Q_1, will now pay a lower price, P_1. This lower price for drugs will lead to fewer drug-related crimes, *ceteris paribus*.

It is also possible that the elasticity of demand for illegal drugs may be more elastic in the long run than the short run. In the short run, as the price rises, the quantity demanded falls less than proportionately because of the addictive nature of illegal drugs (this is also true for goods like tobacco and alcohol). However, in the long run, the demand for illegal drugs may be more elastic; that is, the higher price may deter many younger, and poorer, people from experimenting with illegal drugs.

Section Check

1. The relative elasticity of supply and demand determines the distribution of the tax burden for a good.
2. If demand is more elastic than supply, producers bear the greater burden of the tax.
3. If supply is more elastic than demand, consumers bear the greater burden of the tax.

Summary

Section 5.1

- The price elasticity of demand measures how responsive a change in quantity demanded is to a price change.
- The price elasticity of demand is calculated by finding the percentage change in quantity demanded divided by the percentage change in price.
- If the price elasticity of demand is greater than 1, demand is price elastic ($E_D > 1$).
- If the price elasticity of demand is less than 1, demand is price inelastic ($E_D < 1$).
- If the price elasticity of demand is 1, demand is unit elastic.
- The price elasticity of demand depends on (1) the availability of close substitutes, (2) the proportion of income spent on the good, and (3) the amount of time that buyers have to respond to a price change.
- The midpoint method to calculating percentage change uses the average of the initial and final values when calculating percentage change.

Section 5.2

- If demand is elastic, total revenue will vary inversely with a price change.
- If demand is inelastic, total revenue will vary in the same direction as a change in price.
- Along a linear demand curve, price is more elastic at higher price ranges, more price inelastic at lower price ranges, and unit elastic at the midpoint.

Section 5.3

- Cross-price elasticity of demand measures the impact that a price change of one good will have on the quantity demanded of another good.
- Cross-price elasticity of demand is calculated by finding the percentage change in the quantity demanded on one good divided by the percentage change in the price of another good.
- Cross-price elasticity is positive for substitute goods and negative for complement goods.
- Income elasticity of demand measures how responsive a change in quantity demanded is to a change in consumer income.
- Income elasticity of demand is calculated by finding the percentage change in the quantity demanded and dividing by the percentage change in income.
- Income elasticity is positive for normal goods and negative for inferior goods.

Section 5.4

- The price elasticity of supply measures how responsive a change in quantity supplied is to a price change.
- The price elasticity of supply is calculated by finding the percentage change in quantity supplied divided by the percentage change in price.
- If the price elasticity of supply is greater than 1, supply is price elastic ($E_S > 1$).
- If the price elasticity of supply is less than 1, supply is price inelastic ($E_S < 1$).
- If the price elasticity of supply is 1, supply is unit elastic.
- Time is usually critical in supply elasticity.

Section 5.5

- If demand is relatively more elastic than supply in the relevant tax region, the largest portion of the tax is paid by the producer.
- If demand is relatively less elastic than supply in the relevant tax region, the largest portion of the tax is paid by the consumer.

Key Terms and Concepts

For a complete glossary of chapter key terms, visit the textbook's Web site at http://www.sextonmicro2e.nelson.com.

price elasticity of demand 115
elastic demand segment 116
inelastic demand segment 117

unit elastic demand 118
cross-price elasticity of demand 125
income elasticity of demand 125

price elasticity of supply 126
tax incidence 129

Review Questions

1. The Winnipeg Blue Bombers seek to boost revenues from ticket sales next season. You are hired as an economic consultant and asked to advise the CFL franchise whether to raise or lower ticket prices next year. If the elasticity of demand for Blue Bombers game tickets is estimated to be 1.6, what would you advise? If the elasticity of demand equals 0.4?

2. How might your elasticity of demand for copying and binding services vary if your work presentation is due next week versus in two hours?

3. For each of the following pairs, identify which one is likely to exhibit more elastic demand:

    a. shampoo; Paul Mitchell Shampoo

    b. air travel prompted by an illness in the family; vacation air travel

    c. paper clips; an apartment rental

    d. prescription heart medication; generic aspirin

4. If the elasticity of demand for hamburgers equals −1.5 and the quantity demanded equals 40 000, predict what will happen to the quantity demanded of hamburgers when the price increases by 10 percent. If the price falls by 5 percent, what will happen?

5. Evaluate the following statement: "Along a downward-sloping linear demand curve, the slope, and therefore the elasticity of demand, are both constant."

6. A movie production company faces a linear demand curve for its film and it seeks to maximize total revenue from the film's distribution. At what level should the price be set? Where demand is elastic, inelastic, or unit elastic? Explain.

7. Isabella always spends $50 on red roses each month and simply adjusts the quantity she purchases as the price changes. What can you say about Isabella's elasticity of demand for roses?

8. If the government's goal is to raise tax revenue, which of the following are good markets to tax?

    a. luxury yachts

    b. alcohol

    c. movies

    d. gasoline

    e. grapefruit juice

9. Elasticity of demand in the market for one-bedroom apartments is 2.0, elasticity of supply is 0.5, the current market price is $1000, and the equilibrium number of one-bedroom apartments is 10 000. If the government imposes a price ceiling of $800 on this market, predict the size of the resulting apartment shortage.

10. Indicate whether a pair of products are substitutes, complements, or neither, based upon the following estimates for the cross-price elasticity of demand:

    a. 0.5

    b. −0.5

11. Indicate whether the products are normal, inferior or neither, based on the following estimates for the income elasticity of demand:

    a. 1.7

    b. −1.7

12. Bad weather spoils the orange crop. As a result, the price rises from $3 to $5 a basket and the quantity demanded decreases from 1500 to 900 baskets a week. Over this price range calculate the price elasticity of demand (using the midpoint method).

13. If a 10 percent rise in the price of coffee increases the quantity of tea demanded by 25 percent and decreases the quantity of coffee demanded by 20 percent, calculate the cross elasticity of demand between coffee and tea.

Fill in the Blanks

Section 5.1

1. The price elasticity of demand measures the responsiveness of quantity _____ to a change in price.

2. If the price elasticity of demand is elastic, it means the quantity demanded changes by a relatively _____ amount than the price change.

3. If the price elasticity of demand is inelastic, it means the quantity demanded changes by a relatively _____ amount than the price change.

4. For the most part, the price elasticity of demand depends on the availability of _____, the _____ spent on the good, and the amount of _____ people have to adapt to a price change.

5. The elasticity of demand for a Ford automobile would likely be _____elastic than the demand for automobiles because there are more and better substitutes for a certain type of car than for a car itself.

6. The more time that people have to adapt to a new price change, the _____ the elasticity of demand. The more time that passes, the more time consumers have to find or develop suitable _____ and to plan and implement changes in their patterns of consumption.

7. The _____ uses a midpoint (or average) of the initial and final values in calculating percentage change as opposed to an initial value.

Section 5.2

8. When demand is price elastic, total revenues will _____ as the price declines because the percentage increase in the _____ is greater than the percentage reduction in price.

9. When demand is price inelastic, total revenues will _____ as the price declines because the percentage increase in the _____ is less than the percentage reduction in price.

10. When the price falls on the upper half of a straight-line demand curve, demand is relatively _____. When the price falls on the lower half of a straight-line demand curve, demand is relatively _____.

Section 5.3

11. Income elasticity of demand measures the responsiveness of quantity demanded to a change in _____ .

12. The cross-price elasticity of demand is defined as the percentage change in the _____ of one good divided by the percentage change in _____ of another good.

13. If the cross-price elasticity coefficient is positive, it can be concluded that the two goods are _____.

Section 5.4

14. The price elasticity of supply measures the sensitivity of the quantity _____ to the changes in the price of the good.

15. The price elasticity of supply is defined as the percentage change in the _____ divided by the percentage change in _____.

16. Goods with a supply elasticity that is greater than 1 are called relatively _____ in supply.

17. When supply is inelastic, a 1 percent change in the price of a good will induce a _____ 1 percent change in the quantity supplied.

18. Time is usually critical in supply elasticities because it is _____ costly for producers to bring forth and release resources in a shorter period of time.

Section 5.5

19. The relative _____ determines the distribution of the tax burden for a good.

20. If demand is relatively _____ elastic than supply in the relevant region, the largest portion of a tax is paid by the producer.

True or False

Section 5.1

1. A segment of a demand curve has an elasticity less than 1 if the percentage change in quantity demanded is less than the percentage change in price that caused it.

2. A perfectly elastic demand curve would be horizontal, but a perfectly inelastic demand curve would be vertical.

3. Along a segment of a demand curve that was unit elastic, quantity demanded would change by 10 percent as a result of 10 percent change in the price.

4. Goods with close substitutes tend to have more elastic demands, and goods without close substitutes tend to have less elastic demand.

5. We would expect that the elasticity of demand for Ford automobiles would be greater than the demand for insulin by diabetics.

6. Based on the percentage of a person's budget devoted to a particular item, you would expect that the elasticity of demand for salt would be greater than the elasticity of demand for attending a university.

7. The midpoint between 7 and 9 is 8.

Section 5.2

8. Along a demand curve, if the price rises and total revenue falls as a result, then demand must be relatively elastic along that range of the demand curve.

9. If demand is inelastic, the price and total revenue will move in opposite directions along the demand curve.

10. A straight-line demand curve will have a constant elasticity of demand along its length.

Section 5.3

11. Since quantity demanded and incomes move in the same direction (either both increasing or both decreasing) for *normal goods,* their income elasticities are negative.

12. Since the price of one good and the demand for another move in opposite directions for complementary goods, their cross-price elasticities are negative.

13. A good with an income elasticity coefficient of -1.5 would be considered an inferior good.

14. A 5 percent increase in the price of good A has resulted in a 20 percent decline in the quantity of good B demanded. In this case, the cross-price elasticity of demand is 4.

Section 5.4

15. The price elasticity of supply measures the relative change in the quantity supplied that results from a change in price.

16. When supply is relatively elastic, a 10 percent change in price will result in a greater than 10 percent change in quantity supplied.

17. A perfectly elastic supply curve would be vertical, but a perfectly inelastic supply curve would be horizontal.

18. Goods with a supply elasticity that is less than 1 are called relatively inelastic in supply.

19. Unlike demand, supply tends to be more elastic in the long run than the short run.

Section 5.5

20. If demand has a lower elasticity than supply in the relevant region, the largest portion of a tax is paid by the producer.

21. Who bears the burden of a tax has nothing to do with who actually pays the tax at the time of the purchase.

Multiple Choice

Section 5.1

1. Demand is said to be _____ when the quantity demanded is not very responsive to changes in price.
   a. independent
   b. inelastic
   c. unit elastic
   d. elastic

2. When demand is inelastic,
   a. price elasticity of demand is less than 1.
   b. consumers are not very responsive to changes in price.
   c. the percentage change in quantity demanded resulting from a price change is less than the percentage change in price.
   d. all of the above are correct.

3. Which of the following would tend to have the most elastic demand curve?
   a. automobiles
   b. Chevrolet automobiles
   c. Both a and b would be the same.
   d. none of the above

4. Iron Mike's steel mill finds that a 10 percent increase in its price leads to a 14 percent decrease in the quantity it is able to sell. The demand curve for the mill's output is
   a. elastic.
   b. inelastic.
   c. unit elastic.
   d. perfectly elastic.

5. If recent sharp increases in the price of insulin have had only a small effect on the amount of insulin purchased, then the demand for insulin is
   a. elastic.
   b. inelastic.
   c. unit elastic.
   d. perfectly elastic.

6. The price elasticity of demand coefficient for herbal tea is estimated to be equal to 0.5. It is expected, therefore, that a 10 percent decrease in price would lead to a _____ in the quantity of herbal tea demanded.
   a. 5 percent decrease
   b. 5 percent increase
   c. 10 percent decrease
   d. 10 percent increase
   e. 0.5 percent increase

7. The long-run demand curve for gasoline is likely to be
   a. more elastic than the short-run demand curve for gasoline.
   b. more inelastic than the short-run demand curve for gasoline.
   c. the same as the short-run demand curve for gasoline.
   d. more inelastic than the short-run supply of gasoline.

8. When gasoline prices increased from $1.15/litre to $1.20/litre, the quantity of gasoline demanded by consumers declined from 10000 litres/day to 9400 litres/day. Using the midpoint method, the price elasticity of demand for gasoline is _____.
   a. 1.45
   b. 0.68
   c. 1.38
   d. 1.53

Section 5.2

9. When the local symphony recently raised its ticket price for its summer concerts in the park, the symphony was surprised to see that its total revenue had actually decreased. The reason was that the elasticity of demand for tickets was
   a. unit elastic.
   b. unit inelastic.
   c. inelastic.
   d. elastic.

10. A price hike (increase) will increase the total revenue a firm receives if the demand for its product is
    a. elastic.
    b. inelastic.
    c. unit elastic.
    d. unit inelastic.

Section 5.3

11. In response to a decline in average consumer income from $55000/year to $53000/year, the demand for Florida vacations declined from 12000/year to 10200/year. According to the calculation for income elasticity, Florida vacations are a(n) _____ .
    a. inferior good.
    b. normal good.
    c. substitute good.
    d. complementary good.

12. If the cross-price elasticity of demand between two goods is negative, we know that
    a. they are substitutes.
    b. they are complements.
    c. they are both inferior goods.
    d. they are both normal goods.

13. If the income elasticity of demand for a good A is 0.5 and the income elasticity of demand for a good B is 1.5, then
    a. both A and B are normal goods.
    b. both A and B are inferior goods.
    c. A is a normal good, but B is an inferior good.
    d. A is an inferior good, but B is a normal good.

14. If good X has a negative cross-price elasticity of demand with good Y and good X also has a negative income elasticity of demand, then
    a. X is a substitute for Y, and X is a normal good.
    b. X is a substitute for Y, and X is an inferior good.
    c. X is a complement for Y, and X is a normal good.
    d. X is a complement for Y, and X is an inferior good.

Section 5.4

15. For a given increase in price, the greater is the elasticity of supply, the greater is the resulting
    a. decrease in quantity supplied.
    b. decrease in supply.
    c. increase in quantity supplied.
    d. increase in supply.

16. An increase in demand will increase the price but not the quantity sold in a market if
    a. supply is perfectly elastic.
    b. supply is perfectly inelastic.
    c. supply is relatively elastic.
    d. supply is relatively inelastic.

Section 5.5

17. If the demand for gasoline is highly inelastic and the supply is highly elastic, then if a tax is imposed on gasoline it will be paid
    a. largely by the sellers of the product.
    b. largely by the buyers of the product.
    c. equally by the buyers and sellers of the product.
    d. by the government.

18. A tax is imposed on coffee. Sellers will bear no burden from this tax if the
    a. demand for coffee is perfectly inelastic.
    b. demand for coffee is perfectly elastic.
    c. demand for coffee is unit elastic.
    d. none of the above.

Problems

1. [Section 5.1]
Good weather produces a bumper crop of apples. As a result, the price falls from $6 to $3 a basket and the quantity demanded increases from 600 to 1100 baskets a week. Over this price range calculate the price elasticity of demand (using the midpoint method).

2. [Section 5.2]
If the midpoint on a straight-line demand curve is at a price of $7, what can we say about the elasticity of demand for a price change from $12 to $10? What about from $6 to $4?

3. [Section 5.2]
If the local bus company raises its price per rider from $2.50 to $2.75, and its total revenues rise, what can we say about its elasticity of demand? What if total revenues fall as a result of the price increase?

4. [Section 5.3]
How does the income elasticity of demand tell you whether a good is normal? Inferior?

5. [Section 5.3]
If a 10 percent decline in the price of cameras increases the quantity of film demanded by 20 percent and increases the quantity of cameras demanded by 15 percent, calculate the cross-price elasticity of demand between cameras and film.

6

Market Efficiency and Market Failure

6.1 CONSUMER AND PRODUCER SURPLUS
What is consumer and producer surplus?

6.2 EXTERNALITIES
What are externalities?

6.3 PUBLIC GOODS
What is a public good?

6.4 ASYMMETRIC INFORMATION
What is asymmetric information?

Consumer and Producer Surplus

■ What is consumer surplus?
■ What is producer surplus?
■ How do we measure the total gains from trade?

CONSUMER SURPLUS

In a competitive market, consumers and producers buy and sell at the market equilibrium price. However, what a consumer actually pays for a unit of a good is usually less than the amount she is *willing* to pay. For example, you would be willing and able to pay far more than the market price for a rope ladder to get out of a burning building. You would be willing to pay more than the market price for a tank of gasoline if you had run out of gas on a desolate highway. **Consumer surplus** is the monetary difference between the amount a consumer is willing and able to pay for an additional unit of a good and what the consumer actually pays—the market price. Consumer surplus for the whole market is the sum of all the consumer surpluses of the individual consumers who have purchased the good.

consumer surplus
the difference between the price a consumer is willing and able to pay for an additional unit of a good and the price the consumer actually pays; for the whole market it is the sum of all the individual consumer surpluses

MARGINAL WILLINGNESS TO PAY FALLS AS MORE IS CONSUMED

Suppose it is a very hot day and iced tea is going for $1 per glass, but a consumer is willing to pay $4 for the first glass, $2 for the second glass, and $0.50 for the third glass, reflecting the law of demand. How much consumer surplus will this consumer receive? First, it is important to note the general fact that if the consumer is a buyer of several units of a good, the earlier units will have greater marginal value and therefore create more consumer surplus, because *marginal willingness to pay* falls as greater quantities are consumed in any period. This is demonstrated by the consumer's willingness to pay $4 and $2 successively for the first two glasses of iced tea. Thus, the consumer will receive $3 of consumer surplus for the first glass ($4 − $1) and $1 of consumer surplus for the second glass ($2 − $1), for a total of $4, as seen in Exhibit 1. The consumer will not be willing to purchase the third glass because it would provide less value than its price warrants ($0.50 versus $1) and reduce consumer surplus as a result.

In Exhibit 2, consumer surplus is shown as the area under the market demand curve and above the market price (area A). Areas A and B together represent *total* willingness to pay for Q units of the good, whereas area B is the amount the consumer is required to pay for that quantity ($P \times Q$). The difference is consumer surplus, the shaded area, A.

PRICE CHANGES AND CHANGES IN CONSUMER SURPLUS

Imagine that the price of your favourite beverage fell because of an increase in supply. Wouldn't you feel better off? An increase in supply and a lower price will increase your consumer surplus for each of the units you were already consuming, and will also increase consumer surplus from increased purchases at the lower price. Conversely, a decrease in supply will cause an increase in price and will lower the amount of consumer surplus.

Exhibit 3 shows the gain in consumer surplus associated with a technological advance that shifts the supply curve to the right. As a result, equilibrium price falls (from P_0 to P_1) and quantity rises (from Q_0 to Q_1). Consumer surplus then increases from area P_0AB to area P_1AC, or a gain in consumer surplus of P_0BCP_1. The increase in consumer surplus has two parts. First, there is an increase in consumer surplus because Q_0 can now be purchased at a lower price; this amount of additional consumer surplus is illustrated by area P_0BDP_1 in Exhibit 3. Second, the lower price makes it advantageous for buyers to expand their purchases from Q_0 to Q_1. The net benefit to buyers from expanding their consumption from Q_0 to Q_1 is illustrated by the area BCD.

PRODUCER SURPLUS

As we have just seen, the difference between what a consumer would be willing and able to pay for a quantity of a good and what a consumer actually has to pay is called consumer

Imagine it is 30 degrees in the shade. Do you think you would get more consumer surplus from your first glass of iced tea than you would from a fifth glass?

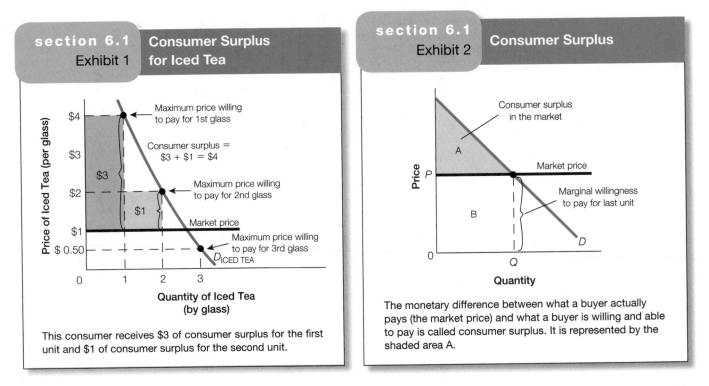

section 6.1
Exhibit 1
Consumer Surplus for Iced Tea

This consumer receives $3 of consumer surplus for the first unit and $1 of consumer surplus for the second unit.

section 6.1
Exhibit 2
Consumer Surplus

The monetary difference between what a buyer actually pays (the market price) and what a buyer is willing and able to pay is called consumer surplus. It is represented by the shaded area A.

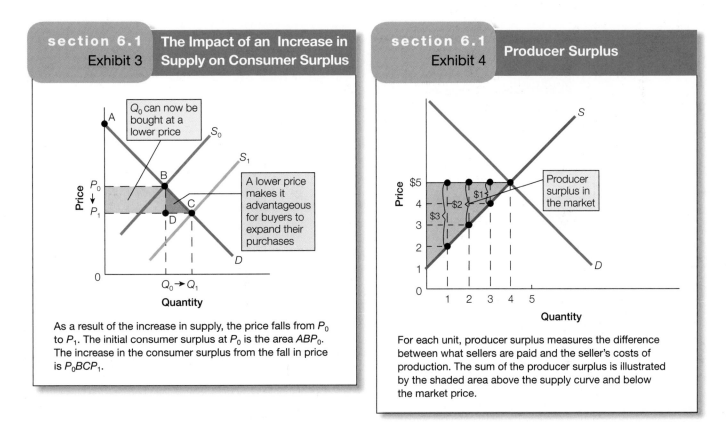

section 6.1
Exhibit 3
The Impact of an Increase in Supply on Consumer Surplus

Q_0 can now be bought at a lower price

A lower price makes it advantageous for buyers to expand their purchases

As a result of the increase in supply, the price falls from P_0 to P_1. The initial consumer surplus at P_0 is the area ABP_0. The increase in the consumer surplus from the fall in price is P_0BCP_1.

section 6.1
Exhibit 4
Producer Surplus

Producer surplus in the market

For each unit, producer surplus measures the difference between what sellers are paid and the seller's costs of production. The sum of the producer surplus is illustrated by the shaded area above the supply curve and below the market price.

surplus. The parallel concept for producers is called producer surplus. **Producer surplus** is the difference between what a producer is paid for a good and the cost of producing that unit of the good. Because some units can be produced at a cost that is lower than the market price, the seller receives a surplus, or a net benefit, from producing those units. For example, in Exhibit 4, the market price is $5. Say the firm's cost is $2 for the first unit, $3 for the second unit, $4 for the third unit, and $5 for the fourth unit. Since producer surplus for a particular unit is the difference between the market price and the seller's cost of producing that unit, producer surplus would be as follows: The first unit would yield $3, the second unit would yield $2, the third unit would yield $1, while the fourth unit would add no more to producer surplus, as the market price equals the seller's cost.

For the market, producer surplus is obtained by summing all the producer surplus of all the sellers—the area above the market supply curve and below the market price. Producer surplus is a measurement of how much sellers gain from trading in the market.

Suppose there is an increase in demand and the market price rises, say from P_0 to P_1; the seller now receives a higher price per unit, so additional producer surplus is generated. In Exhibit 5, we see the additions to producer surplus. Part of the added surplus (area P_1DBP_0) is due to a higher price for the quantity already being produced (up to Q_0) and part (area DCB) is due to the expansion of output made profitable by the higher price (from Q_0 to Q_1).

producer surplus
the difference between what a producer is paid for a good and the cost of producing that unit of the good; for the market, it is the sum of all the individual sellers' producer surpluses— the area above the market supply curve and below the market price

MARKET EFFICIENCY AND PRODUCER AND CONSUMER SURPLUS

With the tools of consumer and producer surplus, we can better analyze the total gains from exchange. The demand curve represents a collection of maximum prices that consumers are willing and able to pay for additional quantities of a good or service. The supply curve represents a collection of minimum prices that suppliers require to be

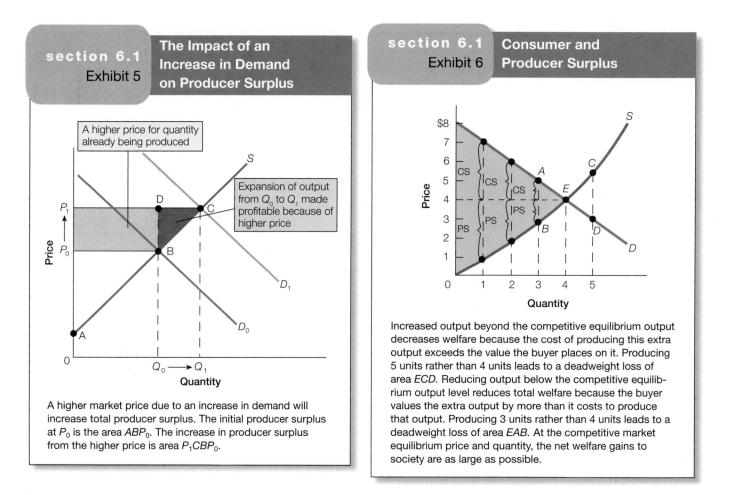

section 6.1
Exhibit 5

The Impact of an Increase in Demand on Producer Surplus

A higher price for quantity already being produced

Expansion of output from Q_0 to Q_1 made profitable because of higher price

A higher market price due to an increase in demand will increase total producer surplus. The initial producer surplus at P_0 is the area ABP_0. The increase in producer surplus from the higher price is area P_1CBP_0.

section 6.1
Exhibit 6

Consumer and Producer Surplus

Increased output beyond the competitive equilibrium output decreases welfare because the cost of producing this extra output exceeds the value the buyer places on it. Producing 5 units rather than 4 units leads to a deadweight loss of area *ECD*. Reducing output below the competitive equilibrium output level reduces total welfare because the buyer values the extra output by more than it costs to produce that output. Producing 3 units rather than 4 units leads to a deadweight loss of area *EAB*. At the competitive market equilibrium price and quantity, the net welfare gains to society are as large as possible.

willing and able to supply each additional unit of a good or service, as seen in Exhibit 6. For example, for the first unit of output, the buyer is willing to pay up to $7 and the seller would have to receive at least $1 to produce that unit. However, the equilibrium price is $4, as indicated by the intersection of the supply and demand curves. It is clear that the two would gain from getting together and trading that unit because the consumer would receive $3 of consumer surplus ($7 − $4) and the producer would receive $3 of producer surplus ($4 − $1). Both would also benefit from trading the second and third units of output—in fact, both would benefit from trading every unit up to the market equilibrium output. That is, buyers purchase each good, except for the very last unit, for less than the maximum amount that they would have been willing to pay; sellers receive, except for the very last unit, more than the minimum amount that they would have been willing to accept to supply the good. Once the equilibrium output is reached at the equilibrium price, all of the mutually beneficial trade opportunities between the suppliers and the demanders will have taken place, and the sum of consumer surplus and producer surplus is maximized. Both buyers and sellers are better off from each of the units traded than they would have been if they had not exchanged them.

It is important to recognize that, in this case, the **total welfare gains** to the economy from trade in this good is the sum of the consumer and producer surplus created. That is, consumers benefit from additional amounts of consumer surplus and producers benefit from additional amounts of producer surplus. Improvements in welfare come from additions to both consumer and producer surplus. In competitive markets, where there are large numbers of buyers and sellers, at the market equilibrium price and quantity, the net gains to society are as large as possible.

total welfare gains
the sum of consumer and producer surplus

Why would it be inefficient to produce only 3 units? The demand curve in Exhibit 6 indicates that the buyer is willing to pay $5 for the third unit. The supply curve shows that it only costs the seller $3 to produce that unit. That is, as long as the buyer values the extra output by more than it costs to produce that unit, total welfare would increase by expanding output. In fact, if output is expanded from 3 units to 4 units, total welfare (the sum of consumer and producer surpluses) will increase by area *AEB* in Exhibit 6.

What if 5 units are produced? The demand curve shows that the buyer is only willing to pay $3 for the fifth unit. However, the supply curve shows that it would cost about $5.50 to produce the fifth unit. Thus, increasing output beyond equilibrium decreases total welfare because the cost of producing this extra output is greater than the value the buyer places on it. If output is reduced from 5 units to 4 units, total welfare will increase by the area *ECD* in Exhibit 6.

Not producing the efficient level of output leads to what economists call a **dead-weight loss.** A deadweight loss is the net loss of total surplus that results from the misallocation of resources.

deadweight loss
net loss of total surplus that results from an action that alters a competitive market equilibrium

Section Check

SECTION CHECK

1. The difference between how much a consumer is willing and able to pay and how much a consumer has to pay for a unit of the good is called consumer surplus.
2. An increase in supply will lead to a lower price and an increase in consumer surplus; a decrease in supply will lead to a higher price and a decrease in consumer surplus.
3. Producer surplus is the difference between what a producer is paid for a good and the cost of producing that good.
4. An increase in demand will lead to a higher market price and an increase in producer surplus; a decrease in demand will lead to a lower market price and a decrease in producer surplus.
5. Total welfare gains from trade to the economy can be measured by the sum of consumer and producer surplus.

section

6.2

Externalities

- What is a market failure?
- What is a negative externality?
- How are negative externalities internalized?
- What is a positive externality?
- How are positive externalities internalized?

externalities
a benefit or cost from consumption or production that spills over onto those that are not consuming or producing the good

negative externality
occurs when costs spill over to an outside party that is not involved in producing or consuming the good

The forces represented by supply and demand perform an extremely complicated and valuable function. However, these market forces do not always produce the "right" amount of all goods and services. That is, sometimes the market system fails to produce efficient outcomes because of side effects economists call **externalities.** An externality is said to

There is nothing worse than having a public place spoiled by the inconsiderate behaviour of others. Some laws, such as this "pooper scooper" law, are intended to minimize negative externalities in public areas.

positive externality

occurs when benefits spill over to an outside party that is not involved in producing or consuming the good

occur whenever there are physical impacts (benefits or costs) of an activity on individuals not directly involved in the activity. If the impact on the outside party is negative, it is called a **negative externality;** if the impact is positive, it is called a **positive externality.** Externalities, therefore, result in market failure, because the market system fails to produce an efficient level of output.

NEGATIVE EXTERNALITIES

The classic example of a negative externality is pollution from an air-polluting factory, such as a steel mill. If the firm uses clean air in production and returns dirty air to the atmosphere, it has created a negative externality. The polluted air has "spilled over" to outside parties. Now people in the neighbouring communities may experience higher incidences of disease, dirtier houses, and other property damage. Such damages are real costs, but because no one owns the air, the firm does not have to pay for its use, unlike the other resources the firm uses in production. A steel mill has to pay for labour, capital, energy, and raw materials because it must compensate the owners of those inputs for their use. If a firm can avoid paying the cost it imposes on others—the external costs—it has lowered its own costs of production, but not the true cost to society.

Examples of negative externalities are numerous: the roommate who plays his stereo too loud at 2:00 A.M.; the neighbour's dog that barks all night long or leaves "messages" on your front lawn; the gardener who runs his leaf blower on full power at 7:00 A.M. on a Saturday.

Graphing Negative External Costs

Let's take another look at the steel industry. In Exhibit 1, we see the market for steel. Notice that at each level of output, the first supply curve, $S_{PRIVATE}$, is lower than the second, S_{SOCIAL}. The reason for this is simple: $S_{PRIVATE}$ only includes the private costs to the firm—the capital, entrepreneurship, land, and labour for which it must pay. However, S_{SOCIAL} includes all of those costs, plus the external costs that production imposes on others. That is, if the firm could somehow be required to compensate those damaged, it would increase the cost of production for the firm and cause a leftward shift in the supply curve. In Exhibit 1, we see that if the government stepped in and made the firm pay for the external costs, then the output of steel would fall to Q_{SOCIAL}, the social optimal (or best) level of output. From society's standpoint, Q_{SOCIAL} is the best level of output because it represents all the costs (private + external costs) associated with the production of this good. If the suppliers of steel are not aware of or are not responsible for the external costs, they will tend to produce too much from society's standpoint. This means that there is an *overallocation* of scarce resources to the production of this good.

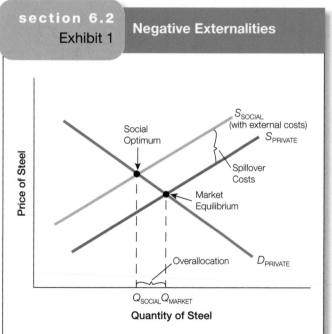

section 6.2 Exhibit 1   **Negative Externalities**

When there are negative externalities, the equilibrium market output level, Q_{MARKET}, will exceed the socially optimum quantity, Q_{SOCIAL}, and there is an overallocation of scarce resources in the production of this good.

Canadians deposit litter on beaches, campgrounds, highways, and vacant lots. Some of this is removed by government agencies, and some of it biodegrades over many years. There are several solutions to the litter problem. Stiffer fines and penalties and more aggressive monitoring could be employed. Alternatively, through education and civic pride, individuals and groups could be encouraged to pick up trash.

© SAMI SARKIS/PHOTODISC/GETTY ONE IMAGES

WHAT CAN THE GOVERNMENT DO TO CORRECT FOR NEGATIVE EXTERNALITIES?

How could society correct this market failure? The government can intervene in market decisions in an attempt to take account of these negative externalities. It may do this by estimating the amount of those external costs and then taxing the manufacturer by that amount, forcing the manufacturer to internalize (bear) the costs.

Pollution Taxes

Pollution taxes are designed to internalize negative externalities. If government could impose a pollution tax equal to the exact size of the external cost, then the firm would produce at the socially desired level of output, Q_{SOCIAL}. That is, the tax would shift the supply curve for steel leftward to S_{SOCIAL} and would provide an incentive for the firm to produce at the social optimum level of output. Additionally, tax revenues would be generated that could be used to compensate those who had suffered damage from the pollution, or that could be used in some other productive way, such as developing new technologies to reduce pollution.

Regulation

Alternatively, the government could use regulation. The government might simply prohibit certain types of activities causing pollution, or might force firms to reduce their emissions. The purchase and use of new pollution-control devices can also increase the cost of production and shift the supply curve to the left, from $S_{PRIVATE}$ to S_{SOCIAL}.

What Is Better—Pollution Taxes or Regulation?

Most economists would agree that a pollution tax, or corrective tax, is more efficient than regulation. The pollution tax is good because it gets rid of the externality and moves society closer to the efficient level of output. The tax also gives firms an incentive to find and apply new technology to further reduce pollution levels in their plant. Under regulation, a firm has little incentive to further reduce emissions once it reaches the predetermined level set by the regulated standard.

For example, a gas tax is a form of pollution tax; it helps reduce the externalities of pollution and congestion. The higher the tax, the fewer the vehicles on the road, the fewer kilometres driven, and the more fuel-efficient vehicles purchased, all of which leads to less congestion and pollution.

Pollution Permits

Although a system of pollution taxes would be effective in solving the externality problem, it would be ineffective in allowing the government to set limits on the amount of pollution generated. Under a system of pollution permits, companies are issued licences to pollute at a certain level by the government. These levels can then be regulated by the government in accordance with their overall pollution-level targets. Companies are allowed to buy, sell, and trade the permits on the market.

If a company's pollution exceeded the allowable limit set out by their assigned permit, they would have to buy additional permits from other companies (thereby incurring additional costs of production). However, a company that managed to pollute less than their permit allowed could profit by selling the unused portion of their permit to another company. From a rational standpoint, the incentive would be for companies to pollute as little as possible.

One problem with pollution permits is that they do not outright prohibit all producers from polluting—so the shift from $S_{PRIVATE}$ to S_{SOCIAL} (in Exhibit 1) is less certain. If a company chooses to pollute, they can buy the necessary licence to do so under a system of tradable pollution permits. Therefore, as opposed to achieving overall reductions in pollution, a system of permits could have the effect of concentrating pollution in certain industries or in certain areas of the world.

POSITIVE EXTERNALITIES

Unlike negative externalities, positive externalities benefit others. For some goods, the individual consumer receives all of the benefits. If you buy a hamburger, for example, you get all of its benefits. But take, for example, a company that landscapes its property with beautiful flowers and sculptures. The landscaping may create a positive externality for those who walk or drive by the company grounds. Or consider education. Certainly, when you "buy" an education, you receive many of its benefits: greater future income, more choice of future occupations, and the consumption value of knowing more about life as a result of classroom (and extracurricular) learning. These benefits, however, great as they may be, are not all of the benefits associated with your education. You may be less likely to be unemployed or commit crimes, or you may end up curing cancer or solving some other social problem. These nontrivial benefits are the positive external benefits of education.

The government frequently subsidizes education. Why? Presumably because the private market does not provide enough. It is argued that the education of a person benefits not only that person, but all of society, because a more informed citizenry can make more intelligent collective decisions that benefit everyone. Another example: Why do public-health departments sometimes offer "free" inoculations against certain communicable diseases, such as influenza? Partly because by protecting one group of citizens, everyone gets some protection; if the first citizen does not get the disease, it prevents that person from passing it on to others. Many governmental efforts in the field of health and education are justified on the basis of perceived positive externalities. Of course, because positive externalities are often difficult to measure, it is hard to empirically demonstrate whether many governmental educational and health programs achieve their intended purpose.

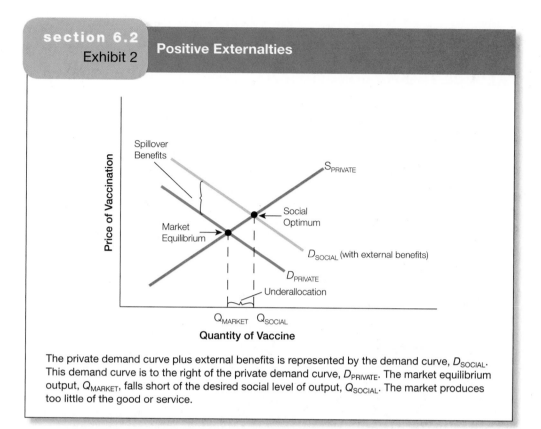

section 6.2
Exhibit 2

Positive Externalties

The private demand curve plus external benefits is represented by the demand curve, D_{SOCIAL}. This demand curve is to the right of the private demand curve, $D_{PRIVATE}$. The market equilibrium output, Q_{MARKET}, falls short of the desired social level of output, Q_{SOCIAL}. The market produces too little of the good or service.

Graphing Positive External Benefits

Let's take the case of a new vaccine against the common cold. The market for the vaccine is shown in Exhibit 2. The demand curve $D_{PRIVATE}$ represents the prices and quantities that buyers would be willing to pay in the private market to reduce their probability of catching the common cold. The supply curve shows the amounts that suppliers would offer for sale at different prices. However, at the equilibrium market output, Q_{MARKET}, we are far short of the socially optimum level of output for vaccinations, Q_{SOCIAL}. Why? Many people benefit from the vaccines, including those who do not have to pay for them; they are now less likely to be infected because others took the vaccine. If we could add the benefits derived by nonpaying consumers, the demand curve would shift to the right, from $D_{PRIVATE}$ to D_{SOCIAL}. The greater level of output, Q_{SOCIAL}, which would result if D_{SOCIAL} were the observed demand, reflects the socially optimal output level. However, because producers are unable to collect payments from all of those who are benefiting from the good or service, the market has a tendency to underproduce. In this case, the market is not producing enough vaccinations from society's standpoint. In this case, there is an *underallocation* of resources because from society's standpoint we are producing too little of this good or service (producing Q_{MARKET} rather than Q_{SOCIAL}).

WHAT CAN THE GOVERNMENT DO TO CORRECT FOR POSITIVE EXTERNALITIES?

How could society correct for this market failure? Two particular methods of achieving the higher preferred output are subsidies and regulation.

In The **NEWS**

PAYING TO REDUCE TRAFFIC CONGESTION

BY DAVID CRANE

Imagine. Every time you wanted to drive into the Toronto downtown core, say from St. Clair Ave. to Lake Ontario between Parliament and Bathurst Sts., you had to pay a traffic congestion fee of slightly more than $12 (Canadian).

London, England, plans this effective Feb. 17 [2003] for people driving in the 21-square-kilometre city centre between 7:00 in the morning and 6:30 in the evening. The charge will not apply on weekends or public holidays. Motorists will have to pay £5.

The whole idea behind this, as officials here explained, is to reduce serious traffic congestion by getting more people to use public transportation, avoid the city centre altogether or drive there in non-peak hours. Some 250,000 vehicles enter the city centre every day, and Mayor Ken Livingstone is hoping to reduce this as much as 15 per cent, though nobody really has any idea how this plan is going to work.

What they do know is that Murphy's Law is out there. If something can go wrong, it will. In fact, the computer system for registration has already had glitches. Also, there's the law of unintended consequences to worry about.

But people also know London has a serious problem of traffic congestion that every day leaves lines of motorists polluting the air, raising stress levels and wasting time. Traffic congestion is unhealthy, expensive and damaging to the environment.

So Livingstone, long known as Red Ken for his radical left-wing views, is employing a market-based solution: the price system to ration the use of city streets.

Not surprisingly, Livingstone has faced a barrage of opposition, from those claiming he is undermining freedom itself by taking away the right of individuals to drive wherever they want, to more specific concerns about costs to small businesses and a burden for low-paid workers who have to drive because of unusual working hours. There's even an anti-Livingstone Web site, a flood of letters to the editor in London's many newspapers and rallies against the plan.

But city planners, health officials and environmentalists argue something has to be done about traffic congestion and this plan should be given a chance. Livingstone has promised to scrap the program if it doesn't work.

© GREG HENRY/SHUTTERSTOCK

While there is a noisy campaign against the plan, much like the campaign against compulsory seat-belts in Ontario in the late 1970s, other people are more balanced.

"We must give congestion charging a chance," says Julia Lalla-Maharajh, director of transportation issues at London First, a business lobby group.

Drivers must register their vehicles and pay the daily fee, which can be done through the mail; through machines; at various convenience stores, gas stations, parking lots and the like; over the Internet; or by cellphone.

Each day, some 700 cameras, mounted on high poles, will capture on video all cars entering the city centre. Other camera systems will monitor vehicles belonging to people and businesses within the city centre.

This information will be converted to digital form and matched against registrations and payments by drivers. Anyone who doesn't pay will face a big fine and even the loss of his or her car or truck.

Setting up the system has cost the estimated equivalent of $490 million. Officials say they expect the system will yield about $330 million a year.

The law requires all of that money be invested in improving public transportation within London. Transport for London, the public transportation corporation, has already purchased 300 new buses to facilitate the system.

This is a huge experiment. If it works, we can expect more cities to experiment with this and other pricing systems. At some point in the future, most cities will find a way to make motorists pay for driving in congested city centres.

SOURCE: Adapted from David Crane, "Tomorrow You'll Pay to Drive in Busy City Core," *Toronto Star*, January 23, 2003, p. C02. Reprinted with permission from the *Toronto Star*.

CONSIDER THIS:
If a road is crowded, it creates a negative externality. That is, when one person enters a road, it causes all other people to drive a little more slowly. Road space is overused because we pay so little for it. At least at some particular times like at rush hours, if we charge a zero money price, there will be a shortage of road space, as seen in Exhibit 3. A toll raises the price and brings the market closer to equilibrium.

IN THE NEWS *(continued)*

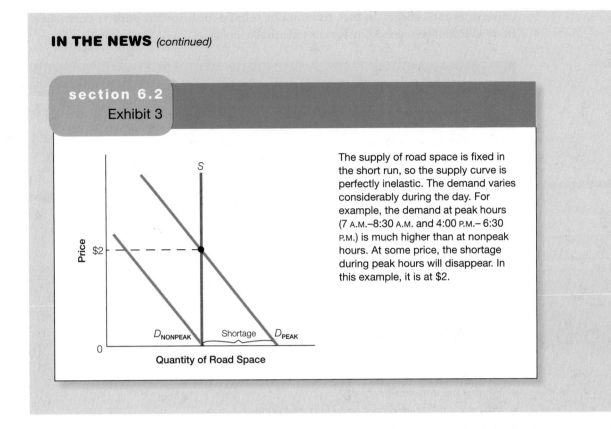

section 6.2
Exhibit 3

The supply of road space is fixed in the short run, so the supply curve is perfectly inelastic. The demand varies considerably during the day. For example, the demand at peak hours (7 A.M.–8:30 A.M. and 4:00 P.M.– 6:30 P.M.) is much higher than at nonpeak hours. At some price, the shortage during peak hours will disappear. In this example, it is at $2.

Subsidies

Government could give a subsidy—either give refunds to individuals who receive an inoculation or provide an incentive for businesses to give their employees "free" inoculations at the office. If the subsidy was exactly equal to external benefits of inoculation, the demand curve would shift from $D_{PRIVATE}$ to D_{SOCIAL}, resulting in an efficient level of output, Q_{SOCIAL}.

Regulation

The government could also pass a regulation requiring each person to get an inoculation. This would also shift the demand curve to the right toward the efficient level of output.

In summary, when there are positive externalities, the private market supplies too little of the good in question (such as education or inoculations for communicable diseases). When there are negative externalities, the market supplies too much. In either case, buyers and sellers are receiving the wrong signals. The free market works fine in providing most goods because most goods do not have externalities. When there are externalities, the market fails to allocate resources efficiently.

NONGOVERNMENTAL SOLUTIONS TO EXTERNALITIES

Sometimes the externality problems can be handled by individuals without the intervention of government, and people may decide to take steps on their own to minimize negative externalities. Moral and social codes may prevent some people from littering, driving gas-guzzling cars, or using gas-powered mowers. The same self-regulation also applies to positive externalities. Philanthropists, for example, frequently donate money to

COURTESY OF ROBERT SEXTON

People may take steps on their own to minimize negative externalities. For example, some people might use battery-powered mowers, or even old-fashioned push mowers, rather than gasoline mowers.

universities and colleges. In part, this must be because they view the positive externalities from education as a good buy for their charitable dollars.

section 6.3

Public Goods

- What is a public good?
- What is the free-rider problem?
- Why does the government provide public goods?
- What is a common resource?
- What is the tragedy of the commons?

PRIVATE GOODS VERSUS PUBLIC GOODS

public good
a good that is nonrivalrous in consumption and nonexcludable

Externalities are not the only cause of market failure. A **public good** is another source of market failure. As used by economists, this term refers not to how particular goods are purchased—by a government agency rather than some private economic agent—but to the properties that characterize them. In this section, we learn the difference between private goods, public goods, and common resources.

Private Goods

private good
a good with rivalrous consumption and excludability

A **private good** such as a cheeseburger has two critical properties in this context; it is rival and excludable. First, a cheeseburger is rival in consumption because if one person eats a particular cheeseburger, nobody else can eat the same cheeseburger. Second, a cheeseburger is excludable. It is easy to keep someone from eating your cheeseburger by not giving it to them. Most goods in the economy like food, clothing, cars, and houses are private goods that are rival and excludable.

Public Goods

The consumption of public goods, unlike private goods, is neither excludable nor rival. A public good is not rival because everyone can consume the good simultaneously; that is, one person's use of it does not diminish another's ability to use it. A public good is likewise *not excludable* because once the good is produced, it is prohibitively costly to exclude anyone from consuming the good. Consider national defence. Everyone enjoys the benefits of national defence (not rival) and it would be too costly to exclude anyone from those benefits (not excludable). That is, once the military has its defence in place, everyone is protected simultaneously (not rival) and it would be prohibitively costly to exclude anyone from consuming national defence (not excludable).

Another example of a public good is a flood control project. A flood control project would allow all the people who live in the flood-plain area to enjoy the protection of the new program simultaneously. It would also be very difficult to exclude someone who lived in the middle of the project who said she did not want to pay. Like national defence, the good is neither rival nor excludable in consumption. Other examples of public goods include outdoor fireworks displays and tornado sirens in small towns.

PUBLIC GOODS AND THE FREE-RIDER PROBLEM

The fact that a public good is not rival and not excludable makes the good difficult to produce privately. Some people would know they could derive the benefits from the good without paying for it because once it is produced, it is too difficult to exclude them. Some people would try to take a *free ride*—derive benefits for something they did not pay for.

free rider
deriving benefits from something not paid for

Let's return to our public good example of national defence. Suppose national defence is actually worth $100 to you. Assume that 10 million households in Canada are each willing to make a $100 contribution for national defence. This would add up to $1 billion. You might write a cheque for $100. Or you might reason as follows: "If I don't give $100 and everybody else does, I will be equally well protected plus derive the benefits of the $100 in my pocket." Taking the latter course represents a rational attempt to be a **free rider.** The rub is that if everyone attempts to take a free ride, the ride will not exist.

The free-rider problem prevents the private market from supplying the efficient amount of the public goods. That is, little incentive exists for individuals in the private sector to provide public goods because it is to difficult to make a profit. Therefore, the government provides important public goods such as national defence.

Government provides important public goods, such as national defence. Voters may disagree on whether we have too much or too little, but most agree that we must have national defence. If national defence were provided privately and people were asked to pay for the use of national defence, many would free ride, knowing they could derive the benefits of the good without paying for it.

THE GOVERNMENT AND BENEFIT—COST ANALYSIS

Everything the government provides has an opportunity cost. What is the efficient level of national defence? More national defence means less of something else that society may value more, like health care or education. To be efficient, public goods must also follow the rule of rational choice—pursue additional government activities only if the expected marginal benefits exceed the expected marginal costs. It all comes back to the saying "There are no free lunches."

In addition, there is also the problem of assessing the value of these goods. Consider the case of a new highway. Before it builds the highway, the appropriate government agency will undertake a benefit–cost analysis of the situation. In this case, it must evaluate consumers' willingness to pay for the highway against the costs that will be incurred for construction and maintenance. However, those individuals who want the highway have an incentive to exaggerate their desire for it. At the same time, individuals who will be displaced or otherwise harmed by the highway have an incentive to exaggerate the harm that will be done to them. Together, these elements make it difficult for the government to assess benefits and costs accurately. Ultimately, their evaluations are reduced to educated guesses about the net impact of the highway on all parties concerned.

COMMON RESOURCES AND THE TRAGEDY OF THE COMMONS

In many cases we do not have exclusive private-property rights to things such as the air around us or the fish in the sea. They are common resources—goods that are owned by everyone and therefore not owned by anyone. When a good is not owned by anyone, individuals feel little incentive to conserve or use the resource efficiently.

common resource
a rival good that is not excludable

    A **common resource** is a rival good that is not excludable; that is, nonpayers cannot be easily excluded from consuming the good, and when one unit is consumed by one person, it means that it cannot be consumed by another. Fish in the vast ocean waters are a good example of a common resource. They are rival because fish are limited—a fish taken by one person is not available for others. They are not excludable because it is prohibitively costly to keep anyone from catching them—almost anyone with a boat and a fishing rod could catch one. Common resources can lead to tragedy—see the following In the News story.

In The **NEWS**

A NOBEL LAUREATE'S WARNING ON THE NET'S SHARED RESOURCES

BY DANIEL MCFADDEN

Immigrants to New England in the 17th century formed villages in which they had privately owned homesteads and gardens, but they also set aside community-owned pastures, called commons, where all of the villagers' livestock could graze. Settlers had an incentive to avoid overuse of their private lands, so they would remain productive in the future. However, this self-interested stewardship of private lands did not extend to the commons. As a result, the commons were overgrazed and degenerated to the point that they were no longer able to support the villagers' cattle. This failure of private incentives to provide adequate maintenance of public resources is known to economists as "the tragedy of the commons."

    Contemporary society has a number of current examples of the tragedy of the commons: the depletion of fish stocks in international waters, congestion on urban highways, and the rise of resistant diseases due to careless use of antibiotics. However, the commons that is likely to have the greatest impact on our lives in the new century is the digital commons, the information available on the Internet through the portals that provide access. The problem with digital information is the mirror image of the original grazing commons: Information is costly to generate and organize, but its

value to individual consumers is too dispersed and small to establish an effective market. The information that is provided is inadequately catalogued and organized. Furthermore, the Internet tends to fill with low-value information: The products that have high commercial value are marketed through revenue-producing channels, and the Internet becomes inundated with products that cannot command these values. Self-published books and music are cases in point. . . .

    The solutions that resolve the problem of the digital commons are likely to be ingenious ways to collect money from consumers with little noticeable pain, and these should facilitate the operation of the Internet as a market for goods and services. Just don't expect it to be free.

SOURCE: Daniel McFadden, "The Tragedy of the Commons," *Forbes Magazine*, September 10, 2001. Reprinted with permission from the author.

CONSIDER THIS:

Just as the early settlers discovered, failure to manage a common resource adequately can ultimately lead to its demise. Today's digital commons—the Internet—is no different. The solution in this case is finding ways to collect money from consumers.

SECTION CHECK

Section Check

1. A public good is both nonrivalrous in consumption (one person's usage of it does not diminish another's ability to use it) and nonexclusive (no one can be excluded from using it).
2. A free rider is someone who attempts to enjoy the benefits of a good without paying for it.
3. The free-rider problem prevents the private market from supplying the efficient amount of public goods.
4. A common resource good is rival in consumption but not excludable.
5. The failure of private incentives to maintain public resources leads to the tragedy of the commons.

Asymmetric Information

- What is asymmetric information?
- What is adverse selection?
- What is moral hazard?

WHAT IS ASYMMETRIC INFORMATION?

When available information is initially distributed in favour of one party relative to another, **asymmetric information** is said to exist. Suppose you bought a new car for $25 000 and about a month later you decide that you would be much happier with your old car and the money. So you call your salesperson and ask what your car is worth—perfect condition and less than 1000 kilometres on the odometer. The salesperson tells you about $20 000. Why did your "new" car depreciate $5000 in just one month? The problem is that a potential buyer is going to be skeptical. Why is that new car being sold? Is it a lemon?

Sellers are at an information advantage over potential buyers when selling a car because they have more information about the car than does the potential buyer. However, potential buyers know that sellers are more likely to sell a lemon. As a result, potential buyers will offer a lower price than they would if they could be certain of the quality. This is known as the lemon problem. Without incurring significant quality-detection costs, such as having it inspected by a mechanic, the potential buyer is at an informational disadvantage relative to the seller. It is rational for the seller to claim that the car is in good shape and has no known defects, but the potential buyer cannot detect whether the car is a lemon or not without incurring costs. If the quality-detection costs are sufficiently high, a solution is to price all used cars as if they are average quality. That is, used cars of the same year, make, and model generally will be offered at the same price, regardless of their known conditions. The seller of a lemon will then receive a payment that is more than the car is worth, and the seller of a rel-atively high-quality car will receive less than the car is worth. However, if a seller of a high-quality car does *not* receive what the car would sell for if the potential buyer knew its quality, the seller will rationally withdraw the offer to sell the car. Given the logical response of sellers of higher-than-average-quality cars, the average quality of used cars on the market will fall, and consequently, many people will avoid buying in the used car market. In other words, the bad cars will drive the good cars out of the market. Thus, fewer used cars are bought and sold because fewer good cars are offered for sale. That is, information problems reduce economic

asymmetric information
occurs when the available information is initially distributed in favour of one party relative to another in an exchange

adverse selection

a situation where an informed party benefits in an exchange by taking advantage of knowing more than the other party

When players get traded from one team to another, a potential asymmetric information and adverse selection problem occurs—especially with pitchers. The team that is trading the pitcher knows more about his medical past, his pitching mechanics, his demeanour on and off the field, and so on, than the team that is trading for him. Even though trades are not finalized until the player passes a physical, many ailments or potential problems may go undetected.

efficiency and thus are another source of market failure. A situation where an informed party benefits in an exchange by taking advantage of knowing more than the other party is called **adverse selection.**

This distortion in the used car market resulting from adverse selection can be reduced by the buyer acquiring more information so that the buyer and seller have equal information. In the used car example, it might mean that an individual buyer would demand that an independent mechanic do a detailed inspection of the used car or that the dealership provide an extended warranty. A warranty provides a credible signal that this dealer is not selling lemons. In addition, new services such as carfax.com allow you to pay to find the history of a used car before you buy it. These services help in eliminating the adverse selection problem because buyers would have more information about the product they are buying.

The least-cost solution would have sellers reveal their superior information to potential buyers. The problem is that it is not individually rational for the seller to provide a truthful and complete disclosure, a point that is known by a potential buyer. Only if the seller is punished for not truthfully revealing exchange-relevant information will a potential buyer perceive the seller's disclosure as truthful.

Adverse selection also occurs in the insurance market. Imagine an auto insurance company that has a one-size-fits-all policy for their insurance premiums. Careful drivers would be charged the same premium as careless drivers. The company would assess the average risk of accidents for all drivers and then set the premium. Of course, this would be very appealing to careless drivers, who are more likely to get in an accident but not very appealing to careful drivers who have a much lower probability of getting in an accident. Under this pricing scheme, the bad drivers would drive the good drivers out of the market. Good drivers would be less likely to buy a policy, thinking that they are paying too much, since they are less likely to get in an accident than a careless driver. Many good drivers would exit the market, leaving a disproportionate share of bad drivers—exactly what the insurance companies do not want—people with a higher risk of getting in accidents. So what do they do?

Insurance companies set premiums according to the risk associated with particular groups of drivers, so good drivers do not exit the market. One strategy they use for dealing with adverse selection is called *screening,* where they use observable information about people to reveal private information. For example, a 17-year-old male driving a sports car will be charged a much higher premium than a 40-year-old female driving a minivan, even if he is a careful driver. Or someone with a good driving record or good grades gets a discount on their insurance. Insurance companies have data on different types of drivers and the probability of those drivers being in accidents, and they use this data to set insurance premiums. They may be wrong on an individual case (the teenager may be accident-free for years), but they are likely to be correct on average.

Reputation and Standardization

Asymmetric information is also present in other markets like rare stamps, coins, paintings, and sports memorabilia where the dealer (seller) knows more about the product than does the potential buyer. Potential buyers want to be assured that these items are authentic, not counterfeits. Unless the seller can successfully provide evidence of the quality of the product, bad products will tend to drive good products out of the market, resulting in a market failure.

One method that sellers can use to convince potential buyers that their products are high quality is *reputation.* For example, if a supermarket has a reputation of selling fresh produce, you are more likely to shop there. The same is true when you choose an electrician, plumber, or physician. In the used car market, the dealer might advertise how

© DENNIS KU/SHUTTERSTAK

long he has been in business. This provides a signal that he has many satisfied customers. Therefore, he is likely to sell more used cars at a higher price. In short, if there is a reputation of high quality, it will minimize the market failure problem.

However, there may be cases where it is difficult to develop a reputation. For example, take a restaurant or a motel on a desolate highway. These establishments may not receive repeat customers. Customers have little idea of the quality of food, the probability of bedbugs, and so on. In this case, *standardization* is important. A national restaurant or a motel chain provides standardization. Although you may not frequent McDonald's when you are at home, when confronted with the choice between a little-known restaurant and McDonald's, you may pick McDonald's because of the standardized products backed by a large corporation.

Asymmetric Information in the Labour Market

The existence of asymmetric information may give rise to signalling behaviour. For example, consider a person looking for a job. The job hunter—the prospective employee—knows much more about the quality of the labour he or she can provide than the firm does. A potential employer has little knowledge of the candidate's abilities: Is the candidate a hardworking, responsible, skilled worker, or a slacker? The firm cannot find out answers to these questions until much later. That is, asymmetric information in the labour market means one party has more information than the other. It would be in the best interest of the job candidate to supply as much valuable information as possible about personal characteristics not on the resume. Therefore, it is rational for prospective job candidates to send signals identifying their unique characteristics. The problem is that some of the candidates will possess superior characteristics, but which candidates? If knowledge and intelligence are important for the job, then years of education send a strong signal in the labour market. Although a college education may increase an individual's productivity, the diploma or degree may send a more important signal about the person's intelligence and perseverance. A college education sends a signal about a person's character that the applicant presumably possessed even *before* entering college. And according to the *signalling model,* this signal is even more important than the skills learned in college. So, education may provide an important signal that helps firms make better choices as they screen their pool of prospective applicants. More productive workers will likely obtain greater levels of education to signal their productivity to employers in the hope of achieving even higher-paying jobs. Of course, there is an alternative explanation for why workers with more education receive higher wages: Additional education provides skills and information that firms value. Recent empirical evidence suggests that higher incomes of college graduates reflect their greater productivity, not just a signal.

WHAT IS MORAL HAZARD?

Another information problem is associated with the insurance market and is called moral hazard. If an individual is fully insured for fire, theft, auto, life, and so on, what incentives will this individual have to take additional precautions from risk? For example, a person with auto insurance may drive less cautiously than would a person without auto insurance.

Insurance companies do, however, try to remedy the adverse selection problem by requiring regular checkups, discounts for nonsmokers, charging different deductibles and different rates for different age and occupational groups, and so on.

Additionally, those with health insurance may devote less effort and resources to staying healthy than those who are not covered. The problem, of course, is that if the insured are behaving more recklessly than they would if they were not insured, the result might be much higher insurance rates. The **moral hazard** arises from the fact that it is

moral hazard
taking additional risks because you are insured

ACTIVE LEARNING EXERCISE

ADVERSE SELECTION

Q: If individuals know a lot more about their health condition than an insurance company, do we have a case of adverse selection?

A: Yes. Even after a medical examination, individuals will know more about their health than the insurance company. That is, the buyers of health insurance have a better idea about their overall body conditions and nutritional habits than the seller, the insurance company. People with greater health problems tend to buy more health insurance than those who are healthy. This tendency drives up the price of health insurance to reflect the costs of sicker-than-average people, which drives people of average health out of the market. So the people who end up buying insurance will be the riskiest group.

costly for the insurer to monitor the behaviours of the insured party. Suppose an individual knew that his car was protected with a "bumper to bumper" warranty. He might have less incentive to take care of the car, despite the manufacturer's contract specifying that the warranty was only valid under "normal wear and tear." It would be too costly for the manufacturer to detect if a product failure was the consequence of a manufacturing defect or the abuse of the owner-user.

Adverse Selection versus Moral Hazard

Don't confuse adverse selection and moral hazard. Adverse selection is the phenomenon that occurs when one party in the exchange takes advantage of knowing more than the other party. Moral hazard involves the action taken *after* the exchange, such as, if you were a non-smoker who had just bought a life insurance policy and then started smoking heavily.

Section Check

1. Asymmetric information occurs when the available information is initially distributed in favour of one party relative to another in an exchange.
2. Adverse selection is a situation where an informed party benefits in an exchange by taking advantage of knowing more than the other party.
3. Moral hazard occurs when one party to a contract passes on the cost of its behavior to the other party.
4. Asymmetric information, adverse selection, and moral hazard are information problems that can distort market signals.

Summary

Section 6.1
- The difference between a consumer's willingness to pay and how much a consumer actually pays is called consumer surplus; it is the area below the demand curve and above the market price.
- Producer surplus is the difference between what the seller receives for the good—the market price and the seller's cost of production; it is the area below the market price and above the supply curve.

- In competitive markets, at the market equilibrium price and quantity, net welfare gains to society are as large as possible.
- Not producing at the efficient level of output leads to deadweight loss.

Section 6.2
- If a market activity has a negative physical impact on an outside party, that side effect is called a negative externality.

- The government can use taxes or other forms of regulation to correct the overallocation problem associated with negative externalities.
- If a market activity has a positive physical impact on an outside party, that side effect is called a positive externality.
- The government can provide subsidies or other forms of regulation to correct the underallocation problem associated with positive externalities.

Section 6.3

- A public good is neither rival in consumption (one person's usage of it does not diminish another's ability to use it) nor excludable (no one can be excluded from using it).
- A free rider is someone who attempts to enjoy the benefits of a good without paying for it.
- The government provides public goods because the free-rider problem results in underproduction of these goods in the marketplace.

- A common resource good is a rival good (one person's usage of it does diminish another's ability to use it) that is not excludable.
- The tragedy of the commons refers to the failure of private incentives to provide adequate maintenance of public resources.

Section 6.4

- A situation of asymmetric information occurs when available information is initially distributed in favour of one party relative to another in an exchange.
- Adverse selection is a situation where an informed party benefits in an exchange by taking advantage of knowing more than the other party.
- Moral hazard occurs when one party to a contract passes on the cost of its behaviour to the other party.

Key Terms and Concepts

For a complete glossary of chapter key terms, visit the textbook's Web site at http://www.sextonmicro2e.nelson.com.

consumer surplus 141
producer surplus 143
total welfare gains 144
deadweight loss 145
externalities 145

negative externality 145
positive externality 146
public good 152
private good 152
free rider 153

common resource 154
asymmetric information 155
adverse selection 156
moral hazard 157

Review Questions

1. If a freeze ruined this year's lettuce crop, show what would happen to consumer surplus.

2. If demand for apples increased as a result of a news story that highlighted the health benefits of two apples a day, what would happen to producer surplus?

3. How is total surplus (the sum of consumer and producer surplus) related to the efficient level of output? Using a supply and demand curve, demonstrate that producing less than the equilibrium output will lead to an inefficient allocation of resources—a deadweight loss.

4. Indicate which of the following activities create a positive externality, a negative externality, or no externality at all:

   a. During a live-theatre performance, an audience member's cellphone loudly rings.

   b. You are given a flu shot.

   c. You purchase and drink a soft drink during a break from class.

   d. A local youth group cleans up trash along a 2-kilometre stretch of highway.

   e. A firm dumps chemical waste into a local stream.

   f. The person down the hall in your residence plays a Britney Spears CD loudly while you are trying to sleep.

5. Is a lighthouse a public good if it benefits many shipowners? What if it primarily benefits ships going to a port nearby?

6. What kind of problems does the government face when trying to perform a benefit–cost analysis of whether and/or how much of a public project to produce?

7. How does a TV broadcast have characteristics of a public good? What about cable services like The Movie Network?

Fill in the Blanks

Section 6.1

1. The monetary difference between the price a consumer is willing and able to pay for an additional unit of a good and the price the consumer actually pays is called _____ .

2. Consumer surplus for the whole market is shown graphically as the area under the market _____ (willingness to pay for the units consumed) and above the _____ (what must be paid for those units).

3. A lower market price due to an increase in supply will _____ consumer surplus.

4. _____ is the difference between what a producer is paid for a good and the cost of producing that unit of the good.

5. Part of the added producer surplus when the price rises, as a result of an increase in demand, is due to a higher price for the quantity _____ being produced, and part is due to the expansion of _____ made profitable by the higher price.

6. The demand curve represents a collection of _____s__ prices that consumers are willing and able to pay for additional quantities of a good or service, whereas the supply curve represents a collection of _____ prices that suppliers require to be willing to supply additional quantities of that good or service.

7. The total welfare gain to the economy from trade in a good is the sum of the _____ and _____ created.

Section 6.2

8. Sometimes the market system fails to produce efficient outcomes because of what economists call _____ .

9. Whenever there are physical impacts of an activity on individuals not directly involved in the activity, if the impact on the outside party is negative, it is called a _____ ; if the impact is positive, it is called a _____ .

10. If a firm can avoid paying the external costs it imposes on others, it _____ its own costs of production but not the _____ cost to society.

11. If the government taxed a manufacturer by the amount of those external costs it imposes on others, it would force the manufacturer to _____ the costs.

12. The benefits of a product or service that spill over to an outside party that is not involved in producing or consuming the good are called _____ .

13. If suppliers are unaware of or are not responsible for the external costs created by their production, there is an _____ of scarce resources to the production of the good.

14. Because producers are unable to collect payments from all of those that are benefiting from the good or service, the market has a tendency to _____ goods with external benefits.

Section 6.3

15. Unlike the consumption of private goods, the consumption of public goods is both _____ and _____ .

16. If once a good is produced it is prohibitively costly to exclude anyone from consuming the good, consumption of that good is called _____ .

17. If everyone can consume a good simultaneously, it is _____ .

18. When individuals derive the benefits of a good without paying for it, it is called a _____ .

19. Public goods can lead to the _____ problem because people have little incentive to pay for the benefits they will receive, as they cannot be prevented from receiving the benefits.

20. The government may be able to overcome the free-rider problem by _____ the public good and imposing taxes to pay for it.

Section 6.4

21. When the available information is initially distributed in favour of one party relative to another, _____ is said to exist.

22. When one party enters into an exchange with another party that has more information, we call it _____ selection.

23. _____ arises from the cost involved for the insurer to monitor the behaviours of the insured party.

24. Goods that are owned by everyone and therefore not owned by anyone are called _____ resources.

25. The failure of private incentives to provide adequate maintenance of the public resources is known to economists as the _____ .

True or False

Section 6.1

1. A lower price will increase your consumer surplus for each of the units you were already consuming and will also increase consumer surplus from increased purchases at the lower price.

2. Because some units can be produced at a cost that is lower than the market price, the seller receives a surplus, or net benefit, from producing those units.

3. Producer surplus is shown graphically as the area under the demand curve and above the supply curve.

4. If the market price of a good falls as a result of a decrease in demand, additional producer surplus is generated.

5. At the market equilibrium both consumers and producers benefit from trading every unit up to the market equilibrium output.

6. Once the equilibrium output is reached at the equilibrium price, all of the mutually beneficial trade opportunities between the suppliers and the demanders will have taken place, and the sum of consumer and producer surplus is maximized.

Section 6.2

7. An externality is said to occur whenever there are physical impacts (benefits or costs) of an activity on individuals not directly involved in the activity.

8. Negative externalities are real costs, but because no one owns the air, unlike the other resources a firm uses in production, a firm does not have to pay for its use.

9. If government could impose a pollution tax equal to the exact size of the external costs imposed by a firm, then the firm would produce at the socially desired level of output.

10. Alternatives to pollution taxes include the government prohibiting certain types of activities causing pollution and forcing firms to clean up their emissions.

11. In the case of external benefits, a tax equal to external benefits would result in an efficient level of output.

Section 6.3

12. In the case of goods where all those affected benefit simultaneously and it is prohibitively costly to exclude anyone from consuming them, market failures tend to arise.

13. In the case of public goods, when people act as free riders, some goods having benefits greater than costs will not be produced.

14. In the case of public goods, the government accurately assesses the benefits and costs of those affected, and the resulting output is at its most efficient level.

15. In those areas where markets have failed to generate efficient results, the government will always do a better job.

Section 6.4

16. Asymmetric information exists when the available information is initially distributed in favour of one party to a transaction relative to another.

17. In adverse selection situations, it is rational for the seller with more information about a product to provide a truthful and complete disclosure and make that fact known to a potential buyer.

18. Warranty can be one method of controlling adverse selection problems.

19. In the market for insurance, the adverse selection problem leads those most likely to collect on insurance to buy it.

20. In the market for insurance, moral hazard can lead those who buy insurance to take fewer precautions and take on more risk.

Multiple Choice

Section 6.1

Use the following demand schedule to answer questions 1 and 2.

Fred's demand schedule for DVDs is as follows: At $30 each, he would buy 1; at $25, he would buy 2; at $15, he would buy 3; and at $10, he would buy 4.

1. If the price of DVDs equals $20, the consumer surplus Fred receives from purchasing DVDs would be
   a. $10.
   b. $15.
   c. $20.
   d. $55.
   e. $90.

2. If the price of DVDs equals $25, the consumer surplus Fred receives from purchasing DVDs would be
   a. $0.
   b. $5.
   c. $25.
   d. $55.
   e. $70.

3. Which of the following is not true about consumer surplus?
   a. Consumer surplus is the difference between what consumers are willing to pay and what they actually pay.
   b. Consumer surplus is shown graphically as the area under the demand curve but above the market price.
   c. An increase in the market price due to a decrease in supply will increase consumer surplus.
   d. A decrease in market price due to an increase in supply will increase consumer surplus.

4. Which of the following is not true about producer surplus?
   a. Producer surplus is the difference between what sellers are paid and their cost of producing those units.
   b. Producer surplus is shown graphically as the area under the market price but above the supply curve.
   c. An increase in the market price due to an increase in demand will increase producer surplus.
   d. All of the above are true about producer surplus.

Section 6.2

5. The presence of negative externalities leads to a misallocation of societal resources because
   a. whenever external costs are imposed on outside parties, the good should not be produced at all.
   b. less of the good than is ideal for society is produced.
   c. there are some costs associated with production that the producer fails to take into consideration.
   d. the government always intervenes in markets when negative externalities are present, and the government is inherently inefficient.

6. A tax equal to the external cost on firms that emit pollutants would
  a. provide firms with the incentive to increase the level of activity creating the pollution.
  b. provide firms with the incentive to decrease the level of activity creating the pollution.
  c. require firms to search for less environmentally damaging production methods.
  d. not reduce pollution levels at all.

7. In the case of a good whose production generates negative externalities,
  a. those not directly involved in the market transactions are harmed.
  b. internalizing the externality would tend to result in a lower price of the good.
  c. too little of the good tends to be produced.
  d. a subsidy would be the appropriate government corrective action.
  e. all of the above are true.

8. If firms were required to pay the full social costs of the production of goods, including both private and external costs, other things being equal, there would probably be
  a. an increase in production.
  b. a decrease in production.
  c. a greater misallocation of resources.
  d. a decrease in the market price of the product.

9. Which of the following will most likely generate positive externalities?
  a. a hot-dog vendor
  b. public education
  c. an automobile
  d. a city bus
  e. a polluting factory

10. Socially inefficient outcomes may occur in markets where there are
  a. free riders.
  b. negative externalities present.
  c. positive externalities present.
  d. any of the above.

11. In the case of externalities, appropriate government corrective policy would be
  a. taxes in the case of external benefits and subsidies in the case of external costs.
  b. subsidies in the case of external benefits and taxes in the case of external costs.
  c. taxes in both the case of external benefits and the case of external costs.
  d. subsidies in both the case of external benefits and the case of external costs.
  e. none of the above; the appropriate thing to do would be to do nothing.

Section 6.3

12. Which of the following is true?
  a. Consumption of a public good by one individual reduces the availability of the good for others.
  b. It is extremely difficult to limit the benefits of a public good to the people who pay for it.
  c. Public goods are free whenever the government produces them.
  d. From an efficiency standpoint, a market economy will generally supply too much of a public good.
  e. None of the above is correct.

13. Which of the following is not true?
    a. The government may be able to overcome the free-rider problem with public goods by providing the public goods and imposing taxes to pay for them.
    b. The nature of public goods is such that the government cannot accurately assess the benefits and costs of those affected.
    c. National defence and flood control are illustrations of public goods.
    d. Just as in the case of external costs, public goods tend to be underprovided by the private sector.

14. Public goods are
    a. nonexcludable and nonrivalrous.
    b. nonexcludable and rivalrous.
    c. excludable and rivalrous.
    d. excludable and nonrivalrous.

15. Public goods
    a. can be consumed only by those who have paid for them.
    b. can be consumed by people whether they have paid for their production or not.
    c. can be consumed only by free riders.
    d. tend to be underprovided by the private market.
    e. are characterized by both b and d.

Section 6.4

16. Adverse selection refers to
    a. the phenomenon that occurs when one party in an exchange takes advantage of knowing more than another party.
    b. the tendency for individuals to alter their behaviour once they are insured against loss.
    c. the tendency for individuals to engage in insurance fraud.
    d. both b and c.

17. Which of the following is not true of adverse selection?
    a. It can result when both parties to a transaction have little information about the quality of the goods involved.
    b. It can cause the quality of goods traded to fall, if quality-detection costs are high.
    c. If can be a difficult problem to overcome because it is not rational for the transactor with the superior information to provide a truthful and complete disclosure.
    d. All of the above are true.

18. If a company offers a medical and dental-care plan that offers benefits to all of the members of each employee's family for a given monthly premium, an employee who is a mother of five children and who has bad teeth who elects that plan would be an illustration of
    a. the moral hazard problem.
    b. the free-rider problem.
    c. the adverse selection problem.
    d. the "lemon" problem.

19. If, after you buy a car with air bags, you start to drive recklessly, it would be an illustration of
   a. the moral hazard problem.
   b. the free-rider problem.
   c. the adverse selection problem.
   d. the "lemon" problem.

20. In the market for insurance, the moral hazard problem leads
   a. those most likely to collect on insurance to buy it.
   b. those who buy insurance to take fewer precautions to avoid the insured risk.
   c. those with more prior insurance claims to be charged a higher premium.
   d. to none of the above.

Problems

1. [Section 6.1]
Suppose Phil's supply curve for widgets is as follows: At $20, he will supply 1; at $30, he will supply 2; at $40, he will supply 3; at $50, he will supply 4; and at $60, he will supply 5.
   a. If the price of widgets is $40, what is his producer surplus?
   b. If the price of widgets rises from $40 to $50, how much will his producer surplus change?

2. [Section 6.2]

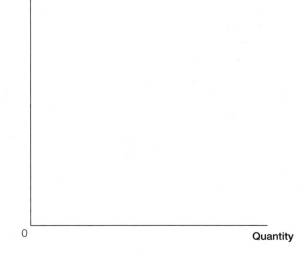

Draw a standard supply and demand diagram for widgets, and indicate the equilibrium price and output.

3. [Section 6.2]
Assuming that the production of widgets generates external costs, illustrate the effect of the producer being forced to pay a tax equal to the external costs generated, and indicate the equilibrium output.

4. [Section 6.2]
If instead of generating external costs widgets generate external benefits, illustrate the effect of a subsidy equal to the external benefits generated, and indicate the equilibrium output.

chapter

7

Production and Costs

section 7.1

Profits: Total Revenues Minus Total Costs

- What are explicit and implicit costs?
- What are accounting profits?
- What are economic profits?
- Do firms really maximize profits?

THE CONCEPT OF COSTS

As we discussed in Chapter 1, costs exist because resources are scarce and have competing uses—to produce more of one good means foregoing the production of another good. The cost of producing a good is measured by the worth of the most valuable alternative that was given up to obtain the resource. As you may recall, this is called the *opportunity cost*.

In Chapter 2, the production possibilities curve highlighted this trade-off. Recall that the opportunity cost of producing additional shelter was the units of food that had to be sacrificed. Other examples of opportunity costs abound: Paper used in this text could have been used in other books or for hundreds of other uses, and the steel used in the construction of a new building could have been used in the production of an automobile or a washing machine.

But what exactly makes up a firm's costs? Let's look at the two distinct components that make up the firm's costs: explicit costs and implicit costs.

ACTIVE LEARNING EXERCISE

EXPLICIT AND IMPLICIT COSTS

Q: True or false? If a company owns its own building in a growing urban area, it can protect itself from rising rents.

A: False; the company cannot avoid implicit costs. If the company owned the building and rents increased, so would the opportunity cost of owning the building. That is, by occupying the building, the company is giving up the new higher rents it could receive from renters if it leased out the space. That is, even though the firm pays zero rent by owning the building, the rent that it could receive by leasing it to another company is a very real economic cost (but not an accounting cost) to the firm.

EXPLICIT COSTS

explicit costs
the opportunity costs of production that require a monetary payment

Explicit costs are the input costs that require a monetary payment—the out-of-pocket expenses that pay for labour services, raw materials, fuel, transportation, utilities, advertising, and so on. It is important to note that the explicit costs are opportunity costs to the firm. For example, money spent on electricity cannot be used for advertising. Remember, in a world of scarcity, we are always giving up something to get something else. Trade-offs are pervasive. The costs that we have discussed so far are relatively easy to measure and an economist and an accountant would most likely arrive at the same amounts. But that will generally not be the case.

IMPLICIT COSTS

implicit costs
the opportunity costs of production that do not require a monetary payment

Some of the firm's (opportunity) costs of production are implicit. **Implicit costs** do not require an outlay of money. This is where the economist's and the accountant's ideas of costs diverge because accountants do not include implicit costs. For example, whenever an investment is made, opportunities to invest elsewhere are forgone. This lost opportunity is an implicit cost that economists include in the total cost of the firm, even though no money is expended. A typical farmer or small business owner may perform work without receiving formal wages, but the value of the alternative earnings forgone represents an implicit opportunity cost to the individual. Because other firms could have used the resources, what the resources could have earned elsewhere is an implicit cost to the firm. It is important to emphasize that whenever we are talking about costs—explicit or implicit—we are talking about opportunity costs.

PROFITS

profits
the difference between total revenue and total cost

Economists generally assume that the ultimate goal of the firm is to maximize **profits.** In other words, firms try to maximize the difference between what they give up for their inputs—their total costs (explicit and implicit)—and the amount they receive for their goods and services—their total revenue. Like revenues and costs, profits refer to flows over time. When we say that a firm earned $5 million in profits, we must clarify the time period in which the profits were earned—a week, month, year, and so on.

ARE ACCOUNTING PROFITS THE SAME AS ECONOMIC PROFITS?

A firm can make a profit in the sense that the total revenues that it receives exceed the explicit costs that it incurs in the process of doing business. We call these **accounting profits**—profits as accountants record them are based on total revenues and explicit costs. In other words, accounting profits do not include implicit costs.

Economists prefer an alternative way of measuring profits; they are interested in total revenue minus all costs (both explicit and implicit). In calculating a firm's total costs, economists include the implicit costs—as well as the explicit costs.

Summing up, measured in terms of accounting profits, like those reported in real-world financial statements, a firm has a profit if its total revenues exceed explicit costs. In terms of **economic profits,** a firm has a profit if its total revenues exceed its total opportunity cost—both its explicit costs and implicit costs. Exhibit 1 illustrates the difference between accounting profits and economic profits.

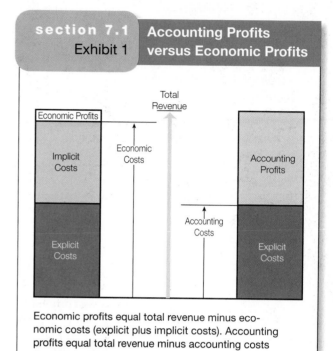

section 7.1
Exhibit 1

Accounting Profits versus Economic Profits

Economic profits equal total revenue minus economic costs (explicit plus implicit costs). Accounting profits equal total revenue minus accounting costs (explicit costs).

A ZERO ECONOMIC PROFIT IS A NORMAL PROFIT

As we just discussed, an economic profit is less than an accounting profit because economic profits include implicit as well as explicit costs. In fact, an economist considers a zero economic profit a normal profit. Recall that zero economic profit means that the firm is covering both explicit and implicit costs—the total opportunity costs of its resources. In other words, the firm's total revenue is sufficient to compensate the time and money that owners have put in the business. This is clearly different from making zero accounting profits because then revenues would not cover the implicit costs. (We will return to this important point in the next chapter.)

accounting profits
total revenues minus total explicit costs

economic profits
total revenues minus explicit and implicit costs

SUNK COSTS

We have just seen how opportunity costs are often hidden, as in the case of implicit costs. However, there is another type of cost that should be discussed—sunk costs. **Sunk costs** are costs that have already been incurred and cannot be recovered. Suppose, for example, that you bought a CD that looked interesting, but when you got home and played it you wished you hadn't. Now your friend comes over and says he likes that CD and will buy it from you for $5. You say "no way" because you paid $15 for the CD. Are you acting rationally? Economists believe that what you paid for the CD is now irrelevant. Now, you must decide whether you would rather have the $5 or the CD. If you decide to keep the CD, the cost is the $5 you could have received from your friend—the rest is sunk.

Or suppose a donut shop has a one-year lease and after three months the owner decides that the shop would do much better by relocating to a new mall that has just opened. Should the donut shop just stay put until the end of the year because it is legally obligated to pay the 12-month lease? No, the nonrefundable lease payment is sunk and

sunk costs
costs that have been incurred and cannot be recovered

ACTIVE LEARNING EXERCISE

ACCOUNTING PROFITS AND ECONOMIC PROFITS

Q: Emily, an energetic 10-year-old, set up a lemonade stand in front of her house. One Saturday, she sold 50 cups of lemonade at 50 cents apiece to her friends, who were hot and thirsty from playing. These sales generated $25 in total revenues for Emily. Emily was pleased because she knew that her total costs—lemonade mix, cups, and so on—were only $5. As she was closing up shop for the day, her neighbour, an accountant, stopped by to say hello. Emily told him about her successful day. He said, "What a great job! You made a $20 profit!" Excited, Emily rushed into the house to tell her mother, an economist, the great news. Will Emily's mother agree with the accountant's calculation of Emily's profits? If not, why?

A: No, Emily's mother will not agree with the accountant because he forgot to include the implicit costs when calculating Emily's profits. That is, he neglected to take into account what Emily could have been doing with her time if she had not been selling lemonade. For example, she could have been playing with her friends, cleaning her room, or perhaps helping her friends make money at their garage sale. These lost opportunities are implicit costs that should be included in the calculation of Emily's economic profits.

irrelevant to the decision to relocate. The decision to relocate should be based on the prospects of future profits regardless of the length of the current lease. In short, sunk costs are irrelevant for any future action because they have already been incurred and cannot be recovered.

Section Check
SECTION CHECK

1. Total cost consists of explicit costs and implicit costs.
2. Explicit costs are the opportunity costs of production that require a monetary payment.
3. Some opportunity costs of the firm are implicit—they do not represent an outlay of money or a contractual obligation.
4. Profits are the difference between the total revenues of a firm and its total costs.
5. Accounting profits are revenues minus explicit costs.
6. Economic profits are revenues minus total opportunity costs—both explicit and implicit costs.
7. Sunk costs are irretrievable and irrelevant to the firm.

section
7.2   Production in the Short Run

- What is the difference between the short run and the long run?
- What is a production function?
- What is diminishing marginal product?

THE SHORT RUN VERSUS THE LONG RUN

Of fundamental importance for cost and production behaviour is the extent to which a firm is able to adjust inputs as it varies output. Since it takes more time to vary some inputs than others, we must distinguish between the short run and the long run. The **short run** is defined as a period too brief for some inputs to be varied. For example, the current size of a plant cannot be altered and new equipment cannot be obtained or built overnight. If demand increases for the firm's product and the firm chooses to produce more output in the short run, it must do so with its existing equipment and factory. Inputs like buildings and equipment that do not change with output are called *fixed* inputs.

short run
a period too brief for some production inputs to be varied

The **long run** is a period of time in which the firm can adjust all inputs. That is, in the long run all inputs to the firm are *variable,* and will change as output changes. The long run can vary considerably from industry to industry. For a chain of coffeehouses that wants to add a few more stores, the long run may only be a few months. In other industries, like the automobile or steel industry, the long run might be a couple of years, as a new plant or factory in this type of industry will take much longer to build.

long run
a period over which all production inputs are variable

PRODUCTION IN THE SHORT RUN

Suppose that Moe's Bagel Shop has just one input that is variable, labour, whereas the size of the bagel shop is fixed in the short run. What will happen to **total product (*TP*),** the total amount of output (bagels) generated by Moe's shop, as the level of the variable input, labour, is increased? Common sense suggests that total product will start at a low level and increase—perhaps rapidly at first, and then more slowly—as the amount of the variable

total product (*TP*)
the total output of a good produced by the firm

input increases. It will continue to increase until the quantity of the variable input (labour) becomes so large in relation to the quantity of other inputs—like the size of the bagel shop—that further increases in output become more and more difficult or even impossible. In the second column of Exhibit 1, we see that as we increase the number of workers in Moe's Bagel Shop, Moe is able to produce more bagels. The addition of the first worker results in a total output of 10 bagels per hour. When Moe adds a second worker, bagel output climbs to 24, an increase of 14 bagels per hour. Total product continues to increase even with the sixth worker hired, but you can see that it has slowed considerably, with the sixth worker increasing total product by only one bagel per hour. Beyond this point, additional workers may even result in a decline in total bagel output as workers bump into each other in the small bagel shop. This outcome is evident both in the table in Exhibit 1, as well as in the total product curve shown in Exhibit 2(a).

section 7.2
Exhibit 1

Moe's Production Function with One Variable Input, Labour

Variable Input Labour (Workers)	Total Output (Bagels per hour) Q	Marginal Product of Labour (Bagels per hour) ΔQ/ΔL
0	0	
		10
1	10	
		14
2	24	
		12
3	36	
		10
4	46	
		4
5	50	
		1
6	51	

DIMINISHING MARGINAL PRODUCT

The **marginal product (*MP*)** of any single input is defined as the change in total product resulting from a small change in the amount of input used. This concept is shown in the final column in Exhibit 1, and is illustrated by the *MP* curve in Exhibit 2(b). As you can see in Exhibit 2(b), the *MP* curve first rises and then falls.

marginal product (*MP*)
the change in total output of a good that results from a unit change in input

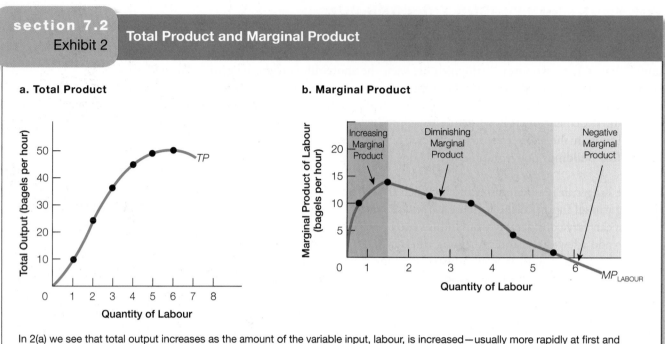

a. Total Product

b. Marginal Product

In 2(a) we see that total output increases as the amount of the variable input, labour, is increased—usually more rapidly at first and then more slowly. In 2(b), we see that the marginal product first rises (increasing marginal product) as workers are added to the fixed input (for example, a machine), which is thus used more efficiently. Then the marginal product falls; the crowding of the fixed input with more and more workers causes marginal product to fall. Lastly, negative marginal product occurs where additional inputs cause output to fall.

The Rise in Marginal Product

The initial rise in the marginal product is the result of more effective use of fixed inputs (the bagel shop) as the number of workers increases (due to specialization and division of labour). For example, certain types of capital equipment may require a minimum number of workers for efficient operation, or perhaps any operation at all. With a small number of workers (the variable factors), some machines cannot operate at all, or only at a very low level of efficiency. As additional workers are added, machines are brought into efficient operation, and thus the marginal product of the workers rises. Similarly, if one person tried to operate a large department store alone—doing work of all types necessary in the store—her energies would be spread so thinly in so many directions that total output (sales) might be less than if she were operating a smaller store (working with less capital). As successive workers are added, up to a certain number, each worker adds more to total product than the previous one and the marginal product rises. This is seen in the shaded area of Exhibit 2(b), labelled increasing marginal product.

The Fall in Marginal Product

diminishing marginal product

as a variable input increases, with other inputs fixed, a point will be reached where the additions to output will eventually decline

But why does marginal product then fall? The answer is **diminishing marginal product,** which stems from the crowding of the fixed input. Specifically, as the amount of a variable input is increased, the amount of other (fixed) inputs being held constant, a point ultimately will be reached beyond which marginal product will decline. Beyond this point, output increases, but at a decreasing rate. It is the crowding of the fixed input with more and more workers that causes the decline in the marginal product. Too many workers in a store make it more difficult for customers to shop; too many workers in a factory get in each other's way. Adding more and more of a variable input to a fixed input will eventually lead to diminishing marginal product.

The point of this discussion is that production functions conform to the same general pattern as that shown by Moe's Bagel Shop in the third column of Exhibit 1 and illustrated in Exhibit 2(b). In the third column of Exhibit 1, we see that as we increase the number of workers in Moe's Bagel Shop, Moe is able to produce more bagels. The first worker is able to produce 10 bagels per hour. When Moe adds a second worker, total bagel output climbs to 24, an increase of 14 bagels per hour. However, when Moe hires a third worker, bagel output still increases, but a third worker's marginal production (12 bagels per hour) is less than that of the second worker. In fact, the marginal product continues to drop as more and more workers are added to the bagel shop. This is diminishing marginal product at work. Note that it is not because the third worker is not as "good" as the second worker that marginal product fell. Even with identical workers, the increased "crowding" of the fixed input causes marginal output to eventually fall.

A firm never *knowingly* allows itself to reach the point where the marginal product becomes negative, the situation in which the use of additional variable input units actually reduces total product. In such a situation, there are so many units of the variable input—inputs with positive opportunity costs—that efficient use of the fixed input units is impaired. In such a situation, *reducing* the number of workers would actually *increase* total product.

© Christine Gonzalves/Shutterstock

How many workers could be added to this jackhammer and still be productive (not to mention safe)? If more workers were added, how much output would be derived from each additional worker? There may be slightly more total output from the second worker because the second worker will be using the jackhammer while the first worker is taking a break from "the shakes." However, the fifth or sixth worker would clearly not create any additional output, as workers would just be standing around for their turn. That is, the marginal product (additional output) would eventually fall because of diminishing marginal product.

Section Check

1. The short run is defined as a period too brief for some inputs to be varied. Inputs like buildings and equipment that do not change with output are called fixed inputs.
2. The long run is a period of time long enough to allow the firm to adjust all inputs. That is, in the long run all inputs are variable and will change as output changes.
3. The production function describes the maximum amount of a product that a firm can produce with any combination of inputs, using existing technology.
4. A diminishing marginal product occurs when the amount of a variable input keeps increasing while the amount of fixed inputs holds constant; eventually, the marginal product declines.

section
7.3

Costs in the Short Run

- What are fixed costs?
- What are variable costs?
- What is average fixed, average variable, and average total cost?
- What is marginal cost?

In the last section we learned about the relationship between a firm's inputs and its level of output. But that is only one part of the discussion; we must also consider how much it will cost the firm to use each of these inputs in production. In this section, we will examine the short-run costs of the firm—what they are and how they vary with the output levels that are produced. The short-run total costs of a business fall into two distinct categories: fixed costs and variable costs.

FIXED COSTS, VARIABLE COSTS, AND TOTAL COSTS

fixed costs
costs that do not vary with the level of output

Fixed costs are those that do not vary with the level of output. For example, the rent on buildings or equipment is usually fixed at least for some period of time; whether the firm produces lots of output or little output, the rent stays the same. Insurance premiums, property taxes, and interest payments on debt used to finance capital equipment are other examples of fixed costs—they have to be paid even if no output is produced. In the short run, fixed costs cannot be avoided. The only way a firm can avoid a fixed cost is by going out of business. The sum of the firm's fixed costs is called the **total fixed cost (*TFC*).**

total fixed cost (*TFC*)
the sum of the firm's fixed costs

variable costs
costs that vary with the level of output

Variable costs vary with the level of output. As more variable inputs like labour and raw materials are added, output increases. The variable cost, the expenditures for wages and raw materials, increases as output increases. The sum of the firm's variable costs is called **total variable cost (*TVC*).** The sum of the total fixed costs and total variable costs is called the firm's **total cost (*TC*).**

total variable cost (*TVC*)
the sum of the firm's variable costs

total cost (*TC*)
the sum of the firm's total fixed costs and total variable costs

AVERAGE TOTAL COST

Although we are often interested in the total amount of costs incurred by the firm, sometimes we find it convenient to discuss these costs on a per-unit-of-output, or an average, basis. For example, if Pizza Shack Company has $1600 in total fixed cost and $2400 in total variable, its total cost is $4000. If it produces 800 pizzas in the time period in question, its total cost per unit of output equals $5 ($4000 total cost divided by 800 units of output). We call this per-unit, cost the **average total cost (*ATC*).** Likewise, we might talk about the fixed cost per unit of output, or **average fixed cost (*AFC*).** In the case of Pizza Shack, the average fixed cost, or *AFC,* would equal $2 ($1600 is the fixed cost divided by 800 units of output). Similarly, we can speak of per-unit variable cost, or **average variable cost (*AVC*).** In this example, the average variable cost would equal $3 ($2400 is the variable cost divided by 800 units of output).

average total cost (*ATC*)
a per-unit cost of operation; total cost divided by output

average fixed cost (*AFC*)
a per-unit measure of fixed costs; fixed costs divided by output

average variable cost (*AVC*)
a per-unit measure of variable costs; variable costs divided by output

MARGINAL COST

To this point, six different short-run cost concepts have been introduced: total cost, total fixed cost, total variable cost, average total cost, average fixed cost, and average variable cost. All of these concepts are relevant to a discussion of firm behaviour and profitability. However, the most important single cost concept has yet to be mentioned: marginal (or additional) cost. You may recall this concept from Chapter 2, where we highlighted the importance of using marginal analysis—that is, analysis that focuses on *additional* or marginal choices. Specifically, **marginal cost (*MC*)** shows the change in total costs associated with a change in output by one unit ($\Delta TC/\Delta Q$). Put a bit differently, marginal cost is the cost of producing one more unit of output. As such, marginal costs are really just a very useful way to view variable costs—costs that vary as output varies. Marginal cost represents the added labour, raw materials, and miscellaneous expenses that are incurred in making an additional unit of output. Marginal cost is the additional, or incremental, cost associated with the "last" unit of output produced.

marginal cost (*MC*)
the change in total costs resulting from a one-unit change in output

ACTIVE LEARNING EXERCISE

MARGINAL COST VERSUS AVERAGE TOTAL COST

Q: Suppose an oil producer's average total cost of producing a barrel of oil has been $20 a barrel and the oil producer can sell that oil to a distributor for $23 a barrel. On average, this seems like a profitable business. Should the oil producer expand production given this profitability?

A: Not necessarily. It is marginal cost that is critical. The next barrel of oil might cost $30 to produce because the well may be drying up or the company might have to drill deeper to get additional oil, making it even more costly to retrieve. It is possible that the *marginal cost* of the additional barrels of oil may be greater than the market price and, thus, no longer profitable.

HOW ARE THESE COSTS RELATED?

Exhibit 1 summarizes the definitions of the seven different short-run cost concepts introduced in this chapter. To further clarify these concepts and to illustrate the relationships between them, we will now return to our discussion of the costs faced by Pizza Shack.

Exhibit 2 presents the costs incurred by Pizza Shack at various levels of output. Note that the total fixed cost is the same at all output levels and that at very low output levels (four or fewer units in the example), total fixed cost is the dominant portion of total costs. At high output levels (eight or more units in the example), total fixed cost becomes quite small relative to total variable cost. As the firm increases its output, it spreads its total fixed cost across more units; as a result, average fixed cost declines continuously.

It is often easier to understand the cost concepts by examining graphs that show the levels of the various costs at different output levels. The graph in Exhibit 3 shows the first three cost concepts: fixed, variable, and total costs for Pizza Shack. The total fixed cost (TFC) curve is always a horizontal line because, by definition, fixed costs are the same at all output levels—even at zero level of output. In Exhibit 3, notice that $TVC = 0$ when $Q = 0$; if there is no output being produced, there are no variable costs.

section 7.3
Exhibit 1 **A Summary of the Short-Run Cost Concepts**

Concept	Abbreviation	Definition
Total fixed cost	TFC	Costs that are the same at all output levels (e.g., insurance, rent).
Total variable cost	TVC	Costs that vary with the level of output (e.g., hourly labour, raw materials).
Total cost	TC	The sum of the firm's total fixed costs and total variable costs at a level of output ($TC = TFC + TVC$).
Marginal cost	MC	The added cost of producing one more unit of output; change in TC associated with one more unit of output ($\Delta TC/\Delta Q$).
Average total cost	ATC	TC per unit of output; TC divided by output (TC/Q).
Average fixed cost	AFC	TFC per unit of output; TFC divided by output (TFC/Q).
Average variable cost	AVC	TVC per unit of output; TVC divided by output (TVC/Q).

Hourly Output (Q)	Total Fixed Cost (TFC)	Total Variable Cost (TVC)	Total Cost (TC = TVC + TFC)	Marginal Cost (MC = ΔTC/ΔQ)	Average Fixed Cost (AFC = TFC/Q)	Average Variable Cost (AVC = TVC/Q)	Average Total Cost (ATC = TC/Q or AFC + ATC)
0	$40	$ 0	$ 40		—	—	—
1	40	10	50	$10	$40.00	$10.00	$50.00
2	40	18	58	8	20.00	9.00	29.00
3	40	25	65	7	13.33	8.33	21.66
4	40	35	75	10	10.00	8.75	18.75
5	40	47	87	12	8.00	9.40	17.40
6	40	60	100	13	6.67	10.00	16.67
7	40	75	115	15	5.71	10.71	16.42
8	40	95	135	20	5.00	11.88	16.88
9	40	120	160	25	4.44	13.33	17.77
10	40	150	190	30	4.00	15.00	19.00

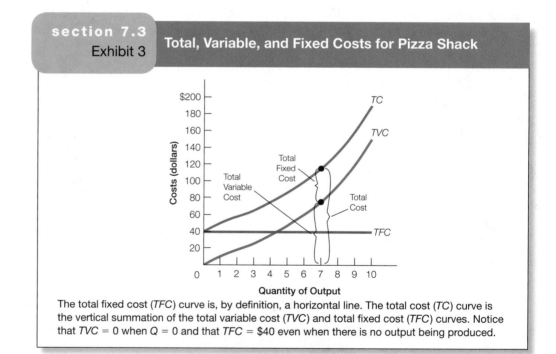

The total fixed cost (*TFC*) curve is, by definition, a horizontal line. The total cost (*TC*) curve is the vertical summation of the total variable cost (*TVC*) and total fixed cost (*TFC*) curves. Notice that *TVC* = 0 when *Q* = 0 and that *TFC* = $40 even when there is no output being produced.

The total cost (*TC*) curve is the summation of the total variable cost (*TVC*) and total fixed cost (*TFC*) curves. Because the total fixed cost curve is horizontal, the total cost curve lies above the total variable cost curve by a fixed (vertical) amount.

Exhibit 4 shows the average fixed cost curve, the average variable cost curve, the average total cost curve, and the associated marginal cost curve for Pizza Shack. In this exhibit, note how the average fixed cost (*AFC*) curve constantly declines, approaching but never reaching zero. Remember, the *AFC* is simply *TFC/Q*, so as output expands, *AFC* declines, because

section 7.3
Exhibit 4 **Average and Marginal Costs for Pizza Shack**

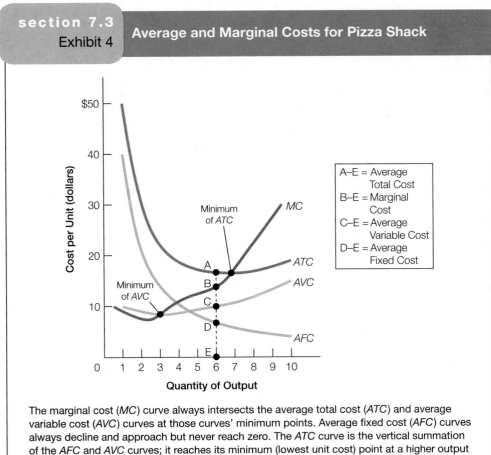

A–E = Average Total Cost
B–E = Marginal Cost
C–E = Average Variable Cost
D–E = Average Fixed Cost

The marginal cost (*MC*) curve always intersects the average total cost (*ATC*) and average variable cost (*AVC*) curves at those curves' minimum points. Average fixed cost (*AFC*) curves always decline and approach but never reach zero. The *ATC* curve is the vertical summation of the *AFC* and *AVC* curves; it reaches its minimum (lowest unit cost) point at a higher output than the minimum point of the *AVC* curve.

the total fixed cost is being spread over successively larger volumes of output. Also observe how the marginal cost (*MC*) curve crosses the average variable cost (*AVC*) and average total cost (*ATC*) curves at their lowest points. At higher output levels, high marginal costs pull up the average variable cost and average total cost curves, whereas at low output levels, low marginal costs pull the curves down. In the next section, we will explain why the marginal cost curve intersects the average variable cost curve and the average total cost curve at their minimum points.

Section Check

1. Fixed costs do not change with the level of output.
2. Variable costs are not fixed. Variable costs change as the level of output changes.
3. Average total cost (*ATC*) is total cost divided by output.
4. Average fixed cost (*AFC*) is fixed cost divided by output.
5. Average variable cost (*AVC*) is variable cost divided by output.
6. Marginal cost (*MC*) is the added cost of producing one more unit of output; it is the change in total cost associated with one more unit of output. It is this cost that is relevant to decisions to produce more or less.

section

7.4

The Shape of the Short-Run Cost Curves

- Why is the average total cost curve U-shaped?
- When marginal cost is greater than average cost, what happens to the average?

THE RELATIONSHIP BETWEEN MARGINAL AND AVERAGE AMOUNTS

The relationship between the marginal and the average is simply a matter of arithmetic; when a number (the marginal cost) being added into a series is smaller than the previous average of the series, the new average will be lower than the previous one. Likewise, when the marginal number is larger than the average, the average will rise. For example, if you have taken two economics exams and received a 90 percent on your first exam and 80 percent on your second exam, you have an 85 percent average. If after some serious studying, you get a 100 percent on the third exam (the marginal exam), what happens to your average? It rises to 90 percent. Because the marginal is greater than the average, it "pulls" the average up. However, if the score on your third (marginal) exam is lower, a 70 percent, your average will fall to 80 percent because the marginal is below the average.

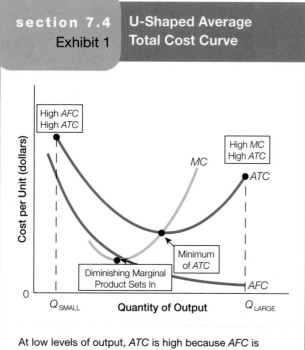

section 7.4
Exhibit 1

U-Shaped Average Total Cost Curve

At low levels of output, *ATC* is high because *AFC* is high—the fixed plant is underutilized. At high levels of output (close to capacity), the fixed plant will be overutilized, leading to high *MC* and, consequently, high *ATC*. It is diminishing marginal product that causes the *MC*, and eventually the *AVC* and *ATC*, to rise.

WHY IS THE AVERAGE TOTAL COST CURVE U-SHAPED?

The average total cost curve is usually U-shaped, as seen in Exhibit 1. Why is this? At very small levels of output and very large levels of output, average total cost is very high. The reason for the high average total cost when the firm is producing a very small amount of output is the high average fixed cost—when the output rate of the plant is small relative to its capacity, the plant is being underutilized. But as the firm expands output beyond this point, the average total cost falls. Why? Remember that $ATC = AFC + AVC$, and average fixed cost always falls when output expands because the fixed costs are being spread over more units of output. Thus, it is the declining *AFC* that is primarily responsible for the falling *ATC*.

The average total cost rises at high levels of output because of diminishing marginal product. For example, as more and more workers are put to work using a fixed quantity of machines, the result may be crowded working conditions and/or increasing maintenance costs as equipment is used more intensively, or older, less efficient machinery is called upon to handle the greater output. In fact, diminishing marginal product sets in at the very bottom of the marginal cost curve, as seen in Exhibit 1. That is, it is diminishing marginal product that causes the marginal cost to increase, eventually causing the average variable cost and the average total cost curves to rise. At very large levels of output, where the plant approaches full capacity, the fixed plant is overutilized, and this leads to high marginal cost that causes a high average total cost.

THE RELATIONSHIP BETWEEN MARGINAL COST AND AVERAGE VARIABLE AND AVERAGE TOTAL COST

Certain relationships exist between marginal cost and average variable and average total cost. For example, when average variable cost is falling, marginal cost must be less than average variable cost; and when average variable cost is rising, marginal cost is greater than average variable cost. Marginal cost is equal to average variable cost at the lowest point of the average variable cost curve, as seen in Exhibit 2. In the left-hand (shaded) portion of Exhibit 2, marginal cost is less than average variable cost and the average is falling. On the right-hand side, marginal cost is greater than average variable cost and the average is rising. The same relationship holds for the marginal cost curve and the average total cost curve. In the left-hand (shaded) portion of Exhibit 3, marginal cost is less than average total cost and the average is falling. On the right-hand side, marginal cost is greater than average total cost and the average is rising.

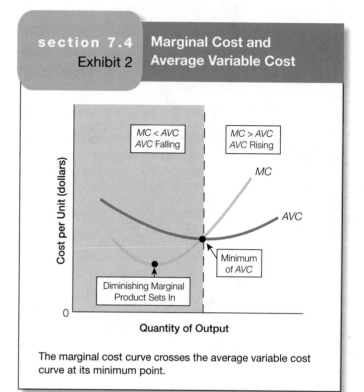

section 7.4
Exhibit 2
Marginal Cost and Average Variable Cost

The marginal cost curve crosses the average variable cost curve at its minimum point.

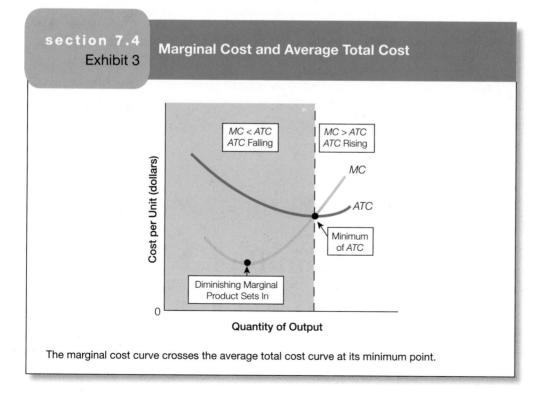

section 7.4
Exhibit 3
Marginal Cost and Average Total Cost

The marginal cost curve crosses the average total cost curve at its minimum point.

ACTIVE LEARNING EXERCISE

MARGINAL VERSUS AVERAGE AMOUNTS

Q: If a small horse-racing jockey decided to join your economics class of ten students, what would happen to the *average* height of the class?

A: The *marginal* addition, the jockey, would presumably be smaller than the *average* person in the class, so the *average* height in the class would fall. Now, if the star centre on the men's basketball team joined your class, the *average* height would rise, as, presumably, the newer marginal member would be taller than the average person. In sum, if the margin is greater (less) than the average, the average will rise (fall).

If Chris Bosh joined your class of ten students, what would happen to the average class height?

© PETER JONES/REUTERS/CORBIS

Section Check

1. Average total cost declines as output expands, but then increases as output expands beyond a certain point.
2. When marginal cost is less than average variable cost, average variable cost must be falling; when marginal cost is less than average total cost, average total cost must be falling.
3. When marginal cost is greater than average variable cost, average variable cost must be rising; when marginal cost is greater than average total cost, average total cost must be rising.

section
7.5   Cost Curves: Short Run and Long Run

- What are economies of scale?
- What are diseconomies of scale?
- What are constant returns to scale?

LONG-RUN VERSUS SHORT-RUN COST CURVES

Over long enough periods of time, firms can vary all of their productive inputs. For example, time provides an opportunity to substitute lower-cost capital, like larger plants or newer, more sophisticated equipment, for more expensive labour inputs. However, in the short run, a company cannot vary its plant size and equipment. These inputs are fixed in the short run, so the firm can only expand output by employing more variable inputs (e.g., workers and raw materials) in order to get extra output from the existing factory. For example, if a company has to pay lots of workers overtime wages to get expanded output in the short run, over longer periods, new highly automated machinery may be introduced that conserves on expensive labour. That is, in the long run (perhaps several years), the company can expand the size of its factories, build new ones, or shut down unproductive ones. Of course, the time it takes for a firm to get to the long run varies from firm to firm. For example, it may take only a couple of months to build a new coffee shop, whereas it may take a few years to build a new automobile plant.

Creating the Long-Run Average Total Cost Curve

In Exhibit 1, the firm has three possible plant sizes—a small plant, $SRATC_1$, a medium-sized plant, $SRATC_2$, and a large plant, $SRATC_3$. As we move along the $LRATC$ (the blue line) in Exhibit 1, the factory size changes with the quantity of output. Certain relationships among the successive curves should be emphasized. For very small output levels, q_1, costs are lowest with plant size $SRATC_1$, point A. Costs with plant size $SRATC_2$ (the medium plant size) are relatively high for these low levels of output because the plant's fixed costs are far too high for low levels of output; machinery, buildings, and so on would be poorly utilized. In Exhibit 1, we can see that if q_1 output is produced with plant size $SRATC_2$, the plant

section 7.5
Exhibit 1   **Short- and Long-Run Average Total Costs**

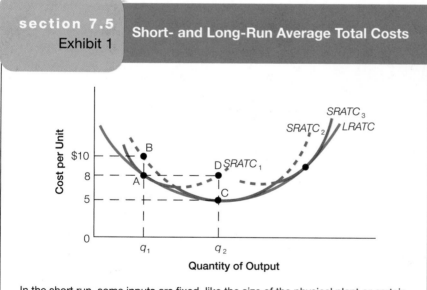

In the short run, some inputs are fixed, like the size of the physical plant or certain machinery. In the long run, firms can increase their capital inputs as well as their inputs that are variable in the short run, in some cases lowering average costs per unit. The curve thus has a shallower U-shape than the short-run average total cost curves. In the long run, all inputs are variable. The *LRATC* is the solid blue line that traces out the three different possible plant sizes, $SRATC_1$, $SRATC_2$, and $SRATC_3$. The *LRATC* shows the lowest average total cost for producing each output in the long run.

By having several screens in one complex, the cinema company can cut down on advertising and employee costs as well as rent. Because of economies of scale, it may be less expensive to have eight screens in one building with one concession area than eight separate theatres, each with one screen and a concession area.

would be operating below capacity, point B, and the cost would be higher at $10 per unit rather than at $8 per unit, at point A. However, if the firm planned to produce output level q_2, costs with plant size $SRATC_2$ are lower that those with $SRATC_1$. If output levels in this range were produced with the smaller plant, $SRATC_1$, the plant would be operating beyond designed capacity, point D, and the cost would be higher at $8 per unit rather than at $5 per unit, at point C. That is, plant $SRATC_2$, designed for a larger volume of output than the small plant, would minimize costs for producing quantity q_2.

If a straight line were extended upward from the horizontal output axis on a graph containing the various $SRATC$ curves for different-sized plants, the point at which it first struck an $SRATC$ curve would indicate the relevant value of $LRATC$ for that output level. Thus, in Exhibit 1, for low levels of output, q_1, the lowest average cost point is on curve $SRATC_1$; at output, q_2, it is on $SRATC_2$, and so on. The $LRATC$ curve is identical with $SRATC$ at the solid scalloped portion of the three short-run cost curves. When there are many possible plant sizes, the successive $SRATC$ curves will be close to one another, and the $LRATC$ curve will be smooth and U-shaped like the dark solid blue line in Exhibit 1.

The $LRATC$ curve is often called a *planning curve,* since it represents the cost data relevant to the firm when it is planning policy relating to scale of operations, output, and price over a long period of time. At a particular time, a firm already in operation has a certain plant and must base its current price and output decisions on the costs with the existing plant. However, when the firm considers the possibility of adjusting its scale of operations, long-run cost estimates are necessary.

economies of scale
occur in an output range where LRATC falls as output increases

constant returns to scale
occur in an output range where LRATC does not change as output varies

diseconomies of scale
occur in an output range where LRATC rises as output expands

minimum efficient scale
the output level where economies of scale are exhausted and constant returns to scale begin

THE SHAPE OF THE LONG-RUN ATC CURVE

By examining the long-run average total cost in Exhibit 2, we can see three possible production patterns. When $LRATC$ falls as output expands, we say that there are **economies of scale** present. And when the $LRATC$ does not vary with output, the firm is facing **constant returns to scale.** And when $LRATC$ rises as output expands, we say that the firm is facing **diseconomies of scale.**

The typical firm in an industry may well experience economies of scale at low levels of output, constant returns to scale at higher levels of output, and diseconomies of scale at still higher levels of output, as seen in Exhibit 2. At the **minimum efficient scale,** a plant has exhausted its economies of scale and the long-run average total costs are minimized. This is shown in Exhibit 2. In this constant returns to scale range (the flat portion of the $LRATC$), firms of differing size can compete on a roughly equal basis as far as costs are concerned—that is, they have no cost advantage over firms that are operating at the minimum efficient scale.

WHY DO ECONOMIES AND DISECONOMIES OF SCALE OCCUR?

As we have just seen, economies of scale exist when there is a reduction in the firm's long-run average costs as output expands. This may occur because a firm can use mass production techniques like assembly line produc-

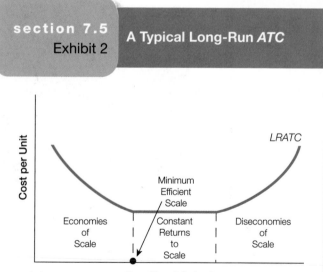

section 7.5
Exhibit 2

A Typical Long-Run *ATC*

All firms are different but most firms will probably have a long-run *ATC* that declines at low levels of output and then remains constant and eventually will rise at the higher levels of output. The minimum efficient scale is the lowest level of output at which average total costs are minimized.

tion or capture gains from labour specialization that might not be possible if the firm were producing at lower levels of output. For example, workers might experience greater proficiency gains if they concentrated on a few specific tasks rather than on many different tasks; that is, people who try to do everything may end up doing nothing very well. As well, larger firms may also enjoy cost advantages relative to smaller competitors when borrowing money or when purchasing inputs.

Recall that diseconomies of scale exist when there is an increase in the firm's long-run average costs as output expands. This may occur as the firm finds it increasingly difficult to handle the complexities of large-scale management. For example, information and coordination problems tend to increase when a firm becomes very large. As well, workers may feel alienated in a large plant and hence productivity and creativity may be stifled.

SHIFTING THE COST CURVES

Any cost curve is based on the assumption that input prices, taxes, regulation, and technology are constant. When these factors change, the cost curves of the firm will shift. For example, in Exhibit 3(a) we see how a per-unit tax increases the marginal cost of each unit of output, shifting the *MC* curve and the *ATC* up by the tax amount. The tax does not affect the firm's fixed cost because it is a tax on units produced. If a licence-to-operate fee increased, it would act like a fixed cost and affect only the average total cost curve—shifting *ATC* up by the amount of the fee increase. Improved technology will reduce marginal costs, shifting *MC* downward along with *ATC*, as in Exhibit 3(b).

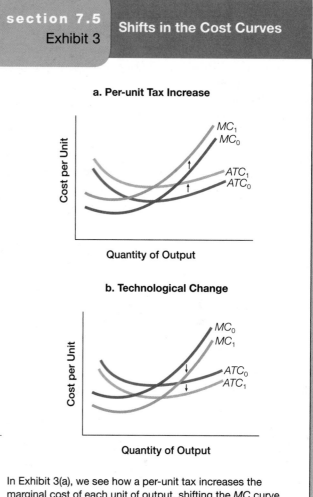

section 7.5
Exhibit 3

Shifts in the Cost Curves

a. Per-unit Tax Increase

b. Technological Change

In Exhibit 3(a), we see how a per-unit tax increases the marginal cost of each unit of output, shifting the *MC* curve and the *ATC* up by the amount of the tax. In Exhibit 3(b), improved technology will reduce marginal costs, shifting *MC* downward along with *ATC*.

In The **NEWS**

ADVANCED TECHNOLOGY BENEFITS MANUFACTURING COMPANIES

BY ERIC BEAUCHESNE

Competition and the survival of the fittest have done more to boost the productivity of Canadian factories than anything else over the past three decades, Statistics Canada says in one of two studies into what makes firms more productive.

Competition and the ensuing shift in market share toward more efficient plants have been a main source of productivity growth in most manufacturing industries, it said.

In fact, shifts in market share accounted for more than half of the overall growth in manufacturing productivity from the late 1970s through the mid-1990s, it said.

"Higher productivity, as measured by production per hour worked, occurs when output increases faster than hours worked," it noted. "In general, productivity growth helps improve prosperity and standards of living."

In more recent years, the use of advanced technology has also tended to boost productivity and, in turn, the market share of manufacturing firms, a separate but related Statistics Canada study says.

(continued)

IN THE NEWS (continued)

"Manufacturing companies that increased their use of advanced technology during the mid-1990s also experienced greater growth in labour productivity," it said, adding it also found a significant link between productivity growth and the increase in market share.

But the other study noted competition itself boosts productivity because it leads to the survival of the fittest firms.

For example, between 1988 and 1997, the shift of production from one plant to another helped to boost productivity growth in all the manufacturing sectors it studied and was responsible for more than half of productivity growth in 13 of the 22 sectors.

"Dynamic, competitive markets provide the foundation for economic prosperity," it said.

Gains in productivity come not so much from the productivity growth in long-established firms but from their replacement by new, more dynamic competitors who gain market share, it said.

The pace at which that Darwinian process was occurring increased in the 1990s as the manufacturing sector underwent a major restructuring to respond to the challenges posed by free trade—and the shifts in market share have been huge.

From 1988 to 1997, more than one-third of market share in an industry was transferred from plants that either contracted or closed to new plants or plants that expanded, it said.

The competitive process was also an important driver of the rapid productivity growth in the high-tech sector during the 1990s, it found.

© AJT/SHUTTERSTOCK

But, in the 1990s, another process—the increased use of advanced technology—was also a key driver of productivity growth, according to the other study. That report investigated the extent to which the adoption of advanced technologies by manufacturing plants between 1993 and 1998 was associated with superior growth and productivity performance.

"Advanced technology use led to growth in labour productivity, which in turn led to growth in market share," it said, reiterating that "the efficiency with which labour is employed in the production process . . . is an essential contributor to the prosperity of Canadians over the long run."

"The more capital-intensive a firm is, the greater the productivity growth," it said. "Plants that had invested heavily in advanced technologies were more likely to enjoy higher productivity growth."

SOURCE: Material reprinted with the express permission of: "CANWEST NEWS SERVICE," a CanWest Partnership.

CONSIDER THIS:

The use of advanced technology by Canadian manufacturing plants has boosted the productivity and the market share of those plants. The increase in production efficiency results in lower marginal costs and lower average total costs.

Section Check

1. In the long run, firms can vary inputs that are fixed in the short run, such as plant size and equipment.
2. At low output levels, when all inputs can be varied, some firms will experience economies of scale, where their per-unit costs are decreasing as output increases.
3. Firms that expand all inputs beyond a certain point will encounter diseconomies of scale, incurring rising per-unit costs as output grows in the long run.
4. In intermediate output ranges, firms may exhibit roughly constant returns to scale; in this range, their per-unit costs remain stable as output increases.
5. Input prices, taxes, technology, and regulation can shift the cost curves.

Summary

Section 7.1

- Total opportunity costs include both explicit costs and implicit costs.
- Explicit costs are the opportunity costs of production that require a monetary payment.
- Implicit costs represent the opportunity costs of production that do not require a monetary payment.
- Profits are the difference between the total revenues of a firm and its total costs.
- Accounting profits are based on revenues minus explicit costs.
- Economic profits occur when the firm is covering its total opportunity cost—both explicit and implicit costs.

Section 7.2

- The production function describes the maximum amount of a product that a firm can produce with any combination of inputs, using existing technology.
- Diminishing marginal product states that as the amount of a variable input is increased, the amount of other (fixed) inputs being held constant, a point ultimately will be reached where the additions to output will decline.

Section 7.3

- Fixed costs are expenses that stay constant regardless of the level of output.
- Variable costs change as the level of output changes.
- Marginal cost is the added cost of producing one more unit of output; it is this cost that is relevant to decisions to produce more or less.

Section 7.4

- When marginal costs are less than average total costs, average total costs must be falling.
- When marginal costs are greater than average total costs, average total costs must be rising.

Section 7.5

- In the long run, at low output levels, some firms will experience economies of scale, where their per-unit costs are decreasing as output increases.
- At a higher level of output, firms may experience constant returns to scale; in this range, their per-unit costs remain stable as output increases.
- At an even higher level of output, firms may experience diseconomies of scale, rising per-unit costs as output grows.

Key Terms and Concepts

For a complete glossary of chapter key terms, visit the textbook's Web site at http://www.sextonmicro2e.nelson.com.

explicit costs 168
implicit costs 168
profits 168
accounting profits 169
economic profits 169
sunk costs 169
short run 171
long run 171

total product (TP) 171
marginal product (MP) 171
diminishing marginal product 172
fixed costs 174
total fixed costs (TFC) 174
variable costs 174
total variable cost (TVC) 174
total cost (TC) 174

average total cost (ATC) 174
average fixed cost (AFC) 174
average variable cost (AVC) 174
marginal cost (MC) 174
economies of scale 182
constant returns to scale 182
diseconomies of scale 182
minimum efficient scale 182

Review Questions

1. What happens to the cost of growing strawberries on your own land if a housing developer offers you three times what you thought your land was worth?

2. As a farmer, you work for yourself using your own tractor, equipment, and farm structures, and you cultivate your own land. Why might it be difficult to calculate your economic profits from farming?

3. Say that your firm's total product curve includes the following data: 1 worker can produce 8 units of output; 2 workers, 20 units; 3 workers, 34 units; 4 workers, 50 units; 5 workers, 60 units; 6 workers, 70 units; 7 workers, 76 units; 8 workers, 78 units; and 9 workers, 77 units.

   a. What is the marginal product of the seventh worker?

   b. When does the law of diminishing product set in?

   c. Under these conditions, would you ever choose to employ nine workers?

4. Why does the law of diminishing marginal product imply the law of increasing costs?

5. What is likely to happen to your marginal costs when adding output requires working beyond an eight-hour day, if workers must be paid time-and-a-half wages beyond an eight-hour day?

6. A one-day ticket to visit the Screaming Coasters theme park costs $36, but you can also get a two-consecutive-day ticket for $40. What is the average cost per day for the two-day ticket? What is the marginal cost of the second consecutive day?

7. As a movie exhibitor, you can choose between paying a flat fee of $5000 to show a movie for a week or paying a fee of $2 per customer. Will your choice affect your fixed and variable costs? How?

8. If your university pays lecture notetakers $20 per hour to take notes in your economics class, and then sells subscriptions for $15 per student, is the cost of the lecture notetaker a fixed or variable cost of selling an additional subscription?

9. How might a high-school cafeteria cooking for 400 students rather than for 3 students be subject to economies of scale in the long run?

Fill in the Blanks

Section 7.1

1. Profits are defined as _____ minus _____.

2. The cost of producing a good is measured by the worth of the _____ alternative that was given up to obtain the resource.

3. Explicit costs are input costs that require a _____ payment.

4. Whenever we talk about costs—explicit or implicit—we are talking about _____ cost.

5. Economists generally assume that the ultimate goal of a firm is to _____ profits.

6. Accounting profits equal actual revenues minus actual expenditures of cash (explicit costs), so they do not include _____ costs.

7. Economists consider a zero economic profit a normal profit because it means that the firm is covering both _____ and _____ costs—the total opportunity cost of its resources.

8. _____ costs are costs that have already been incurred and cannot be recovered.

Section 7.2

9. Because it takes more time to vary some inputs than others, we must distinguish between the _____ run and the _____ run.

10. The long run is a period of time in which the firm can adjust _____ inputs.

11. In the long run, all costs are _____ costs and will change as output changes.

12. The total product schedule shows the total amount of _____ generated as the level of the variable input increases.

13. The marginal product of any single input is the change in total product resulting from a _____ change in the amount of that input used.

14. As the amount of a variable input is increased, the amount of other fixed inputs being held constant, a point ultimately will be reached beyond which marginal product will decline. This is called _____.

Section 7.3

15. The short-run total costs of a business fall into two distinct categories: _____ costs and _____ costs.

16. Fixed costs are costs that _____ with the level of output.

17. In the short run, fixed costs cannot be avoided without _____.

18. Costs that are not fixed are called _____ costs.

19. The sum of a firm's total _____ costs and total _____ costs is called its total cost.

20. Average total cost equals _____ divided by the _____ produced.

21. _____ equals total variable cost divided by the level of output produced.

22. Marginal costs are the _____ costs associated with the "last" unit of output produced.

Section 7.4

23. A fixed cost curve is always a _____ line because, by definition, fixed costs are the same at all output levels.

24. The reason for high average total costs when a firm is producing a very small amount of output is the high _____ costs.

25. The average total cost curve rises at high levels of output because of _____ product.

26. When AVC is falling, MC must be _____ than AVC; and when AVC is rising, MC must be _____ than AVC.

Section 7.5

27. In the _____ run, a company cannot vary its plant size and equipment, so the firm can only expand output by employing more _____ inputs.

28. The $LRATC$ curve is often called a _____ curve because it represents the cost data relevant to a firm when it is planning policy relating to scale of operations, output, and price over a long period of time.

29. When $LRATC$ falls as output expands, there are _____ of scale. When the $LRATC$ does not vary with output, the firm faces _____ to scale. When the $LRATC$ rises as output expands, there are _____ of scale.

30. At the _____ scale, a plant has exhausted its economies of scale and the long-run average total costs are minimized.

31. Any particular cost curve is based on the assumption that _____ prices and _____ are constant.

32. _____ may occur as a firm finds it increasingly difficult to handle the complexities of large-scale management.

True or False

Section 7.1

1. Explicit costs include both wages paid to workers and the opportunity cost of using one's own land, labour, or capital.

2. Because implicit costs do not represent an explicit outlay of money, they are not real costs.

3. When economists say firms try to maximize profits, they mean that firms try to maximize the difference between what they receive for their goods and services—their total revenue—and what they give up for their inputs—their total costs (explicit and implicit).

4. Economic profits equal actual revenues minus all explicit and implicit costs.

5. Economists consider a zero economic profit to be less than a normal profit rate.

6. Earning zero economic profit is different from earning zero accounting profit.

7. Sunk costs are irrelevant for any future action.

Section 7.2

8. The short run is defined as a period too brief for some inputs to be varied.

9. In the long run, the inputs that do not change with output are called fixed inputs or fixed factors of production.

10. The long run can vary considerably in length from industry to industry.

11. Total product will typically start at a low level and increase slowly at first and then more rapidly as the amount of the variable input increases.

12. Marginal product first rises as the result of more effective use of fixed inputs and then falls.

13. Diminishing marginal product stems from the crowding of the fixed inputs with more and more of the variable input.

14. A firm never knowingly allows itself to reach the point where the marginal product becomes negative.

15. If a firm were producing at the level where the marginal product of an input was negative, its profits would be lower as a result.

Section 7.3

16. Fixed costs for a given period have to be paid only if a firm produces output in that period.

17. Variable costs vary with the level of output, whereas fixed costs do not.

18. Marginal cost shows the change in total costs associated with a change in output by one unit, or the costs of producing one more unit of output.

19. Marginal costs are really just a useful way to view changes in fixed costs as output changes.

20. The total cost curve is the summation of the total variable cost and total fixed cost curves.

21. The average fixed cost curve is always a horizontal line, since fixed costs do not change with output.

22. The marginal cost curve crosses the average variable cost and average total cost curves at those curves' lowest points.

Section 7.4

23. At output levels where average total cost is rising, marginal cost must be greater than average total cost.

24. The average fixed cost curve declines whether the marginal cost curve is rising or falling.

25. The average total cost curve is usually U-shaped.

26. It is the declining average variable cost curve that is primarily responsible for the falling segment of the average total cost curve.

27. Diminishing marginal product first sets in at the minimum point of the average total cost curve.

28. Diminishing marginal product causes the marginal cost curve to increase, eventually causing the average variable cost and average total cost curves to rise.

29. *MC* is equal to *AVC* at the lowest point on the *AVC* curve, and it is equal to *ATC* at the lowest point on the *ATC* curve.

Section 7.5

30. Over long enough time periods, firms can vary all of their productive inputs.

31. As we move along the *LRATC*, the factory size changes with the quantity of output.

32. A typical firm experiences economies of scale at low levels of output, constant returns to scale at higher levels of output, and diseconomies of scale at still higher levels of output.

33. Diseconomies of scale may exist because a firm can use mass production techniques or capture gains from further labour specialization not possible at lower levels of output.

34. When input prices or technology changes, the cost curves of a firm will shift.

35. A lower wage will reduce *MC, AVC,* and *ATC.*

Multiple Choice

Section 7.1

1. An explicit cost
   a. is an opportunity cost.
   b. is an out-of-pocket expense.
   c. does not require an outlay of money.
   d. is characterized by both a and b.
   e. is characterized by both a and c.

2. Which of the following is *false?*
   a. Explicit costs are input costs that require a monetary payment.
   b. Implicit costs do not represent an explicit outlay of money.
   c. Both implicit and explicit costs are opportunity costs.
   d. Sunk costs are irrelevant for any future action.
   e. All of the above are true.

3. Which of the following is *false?*
   a. Profits are a firm's total revenue minus its total costs.
   b. Accounting profits are actual revenues minus actual expenditures of money.
   c. Economic profits are actual revenues minus all explicit and implicit costs.
   d. If a firm has any implicit costs, its economic profits exceed its accounting profits.
   e. All of the above are true.

4. The crucial difference between how economists and accountants analyze the profitability of a business has to do with whether or not _____ are included when calculating total production costs.
   a. implicit costs
   b. cash payments
   c. sunk costs
   d. explicit costs

5. Which of the following is *true?*
   a. If a firm's implicit costs are zero, accounting profits equal economic profits.
   b. If a firm's implicit costs are positive, accounting profits exceed economic profits.
   c. If a firm's implicit costs are positive, economic profits exceed accounting profits.
   d. Both a and b are true.
   e. Both a and c are true.

6. Cassie produces and sells 300 jars of homemade jelly each month for $3 each. Each month, she pays $200 for jars and $150 for ingredients, and uses her own time, with an opportunity cost of $300. Her economic profits each month are
   a. $250.
   b. $400.
   c. $550.
   d. $600.
   e. minus $350.

7. Sunk costs
   a. should be included when weighing the marginal costs of production against the marginal benefits received.
   b. have already been incurred and cannot be recovered.
   c. plus variable costs equal the total costs of production.
   d. are relevant to future decisions and should be carefully considered.

Section 7.2

8. The short run
   a. is a period too brief for any inputs to be varied.
   b. is a period in which there are no fixed costs.
   c. is normally a period of one year.
   d. is none of the above.

9. The long run
   a. is a period in which a firm can adjust all its inputs.
   b. can vary in length from industry to industry.
   c. is a period in which all costs are variable costs.
   d. is characterized by all of the above.

10. The long-run production period
    a. is a time when all inputs are variable.
    b. varies in length according to how capital goods are specialized.
    c. is likely longer for a steel manufacturer than for a retailer who sells watches off a cart at the local mall.
    d. is characterized by all of the above.

11. Which of the following most accurately describes the long-run period?
    a. The long run is a period of time in which a firm is unable to vary some of its factors of production.
    b. In the long run, a firm is able to expand output by utilizing additional workers and raw materials, but not physical capital.
    c. The long run is of sufficient length to allow a firm to alter its plant capacity and all other factors of production.
    d. The long run is of sufficient length to allow a firm to transform economic losses into economic profits.
    e. Both a and b most accurately describe the long-run period.

12. Production in the short run
   a. is subject to the law of diminishing marginal product.
   b. involves some fixed factors.
   c. can be increased by employing another unit of a variable input, as long as the marginal product of that input is positive.
   d. is characterized by all of the above.
   e. is characterized by none of the above.

13. A production function shows the relationship between
   a. variable inputs and fixed inputs.
   b. variable inputs and output.
   c. costs and output.
   d. inputs and costs.
   e. production and sales revenue.

14. Diminishing marginal product
   a. occurs in the long run but not in the short run.
   b. occurs in the short run but not in the long run.
   c. occurs both in the long run and the short run.
   d. occurs in neither the long run nor the short run.

15. Diminishing marginal productivity in a frozen-pizza company means that
   a. hiring additional workers causes the total output of pizza to fall.
   b. hiring additional workers does not change the total output of pizza produced.
   c. hiring additional workers adds fewer and fewer pizzas to total output.
   d. the average total cost of production must be decreasing.

Section 7.3
16. Total fixed costs
   a. do not vary with the level of output.
   b. cannot be avoided in the short run without going out of business.
   c. do not exist in the long run.
   d. are characterized by all of the above.

17. Which of the following is most likely a variable cost for a business?
   a. the loan payment on funds borrowed when a new building is constructed
   b. payments for electricity
   c. the lease payment on a warehouse used by the business
   d. the opportunity cost of the heavy equipment installed in a factory

18. The change in total cost that results from the production of one additional unit of output is called
   a. marginal revenue.
   b. average variable cost.
   c. marginal cost.
   d. average total cost.
   e. average fixed cost.

19. Which short-run curve typically declines continuously as output expands?
   a. average variable cost
   b. average total cost
   c. average fixed cost
   d. marginal cost
   e. none of the above

Section 7.4

20. Which of the following is true?
   a. The short-run *ATC* exceeds the short-run *AVC* at any given level of output.
   b. If the short-run *ATC* curve is rising, the short-run *AVC* curve is also rising.
   c. The short-run *AFC* is always falling with increased output, whether the short-run *MC* curve is greater or less than short-run *AFC*.
   d. If short-run *MC* is less than short-run *AVC*, short-run *AVC* is falling.
   e. All of the above are true.

21. Which of the following is false in the short run?
   a. *ATC* is usually U-shaped.
   b. Declining *AFC*s are the primary reason *ATC* decreases at low levels of output.
   c. *ATC* increases at high levels of output because of diminishing marginal product.
   d. Diminishing marginal product sets in at the minimum point of *ATC*.
   e. All of the above are true in the short run.

22. Typically, what is the shape of the average total cost curve for a firm in the short run?
   a. Typically, an average total cost curve is U-shaped.
   b. Typically, an average total cost curve constantly slopes upward as output expands and eventually approaches an infinite dollar amount at high rates of output.
   c. Typically, an average total cost curve is a vertical line.
   d. Typically, an average total cost curve slopes downward as output expands and approaches the *X*-axis when output is very large.

23. Which of the following is true in the short run?
   a. *MC* equals *ATC* at the lowest point of *ATC*.
   b. *MC* equals *AVC* at the lowest point of *AVC*.
   c. When *AVC* is at its minimum point, *ATC* is falling.
   d. When *ATC* is at its minimum point, *AVC* is rising.
   e. All of the above are true.

24. Which of the following is always true?
   a. When marginal cost is less than average total cost, average total cost is increasing.
   b. When average fixed cost is falling, marginal cost must be less than average fixed cost.
   c. When average variable cost is falling, marginal cost must be greater than average variable cost.
   d. When marginal cost is greater than average total cost, average total cost is increasing.

25. When marginal product is increasing,
   a. marginal cost is increasing.
   b. marginal cost is decreasing.
   c. average variable cost is increasing.
   d. average total cost is increasing.
   e. total cost is decreasing.

26. Luke Spacewalker realizes that his space-taxi service is operating in the region of diminishing marginal product. As he provides more taxi service in the short run, what will happen to the marginal cost of providing the additional service?
   a. It is impossible to say anything about marginal cost with the information provided.
   b. Marginal cost will decrease.
   c. Marginal cost will increase.
   d. Marginal cost will stay the same.

Section 7.5

27. If Bob's Burger Barn's city permit to operate rose by $3000 per year,
  a. that would shift its *MC* curve upward.
  b. that would shift its *AVC* curve upward.
  c. that would shift its *ATC* curve upward.
  d. that would shift its *MC, AVC,* and *ATC* curves upward.

28. If a firm's *ATC* is falling in the long run, then
  a. it is subject to economies of scale over that range of output.
  b. it is subject to diseconomies of scale over that range of output.
  c. it is subject to constant return to scale over that range of output.
  d. it has reached the minimum efficient scale of production.
  e. both c and d are true.

29. In the long run,
  a. the average fixed cost curve is U-shaped.
  b. the average fixed cost exceeds the average variable cost of production.
  c. all costs are variable.
  d. all costs are fixed.
  e. none of the above is correct.

30. When there are economies of scale in production,
  a. long-run average total cost declines as output expands.
  b. long-run average total cost increases as output expands.
  c. marginal cost increases as output expands.
  d. the marginal product of an input diminishes with increased utilization.

31. The lowest level of output at which a firm's goods are produced at minimum long-run average total cost is called
  a. the point of zero marginal cost.
  b. the point of diminishing returns.
  c. the minimum total product.
  d. the minimum efficient scale.
  e. plant capacity.

Problems

1. [Section 7.2]

Fill in the rest of the production function for Candy's Candies from the information provided.

Labour (workers)	Total Product (kilograms)	Marginal Product (kilograms)
0		
1	20	
2	44	
3	62	
4		12
5		6
6	78	

  a. Candy's Candies begins to experience diminishing marginal product with which worker?
  b. Does Candy's Candies ever experience negative marginal product? If so, with the addition of which worker?

2. **[Section 7.3]**

   Use the graph below to answer the following questions.
   a. Curve A represents which cost curve?
   b. Curve B represents which cost curve?
   c. Curve C represents which cost curve?
   d. Curve D represents which cost curve?
   e. Why must curve D pass through the minimum points of both curve B and curve C?
   f. What significance does the point where curve A intersects curve D have?

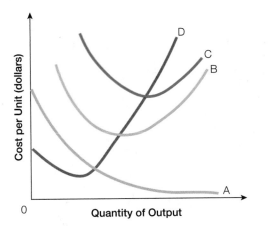

3. **[Section 7.3]**

   Fill in the rest of the cost function for Bob's Beautiful Bowling Balls.

Output	Total Fixed Costs	Total Variable Costs	Total Costs	Average Fixed Cost	Average Variable Cost	Average Total Cost	Marginal Cost
1	$200	$ 60	$	$	$	$	$
2		100					
3		120					
4		128					
5		158					
6		218					
7		326					
8		480					

chapter

8

Perfect Competition

section

8.1

The Four Different Market Structures

- What are the four market structures?
- What are the characteristics of a perfectly competitive firm?
- What is a price taker?

Economists have identified four different market structures in which firms operate: perfect competition, monopoly, monopolistic competition, and oligopoly. Each structure or environment has certain key characteristics that distinguish it from the other structures. In practice it is sometimes difficult to decide precisely which structure a given firm or industry most appropriately fits, since the dividing line between the structures is not entirely crystal clear.

Perfect Competition

A competitive market is a market situation where there is a large number of buyers and sellers—perhaps thousands or very conceivably millions. In addition, no single firm produces more than an extremely small proportion of total output. This means that no single firm can influence the market price or quantity. Firms are price takers; they must accept the price for the product as determined by the forces of demand and supply. Individually, they are too small and powerless to alter prices.

Firms in **perfect competition** sell a homogeneous or standardized product. In the wheat market, which approximates the conditions of perfect competition, it is not possible to determine any significant and consistent qualitative differences in the wheat produced by different farmers. New firms can easily enter the market.

perfect competition
a market with many buyers and sellers, selling homogeneous goods, easy market entry and exit, and no firm can affect the market price

Monopoly

On the other end of the continuum of market environments is pure monopoly. In this market structure, there is one firm (a single seller) that produces a good or service that has no close substitutes, and there are significant barriers to potential entrants into the market. Examples of monopoly include government-owned or government-regulated public utilities (electric, water, and natural gas suppliers) and DeBeers, the South African diamond producer.

Monopolistic Competition

Monopolistic competition falls between perfect competition and monopoly. Monopolistic competition is a market structure where firms have both an element of competition and an element of monopoly power. Because each firm's product is differentiated at least slightly from that of other competitors, it has some monopoly power. For example, in a given city of 100 000 there may be 100 restaurants, each slightly different in the type of food that it sells, the services that it provides, and the hours that it stays open. However, because there are so many competing restaurants vying for your business it also has an element of competitive markets. The same is true for service stations, retail businesses, and furniture stores.

Oligopoly

Like monopolistic competition, oligopoly also falls between perfect competition and monopoly. Oligopoly exists when a *few* firms produce similar or identical goods, as opposed to one firm (monopoly) or many (competitive market). Unlike pure monopoly, oligopoly allows for some competition between firms; unlike competition, firms in oligopolistic environments have a significant share of the total market for the good being produced.

The oligopolist is very conscious of the actions of competing firms. In this respect, the oligopoly structure differs from others. In perfect competition, Farmer Jones does not worry about what Farmer Smith does, since neither of them is big enough to have any influence on overall market conditions. In monopoly, there is no other firm to worry about. In true monopolistic competition, there are many relatively small firms, so again a firm usually does not worry much about the impact on it of the behaviour of a competing firm. In oligopoly, though, a firm's behaviour is closely related to that of its competitors. General Motors' pricing decisions influence the pricing decisions of Ford, Chrysler, and other manufacturers, including ones located in other countries. The oligopolist does have some control over price and thus is a price setter. Note that the oligopoly may involve a standardized product (like steel, aluminum, or crude oil) or a differentiated one (automobiles, refrigerators, TV sets).

Economists often distinguish the perfectly competitive market from the imperfectly competitive markets of monopoly, monopolistic competition, and oligopoly. The differences between these markets will become clearer as we look at each model separately in

Can the owner of this orchard charge a noticeably higher price for the same quality of apples? What if she charges a lower price for the same-quality apples? How many apples can she sell at the market price?

© BRUCE HEINEMANN/PHOTODISC/GETTY ONE IMAGES

In The NEWS

GOVERNMENT PANEL CALLS FOR INCREASED COMPETITION

BY JAMIE STURGEON

To improve the competitiveness of Canada's business environment, foreigners should have an easier time investing in the country's telecommunications, air-transportation and uranium-mining industries, and banks should be allowed to merge, a government-appointed panel said yesterday.

These recommendations were among the 61 made in a 134-page report by the five-person Competition Policy Review Panel, commissioned in July 2007 amid rising concerns over foreign takeovers.

"In order to succeed and prosper in the 21st century, Canada must adopt a more globally competitive mindset by thinking and acting more globally and competing more intensively, we will build a stronger economy," panel chairman Lynton (Red) Wilson told reporters after the release of the report, which was presented to Industry Minister Jim Prentice.

"As the pace of change quickens in this rapidly globalizing world, we believe that Canada must and can compete to win," he said, adding that increased competition "will provide Canadians with a higher standard of living."

"Canada must improve its productivity," he added. "Canadian firms will need to become more innovative and entrepreneurial."

"The report focuses on three areas: liberalizing foreign-investment rules, streamlining Canada's competition regime, and creating an internationally competitive business environment," Wilson said.

The panel also called for the creation of a Canadian Competitiveness Council, which would be an independent body charged with advocating competition in both the public and private sectors.

"We are very pleased with the approach taken by the panel," Perrin Beatty, chief executive of the Canadian Chamber of Commerce, said in a statement.

"The report deals in clear terms with the most important issue facing Canadian business today: the ability of Canadians to succeed in a globalized economy where competition grows every day," he said.

However, a group representing Canada's small- and medium-sized businesses criticized the report. Among other things, the Canadian Federation of Independent Business took exception to the suggestion of allowing bank mergers, saying it runs counter to what's supposed to be achieved.

"To enhance our competitiveness, we need more competition, not less competition," said CFIB executive vice-president Garth Whyte.

He said fewer banks could result in higher fees and less access to capital for independent businesses.

SOURCE: Materials reprinted with the express permission of: "CANWEST NEWS SERVICE,"a CanWest Partnership.

CONSIDER THIS:
According to this government-appointed panel, the Canadian economy could benefit from increased levels of competition. A key recommendation from the panel was for increased foreign investment in the air-transport and telecommunications industries. In other words, the panel would like to see certain key Canadian industries face increased competition, moving those industries from an oligopolistic market structure to a more perfectly competitive market structure.

---

the chapters to come. Because we will often compare perfect competition to the other market structures, it is a good starting point for our study of the four market models. Let us take a closer look now at the perfectly competitive model.

A PERFECTLY COMPETITIVE MARKET

This chapter examines perfect competition, a market structure characterized by (1) many buyers and sellers, (2) an identical (homogeneous) product, and (3) easy market entry and exit. Let's examine these characteristics in greater detail.

Many Buyers and Sellers

price taker
a perfectly competitive firm takes the price that it is given by the intersection of the market demand and market supply curves

In a perfectly competitive market there are *many buyers and sellers* trading identical goods. Because each firm is so small in relation to the industry, its production decisions have no impact on the market—each regards price as something over which it has little control. This is why perfectly competitive firms are called **price takers.** That is, they must take the price given by the market because their influence on price is insignificant. If the price of apples in the apple market is $2 a kilogram, then individual apple farmers will receive $2 per kilogram for their apples. Similarly, no single buyer of apples can influence the price of apples because each buyer purchases only a small amount of the apples traded. We will see how this works in more detail in Section 8.3.

Identical (Homogeneous) Products

Consumers believe that all firms in perfectly competitive markets *sell identical (or homogeneous) products*. For example, in the wheat market, it is not possible to determine any significant and consistent qualitative differences in the wheat produced by different farmers. Wheat produced by Farmer Jones looks, feels, smells, and tastes like that produced by Farmer Smith. In short, a bushel of wheat is a bushel of wheat. The products of all the firms are considered to be perfect substitutes.

Easy Entry and Exit

Product markets characterized by perfect competition have no significant *barriers to entry or exit*. This means that it is fairly easy for entrepreneurs to become suppliers of the product or, if they are already producers, to stop supplying the product. "Fairly easy" does not mean that any person on the street can instantly enter the business, but rather that the financial, legal, educational, and other barriers to entering the business are modest, so that large numbers of people can overcome the barriers and enter the business if they so desire in any given time period. If buyers can easily switch from one seller to another and sellers can easily enter or exit the industry, then we have met the perfectly competitive condition of easy entry and exit. Because of this easy market entry, perfectly competitive markets generally consist of a large number of small suppliers.

A perfectly competitive market is approximated most closely in highly organized markets for securities and agricultural commodities, such as the Toronto Stock Exchange or the Winnipeg Commodity Exchange. Wheat, corn, soybeans, cotton, and many other agricultural products are sold in perfectly competitive markets. Although all the criteria for a perfect competitive market are rarely met, a number of markets come close to satisfying them. Even when all the assumptions don't hold, it is important to note that studying the model of perfect competition is useful because there are many markets that resemble perfect competition—that is, markets in which firms face very elastic (flat) demand curves and relatively easy entry and exit. The model also gives us a standard of comparison. In other words, we can make comparisons with the perfectly competitive model to help us evaluate what is going on in the real world.

Section Check

1. There are four main market structures: perfect competition, monopoly, monopolistic competition, and oligopoly.
2. A perfectly competitive market is characterized by many buyers and sellers, an identical (homogeneous) product, and easy market entry and exit.
3. Consumers believe that all firms in perfectly competitive markets sell virtually identical (homogeneous) products. The products of all the firms are considered to be perfect substitutes.
4. Because there are so many buyers and so many sellers, neither buyers nor sellers have any control over price in perfect competition. They must take the going price and are called price takers.
5. Perfectly competitive markets have no significant barriers to entry. That is, the barriers are significantly modest so that many sellers can enter or exit the industry.

An Individual Price Taker's Demand Curve

- Why won't individual price takers raise or lower their prices?
- Can individual price takers sell all they want at the market price?
- Will the position of individual price takers' demand curves change when market price changes?

AN INDIVIDUAL FIRM'S DEMAND CURVE

Perfectly competitive firms are price takers; that is, they must sell at the market-determined price, where the market price and output are determined by the intersection of the market supply and demand curves, as seen in Exhibit 1(a). Individual wheat farmers know that they cannot dispose of their wheat at any figure higher than the current market price; if they attempt to charge a higher price, potential buyers would simply make their purchases from other wheat farmers. And they certainly would not knowingly charge a lower price because they could sell all they want at the market price.

Likewise, in a perfectly competitive market, individual sellers can change their output and it will not alter the market price. This is possible because of the large number of sellers who are selling identical products. Each producer provides such a small fraction

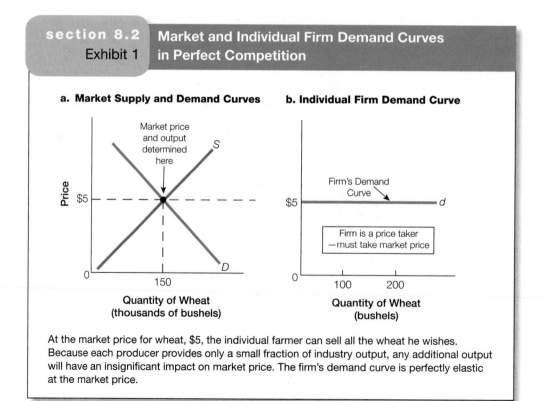

section 8.2
Exhibit 1
Market and Individual Firm Demand Curves in Perfect Competition

a. Market Supply and Demand Curves

Market price and output determined here

Price

$5

S

D

0

150

Quantity of Wheat
(thousands of bushels)

b. Individual Firm Demand Curve

Firm's Demand Curve

$5

d

Firm is a price taker
—must take market price

0

100   200

Quantity of Wheat
(bushels)

At the market price for wheat, $5, the individual farmer can sell all the wheat he wishes. Because each producer provides only a small fraction of industry output, any additional output will have an insignificant impact on market price. The firm's demand curve is perfectly elastic at the market price.

of the total supply that a change in the amount it offers does *not* have a noticeable effect on market equilibrium price. In a perfectly competitive market, then, an individual firm can sell as much as it wishes to place on the market at the prevailing price; the demand, as seen by the seller, is perfectly elastic.

It is easy to construct the demand curve for an individual seller in a perfectly competitive market. Remember, she won't charge more than the market price because no one will buy the good, and she won't charge less because she can sell all she wants at the market price. Thus, the farmer's demand curve is horizontal over the entire range of output that she could possibly produce. If the prevailing market price of the product is $5, the farmer's demand curve will be represented graphically by a horizontal line at the market price of $5, as shown in Exhibit 1(b).

A CHANGE IN MARKET PRICE AND THE FIRM'S DEMAND CURVE

To say that producers under perfect competition regard price as a given is not to say that price is constant. The *position* of the firm's demand curve varies with every change in the market price. In Exhibit 2, we see that when the market price for wheat increases, say as a result of an increase in market demand, the price-taking firm will receive a higher price for all of its output. Or when the market price decreases, say as a result of a decrease in market demand, the price-taking firm will receive a lower price for all of its output.

In effect, sellers are provided with current information about market demand and supply conditions as a result of price changes. It is an essential aspect of the perfectly competitive model that sellers respond to the signals provided by such price movements, so they must alter their behaviour over time in the light of actual experience, revising their production decisions to reflect changes in market price. In this respect, the perfectly competitive model is very straightforward; it does not assume any knowledge on the part of individual buyers and sellers about market demand and supply—they only have to know the price of the good they sell.

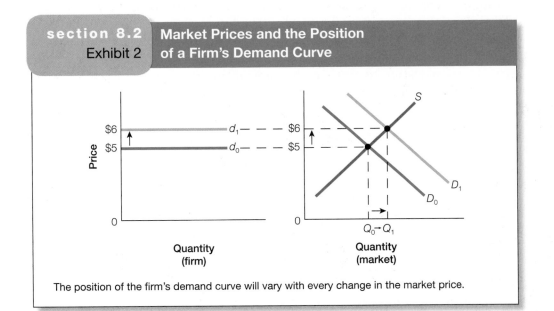

section 8.2
Exhibit 2

Market Prices and the Position of a Firm's Demand Curve

The position of the firm's demand curve will vary with every change in the market price.

section 8.3

Profit Maximization

- What is total revenue?
- What is average revenue?
- What is marginal revenue?
- Why does the firm maximize profits where marginal revenue equals marginal costs?

REVENUES IN A PERFECTLY COMPETITIVE MARKET

The objective of the firm is to maximize profits. To maximize profits the firm wants to produce the amount that maximizes the difference between its total revenues and total costs. In this section, we will examine the different ways to look at revenue in a perfectly competitive market: total revenue, average revenue, and marginal revenue.

TOTAL REVENUE

total revenue (*TR*)
the product price times the quantity sold

Total revenue (*TR*) is the revenue that the firm receives from the sale of its products. Total revenue from a product equals the price of the good (P) times the quantity (q) of units sold ($TR = P \times q$). For example, if a farmer sells 10 bushels of wheat a day for $5 a bushel, his total revenue is $50 ($5 $\times$ 10 bushels). (Note: We will use the small letter q to denote the single firm's output and reserve the large Q for the output of the entire market. For example, q would be used to represent the output of one potato grower, whereas Q would be used to represent the output of all potato growers in the potato market.)

AVERAGE REVENUE AND MARGINAL REVENUE

average revenue (*AR*)
total revenue divided by the number of units sold

Average revenue (*AR*) equals total revenue divided by the number of units sold of the product (TR/q, or $[P \times q]/q$). For example, if the farmer sells 10 bushels at $5 a bushel, total revenue is $50 and average revenue is $5 ($50/10 bushels = $5 per bushel). So, in perfect competition, average revenue is equal to price of the good.

marginal revenue (*MR*)
the increase in total revenue resulting from a one-unit increase in sales

   Marginal revenue (*MR*) is the additional revenue derived from the production of one more unit of the good. In other words, marginal revenue represents the increase in total revenue that results from the sale of one more unit. In a perfectly competitive market, because additional units of output can be sold without reducing the price of the product, marginal revenue is constant at all outputs and equal to average revenue. For example, if the price of wheat per bushel is $5, the marginal revenue is $5. Because total

section 8.3
Exhibit 1   **Revenues for a Perfectly Competitive Firm**

Quantity (q)	Price (P)	Total Revenue (TR = P × q)	Average Revenue (AR = TR/q)	Marginal Revenue (MR = ΔTR/Δq)
1	$5	$ 5	$5	
2	5	10	5	$5
3	5	15	5	5
4	5	20	5	5
5	5	25	5	5

revenue is equal to price multiplied by quantity ($TR = P \times q$), as we add one additional unit of output, total revenue will always increase by the amount of the product price, $5. Marginal revenue facing a perfectly competitive firm is equal to the price of the good.

In perfect competition, then, we know that marginal revenue, average revenue, and price are all equal: $P = MR = AR$. These relationships are clearly illustrated in the calculation presented in Exhibit 1.

HOW DO FIRMS MAXIMIZE PROFITS?

Now that we have discussed both the firm's cost curves (Chapter 7) and the firm's revenues, we are ready to see how a firm maximizes its profits. A firm's profits equal its total revenues minus its total costs. But at what output level will a firm produce and sell in order to maximize profits? There are two methods for identifying this output, the marginal approach and the total cost–total revenue approach. In all types of market environments, firms will maximize profits at that output that maximizes the difference between total revenue and total costs, which is at the same output level where marginal revenue equals marginal costs.

EQUATING MARGINAL REVENUE AND MARGINAL COST

The importance of equating marginal revenue and marginal costs is seen in Exhibit 2. As output expands beyond zero up to q^*, the marginal revenue derived from each unit of the expanded output exceeds the marginal cost of that unit of output, so the expansion of output creates additional profits. This addition to profit is shown as the left-most shaded section in Exhibit 2. As long as marginal revenues exceed marginal costs, profits continue to grow. For example, if the firm decides to produce $q_{\text{TOO LITTLE}}$, the firm sacrifices potential profits because the marginal revenue from

section 8.3
Exhibit 2   **Finding the Profit-Maximizing Level of Output**

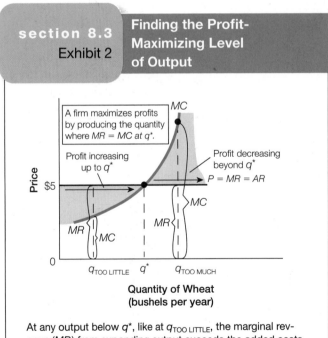

At any output below q^*, like at $q_{\text{TOO LITTLE}}$, the marginal revenue (MR) from expanding output exceeds the added costs (MC) of that output, so additional profits can be made by expanding output. Beyond q^*, like at $q_{\text{TOO MUCH}}$, marginal costs exceed marginal revenue, so output expansion is unprofitable and output should be reduced. The profit-maximizing level of output is at q^*, where the profit-maximizing output rule is followed—the firm should produce the level of output where $MR = MC$.

producing more output is greater than the marginal cost. Only at q^*, where $MR = MC$, is the output level just right—not too large, not too small. Further expansion of output beyond q^* will lead to losses on the additional output (decrease the firm's overall profits) because $MC > MR$. For example, if the firm produces $q_{TOO\ MUCH}$, the firm incurs losses on that output produced beyond q^*; the firm should reduce its output. Only at output q^*, where $MR = MC$, can we find the profit-maximizing level of output. The **profit-maximizing output rule** says a firm should always produce at the level of output where its $MR = MC$.

profit-maximizing output rule

a firm should always produce at the level of output where MR = MC

THE MARGINAL APPROACH

We can use the data in Exhibit 3 to find Farmer John's profit-maximizing position. In the table in Exhibit 3, columns 5 and 6 show the marginal revenue and marginal cost, respectively. We see that output levels of one and two bushels produce outputs that have marginal revenues that exceed marginal cost—John certainly wants to produce those units and more. That is, as long as marginal revenue exceeds marginal costs, producing and selling those units adds more to revenues than to costs; in other words, they add to profits. However, once he expands production beyond four units of output, John's marginal revenues are less than his marginal costs and his profits begin to fall. Clearly, Farmer John should not produce beyond four bushels of wheat.

THE TOTAL COST—TOTAL REVENUE APPROACH

Let us take another look at profit maximization using the table in Exhibit 3. Comparing columns 2 and 3, the calculations of total revenues and total costs, respectively, we see that Farmer John maximizes his profits at output levels of three or four bushels, where he will make profits of $4. In column 4, "Profit," you can see that there is no higher level of profit at any of the other output levels.

In the next section we will use the profit-maximizing output rule to see what happens when changes in the market cause the price to fall below average total cost and even below average variable costs. We will introduce the three-step method to determine whether the firm is making an economic profit, minimizing its losses, or should temporarily shut down.

section 8.3 Exhibit 3	Cost and Revenue Calculations for a Perfectly Competitive Firm				
Quantity (1)	Total Revenue (2)	Total Cost (3)	Profit (TR − TC) (4)	Marginal Revenue ($\Delta TR/\Delta q$) (5)	Marginal Cost ($\Delta TC/\Delta q$) (6)
0	$ 0	$ 2	$−2		
1	5	4	1	$5	$2
2	10	7	3	5	3
3	15	11	4	5	4
4	20	16	4	5	5
5	25	22	3	5	6

1. Total revenue is price times the quantity sold ($TR = P \times q$).
2. Average revenue is total revenue divided by the quantity sold ($AR = TR/q = P$).
3. Marginal revenue is the change in total revenue from the sale of an additional unit of output ($MR = \Delta TR/\Delta q$). In a competitive industry, the price of the good equals both the average revenue and the marginal revenue.
4. As long as marginal revenue exceeds marginal costs, the seller should expand production because producing and selling those units adds more to revenues than to costs, or increases profits. However, if marginal revenue is less than marginal cost, the seller should decrease production.
5. The profit-maximizing output rule says a firm should always produce where $MR = MC$.

Short-Run Profits and Losses

■ How do we determine if a firm is generating an economic profit?
■ How do we determine if there is an economic loss?
■ How do we determine if a firm is making zero economic profits?
■ Why doesn't a firm produce when price is below average variable costs?

In the previous section, we discussed two methods of determining the profit-maximizing output level for a perfectly competitive firm. However, producing at this profit-maximizing level does not mean that a firm is actually generating profits; it merely means that a firm is maximizing its profit opportunity at a given price level. How do we know if a firm is actually making economic profits or losses?

THE THREE-STEP METHOD
What Is the Three-Step Method?

Determining whether a firm is generating economic profits, economic losses, or zero economic profits at the profit-maximizing level of output, q^*, can be done in three easy steps. First, we will walk through these steps, and then we will apply the method to three different situations for a hypothetical firm in the short run in Exhibit 1.

1. Find where marginal revenues equal marginal costs and proceed straight down to the horizontal quantity axis to find q^*, the profit-maximizing output level.
2. At q^*, go straight up to the demand curve and then to the left to find the market price, P^*. Once you have identified P^* and q^*, you can find total revenue at the profit-maximizing output level, because $TR = P \times q$.
3. The last step is to find total costs. Again, go straight up from q^* to the average total cost (ATC) curve and then left to the vertical axis to compute the average total cost *per unit*. If we multiply average total costs by the output level, we can find the total costs ($TC = ATC \times q$).

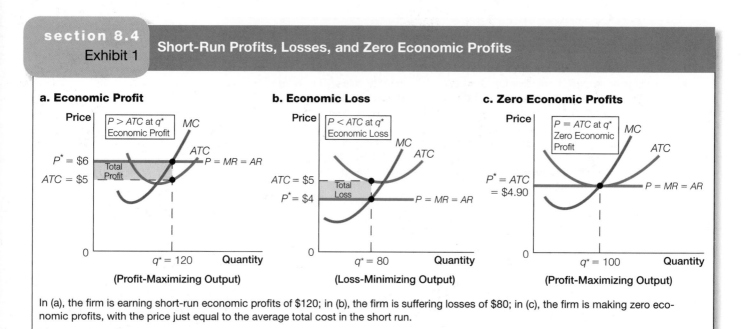

In (a), the firm is earning short-run economic profits of $120; in (b), the firm is suffering losses of $80; in (c), the firm is making zero economic profits, with the price just equal to the average total cost in the short run.

If total revenue is greater than total costs at q^*, the firm is generating economic profits. And if total revenue is less than total costs at q^*, the firm is generating economic losses. Remember, the cost curves include implicit and explicit costs—that is, we are covering the opportunity costs of our resources. So even if there are zero economic profits, no tears should be shed, because the firm is covering both its implicit and explicit costs. Because firms are also covering their implicit costs, or what they could be producing with these resources in another endeavour, economists sometimes call this zero economic profit *a normal rate of return*. That is, the owners are doing as well as they could elsewhere, in that they are getting the normal rate of return on the resources they invested in the firm.

The Three-Step Method in Action

In Exhibit 1, there are three different short-run equilibrium positions; in each case, the firm is producing at a level where marginal revenue equals marginal costs. Each of these alternatives shows that the firm is maximizing profits or minimizing losses in the short run.

Assume that there are three alternative prices for a firm with given costs. In Exhibit 1(a), the firm receives $6 per unit at an equilibrium level of output ($MR = MC$) of 120 units. Total revenue ($P \times q^*$) is 6×120, or $720. The average total cost at 120 units of output is $5, and the total cost ($ATC \times q^*$) is $600. Following the three-step method, we can calculate that this firm is earning total economic profits of $120.

In Exhibit 1(b), the market price has fallen to $4 per unit. At the equilibrium level of output, the firm is now producing 80 units of output at an average total cost of $5 per unit. The total revenue is now $320 ($4 \times 80$), and the total costs are $400 ($5 \times 80$). We can see that the firm is now incurring total economic losses of $80.

In Exhibit 1(c), the firm is earning zero economic profits, or a normal rate of return. The market price is $4.90, and the average total cost is $4.90 per unit for 100 units of output. In this case, economic profits are zero because total revenue, $490, minus total cost, $490, is equal to zero. This firm is just covering all its costs, both implicit and explicit.

EVALUATING ECONOMIC LOSSES IN THE SHORT RUN

A firm generating an economic loss faces a tough choice: Should it continue to produce or shut down its operation in the short run? To make this decision, we need to add another variable to our discussion of economic profits and losses: average variable costs. Variable costs are those costs that vary with output, such as wages, raw material, transportation, and electricity. If a firm cannot generate enough revenues to cover its variable costs, then it will have larger losses if it operates than if it shuts down (losses in that case = fixed costs). Thus, a firm will not produce at all unless the price is greater than its average variable costs.

Operating at a Loss

At price levels greater than or equal to average variable costs, a firm may continue to operate in the short run even if average total costs—variable and fixed costs—are not completely covered. That is, the firm may continue to operate even though it is experiencing an economic loss. Why? Because fixed costs continue whether the firm produces or not; it is better to earn enough to cover a portion of fixed costs rather than earn nothing at all.

In Exhibit 2, price is less than average total cost but more than average variable cost. In this case, the firm produces in the short run, but at a loss. To shut down would make this firm worse off because it can cover at least *some* of its fixed costs with the excess of revenue over its variable costs.

The Decision to Shut Down

Exhibit 3 illustrates a situation in which the price a firm is able to obtain for its product is below its average variable costs at all ranges of output. In this case, the firm is unable to cover even its variable costs in the short run. Because the firm is losing even more than the fixed costs it would lose if it shut down, it is more logical for the firm to cease operations. So if $P < AVC$, the firm can cut its losses by shutting down.

The Short-Run Supply Curve

As we have just seen, at all prices above minimum AVC, a firm produces in the short run even if average total cost (ATC) is not completely covered, and at all prices below the minimum AVC, the firm shuts down. The firm produces above the minimum of the AVC even if it is incurring economic losses because it can still earn enough in total revenues to cover all of its average variable costs and a portion of its fixed costs—this is better than not producing, and earning nothing at all.

In graphical terms, the **short-run supply curve** of an individual competitive seller is identical with that portion

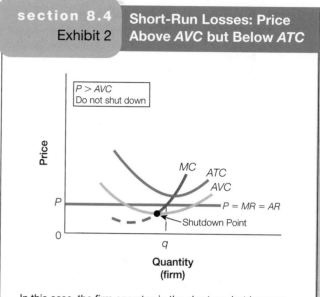

Short-Run Losses: Price Above *AVC* but Below *ATC*

In this case, the firm operates in the short run but incurs a loss because $P < ATC$. Nevertheless, $P > AVC$, and revenues cover variable costs and partially defray fixed costs. This firm will leave the industry in the long run unless prices are expected to rise in the near future, but in the short run it continues to operate at a loss as long as $P > AVC$.

short-run supply curve
as a cost relation, this curve shows the marginal cost of producing any given output; as a supply curve, it shows the equilibrium output that the firm will supply at various prices in the short run

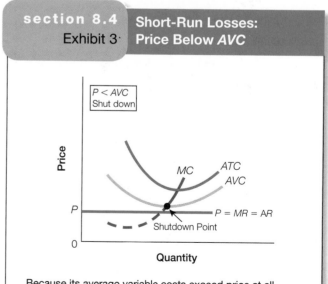

Short-Run Losses: Price Below *AVC*

Because its average variable costs exceed price at all levels of output, this firm would cut its losses by discontinuing production.

section 8.4
Exhibit 4

The Firm's Short-Run Supply Curve

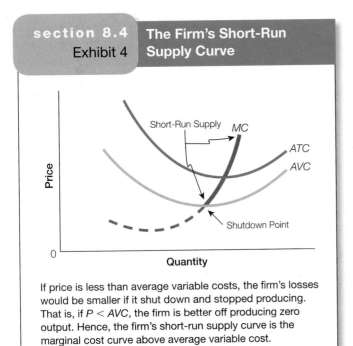

If price is less than average variable costs, the firm's losses would be smaller if it shut down and stopped producing. That is, if $P < AVC$, the firm is better off producing zero output. Hence, the firm's short-run supply curve is the marginal cost curve above average variable cost.

short-run market supply curve

the horizontal summation of the individual firms' supply curves in the market

of the *MC* curve that lies above the minimum of the *AVC* curve. As a cost relation, this curve shows the marginal cost of producing any *given output;* as a supply curve, it shows the *equilibrium output* that the firm will supply at various prices in the short run. The thick line in Exhibit 4 is the firm's supply curve—the portion of *MC* above its intersection with *AVC*. The declining portion of the *MC* curve has no significance for supply, because if the price falls below average variable costs, the firm is better off shutting down—producing no output. Beyond the point of lowest *AVC*, the marginal costs of successively larger amounts of output are progressively greater, so the firm will supply larger and larger amounts only at higher prices. The absolute maximum that the firm can supply, regardless of price, is the maximum quantity that it can produce with the existing plant.

DERIVING THE SHORT-RUN MARKET SUPPLY CURVE

The **short-run market supply curve** is the horizontal summation of the individal firms' supply curves (that is, the portion of the firms' *MC* above *AVC*) in the market. Because the short run is too brief for new firms to enter the market, the market supply curve is the horizontal summation of *existing* firms. For example, in Exhibit 5, at P_0, each of the 1000 identical firms in the industry produce 50 bushels of wheat per day at point a, in Exhibit 5(a) and the quantity supplied in the market is 50 000 bushels of wheat, point A, in Exhibit 5(b). We can again sum horizontally at P_1; the quantity supplied for each of the 1000 identical firms is 80 bushels of wheat

section 8.4
Exhibit 5

Deriving the Short-Run Market Supply Curve

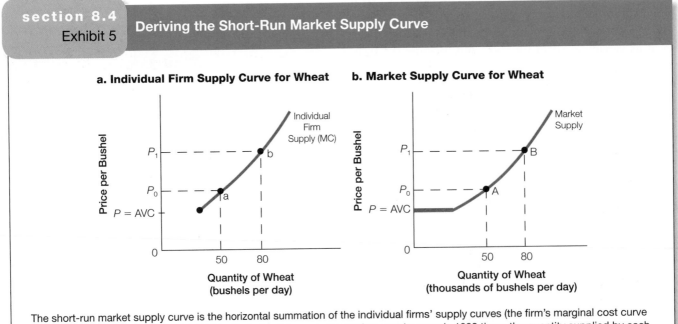

The short-run market supply curve is the horizontal summation of the individual firms' supply curves (the firm's marginal cost curve above *AVC*) in (a). In a market of 1000 identical wheat farmers, the market supply curve is 1000 times the quantity supplied by each firm in (a).

Since the demand for summer camps will be lower during the off-season, it is likely that revenues may be too low for the camp to cover its variable costs and the owner will choose to shut down. Remember, the owner will still have to pay the fixed costs: property tax, insurance, and the costs associated with the building and land. However, if the camp is not in operation during the off-season, the owner will at least not have to pay the variable costs: salary for the camp staff, food, and electricity.

ACTIVE LEARNING EXERCISE

EVALUATING SHORT-RUN ECONOMIC LOSSES

Q: Rosa is one of many florists in a large urban area. That is, we assume that she works in a market similar to a perfectly competitive market and operates, of course, in the short run. Rosa's cost and revenue information is provided in Exhibit 6. Based on this information, what should Rosa do in the short run, and why?

A: Fixed costs are unavoidable unless the firm goes out of business. Rosa really has two decisions in the short run—either to operate or to shut down temporarily. In Exhibit 6, we see that Rosa makes $2000 a day in total revenues but her daily costs (fixed and variable) are $2500. She has to pay her workers, pay for the fresh flowers, and pay for the fuel used by the drivers in picking up and delivering the flowers. She must also pay the electricity bill to heat her shop and keep her refrigerators going to

protect her fresh flowers. That is, every day, poor Rosa is losing $500, but she still might want to operate the shop despite the loss. Why? Rosa's variable costs (flowers, transportation fuel, daily wage earners, and so on) cost her $1500 a day, and her fixed costs (insurance, property taxes, rent for the building, and refrigerator payments) are $1000 a day. Now, if Rosa does not operate, she will save on her variable costs—$1500 a day—but she will be out the $2000 a day she makes in revenues from selling her flowers. So every day she operates, she is better off than if she had not operated at all. That is, if the firm can cover variable costs, it is better off operating than not operating. Suppose Rosa's variable costs were $2100 a day. Then Rosa should not operate, because every day she does, she is $100 worse off than if she shut down altogether.

Why does Rosa even bother operating if she is making a loss? Perhaps the economy is in a recession and the demand for flowers is temporarily down, but Rosa thinks things will pick up again in the next few months. If Rosa is right and demand picks up, her prices and marginal revenue will rise and she may then have a chance to make short-run economic profits.

If Rosa cannot cover her fixed costs, will she continue to operate?

section 8.4 — Exhibit 6 — Rosa's Daily Revenue and Cost Schedule

Total Revenue	$2000
Total Costs	$2500
Variable Costs	1500
Fixed Costs	1000

per day at point b in Exhibit 5(a), so the quantity supplied for the industry is 80 000 bushels of wheat per day, point B in Exhibit 5(b). Continuing this process gives us the market supply curve for the wheat market. In a market of 1000 identical wheat farmers, the market supply curve is 1000 times the quantity supplied by each firm, as long as the price is above *AVC*.

ACTIVE LEARNING EXERCISE

REVIEWING THE SHORT-RUN OUTPUT DECISION

Exhibit 7 shows the firm's short-run output at these various market prices: P_1, P_2, P_3, and P_4.

At a market price of P_1, the firm would not cover its average variable costs—the firm would produce zero output because the firm's losses would be smaller if it shut down and stopped producing. At a market price of P_2, the firm would produce at the loss-minimizing output of q_2 units. It would operate rather than shut down because it could cover all of its average variable costs and some of its fixed costs. At a market price of P_3, the firm would produce q_3 units of output and make zero economic profits (a normal rate of return). At a market price of P_4, the firm would produce q_4 units of output and be making short-run economic profits.

section 8.4
Exhibit 7
The Short-Run Output Decision

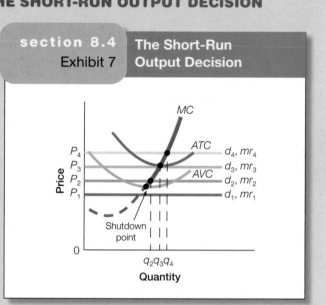

Section Check

1. The profit-maximizing output level is found by equating $MR = MC$ at q^*. If at that output the firm's price is greater than its average total costs, it is making an economic profit.
2. If at the profit-maximizing output level, q^*, the price is less than the average total cost, the firm is incurring an economic loss.
3. If at the profit-maximizing output level, q^*, the price is equal to average total cost, the firm is making zero economic profits; that is, the firm is covering both its implicit and explicit costs (making a normal rate of return).
4. If the price falls below average variable cost, the firm is better off shutting down than operating in the short run because it would incur greater losses from operating than from shutting down.

section 8.5

Long-Run Equilibrium

- If there are profits being earned in an industry, will this encourage the entry of new firms?
- Why do perfectly competitive firms make zero economic profits in the long run?

ECONOMIC PROFITS AND LOSSES DISAPPEAR IN THE LONG RUN

If farmers are able to make economic profits producing wheat, what will their response be in the long run? Farmers will increase the resources that they devote to the lucrative business of producing wheat. Suppose Farmer John is making an economic profit (he is earning an above-normal rate of return) producing wheat. To make even more profits, he may take land out of producing other crops and plant more wheat. Other farmers or people who are holding land for speculative purposes might also decide to plant wheat on their land.

As the word gets out that wheat production is proving profitable, there will be a supply response—the market supply curve will shift to the right as more firms enter the industry and existing firms expand, as in Exhibit 1(a). With this shift, the quantity of wheat supplied at any given price is greater than before. It may take a year or even longer, of course, for the complete supply response to take place, simply because it takes some time for information to spread on profit opportunities, and still more time to plant, grow, and harvest the wheat. Note that the impact of increasing supply, other things equal, is to reduce the equilibrium price of wheat. Suppose that, as a result of the supply response, the price of wheat falls from P_0 to P_1.

The impact of the change in the market price of wheat, over which John has absolutely no control, is very simple. If his costs have not changed, he will move from making a profit ($P_0 > ATC$) to zero economic profits ($P_1 = ATC$), as seen in Exhibit 1(b). In long-run equilibrium, perfectly competitive firms make zero economic profits. Remember, zero economic profits means that the firm is actually earning a normal return on the use of its capital. Zero economic profits is an equilibrium or stable situation because any positive economic (above-normal) profits signal resources into the industry, beating down prices and thus revenues to the firm. Any economic losses signal resources to leave the industry, causing market supply reductions that lead to increased prices and higher firm revenues for the remaining firms. For example, in Exhibit 2 we see a firm that

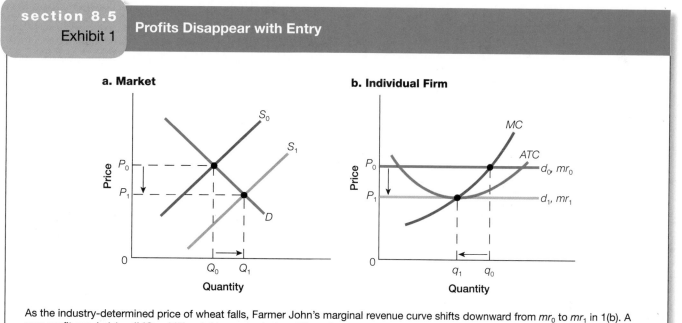

section 8.5
Exhibit 1
Profits Disappear with Entry

a. Market

b. Individual Firm

As the industry-determined price of wheat falls, Farmer John's marginal revenue curve shifts downward from mr_0 to mr_1 in 1(b). A new profit-maximizing ($MC = MR$) point is reached at q_1. When the price is P_0, Farmer John is making a profit because $P_0 > ATC$. But when the market supply increases, causing the market price to fall to P_1, Farmer John's profits disappear because $P_1 = ATC$.

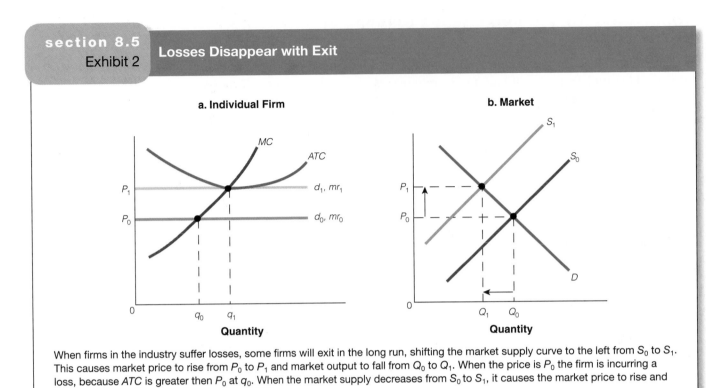

section 8.5
Exhibit 2   **Losses Disappear with Exit**

a. Individual Firm

b. Market

When firms in the industry suffer losses, some firms will exit in the long run, shifting the market supply curve to the left from S_0 to S_1. This causes market price to rise from P_0 to P_1 and market output to fall from Q_0 to Q_1. When the price is P_0 the firm is incurring a loss, because ATC is greater then P_0 at q_0. When the market supply decreases from S_0 to S_1, it causes the market price to rise and the firm's losses disappear, because $P_1 = ATC$.

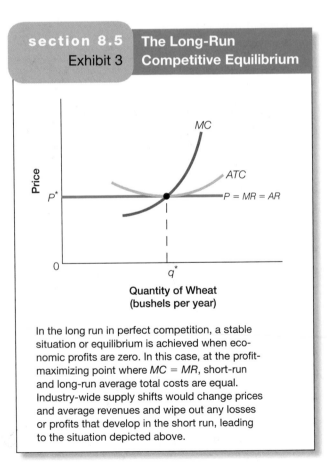

section 8.5
Exhibit 3   **The Long-Run Competitive Equilibrium**

In the long run in perfect competition, a stable situation or equilibrium is achieved when economic profits are zero. In this case, at the profit-maximizing point where $MC = MR$, short-run and long-run average total costs are equal. Industry-wide supply shifts would change prices and average revenues and wipe out any losses or profits that develop in the short run, leading to the situation depicted above.

continues to operate despite its losses—*ATC* is greater than P_0 at q_0. With losses, however, some firms will exit the industry, causing the market supply curve to shift from S_0 to S_1 and driving up the market price to P_1. This price increase reduces the losses for the firms remaining in the industry, until the losses are completely eliminated at P_1. The remaining firms will maximize profits by producing at q_1 units of output, where profits and losses are zero. Only at zero economic profits is there no tendency for firms to either enter or exit the industry.

THE LONG-RUN EQUILIBRIUM FOR THE COMPETITIVE FIRM

The long-run competitive equilibrium for a perfectly competitive firm is graphically illustrated in Exhibit 3. At the equilibrium point (where $MC = MR$), short-run and long-run average total costs are also equal. The average total cost curves touch the marginal cost and marginal revenue (demand)' curves at the equilibrium output point. Because the marginal revenue curve is also the average revenue curve, average revenues and average total costs are equal at the equilibrium point. The long-run equilibrium in perfect competition depicted in Exhibit 3 has an interesting feature. Note that the equilibrium output occurs at the lowest point on the average total cost curve. As you may recall, this occurs because the marginal cost curve must intersect the average total cost curve at the latter curve's lowest point. Hence, the equilibrium condition in the long run in perfect competition is for firms to produce at that output that minimizes average total costs—that is, the firm is operating at its minimum efficient scale. At this long-run equilibrium, all firms in the industry are earning zero economic profit; consequently, new firms have no incentive to enter the market, and existing firms have no incentive to exit the market.

Section Check

SECTION CHECK

1. Economic profits will encourage entry of new firms, which will shift the market supply curve to the right.
2. Any positive economic profits signal resources into the industry, driving down prices and revenues to the firm.
3. Any economic losses signal resources to leave the industry, leading to supply reduction, higher prices, and increased revenues.
4. Only at zero economic profits is there no tendency for firms to either enter or exit the industry.

Long-Run Supply

- What are constant-cost industries?
- What are increasing-cost industries?

The preceding sections have considered the costs of an individual, perfectly competitive firm as it varies output, on the assumption that the prices paid for inputs (costs) are given. However, when the output of an entire industry changes, the likelihood is greater of changes occurring in costs. But how will the changes in the number of firms in an industry affect the input costs of individual firms? In this section we develop the long-run supply curve (*LRS*). As we will see, the shape of the long-run supply curve depends on the extent to which input costs change when there is entry or exit of firms in the industry. We will look at two possible types of industries when considering long-run supply: constant-cost industries and increasing-cost industries.

A CONSTANT-COST INDUSTRY

In a **constant-cost industry,** the prices of inputs do not change as output is expanded. The industry may not use inputs in sufficient quantities to affect input prices. For example, say the firms in the industry use a lot of unskilled labour but the industry is small. So, as output expands, the increase in demand for unskilled labour will not cause the market wage for unskilled labour to rise. Similarly, suppose a paper-clip maker decides to double its output. It is highly unlikely that its demand for steel will have an impact on steel prices because its demand for the input is so small.

Once long-run adjustments are complete, by necessity each firm operates at the point of lowest long-run average total costs because supply shifts with entry and exit, eliminating

constant-cost industry
an industry where input prices (and cost curves) do not change as industry output changes

profits. Therefore, each firm supplies the market the quantity of output that it can produce at the lowest possible long-run average total cost.

In Exhibit 1, we can see the impact of an unexpected increase in market demand. Suppose that recent reports show that blueberries can lower cholesterol, lower blood pressure, and significantly reduce the risk of all cancers. The increase in market demand for blueberries leads to a price increase from P_0 to P_1 as the firm increases output from q_0 to q_1, and blueberry industry output increases from Q_0 to Q_1, as seen in Exhibit 1(b). The increase in market demand generates a higher price and positive profits for existing firms in the short run. The existence of economic profits will attract new firms into the industry, causing the short-run supply curve to shift from S_0 to S_1 and lowering price until excess profits are zero. This shift results in a new equilibrium, point C in Exhibit 1(c). Because the industry is one of constant costs, industry expansion does not alter firms' cost curves, and the industry long-run supply curve is horizontal. That is, the long-run equilibrium price is at the same level that prevailed before demand increased; the only long-run effect of the increase in demand is an increase in industry output, as more firms enter that are just like existing firms as Exhibit 1(c) indicates. However, the long-run supply curve does not have to be horizontal.

AN INCREASING-COST INDUSTRY

increasing-cost industry
an industry where input prices rise (and cost curves rise) as industry output rises

In the **increasing-cost industry,** a more likely scenario, the cost curves of the individual firms rise as the total output of the industry increases. Increases in input prices (upward shifts in cost curves) occur as larger quantities of factors are employed in the industry. When an industry utilizes a large portion of an input whose total supply is not huge, input prices will rise when the industry uses more of the input.

Increasing cost conditions are typical of "extractive" industries, such as agriculture, fishing, mining, and lumbering, which utilize large portions of the total supply of specialized natural resources such as land or mineral deposits. As the output of such an industry expands, the increased demand for the resources raises the prices that must be paid for their use. Because additional resources of given quality cannot be produced, greater supplies can be obtained (if at all) only by luring them away from other industries, or by using lower-quality (and less-productive, thus higher-cost) resources.

Wheat production is a typical example of an increasing-cost industry. As the output of wheat increases, the demand for land suitable for the production of wheat rises, and thus the price paid for the use of land of any given quality increases.

If there were a construction boom in a fully employed economy, would it be more costly to get additional resources like workers and raw materials? Yes, if this is an increasing-cost industry, the industry can only produce more output if it gets a higher price because the firm's costs of production rise as output expands. As new firms enter and output expands, the increase in demand for inputs causes the price of inputs to rise—the cost curves of all construction firms shift upward as the industry expands. The industry can produce more output but only at a higher price, enough to compensate the firm for the higher input costs. In an increasing-cost industry, the long-run supply curve is upward sloping.

Whether the industry is one of constant cost or increasing cost, the basic point is the same. The long-run supply is usually more elastic than the short-run supply because in the long run, firms can enter and exit the industry.

PERFECT COMPETITION AND ECONOMIC EFFICIENCY

We say that the output that results from equilibrium conditions of market demand and market supply in perfectly competitive markets is *economically efficient*. Only at this outcome can maximum output be obtained from our scarce resources.

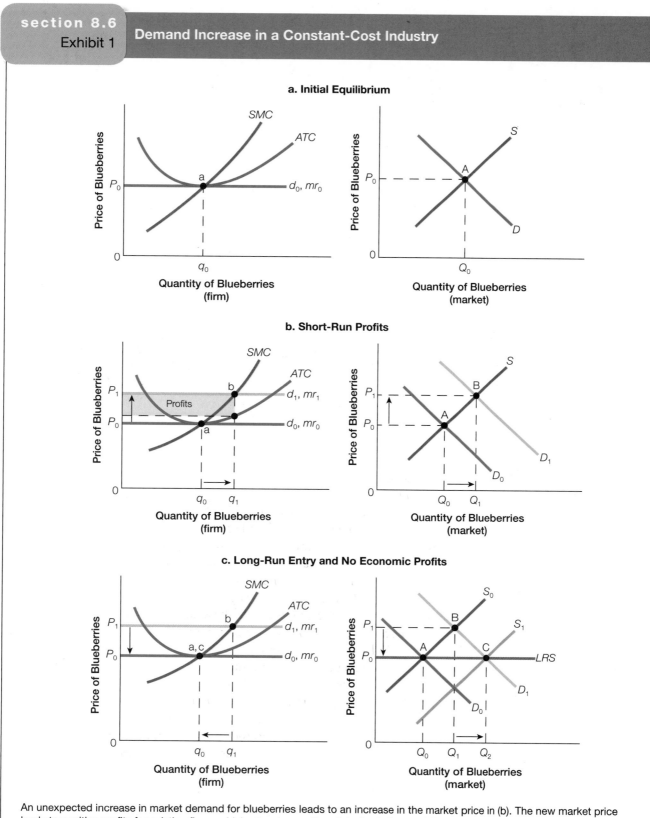

section 8.6
Exhibit 1

Demand Increase in a Constant-Cost Industry

a. Initial Equilibrium

b. Short-Run Profits

c. Long-Run Entry and No Economic Profits

An unexpected increase in market demand for blueberries leads to an increase in the market price in (b). The new market price leads to positive profits for existing firms, which attracts new firms into the industry, shifting market supply from S_0 to S_1 in (c). This increased short-run industry supply curve intersects D_1 at point C. Each firm (of a new larger number of firms) is again producing at q_0 and earning zero economic profit.

Allocative Efficiency and Perfect Competition

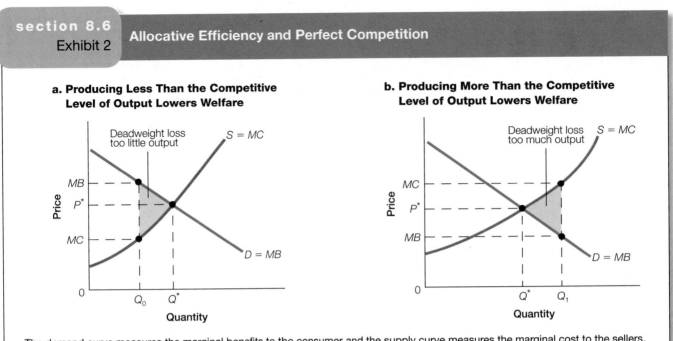

a. Producing Less Than the Competitive Level of Output Lowers Welfare

b. Producing More Than the Competitive Level of Output Lowers Welfare

The demand curve measures the marginal benefits to the consumer and the supply curve measures the marginal cost to the sellers. At P^* and Q^*, resources are being allocated efficiently—the marginal benefits of those resources are equal to the marginal cost of those resources. At this point the sum of consumer and producer surplus is maximized. If Q_0 is produced, then the marginal benefits from producing additional units are greater than the marginal costs. Society gains from expanding output up to the point where $MB = MC$ at Q^*. If output is expanded beyond Q^*, $MC > MB$, society gains from a reduction in output, back to Q^*.

At the intersection of market supply and market demand we find the competitive equilibrium price, P^*, and the competive equilibrium output, Q^*. In competitive markets, market supply equals market demand and $P = MC$. When $P = MC$, buyers value the last unit of output by the same amount that it cost sellers to produce it. If buyers value the last unit by more than the marginal cost of production, resources are not being allocated efficiently, like at Q_0 in Exhibit 2(a). Think of the demand curve as the marginal benefit curve ($D = MB$) and the supply curve as the marginal cost curve ($S = MC$). According to the rule of rational choice, we should pursue an activity as long as the expected marginal benefits are greater than the expected marginal costs. For example in Exhibit 2(a), if Q_0 is produced, then the marginal benefits from producing additional units are greater than the marginal costs. The shaded area is deadweight loss. That is, at Q_0, resources are not being allocated efficiently, and output should be expanded.

We can also produce too much output. For example, if output is expanded beyond Q^* in Exhibit 2(b) the cost to sellers for producing the good is greater than the marginal benefits to consumers. The shaded area is deadweight loss. Society would gain from a reduction in output back to Q^*. Once the competitive equilibrium is reached, the buyers' marginal benefit equals the sellers' marginal cost.

In The **NEWS**

INTERNET CUTS COSTS AND INCREASES COMPETITION

The Internet makes it easier for buyers and sellers to compare prices. It cuts out the middlemen between firms and customers. It reduces transaction costs. And it reduces barriers to entry. To understand this, go back to Ronald Coase, [a U.S.] economist, who argued in 1937 that the main reason why firms exist (as opposed to individuals acting as buyers and sellers at every stage of production) is to minimize transaction costs. Since the Internet reduces such costs, it also reduces the optimal size of firms. Small firms can buy in services from outside more cheaply. Thus, in overall terms, barriers to entry will fall.

In these ways, then, the Internet cuts costs, increases competition, and improves the functioning of the price mechanism. It thus moves the economy closer to the textbook model of perfect competition, which assumes abundant information, zero transaction costs, and no barriers to entry. The Internet makes this assumption less far-fetched. By improving the flow of information between buyers and sellers, it makes markets more efficient, and so ensures that resources are allocated to their most productive use. The most important effect of the "new" economy, indeed, may be to make the "old" economy more efficient.

It is hard to test this conclusion, but some studies seem to support it. Prices of goods bought online, such as books and CDs, are, on average, about 10 percent cheaper (after including taxes and delivery) than in conventional shops, though the non-existent profits of many electronic retailers make this evidence inconclusive. Competition from the Internet is also forcing traditional retailers to reduce prices. The Internet offers even clearer savings in services

such as banking. According to Lehman Brothers [a global financial-services firm prior to its bankruptcy and sale in 2008], a transfer between bank accounts costs [US] $1.27 if done by a bank teller, 27 cents via a cash machine, and only one cent over the Internet.

The biggest economic impact of the Internet is likely to come from business-to-business (B2B) e-commerce. GartnerGroup forecasts that global B2B turnover could reach [US] $4 trillion in America in 2003, compared with less than [US] $400 billion of online sales to consumers.

B2B e-commerce cuts companies' costs in three ways. First, it reduces procurement costs, making it easier to find the cheapest supplier and cutting the cost of processing transactions. Second, it allows better supply-chain management. And third, it makes possible tighter inventory control, so that firms can reduce their stocks or even eliminate them. Through these three channels B2B e-commerce reduces firms' production costs, by increasing efficiency or by squeezing suppliers' profit margins.

SOURCE: WASHINGTON POST by Daniel McFadden. Copyright 2001 by Washington Post Writers Group. Reproduced with permission of Washington Post Writers Group in the format Textbook via Copyright Clearance Center.

CONSIDER THIS:

The Internet cuts costs. This will cause a fall in a firm's marginal and average total costs, as well as an increase in market or industry supply. The result will be lower prices for affected goods and services.

Section Check

1. In constant-cost industries, the cost curves of the firm are not affected by changes in the output of the entire industry. Such industries must be very small demanders of resources in the market.
2. In an increasing-cost industry, the cost curves of the individual firms rise as total output increases. This case is the most typical.

Summary

Section 8.1

■ There are four main market structures: perfect competition, monopoly, monopolistic competition, and oligopoly.

■ The characteristics of a perfectly competitive market are: many buyers and sellers, an identical (homogeneous) product, and easy market entry and exit.

Section 8.2

■ Perfectly competitive firms are price takers, selling at the market-determined price.

■ Demand, for the individual firm, is perfectly elastic (individual firm's demand curve is horizontal).

■ The position of the individual firm's demand curve varies directly with the market price.

Section 8.3

■ The short-run profit-maximizing output level, q^*, is found by equating $MR = MC$.

Section 8.4

■ If at the profit-maximizing output level, q^*, the firm's price is greater than its average total costs, it is making an economic profit.

■ If at the profit-maximizing output level, q^*, the price is less than the average total cost, the firm is incurring an economic loss.

■ If at the profit-maximizing output level, q^*, the price is equal to average total cost, the firm is making zero economic profits.

■ A firm making zero economic profits is covering both its implicit and explicit costs (making a normal rate of return).

■ If the price falls below average variable cost, the firm is better off shutting down than operating in the short run.

Section 8.5

■ Positive economic profits will encourage entry of new firms, which will shift the market supply curve to the right, driving down prices and revenues to the firm.

■ Economic losses signal resources to leave the industry, leading to supply reduction, higher prices, and increased revenues.

■ Only at zero economic profits is there no tendency for firms to either enter or exit the industry.

■ Long-run competitive equilibrium occurs where there are no economic profits and therefore no incentive to enter or exit the industry.

Section 8.6

■ In constant-cost industries, the cost curves of the firm are not affected by changes in the output of the entire industry.

■ In an increasing-cost industry, the cost curves of the individual firms rise as total output increases.

Key Terms and Concepts

For a complete glossary of chapter key terms, visit the textbook's Web site at http://www.sextonmicro2e.nelson.com.

perfect competition 197
price taker 198
total revenue (*TR*) 202
average revenue (*AR*) 202

marginal revenue (*MR*) 202
profit-maximizing output rule 204
short-run supply curve 207
short-run market supply curve 208

constant-cost industry 213
increasing-cost industry 214

Review Questions

1. Which of the following are most likely to be perfectly competitive?

   a. the fishing industry

   b. the fast-food industry

   c. the computer software industry

   d. the Toronto Stock Exchange

   e. the clothing industry

2. Illustrate the *SRATC, AVC, SRMC,* and *MR* curves for a perfectly competitive firm that is operating at a loss. What is the output level that minimizes losses? Why is it more profitable to continue producing in the short run rather than to shut down?

3.

Output	Total Cost	Total Revenue
0	30	0
1	45	25
2	65	50
3	90	75
4	120	100
5	155	125

   Given the data above, determine *AR, MR, P,* and the short-run profit-maximizing (loss-minimizing) level of output.

4. Explain why the following conditions are typical under perfect competition in the long run.

   a. $P = MC$

   b. $P = $ minimum ATC

5. Graph and explain the adjustments to long-run equilibrium when there is a decrease in market demand in a constant-cost industry.

6. Evaluate the following statements. Determine whether each is true or false and explain your answer.

   a. If economic profits are zero, firms will exit the industry in the long run.

   b. A firm cannot maximize profits without minimizing costs.

   c. If a firm is minimizing costs, it must be maximizing profits.

7. What is meant by the term *perfect competition?* Is it possible for a situation that does not conform to the assumptions of perfect competition to still be described by the perfectly competitive price theory? Discuss.

8. Discuss the following questions.

   a. Why must price cover *AVC* if firms are to continue to operate?

   b. If firms are covering *AVC* but not all of their fixed costs, will they continue to operate in the short run? Why or why not?

   c. Why is it possible for price to remain above average total cost in the short run but not the long run?

9. Say that there is a large number of small producers in an industry but very large barriers to entry to new firms. After a large, permanent increase in industry demand, would producers in the industry again earn zero economic profits in long-run equilibrium?

10. What would happen to the equilibrium output if there was a specific tax on a competitive firm? Graph the curve. What happens to the marginal cost curve? the average total cost curve?

Fill in the Blanks

Section 8.1

1. Economists have identified four different market structures in which firms operate: _____, _____, _____, and _____.

2. Perfect competition is a market structure involving a _____ number of buyers and sellers, a _____ product, and _____ market entry and exit.

3. Perfectly competitive firms are _____, who must accept the market price as determined by the forces of demand and supply.

4. In _____, there is a single seller who sets the price that will maximize the seller's profits.

5. In monopolistic competition, there is an element of monopoly power because each firm's product is _____ from that of other competitors, but because there are _____ competitors, it also has an element of competition.

6. In oligopoly, _____ firms, as opposed to one firm or many, produce similar or identical goods.

7. Because perfectly competitive markets have _____ buyers and sellers, each firm is so _____ in relation to the industry that its production decisions have no impact on the market.

8. Because consumers believe that all firms in a perfectly competitive market sell _____ products, the products of all the firms are perfect substitutes.

Section 8.2

9. In a perfectly competitive industry each producer provides such a _____ fraction of the total supply that a change in the amount he or she offers does not have a noticeable effect on the market price.

10. Since perfectly competitive sellers can sell all they want at the market price, their demand curve is _____ at the market price over the _____ range of output that they could possibly produce.

Section 8.3

11. The objective of a firm is to maximize profits by producing the amount that maximizes the difference between its _____ and _____.

12. Total revenue for a perfectly competitive firm equals the _____ times the _____.

13. _____ equals total revenue divided by the number of units of the product sold.

14. _____ is the additional revenue derived from the sale of one more unit of the good.

15. In perfect competition, we know that _____ and price are equal.

16. There are two methods for identifying a firm's profit-maximizing output: the _____ approach and the _____ approach.

17. In all types of market environments, firms will maximize profits at the output that maximizes the difference between _____ and _____, which is the same output level where _____ equals _____.

Section 8.4

18. At the level of output chosen by a competitive firm, total cost equals _____ times quantity, whereas total revenue equals _____ times quantity.

19. If total revenue is greater than total costs at its profit-maximizing output level, a firm is generating _____. If total revenue is less than total costs, the firm is generating _____. If total revenue equals total cost, the firm is earning _____.

20. If a firm cannot generate enough revenues to cover its _____ costs, then it will have larger losses if it operates than if it shuts down in the short run.

21. The loss a firm would bear if it shut down would be equal to _____.

22. When price is less than _____ but more than _____, a firm produces in the short run, but at a loss.

23. The short-run supply curve of an individual competitive seller is identical with that portion of the _____ curve that lies above the minimum of the _____ curve.

24. The short-run market supply curve is the horizontal summation of the individual firms' supply curves, providing that _____ are not affected by increased production of existing firms.

Section 8.5

25. If perfectly competitive producers are currently making economic profits, the market supply curve will shift to the right over time as more firms _____ and existing firms _____.

26. As entry into the profitable industry pushes down the market price, producers will move from a situation where price _____ average total cost to one where price _____ average total cost.

27. Only at _____ is there no tendency for firms either to enter or leave the business.

28. The long-run equilibrium output in perfect competition occurs at the lowest point on the average total cost curve, so the equilibrium condition in the long run in perfect competition is for firms to produce at the output that minimizes _____.

Section 8.6

29. The shape of the long-run supply curve depends on the extent to which _____ change when there is entry or exit of firms in the industry.

30. In a constant-cost industry, the prices of inputs _____ as output is expanded.

31. In an increasing-cost industry, the cost curves of the individual firms _____ as the total output of the industry increases.

32. The output that results from equilibrium conditions of market demand and market supply in perfectly competitive markets is economically _____.

True or False

Section 8.1

1. In practice, it is sometimes difficult to decide precisely which market structure a given firm or industry most appropriately fits.

2. In perfect competition, no single firm produces more than an extremely small proportion of output, so no firm can influence the market price.

3. At the other end of the continuum of market environments from perfect competition is pure monopoly, where there is a single seller.

4. Despite each firm's product being differentiated at least slightly from that of other competitors in monopolistic competition, none has any monopoly power.

5. Unlike monopoly, oligopoly allows for some competition between firms; unlike competition, firms in oligopolistic environments have a significant share of the total market for the good being produced.

6. As in the other market structures, an oligopolist is very conscious of the actions of competing firms.

7. Unlike a perfectly competitive firm, an oligopolist has some control over price and thus is a price-setter.

8. A perfectly competitive market is approximated most closely in markets for agricultural commodities.

Section 8.2

9. A perfectly competitive firm cannot sell at any figure higher than the current market price and would not knowingly charge a lower price because the firm could sell all it wants at the market price.

10. In a perfectly competitive market, individual sellers can change their output and it will not alter the market price.

11. In a perfectly competitive industry, the market demand curve is perfectly elastic at the market price.

12. Because perfectly competitive firms are price takers, each firm's demand curve remains unchanged even when the market price changes.

13. The perfectly competitive model does not assume any knowledge on the part of individual buyers and sellers about market demand and supply—they only have to know the price of the good they sell.

Section 8.3

14. In a perfectly competitive market, marginal revenue is constant and equal to the market price.

15. For a perfectly competitive firm, as long as the price derived from expanded output exceeds the marginal cost of that output, the expansion of output creates additional profits.

Section 8.4

16. Producing at the profit-maximizing output level means that a firm is actually earning economic profits.

17. A competitive firm earning zero economic profit will be unable to continue in operation over time.

18. A firm will not produce at all unless the price is greater than its average variable costs.

19. A perfectly competitive firm will operate in the short run only at price levels greater than or equal to average total costs.

20. The *MC* curve above minimum *AVC* shows the marginal cost of producing any given output, as well as the equilibrium output that the firm will supply at various prices in the short run.

21. Because the short run is too brief for new firms to enter the market, the market supply curve is the vertical summation of the supply curves of existing firms.

Section 8.5

22. As new firms enter an industry where sellers are earning economic profits, the result will include a reduction in the equilibrium price.

23. In long-run equilibrium, perfectly competitive firms make zero economic profits, earning a normal return on the use of their capital.

24. For a perfectly competitive firm, the long-run equilibrium will be the point at which price equals marginal cost as well as short-run average total cost and long-run average cost.

Section 8.6

25. In a constant-cost industry, the industry does not use inputs in sufficient quantities to affect input prices.

26. In a constant-cost competitive industry, industry expansion does not alter a firm's cost curves, and the industry long-run supply curve is upward sloping.

27. In a constant-cost competitive industry, the only long-run effect of an increase in demand is an increase in industry output.

28. When an industry utilizes a large portion of an input, input prices will rise when the industry uses more of that input as it expands output, which will shift firms' cost curves upward.

Multiple Choice

Section 8.1

1. Which market structure has the largest number of firms?
   a. perfect competition
   b. monopolistic competition
   c. oligopoly
   d. monopoly

2. Which of the following is *false?*
   a. Monopolistically competitive firms produce differentiated products.
   b. Oligopolistic firms produce a substantial fraction of the output of their industry.
   c. A monopoly is the single seller of a product without a close substitute.
   d. Only a perfectly competitive firm has no power to influence the market price for its product.
   e. All of the above are *true.*

3. Which of the following is *false* about perfect competition?
   a. Perfectly competitive firms sell homogeneous products.
   b. There is easy entry into, and exit from, a perfectly competitive industry.
   c. A perfectly competitive firm must take the market price as given.
   d. A perfectly competitive firm produces a substantial fraction of the industry output.
   e. All of the above are *true.*

Section 8.2

4. An individual perfectly competitive firm
   a. may increase its price without losing sales.
   b. is a price setter.
   c. has no perceptible influence on the market price.
   d. sells a product that is differentiated from those of its competitors.

5. When will a perfectly competitive firm's demand curve shift?
   a. never
   b. when the market demand curve shifts
   c. when new producers enter the industry in large numbers
   d. when either b or c occurs

6. In a market with perfectly competitive firms, the market demand curve is
   _____ and the demand curve facing each individual firm is _____.
   a. upward sloping; horizontal
   b. downward sloping; horizontal
   c. horizontal; downward sloping
   d. horizontal; upward sloping
   e. horizontal; horizontal

Section 8.3

7. The marginal revenue of a perfectly competitive firm
   a. decreases as output increases.
   b. increases as output increases.
   c. is constant as output increases and equal to price.
   d. increases as output increases and is equal to price.

8. A perfectly competitive firm seeking to maximize its profits would want to
   maximize the difference between
   a. its marginal revenue and its marginal cost.
   b. its average revenue and its average cost.
   c. its total revenue and its total cost.
   d. its price and its marginal cost.
   e. either a or d.

9. If a perfectly competitive firm's marginal revenue exceeded its marginal cost,
   a. it would cut its price in order to sell more output and increase its profits.
   b. it would expand its output but not cut its price in order to increase its profits.
   c. it is currently earning economic profits.
   d. both a and c are true.
   e. both b and c are true.

10. A perfectly competitive firm maximizes its profit at an output in which
   a. total revenue exceeds total cost by the greatest dollar amount.
   b. marginal cost equals the price.
   c. marginal cost equals marginal revenue.
   d. all of the above are true.

Section 8.4

11. The minimum price at which a firm would produce in the short run is the point at
   which
   a. price equals the minimum point on its marginal cost curve.
   b. price equals the minimum point on its average variable cost curve.
   c. price equals the minimum point on its average total cost curve.
   d. price equals the minimum point on its average fixed cost curve.

12. If a perfectly competitive firm finds that price is greater than *AVC* but less than *ATC* at the quantity where its marginal cost equals the market price,

    a. the firm will produce in the short run but may eventually go out of business.

    b. the firm will produce in the short run, and new entrants would tend to enter the industry over time.

    c. the firm will immediately shut down.

    d. the firm will be earning economic profits.

    e. both b and d are true.

Use the following diagram to answer questions 13–16.

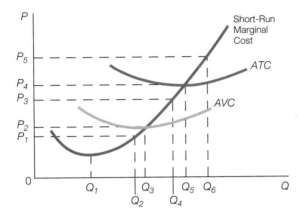

13. When the market price equals P_1, the firm should produce output

    a. Q_1.

    b. Q_2.

    c. Q_3.

    d. Q_4.

    e. none of the above

14. When the market price equals P_3, the firm should produce output

    a. Q_3, operating at a loss.

    b. Q_4, operating at a loss.

    c. Q_4, earning an economic profit.

    d. Q_5, operating at a loss.

    e. Q_5, earning a normal profit.

15. When the market price equals P_4, the firm should produce output

    a. Q_4, operating at a loss.

    b. Q_4, earning an economic profit.

    c. Q_5, operating at a loss.

    d. Q_5, earning a normal profit.

    e. Q_5, earning a positive economic profit.

16. When the market price equals P_5, the firm should produce output

    a. Q_5, operating at a loss.

    b. Q_5, earning an economic profit.

    c. Q_6, operating at a loss.

    d. Q_6, earning a normal profit.

    e. Q_6, earning a positive economic profit.

17. The short-run supply curve of a perfectly competitive firm is
    a. its *MC* curve.
    b. its *MC* curve above the minimum point of *AVC*.
    c. its *MC* curve above the minimum point of *ATC*.
    d. none of the above.

18. Darlene runs a fruit-and-vegetable stand in a medium-sized community where there are many such stands. Her weekly total revenue equals $3000. Her weekly total cost of running the stand equals $3500, consisting of $2500 of variable costs and $1000 of fixed costs. An economist would likely advise Darlene to
    a. shut down as quickly as possible in order to minimize her losses.
    b. keep the stand open because it is generating an economic profit.
    c. keep the stand open for a while longer because she is covering all of her variable costs and some of her fixed costs.
    d. keep the stand open for a while longer because she is covering all of her fixed costs and some of her variable costs.

Section 8.5

19. The entry of new firms into an industry will very likely
    a. shift the industry supply curve to the right.
    b. cause the market price to fall.
    c. reduce the profits of existing firms in the industry.
    d. do all of the above.

20. Which of the following statements concerning equilibrium in the long run is incorrect?
    a. Firms will exit the industry if economic profits equal zero.
    b. Firms are able to vary their plant sizes in the long run.
    c. Economic profits are eliminated as new firms enter the industry.
    d. The market price equals both marginal cost and average total cost.

21. In long-run equilibrium under perfect competition, price does not equal which of the following?
    a. long-run marginal cost
    b. minimum average total cost
    c. average fixed cost
    d. marginal revenue
    e. average revenue

Section 8.6

22. If the domino-making industry is a constant-cost industry, one would expect the long-run result of an increase in demand for dominoes to include
    a. a greater number of firms and a higher price.
    b. a greater number of firms and the same price.
    c. the same number of firms and a higher price.
    d. the same number of firms and the same price.

23. In an increasing-cost industry, an unexpected increase in demand would lead to what result in the long run?
    a. higher costs and a higher price
    b. higher costs and a lower price
    c. no change in costs or prices
    d. impossible to determine from the information given

24. If input prices rise as industry output expands, then a perfectly competitive firm's marginal cost and average cost curves will

  a. shift upward.

  b. shift downward.

  c. not shift. As the firm increases production, however, costs increase as the firm moves upward to the right along these curves.

  d. not shift. As the firm increases production, however, costs decrease as the firm moves downward to the left along these curves.

Problems

1. [Section 8.2]

Use the diagram below to answer a, b, and c.

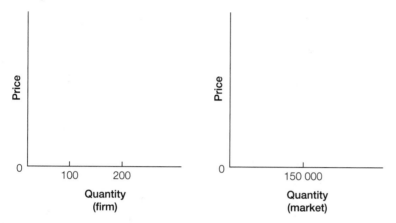

  a. Illustrate the relationship between a perfectly competitive firm's demand curve and the market supply and demand curve.

  b. Illustrate the effects of an increase in market demand on a perfectly competitive firm's demand curve.

  c. Illustrate the effects of a decrease in market demand on a perfectly competitive firm's demand curve.

2. [Section 8.3]

Complete the following table for a perfectly competitive firm, and indicate its profit-maximizing output.

Quantity	Price	Total Revenue	Marginal Revenue	Total Cost	Marginal Cost	Total Profit
6	10			30	3	30
7				35		
8				42		
9				51		
10				62		
11				75		
12				90		

3. [Sections 8.3 and 8.4]

Use the following diagram to answer a–d.

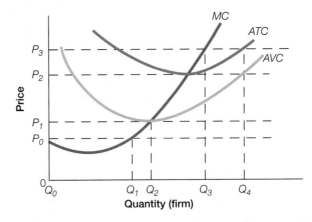

a. How much would a perfectly competitive firm produce at each of the indicated prices?

b. At which prices is the firm earning economic profits? zero economic profits? negative economic profits?

c. At which prices would the firm shut down?

d. Indicate what this firm's supply curve would be.

4. [Section 8.5]

Describe what would happen in the long run to the industry supply curve and the economic profits of the firms in a competitive industry if those firms are currently earning economic profits. What if they are currently earning economic losses?

5. [Section 8.6]

Use the following diagrams to answer a and b.

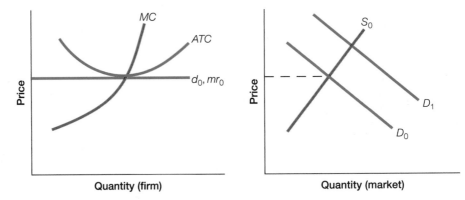

a. Show the effect of the increase in demand on the industry and on the perfectly competitive firm's price, marginal revenue, output, and profits in the short run.

b. Show the long-run effects of the increase in demand for the industry, and the effects on a perfectly competitive firm's price, marginal revenue, output, and profits for a constant-cost industry.

chapter

9

Monopoly

Monopoly: The Price Maker

- What is a monopoly?
- Why is pure monopoly rare?
- What are the sources of monopoly power?
- What is a natural monopoly?

WHAT IS A MONOPOLY?

A true or pure **monopoly** exists where there is only one seller of a product for which no close substitute is available and there are natural or legal barriers to entry that prevent competition. In a monopoly, the firm and "the industry" are one and the same. Consequently, the firm sets the price of the good because the firm faces the industry demand curve and can pick the most profitable point on that demand curve. Monopolists are price makers (rather than price takers) who try to pick the price that will maximize their profits.

monopoly
a market with only one supplier of a product that has no close substitute and there are natural and legal barriers to entry that prevent competition

PURE MONOPOLY IS A RARITY

Few goods and services truly have only one producer. One might think of a small community with a single bank, a single newspaper, or even a single grocery store. Even in these situations, however, most people can bank out of town, use a substitute financial institution, buy out-of-town newspapers or read them on the Web, go to a nearby town to buy groceries, and so on. Near-monopoly conditions exist, but absolute total monopoly is rather unusual.

One area where there is typically only one producer of goods and services within a market area is public utilities. In any given market, usually only one company provides natural gas or supplies water. Moreover, governments themselves provide many services for which they are often the sole providers—sewer services, fire and police protection, and military protection. Most of these situations resemble a pure monopoly. Again, however, for most of the above cited goods and services, substitute goods and services are available. People heating their home with natural gas can switch to electric heat (or vice versa). In some areas, one can even substitute home-collected rainwater or well water for that provided by the local water company.

Although the purist might correctly deny the existence of monopoly, the situations where monopoly conditions are closely approximated are numerous enough to make the study of monopoly more than a theoretical abstraction; moreover, the study of monopoly is useful in clarifying certain desirable aspects of perfect competition.

BARRIERS TO ENTRY

There are several ways that a monopolist may make it virtually impossible for other firms to overcome barriers to entry. For example, a monopolist might prevent potential rivals from entering the market through legal barriers, through economies of scale, or by controlling important inputs.

Legal Barriers

natural monopoly

a firm that can produce at a lower cost than a number of smaller firms could

In the case of legal barriers, the government might franchise only one firm to operate an industry, as is the case for postal services in most countries. The government can also provide licensing designed to ensure a certain level of quality and competence. Many industries require government licensing, such as medical doctors, nurses, electricians, and plumbers.

Also, the government could give a company a patent to encourage inventive activity. It can cost millions of dollars to develop a new drug or a computer chip and without a patent to recoup some of these costs, there would certainly be less inventive activity. As long as the patent is in effect the company has the potential to enjoy monopoly profits for many years. After all, why would a firm engage in costly research if any company could free ride off its discovery and produce and sell the new drug or computer chip?

Economies of Scale

The situation in which one large firm can provide the output of the market at a lower cost than two or more smaller firms is called a **natural monopoly.** With a natural monopoly, it is more efficient to have one firm produce the good. The reason for the cost advantage is economies of scale; that is, *ATC* falls as output expands throughout the relevant output range, as seen in Exhibit 1. Public utilities, such as water, natural gas, and

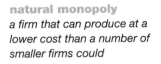

section 9.1
Exhibit 1   **Economies of Scale**

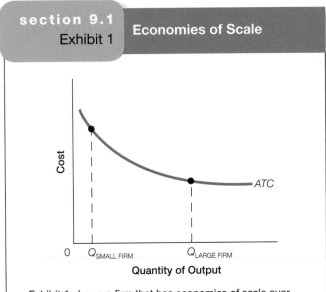

Exhibit 1 shows a firm that has economies of scale over the relevant range of output with declining average total costs. If one firm can produce the total output at a lower cost than several small firms, it is called a natural monopoly.

electricity, are examples of natural monopoly. It is less costly for one firm to lay down pipes and distribute water than for a number of firms to lay down a maze of competing pipes. That is, a single firm can supply water more efficiently than a large number of competing firms.

Control Over an Important Input

Another barrier to entry could occur if a firm had control over an important input. For example, from the late nineteenth century to the early 1940s, the Aluminum Company of America (Alcoa) had a monopoly in the production of aluminum in the United States. Its monopoly power was guaranteed because of its control over an important ingredient in the production of aluminum—bauxite. Similarly, the DeBeers company of South Africa has monopoly power because it controls roughly 75 percent of the world's output of diamonds.

Section Check

1. A pure monopoly exists where there is only one seller of a product for which no close substitute is available.
2. Pure monopolies are rare because there are few goods and services where only one producer exists.
3. Sources of monopoly power include legal barriers, economies of scale, and the control over important inputs.
4. A natural monopoly occurs when one firm can provide the good or service at a lower cost than two or more smaller firms.

Demand and Marginal Revenue in Monopoly

- How does the demand curve for a monopolist differ from that of a perfectly competitive firm?
- Why is marginal revenue less than price in monopoly?

In monopoly, the market demand curve may be regarded as the demand curve for the firm's product because the monopoly firm *is* the market for that particular product. The demand curve indicates the quantities that the firm can sell at various possible prices. In monopoly, the price for the firm's product declines as additional units are placed on the market—the demand curve is downward sloping. In monopoly, the firm cannot set both its price and the quantity it sells. That is, a monopolist would love to sell a larger quantity at a high price, but it can't. If the monopolist reduces output, the price will rise; if the monopolist expands output, the price will fall.

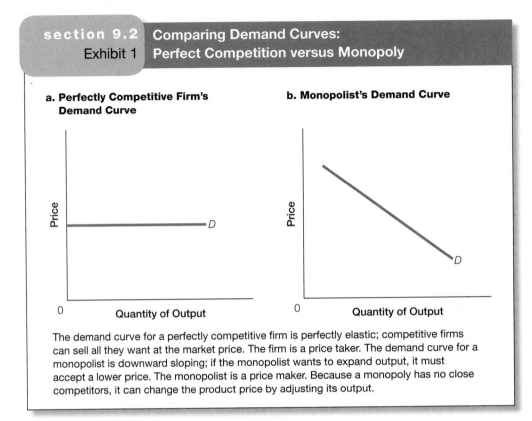

section 9.2
Exhibit 1

Comparing Demand Curves:
Perfect Competition versus Monopoly

a. Perfectly Competitive Firm's
Demand Curve

Price

Quantity of Output

0

D

b. Monopolist's Demand Curve

Price

Quantity of Output

0

D

The demand curve for a perfectly competitive firm is perfectly elastic; competitive firms
can sell all they want at the market price. The firm is a price taker. The demand curve for a
monopolist is downward sloping; if the monopolist wants to expand output, it must
accept a lower price. The monopolist is a price maker. Because a monopoly has no close
competitors, it can change the product price by adjusting its output.

Recall that in perfect competition, because there are many buyers and sellers of homogeneous goods (resulting in a perfectly elastic demand curve for the firm), competitive firms can sell all they want at the market price. They face a horizontal demand curve. The firm takes the price of its output as determined by the market forces of supply and demand. Monopolists, on the other hand, face a downward-sloping demand curve and if the monopolist wants to expand output, it must accept a lower price. The two demand curves are displayed side by side in Exhibit 1.

In Exhibit 2, we see the price of the good, the quantity of the good, the *total revenue* ($TR = P \times Q$), and the *average revenue,* the amount of revenue the firm receives per unit sold ($AR = TR/Q$). The average revenue is just the price per unit sold. We are also given the *marginal revenue*—the amount of revenue the firm receives from selling an additional unit ($MR = \Delta TR/\Delta Q$).

In Exhibit 3, we see that the marginal revenue curve for a monopolist lies below the demand curve. Why is this the case? Suppose the firm initially sets its price at $5. It only sells one unit a day and its total revenue is $5. To increase sales it decides to drop the price to $4. Sales increase to two units a day and total revenue increases to $8. The firm's marginal revenue is only $3. Why? When the firm cuts the price in order to induce the second customer to buy, it now receives only $4 from the first customer even though she is willing to pay $5. That is, because both customers are now paying $4, the company is receiving $4 more from customer two, but it is now earning $1 less from customer one. Remember, the first customer was willing to pay $5. Thus, in order to get revenue from marginal customers, the firm has to lower the price.

In order to induce a third daily customer to purchase the good, the firm must cut its price to $3. In doing so, it gains $3 in revenue from the new, third customer, but it loses

section 9.2
Exhibit 2   **Total, Marginal, and Average Revenue**

Price	Quantity	Total Revenue ($TR = P \times Q$)	Marginal Revenue ($MR = \Delta TR/\Delta Q$)	Average Revenue ($AR = TR/Q$)
$6	0	$0		—
			$5	
5	1	5		$5
			3	
4	2	8		4
			1	
3	3	9		3
			−1	
2	4	8		2
			−3	
1	5	5		1
			−5	
0	6	0		0

$2 in revenue because each of the first two customers are now paying $1 less than previously. The marginal revenue is $1 ($3 − $2), less than the price of the good ($3).

Finally, in order to get a fourth customer, the firm has to cut the price to $2. The firm finds that in doing so, it actually loses revenue, because the new revenue received from the fourth customer ($2) is more than offset by losses in revenues from the first three customers, $3, because each customer pays $1 less than before.

Hence, *the marginal revenue is always less than the price* —that is, the marginal revenue curve will always lie below the demand curve, as shown in Exhibit 3. Recall from Perfect Competition in Chapter 8, the firm could sell all it wanted at the market price and the price was equal to marginal revenue. However, in monopoly, if the seller wants to expand output, it will have to lower its price on *all* units. This means that the monopolist receives additional revenue from the new unit sold but it will receive less revenue on all of the units it was previously selling. So when the monopolist cuts price to attract new customers, the old customers benefit.

In Exhibit 4, we can compare marginal revenue for the perfectly competitive firm with marginal revenue for the monopolist. The firm in perfect competition can sell another unit of output without lowering its price; hence, the marginal revenue from selling its last unit of output is the market price. However, the monopolist has a downward-sloping demand curve. This means that to sell an extra unit of output, if must lower the price from P_0 to P_1, and the monopolist loses area c in Exhibit 4(b).

It is important to note that although a monopolist can set its price anywhere it wants, it will not set its price as high as possible—be careful not to confuse ability with incentive. As we will see in the next section, some prices along the demand curve will not be profitable for a firm. In other words, profits may be enhanced by either lowering the price or raising it.

section 9.2
Exhibit 3   **Demand and Marginal Revenue for the Monopolist**

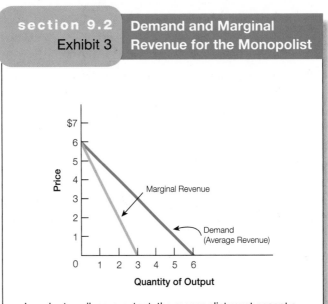

In order to sell more output, the monopolist must accept a lower price on all units sold. This means that the monopolist receives additional revenue from the new unit sold but will receive less revenue on all of the units it was previously selling. Thus, the marginal revenue curve will always lie below the demand curve.

Marginal Revenue—Competitive Firm versus Monopolist

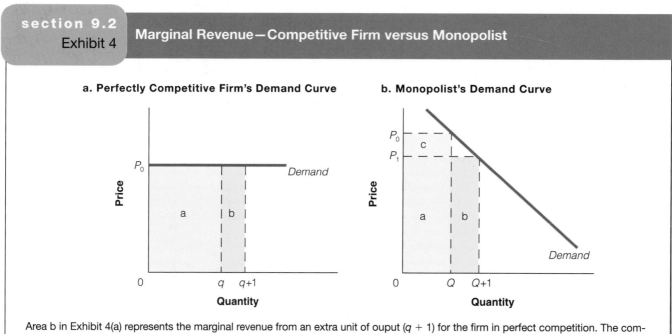

a. Perfectly Competitive Firm's Demand Curve   **b. Monopolist's Demand Curve**

Area b in Exhibit 4(a) represents the marginal revenue from an extra unit of ouput ($q + 1$) for the firm in perfect competition. The competitive firm's marginal revenue (area b) is equal to the market price. In Exhibit 4(b), we see that the monopolist's marginal revenue from an extra unit ($Q + 1$) is less than the price by area c, because the monopolist must lower its price to sell another unit of output.

ACTIVE LEARNING EXERCISE

DEMAND AND MARGINAL REVENUE

Q: Using the concepts of total revenue and marginal revenue, show why marginal revenue is less than price in a monopoly situation. Suppose a monopolist wants to expand output from one unit to two units. In order to sell two units rather than one, the monopolist must lower its price from $10 to $8—see Exhibit 5. Will the marginal revenue be less than the price?

A: In Exhibit 5 we see that to sell two units we have to lower the price on both units to $8. That is, the seller doesn't receive $10 from unit one, and $8 for unit two, but rather, receives $8 for each of the units. So what happens to marginal revenue? There are two parts to this answer. One, there is a loss in revenue, $2, from selling the first unit at $8 instead of $10. Two, there is a gain in revenue from selling the additional output—the second unit at $8. So the marginal revenue is $6 ($8 − $2), which is less than the price of the good, $8. The monopolist's marginal revenue will always be less than price because of the downward-sloping demand curve.

Demand and Marginal Revenue

Price	Quantity	Total Revenue	Marginal Revenue
$10	1	$10	
8	2	16	$6
6	3	18	2

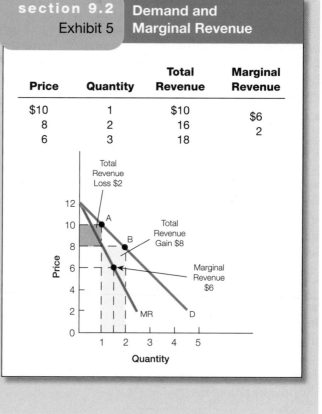

MONOPOLISTS' PRICE IN THE ELASTIC PORTION OF THE DEMAND CURVE

The relationship between the elasticity of demand and marginal and total revenue are shown in Exhibit 6. In Exhibit 6(a), elasticity varies along a linear demand curve. Recall from Chapter 5 that above the midpoint, the demand curve is elastic ($E_D > 1$); below the midpoint, it is inelastic ($E_D < 1$); and at the midpoint, it is unit elastic ($E_D = 1$). How does elasticity relate to total and marginal revenue? In the elastic portion of the curve, when the price falls, total revenue rises in Exhibit 6(b), so that marginal revenue is positive. In the inelastic region of the demand curve, when the price falls, total revenue falls in Exhibit 6(b), so that marginal revenue is negative. At the midpoint of the linear demand curve, the total revenue curve reaches its highest point, as seen in Exhibit 6(b), so that $MR = 0$.

For example, suppose the price falls on the top half of the demand curve in Exhibit 6(a) from $90 to $80; total revenue increases from $90 ($90 × 1) to $160 ($80 × 2); the marginal revenue is positive at $70. Because a reduction in price leads to an increase in total revenue, the demand curve is elastic in this region. Now, suppose the price falls from $20 to $10 on the lower portion of the demand curve; total revenue falls from $160 ($20 × 8) to $90 ($10 × 9); the marginal revenue is negative at −$70. Because a reduction in price leads to a decrease in total revenue, the demand curve is inelastic in this region.

A monopolist will never knowingly operate in the inelastic portion of its demand curve because increased output will lead to lower total revenue in this region. Not only are total revenues falling, but total costs will rise as you produce more output. Similarly, if a monopolist lowered its output, it could increase its total revenue and lower its total costs (because it costs less to produce fewer units), leading to greater economic profits.

section 9.2 Exhibit 6 — **The Relationship Between the Elasticity of Demand and Total and Marginal Revenue**

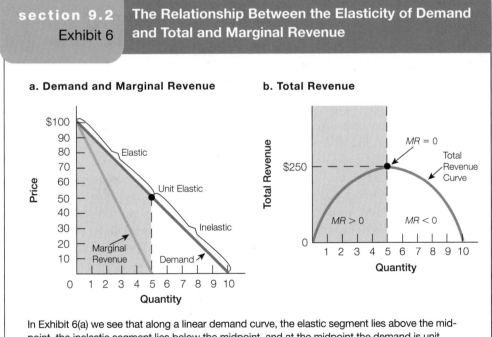

In Exhibit 6(a) we see that along a linear demand curve, the elastic segment lies above the midpoint, the inelastic segment lies below the midpoint, and at the midpoint the demand is unit elastic. When demand is elastic, a decline in price will increase total revenue; when demand is inelastic, a decline in price will lead to a decrease in total revenue. In Exhibit 6(b), we see that over the range from 0 to 5 units, total revenue is rising, so that marginal revenue is positive. Over the range from 5 units to 10 units, total revenue is falling, so that marginal revenue is negative. At 5 units of output, total revenue is maximized at $250 ($50 × 5), so that marginal revenue is zero.

Section Check

1. The monopolist's demand curve is downward sloping because it is the market demand curve. To produce and sell another unit of output, the firm must lower its price on all units. As a result, the marginal revenue curve lies below the demand curve.
2. The monopolist cannot set both price and the quantity it sells. If the monopolist reduces output, the price will rise, and if the monpolist expands output, the price will fall.
3. The monopolist's marginal revenue will always be less than price because there is a downward-sloping demand curve. In order to sell more output, the monopolist must accept a lower price on all units sold. This means that the monopolist receives additional revenue from the new unit sold but receives less revenue on all of the units they were previously selling.
4. The monopolist will operate in the elastic portion of their demand curve.

section 9.3

The Monopolist's Equilibrium

- How does the monopolist decide what output to produce?
- How does the monopolist decide what price to charge?
- How do we know if the monopolist is making a profit?
- How do we know if the monopolist is incurring a loss?
- Can the monopolist's economic profits last into the long run?

HOW DOES A MONOPOLIST DETERMINE THE PROFIT-MAXIMIZING OUTPUT?

In the last section we saw how a monopolist could choose any point along a demand curve. But the monopolist's decision on what level of output to produce depends on more than the marginal revenue derived at various outputs. The firm faces production costs, and the monopolist, like the perfect competitor, will maximize profits at that output where $MR = MC$. This point is demonstrated graphically in Exhibit 1.

As you can see in Exhibit 1, at output level Q_1, the marginal revenue exceeds the marginal cost of that production, so it is profitable for the monopolist to expand output. Profits continue to grow until output Q^* is reached. Beyond that output, say Q_2, the marginal cost of production exceeds the marginal revenue from production, so profits decline. The monopolist should cut production back to Q^*. Therefore, the equilibrium output is Q^*. At this output, marginal costs and marginal revenues are equal.

THREE-STEP METHOD FOR MONOPOLISTS

Let us return to the three-step method we used in Chapter 8. Determining whether a firm is generating economic profits, economic losses, or zero economic profits at the profit-maximizing level of output, Q^*, can be done in three easy steps.

1. Find where marginal revenues equal marginal costs and proceed straight down to the horizontal quantity axis to find Q^*, the profit-maximizing output level.

2. At Q^*, go straight up to the demand curve, then to the left to find the market price, P^*. Once you have identified P^* and Q^*, you can find total revenue at the profit-maximizing output level because $TR = P \times Q$.

3. The last step is to find total costs. Again, go straight up from Q^* to the average total cost (ATC) curve then left to the vertical axis to compute the average total cost. If we multiply average total costs by the output level, we can find the total costs ($TC = ATC \times Q$).

PROFITS FOR A MONOPOLIST

Exhibit 1 does not show what profits, if any, the monopolist is actually making. This is rectified in Exhibit 2, which shows the equilibrium position of a monopolist, this time adding an average total cost (ATC) curve. As we just discussed, the firm produces where $MC = MR$, or 100 units of output. At 100 units of output, the demand curve gives us a price of $6 per unit. The firm's total revenue is $P \times Q$ (6×100), or $600. The firm's total cost is $ATC \times Q$ (4×100), or $400. Thus, the firm has a total profit of $200.

In perfect competition, profits in an economic sense will persist only in the short run, because in the long run, new firms will enter the industry, increasing industry supply, and thus driving down the price of the good. With this, profits are eliminated. In monopoly, however, profits are not eliminated because one of the conditions for monopoly is that barriers to entry exist. Other firms cannot enter, so economic profits persist in the long run.

LOSSES FOR A MONOPOLIST

It is easy to imagine a monopolist ripping off consumers by charging prices resulting in long-run economic profits. However, there are also many companies with monopoly power that have gone out of business. Imagine that you received a patent on a bad idea like a roof ejection seat for a helicopter, or that you had the sole rights to turn an economics textbook into a screenplay for a motion picture. Although you may be the sole supplier of a product, that does not guarantee that consumers will demand your product. There may be no close substitute for your product, but there is always competition for the consumer dollar—other goods may provide greater satisfaction.

Exhibit 3 illustrates loss in a monopoly situation. In this graph, notice that the demand curve is well below the average total cost curve. In this case, the monopolist will incur a loss because there is insufficient demand to cover average total costs at any price and output combination along the demand curve. Total revenue is $600

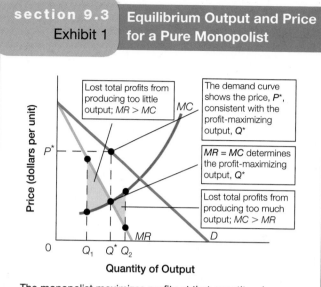

section 9.3
Exhibit 1

Equilibrium Output and Price for a Pure Monopolist

The monopolist maximizes profits at that quantity where $MR = MC$, at Q^*. At Q^* the monopolist finds P^* by extending a vertical line up to the demand curve and over to the vertical axis to find the price. Rather than charging a price equal to marginal cost or marginal revenue at their intersection, however, the monopolist charges the price that customers are willing to pay for that quantity as indicated on the demand curve at P^*. At Q_1, $MR > MC$ and the firm should expand output. At Q_2, $MC > MR$ and the firm should cut back its production.

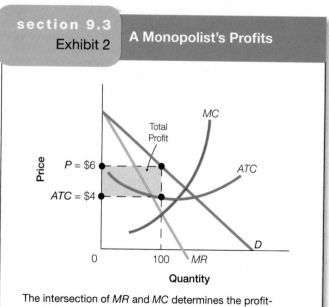

section 9.3
Exhibit 2

A Monopolist's Profits

The intersection of MR and MC determines the profit-maximizing level of output. The demand curve shows the price that can be charged. Total profit is total revenue minus total cost ($600 - 400$), or $200.

section 9.3
Exhibit 3

A Monopolist's Losses

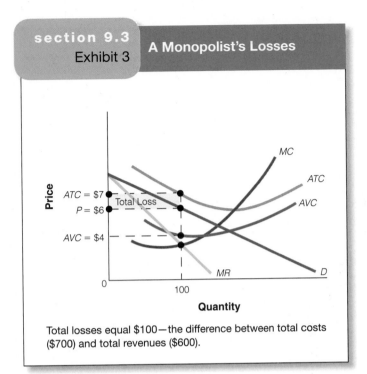

Total losses equal $100—the difference between total costs ($700) and total revenues ($600).

($P \times Q = \$6 \times 100$) and total cost is $700 ($ATC \times Q = \$7 \times 100$), for an economic loss of $100. Notice that the total revenue is great enough to cover the total variable costs of $400 ($TVC = \$4 \times 100$). Thus, the firm can reduce its losses by operating rather than shutting down in the short run. However, in monopoly as in perfect competition, a firm will go out of business in the long run if it cannot generate enough revenue to cover its total costs.

In summary, if total revenue is greater than total costs at Q^*, the firm is generating total economic profits. And if total revenue is less than total costs at Q^*, the firm is generating total economic losses. If total revenue is equal to total costs at Q^*, the firm is earning zero economic profits. Remember, the cost curves include implicit and explicit costs—so in this case, we are covering the total opportunity costs of our resources and are earning a normal profit or rate of return.

PATENTS

One form of monopoly power conferred by governments is provided by patents and copyrights. A patent puts the government's police power behind the patent holder's exclusive right to make a product for a period of time (in Canada, the period of time is 20 years) without anyone else being able to make an identical product. As Exhibit 4 suggests, this gives the supplier at least temporary monopoly power over that good or service. This allows the firm with the patent to price its product well above marginal costs, at P_M. Notice the marginal cost curve is flat. The reason for this is that most of the cost of drugs is in the development stage. Once the drug is available for the market, the marginal costs are close to constant—flat. When patents expire, the price of the patented good or service usually falls substantially with the entry of competing firms. The price will fall towards the perfectly competitive price P_{PC} and the output will increase towards $Q_{NO\ PATENT}$.

section 9.3
Exhibit 4

Impact of Patent Protection on Equilibrium Price and Quality

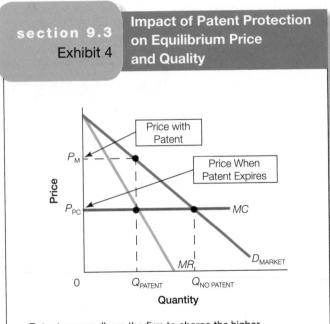

Patent power allows the firm to charge the higher monopoly price, P_M, which is well above the marginal cost of producing that good. However, when the patent expires, the price falls to a position closer to the perfectly competitive price, P_{PC}.

Why does the government give inventors this limited monopoly power, raising the prices of pharmaceutical drugs and other "vital" goods? The rationale is simple. Without patents, inventors would have little incentive to incur millions of dollars in research and development expenses to create new products (e.g., life-saving drugs) if others could immediately copy the idea and manufacture the products without incurring the research expenses. Similarly, copyrights stimulate creative activity of other kinds, giving writers the incentive to write books that earn royalties and are not merely copied freely. Just as the enormous number of computer programs written for home computers reflects the fact that program writers receive royalties from the sale of each copy sold; that is why they and the firms they work for vehemently oppose unauthorized copying of their work.

Without patents, would some life-saving drugs have been invented? Some drugs cost millions of dollars in research. Without the protection of a patent, the firm may not have been able to make profits from its inventive activity for very long, which is why the government issues patents that last up to 20 years. However, after the patent expires, many popular drugs soon lose their protection. In most cases, less costly generic drugs hit the market soon after the patent expiration and prices then move closer to the competitive price, although perhaps not all the way to the competitive level, as some companies are able to keep customers through brand loyalty.

Section Check

1. The monopolist, like the perfect competitor, maximizes profits at that output where marginal revenue equals marginal cost.
2. The monopolist sets the price according to the demand for the product at the profit-maximizing output.
3. Monopoly profits can be found by comparing price per unit and average total cost at Q^*. If $P > ATC$, there are economic profits. If $P < ATC$, there are economic losses.
4. Monopolists' profits can last into the long run because in monopoly, there are barriers to entry.

section

Monopoly and Welfare Loss

9.4

- How does monopoly lead to inefficiencies?
- What is the welfare loss in monopoly?
- Does monopoly hinder innovation?

DOES MONOPOLY PROMOTE INEFFICIENCY?

Monopoly is often considered to be bad. But what is the basis in economic theory for concerns about the establishment of monopoly power? There are two main objections to monopoly. First, on equity grounds, many people feel that it is not "fair" for monopoly owners to have persistent economic profits when they do not work harder than other firms. However, to most economists, the more serious objection is that monopolies result in market inefficiencies. That is, monopoly leads to a lower output and to higher prices than would exist under perfect competition. To demonstrate why this is so, see Exhibit 1. In monopoly, the firm produces output Q_M and charges a price of P_M. Suppose, however, that we had perfect competition and that the industry was characterized by many small firms that could produce output with the same efficiency (at the same cost) as one large

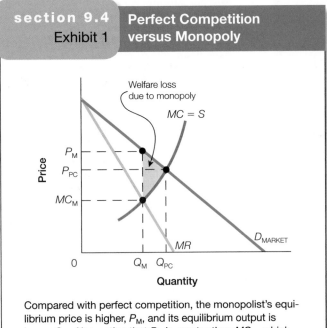

Compared with perfect competition, the monopolist's equilibrium price is higher, P_M, and its equilibrium output is lower, Q_M. Also notice that P_M is greater than MC_M, which means the value of the last unit produced by the monopolist (P_M) is greater than the cost of the last unit (MC_M), so from society's point of view the monopolist is producing too little output.

firm. Then the marginal cost curve shown in Exhibit 1 could be the sum of the individual marginal cost curves of the individual firms, and the upward portion of that curve might be considered the industry supply curve.

Equilibrium price and quantity with perfect competition would be determined where the marginal cost (or supply) curve intersects with the demand curve, at output Q_{PC} and price P_{PC}. Thus, the competitive equilibrium solution provides for more output and lower prices than the solution prevailing in monopoly. This provides the major efficiency objection to monopoly: Monopolists charge higher prices and produce less output. This may also be viewed as "unfair," in that consumers are burdened more than under the alternative competitive arrangement.

Welfare Loss in Monopoly

In addition to the monopolist producing lower levels of output at higher prices, notice that the monopolist produces at an output where the price (P_M) is greater than the marginal cost (MC_M). Because $P > MC$, it means that the value to society from the last unit produced is greater than the cost of the last unit (MC_M). That is, the monopoly is *not* producing enough of the good from society's perspective. We call the shaded area in Exhibit 1 the welfare loss, or deadweight loss, due to monopoly.

The actual amount of the deadweight loss in monopoly is of considerable debate among economists. Estimates across nations vary between one-tenth of 1 percent and 6 percent of national income. The variation depends on the researchers' estimates of elasticity of demand, whether firm or industry data was used, whether adjustments for profits were made (for the inclusion of royalties and intangibles), and last, whether the researcher included some proxy for scarce resources used in attempting to create a monopoly.

DOES MONOPOLY HINDER INNOVATION?

Another argument against monopoly is that a lack of competition tends to hinder technological advancement. Monopolists become comfortable, reaping their monopolistic profits, so they do not work hard at product improvement, technical advances designed to promote efficiency, and so forth. The railroad industry is sometimes cited as an example of this situation. Early in the last century, railroads had a strong amount of monopoly power, but they did not spend much on research or development; they did not aggressively try to improve rail transport. As a consequence, technical advances in other transport modes—like cars, trucks, and airplanes—led to a loss of monopoly power, as transportation substitutes came into existence.

However, the notion that monopoly hinders all innovation can be disputed. Many near-monopolists are, in fact, important innovators. Companies like Microsoft, IBM, Polaroid, and Xerox have all, at one time or another, had very strong market positions, in some instances approaching monopoly secured by patent protection, but they were also important innovators. Indeed, innovation helps firms initially obtain a degree of monopoly status, as patents can give a monopoly new products and/or cost-saving technology. Even the monopolist wants more profits, and any innovation that lowers costs or expands revenues creates profits for the monopolist. In addition, because patents expire, a monopolist may be expected to innovate in order to obtain additional patents and preserve its monopoly power. Therefore, the incentive to innovate may well exist in monopolistic market structures.

Section Check

1. Monopoly results in smaller output and a higher price than would be the case under perfect competition.
2. The monopolist produces at an output where $P > MC$. This means the value to society of the last unit produced is greater than its cost. In other words, the monopoly is not producing enough output from society's standpoint.
3. Monopoly may lead to greater concentration of economic power and could hinder innovation.

Monopoly Policy

■ What is the objective of anti-combine laws?
■ What is regulation?
■ What is average cost pricing?

Because monopolies pose certain problems with respect to efficiency, equity, and power, the public, through its governments, must decide how to deal with the phenomenon. Two major approaches to dealing with the monopoly problem are commonly used: anti-combine laws and government regulation. It should be pointed out that in these discussions, the word "monopoly" is sometimes used in a loose, general sense to refer to imperfectly competitive markets, not just to "pure" monopoly.

ANTI-COMBINE LAWS

The rationale for anti-combine laws is to prevent monopoly, to promote competition, and to enhance economic efficiency. Canada's anti-combine laws started in 1889. Around that time, monopolistic behaviour arose in a number of industries such as twine, sugar, and flour.

Today, Canada's anti-combine laws are covered by the Competition Act of 1986. The act covers business practices that unduly prevent or lessen competition, and it differentiates between criminal and civil offences. Criminal offences are handled by the courts and the standard of evidence is "beyond a reasonable doubt." Penalties range from fines to possible imprisonment of guilty executives. Civil offences are handled by the Competition Tribunal, which is a government body that operates under a civil law framework. The Competition Tribunal can issue orders to restore and maintain competition in the affected industry.

Criminal offences include conspiracy to fix prices, bid-rigging, and predatory pricing. Bid-rigging occurs when firms that bid on contracts arrange among themselves who will win each contract and at what price. Predatory pricing occurs when a firm temporarily reduces the price of its product below the product's average cost in order to drive the firm's competition out of business.

Civil offences include mergers and abuse of a dominant market position. A merger is the combining of two firms into one. The Competition Tribunal assesses the economic impact of proposed mergers. If a merger would significantly reduce competition in an industry, the Competition Tribunal has the power to stop the merger. On the other hand, if a merger would increase efficiency in an industry and consumers would benefit from the resulting lower prices, it could allow the merger. Abuse of a dominant market position occurs when a firm that controls most of the sales in a market uses its dominant position to engage in anti-competitive behaviour.

Recently, a number of high-profile cases have come under the Competition Act. For example, in 1998, the Competition Tribunal recommended against bank mergers when the Royal Bank of Canada and the Bank of Montreal tried to merge. It concluded that the merger would likely lead to a substantial lessening or prevention of competition. In 2004, an extensive review of the proposed merger between Cineplex Galaxy and Famous Players was conducted by the Competition Tribunal. It came to the conclusion that such a merger would result in a substantial lessening of competition of first-run motion pictures in a number of urban areas. As a result of these concerns, Cineplex Galaxy was required to divest itself of theatres in all the affected areas.

GOVERNMENT REGULATION

Government regulation is an alternative approach to dealing with monopolies. Under regulation, a company would not be allowed to charge any price it wants. Suppose the government does not want to break up a natural monopoly in the water or the power industry. Remember that natural monopolies occur when one large firm can produce as much output as many smaller firms but at a lower average cost per unit. The government may decide to regulate the monopoly price, but what price does it let the firm charge? The goal is to achieve the efficiency of large-scale production without permitting the high monopoly prices and low output that can promote allocative *inefficiency*.

The basic policy dilemma that regulators often face in attempting to fix maximum prices can be rather easily illustrated. Consider Exhibit 1. Without regulation, say the

section 9.5
Exhibit 1   Marginal Cost Pricing versus Average Cost Pricing

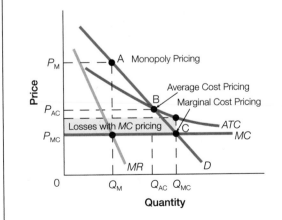

The marginal cost (*MC*) curve is less than the average total cost curve (*ATC*) for a natural monopolist as the average cost falls. If the monopolist is unregulated, it could produce a relatively small level of output, Q_M, at a relatively high price, P_M. If regulators require the natural monopolist to use marginal cost pricing, the monopoly will lose money, because P_{MC} is less than average total costs. Average cost pricing (at point B) would permit firms to make a normal rate of return, where $P_{AC} = ATC$. The monopolist's unregulated output at point A is not optimal from society's standpoint, and the optimal output at point C is not feasible.

In The **NEWS**

IS MICROSOFT A MONOPOLY?

Government prosecutors [in the United States] have argued that Microsoft has engaged in a pattern of using its monopoly power to crush rivals and prevent real competition from developing. In June 2001, a federal appeals court unanimously threw out a lower court order to break up Microsoft into two companies. However, the appeals court did find that the company had repeatedly abused its monopoly power in the software business. It now looks like a Microsoft breakup is unlikely.

What does Larry Ellison, the Oracle Software magnate, think of the Microsoft . . . case? "So they make all the stuff for free and drive Netscape out of business. They thought Netscape was an incredibly dangerous company. They thought that the browser would become the platform for the next-generation application. As it turns out, I think they were mistaken. They should have been shooting at us [Oracle], when they were shooting at Netscape. In fact, we used to refer to Netscape as the heat-shield. They were so busy destroying Netscape, they kind of lost sight of what we were doing. And in the Internet, it's not about the desktop software. It's about the server software. The irony of all of this is they broke into the wrong bank.

"They repeatedly broke the law. They said to Compaq: If you want to get a good price for Windows, you better not put Netscape on that computer. That is using an existing monopoly, Windows, to obtain a new monopoly in browsers. That's an explicit violation of the Sherman Antitrust Act. They did it over and over again."

SOURCE: http://www.businessweek.com/2001/01_09/b3721108.htm. February 26, 2001. © 2001 by the McGraw-Hill Companies, Inc. All rights reserved. Reproduced from the February 26, 2001 issue of Business Week by special permission, copyright © 2009 by The McGraw-Hill Companies, Inc.

CONSIDER THIS:

It appears that the Microsoft case has less to do with the degree of monopoly power and more to do with the abuse of that power. Specifically, the case is about the *actions* taken to form, extend, or maintain the monopoly. However, we have to ask the question: Are consumers necessarily worse off as a result of a few powerful computer companies that temporarily dominate the industry? There may be economies of scale in production and technology. Furthermore, the monopoly might well be short-lived. And are the barriers to entry in the computer industry insurmountable? The history of the computer industry has several success stories of individuals with great ideas that have successfully broken into the industry. In addition, Microsoft and Intel are at least partially responsible for making computer power what it is today. A Dell computer with Intel Core 2 Extreme Processors and Microsoft Vista operating system, available for under $1000, could not be matched in performance ten years ago at many times that price.

However, it is important to remember that if the computer market was more competitive, prices might have gone down even faster and the quality of the products might be even higher. And just because prices are falling now, will they continue to fall if markets do not become more competitive in the future?

---

profit-maximizing monopolist operates at point A, at output Q_M, and price P_M. At that output, the price exceeds the average total cost, so economic profits exist. However, the monopolist is producing relatively little output and is charging a relatively high price, and it is producing at a point where price is above marginal cost. This is not the best point from society's perspective.

Allocative Efficiency

From society's point of view, what would be the best price and output position? As we discussed in Chapter 8, the best position is at the competitive equilibrium output where $P = MC$. This is because the equilibrium price represents the marginal value of output. The marginal cost represents society's opportunity costs in making the good as opposed to something else. Where price equals marginal cost, society matches marginal value and marginal cost or achieves **allocative efficiency;** this is seen at point C in Exhibit 1.

allocative efficiency
production where the price of a good equals marginal cost

Can the Regulated Monopolist Operate at *P = MC*?

Unfortunately, the natural monopoly cannot operate profitably at the allocative efficient point, where $P = MC$, indicated at point C on Exhibit 1. At point C, the intersection of the demand and marginal cost curves, average total costs are greater than price. The optimal output, then, is an output that produces losses for the producer. Any regulated business that produced for long at this "optimal" output would go bankrupt; it would be impossible to attract new capital to the industry.

Therefore, the "optimal" output from a welfare perspective really is not viable because losses are incurred. The regulators cannot force firms to price their product at P_{MC} and to sell Q_{MC} output because the firm would go out of business. Indeed, in the long run, the industry's capital would deteriorate as investors failed to replace old capital when it became worn out or obsolete. If the monopolist's unregulated output at point A is not optimal from society's standpoint, and the short-run optimal output at point C is not feasible from the monopolist's standpoint, where should the regulated monopolist be allowed to operate?

One option to solving the problem is that the government could subsidize the losses associated with marginal cost pricing. However, the burden will ultimately fall on the taxpayers, as the government will have to raise the money to pay for the losses.

The Compromise: Average Cost Pricing

A compromise between monopoly pricing and marginal cost pricing is found at point B on Exhibit 1, output Q_{AC}, which is somewhere between the excessively low output and high prices of an unregulated monopoly and the excessively large output and low prices achieved when prices are equated with marginal cost pricing. At point B, price equals average total costs. The monopolist is permitted to price the product where economic profits are zero, meaning that there is a normal economic profit or rate of return, like firms experience in perfect competition in the long run. This compromise is called **average cost pricing.**

In the real world, regulators often permit utilities to receive a "fair and reasonable" return that is a rough approximation to that suggested by average cost pricing, at point B. Point B would seem "fair" in that the monopolist is receiving rewards equal to those that a perfect competitor would ordinarily receive—no more and no less. Point B permits more output at a significantly lower price than would occur if the monopolist were unregulated, point A, even though output is still somewhat less and price somewhat more than that suggested by point C, the social optimum or best position.

average cost pricing
to set the price equal to average total cost

DIFFICULTIES IN AVERAGE COST PRICING

Accurate Calculations of Costs

The actual implementation of a rate (price) that permits a "fair and reasonable" return is more difficult than the analysis suggests. The calculations of costs and values are difficult. In reality, the firm may not know exactly what its demand and cost curves look like. This forces regulatory agencies to use profits, another somewhat ambiguous target, as a guide. If profits are "too high," lower the price, and if profits are "too low," raise the price.

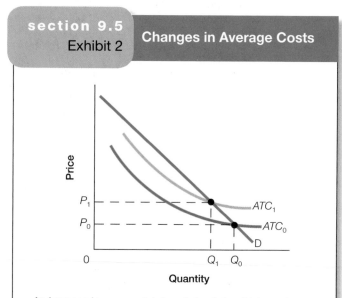

section 9.5
Exhibit 2   **Changes in Average Costs**

An increase in average total costs leads to a higher price and lower output (P_1Q_1); lower average total costs leads to a lower price and greater output (P_0Q_0). However, both situations lead to a normal rate of return. Because the regulated firm has little incentive to minimize costs, average total costs would have a tendency to rise.

No Incentives to Keep Costs Down

Another problem is that average cost pricing gives the monopolists no incentive to reduce costs. That is, if the firm's costs rise from ATC_0 to ATC_1 in Exhibit 2, the price will rise from P_0 to P_1. And if costs fall, the firm's price will fall. In either scenario, the firm will still be earning a normal rate of return. This is equivalent to saying that if the regulatory agency sets the price at any point where the ATC curve intersects the demand curve, the firm will earn a normal rate of return. So if the agency is going to set the price wherever ATC intersects the demand curve, why not let your average costs rise? Let your employees fly first class and dine in the finest restaurants. While you are at it, why not buy concert tickets and season tickets to sporting events? And if the regulated monopolist knows that the regulators will reduce prices if costs fall, the regulated monopolist does not benefit from lower costs. Regulators have tackled this problem by allowing the regulated firm to keep some of the profits that come from lower costs; that is, they do not adhere strictly to average cost pricing.

Special Interest Groups

In the real world, consumer groups are constantly battling for lower rates, while the utilities themselves are lobbying for higher rates so that they can approach the monopoly profits indicated by point A on Exhibit 1. Decisions are not always made in a calm, objective, dispassionate atmosphere free of outside involvement. It is precisely the political economy of rate setting that disturbs some critics of this approach to dealing with the monopoly problem. For example, it is possible that a rate-making commissioner could become friendly with a utility company, believing that he can obtain a nice job after his tenure as a regulator is over. The temptation is great for the commissioner to be generous to the utilities. On the other hand, there may be a tendency for regulators to bow to pressure from consumer groups. A politician who wants to win votes can almost always succeed by attacking utility rates and promising rate "reform" (lower rates). If zealous rate regulators listen too closely to the consumer groups and push rates down to a level indicated by point C in Exhibit 1, the industry might be too unstable to attract capital for expansion.

A review of government behaviour in this case would reveal a trend away from regulation toward competition; for example, between 1980 and 1997, the federal government fully deregulated the telecommunications industry, ending Bell Canada's monopoly. Similar instances of deregulation have also occurred in the transportation industry and natural gas market. Technological advances now allow us to separate the production of electric power or natural gas from the distributor, which will ultimately lead to greater competition in these markets.

In The **NEWS**

DEREGULATION SPURS INVESTMENT

BY WILLIAM WATSON

When it comes to judging deregulation, a recent study by four economists—Alberto Alesina, Silvia Ardagna, Giuseppe Nicoletti and Fabio Schiantarelli of, respectively, Harvard, Wellesley College, the OECD and Boston College—is especially instructive.

The four looked at episodes of deregulation in seven industries (airlines, trucking, railways, telecommunications, postal services and electrical and gas utilities) in 21 industrialized countries from 1975 to 1996 to see what effect the worldwide shift toward reduced government control had on investment spending on capital goods in these industries.

(continued)

IN THE NEWS *(continued)*

The four economists begin with open minds about whether deregulation leads to more investment or less. It leads to more if easier entry into an industry squeezes industry markups and prices, thus leading consumers to buy more product, which requires more investment by firms. Also, with less red tape, firms are better able to respond to profit opportunities that, when they were regulated, they might have forgone.

At least two other forces, however, work in the opposite direction. First, many regulated utilities are (or were) subject to rate-of-return regulation: that is, they are allowed a specific percentage return on their capital base.

But if they can only make money on their capital base, they may have an incentive to over-invest in capital. Deregulate them and they'll get rid of their excess machinery, equipment and structures. So deregulation leads to de-investment. Second, many public enterprises operating in regulated industries are under instruction, whether explicit or implicit, to be heavy on investment, particularly in politically important jurisdictions. Privatize them or make them subject to commercial incentives and they may pare back on their over-investments.

But if the theory is ambiguous on whether deregulation leads to more or less investment, the data are not. Deregulation and subsequent investment are highly positively correlated. In laymen's terms, deregulation leads to greater investment. Big time. Reduce regulation by one point on a six-point scale and the overall rate of investment in the industries studied increases from 6% to 7.1%.

Other rules emerging from their statistical work:

* Barriers to entry are key. Getting rid of protective measures that prevent new firms from entering an industry gives the biggest increases in investment.
* Privatization isn't crucial. Subjecting public companies to greater competition is more important, though deep privatization does lead to accelerated investment.
* Half measures don't count. Countries (like France, Germany and Italy) that reduce their regulation index only slightly and from high levels don't get much payoff in greater investment.
* Deregulation doesn't hurt workers. Greater investment in these industries usually brought higher wages, not lower.

SOURCE: Adapted from William Watson, "Deregulation—It Works," *National Post*, July 31, 2003, p. FP11. Reprinted with permission from the Author.

CONSIDER THIS:

Government regulation has been a popular policy in dealing with certain monopoly industries such as railways and electrical and gas utilities. However, recently, deregulation of a number of key industries has taken place in many countries, including Canada. It appears that deregulation has many benefits, including greater investment in the industry.

Section Check

1. Anti-combine laws are designed to reduce the abuses of monopoly power and push production closer to the social optimum.
2. Privately owned monopolies may be allowed to operate but under regulation of a government agency.
3. Average cost pricing sets price equal to average total cost, where the demand curve intersects average total costs.

section

9.6   Price Discrimination

■ What is price discrimination?
■ Why does price discrimination exist?

PRICE DISCRIMINATION

Sometimes sellers will charge different customers different prices for the same good or service when the cost of providing that good or service does not differ among the customers.

This is called **price discrimination.** For example, kids pay less for the movies than adults; senior citizens get discounts on hotels, restaurants, museums, and zoos; most vacation travellers fly between places for less than business travellers; and so on. Under certain conditions, the monopolist finds it profitable to discriminate among various buyers, charging higher prices to those who are more willing to pay and lower prices to those who are less willing to pay.

price discrimination
the practice of charging different consumers different prices for the same good or service

CONDITIONS FOR PRICE DISCRIMINATION

The ability to practise price discrimination is not available to all sellers. In order to practise price discrimination, the following three conditions must hold:

Monopoly Power. Price discrimination is possible only with monopoly or where members of a small group of firms (firms that are not price takers) follow identical pricing policies. When there is a large number of competing firms, discrimination is less likely because competitors tend to undercut the high prices charged by the firms that are engaging in price discrimination.

Market Segregation. Price discrimination can only occur if the demand curves for markets, groups, or individuals are different. If the demand curves are not different, a profit-maximizing monopolist would charge the same price in both markets. In short, price discrimination requires the ability to separate customers according to their willingness to pay.

No Resale. For price discrimination to work, the person buying at a discount must have difficulty in reselling the product to customers being charged more. Otherwise, those getting the items cheaply would want to buy extra amounts of the product at the discounted price and sell it at a profit to others. Price differentials between groups erode if reselling is easy.

ACTIVE LEARNING EXERCISE

PRICE DISCRIMINATION AND BUSINESS TRAVELLERS

Q: Why do business travellers generally pay more for their flights than vacation travellers?

A: The airline industry has found that business travellers have a more inelastic demand for air travel than vacationers and students do. The airlines know that business travellers are generally unwilling to stay over for the weekend (away from home, family, or their favourite golf course), only spend a day or two at their destination, and often do not make their reservations far in advance. All of which means the business traveller has a more inelastic demand curve for flights (fewer substitutes). If the airlines cut prices for business travellers, airline revenues would fall. Personal travellers (perhaps vacationers) are operating on a much more elastic demand curve—they are much more flexible. For these travellers, many substitutes are available, such as other modes of transportation, different times

© JACK HOLLINGSWORTH/PHOTODISC/GETTY ONE IMAGES

(non–peak times), and so on. Clearly the airlines can make more money by separating the market according to each group's elasticity of demand rather than charging all users the same price.

WHY DOES PRICE DISCRIMINATION EXIST?

Price discrimination results from the profit-maximization motive. In our graphical analysis of monopoly, we suggested that there was a demand curve for the product and a corresponding marginal revenue curve. Sometimes, however, different groups of people have different demand curves and therefore react differently to price changes. A seller can make more money by charging those different buyers different prices. For example, if the price of a movie is increased from $7 to $10, many kids who would attend at $7 may have to stay home at $10, as they (and perhaps their parents) balk at paying the higher price. The impact on attendance of raising prices may be less, however, for adults, for whom the ticket price may represent a smaller part of the expenses of an evening out.

Thus, there is a different demand curve for those, say, under 16, as opposed to those who are older. Specifically, the elasticity of demand with respect to price is greater for children than for adults. This means that there is a different marginal revenue curve for children than for adults. Assume, for simplicity, that the marginal cost is constant. The profit-maximizing movie-theatre owner will price where the constant marginal costs equal marginal revenue for each group. As you can see in Exhibit 1(a), the demand curve for kids is rather elastic. The adult demand curve, shown in Exhibit 1(b), is more downward sloping at any given price and quantity (relatively inelastic), meaning the marginal revenue curve lies well below the demand curve at most output levels. Thus, the price charged adults is way above the point where marginal revenue equals marginal costs, whereas for kids, the price is not as much above the point where marginal revenue equals marginal costs.

EXAMPLES OF PRICE DISCRIMINATION

There are other examples of price discrimination in Canada. Here are just a few.

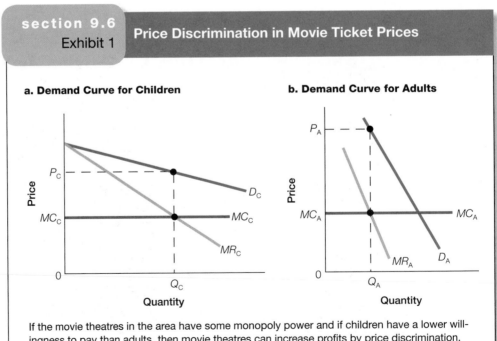

section 9.6
Exhibit 1

Price Discrimination in Movie Ticket Prices

a. Demand Curve for Children

b. Demand Curve for Adults

If the movie theatres in the area have some monopoly power and if children have a lower willingness to pay than adults, then movie theatres can increase profits by price discrimination. Because the demand curve for children is relatively more elastic than the demand curve for adults, the firm finds it profitable to charge the two different groups a different price. The firm sets each price so the *MR* for that group is equal to the constant *MC*.

Airline Tickets

Seats on airplanes usually go for different prices. There are the high-prices, no-strings-attached fares, and there are restricted fares—tickets that require Saturday-night layovers or must be purchased weeks in advance. This airline pricing strategy allows the airlines to discriminate against business travellers, who usually have little advance warning, travel on weekdays, and are not as willing to spend their weekends away from home and family. Because business travellers have a high willingness to pay (a relatively inelastic demand curve), airlines can charge them higher prices. If airlines were to cut prices for these clients, their revenues would fall. On the other hand, the personal traveller (perhaps a vacationer) can choose among many substitutes, such as other modes of transportation and different times. In short, the personal traveller has a lower willingness to pay (a relatively elastic demand curve). Thus, the airlines can clearly make more money by charging a higher price to those who have a higher willingness to pay (less elastic demand) and a lower price to those who have a lower willingness to pay (more elastic demand)—those who are willing to book in advance and stay over on Saturday nights. If airlines charged a higher single price to everyone, those with a lower willingness to pay would not travel; if they charged a lower single price to everyone, they would lose profits by receiving less revenue from those who are willing to pay more.

Coupons

The key to price discrimination is observing the difference in demand curves for different customers. The coupon clipper, who spends an hour looking through the Saturday paper for coupons, will probably have a relatively more elastic demand curve than, say, a busy and wealthy physician or executive. Consequently, firms charge a lower price to customers with a lower willingness to pay (more elastic demand)—the coupon clipper—and a higher price to those who don't use coupons (less elastic demand).

QUANTITY DISCOUNTS

Another form of price discrimination occurs when customers buy in large quantities. This is often the case with public utilities and wholesalers, but even stores will sell a six-pack

ACTIVE LEARNING EXERCISE

PRICE DISCRIMINATION AND COUPONS

Q: Tara loves to go through the Saturday paper and cut out supermarket coupons. How do you think Tara's coupon-clipping habits apply to the concept of price discrimination?

A: Often, the key to price discrimination is observing the difference in demand curves for different customers. For example, Tara, who spends an hour looking through the Saturday paper for coupons, will probably have a relatively more elastic demand curve than, say, a busy executive.

In The **NEWS**

THE ECONOMICS OF PROSTITUTION

BY WILLIAM WATSON

Steven Levitt of Freakanomics fame has just published new work on the economics of prostitution in several Chicago neighbourhoods. He and his colleague Sudhir Alladi Venkatesh paid 159 prostitutes $150 a week to participate in the study and hired trackers, often former prostitutes, to fill out "event tracking sheets" right after the "events" were performed, with details of acts, prices charged, the customer's demographic data and so on.

Chicago prostitutes, they found, average about $27 an hour and work about 13 hours a week during which they average 10 sex acts, for an income of about $20,000 a year—not much given the dangers and degradation of the job, but a lot better than the $7 an hour they average in the daycare, babysitting, hair styling, lawn care and so on that is their typical employment alternative.

Prostitutes who work with pimps charge more—an average $16 per trick more—and net more, even after giving their pimp a quarter of what they earn. You might think they're paying for protection, since they suffer fewer acts of violence at the hands of customers. In reality, the pimps make up for it with violence of their own. Working with a pimp does save girls the hassles of street-walking or making their own bookings.

Pricing follows patterns one would expect. More intimate or intricate acts cost more. Prices are lower on Mondays, when business is slowest (it's most brisk on Fridays). There's a shocking amount of unprotected sex—80% of all acts—and only a small discount for use of a condom. Repeat customers pay less and so do black customers—$8 to $9 less per trick—a strange example of **price discrimination** by race. And the odds of selling services to a cop or giving them away as goodwill are actually greater than the odds of being arrested by one. Using Chicago's Web-posted crime data (http://chicago.everyblock.com/crime/) Mr. Levitt and Mr. Venkatesh calculate that there's an average of 453 tricks per prostitution arrest.

Their most intriguing result is the Fourth of July effect. Because of various Independence Day street festivals there's a 60% increase in demand that week, which brings about a 30% increase in price, which in turn attracts new suppliers to the market—both out-of-towners and women for whom the regular price isn't sufficient inducement but the higher holiday price will do.

Mr. Levitt and Mr. Venkatesh didn't do any sampling during February, so they don't actually know if Valentine's Day is good or bad for business. But whether prices are up because business is booming or down because everyone's home eating chocolate, you're almost certainly better off finding another way to celebrate.

SOURCE: Material reprinted with the express permission of: "The National Post Company," a CanWest Partnership.

CONSIDER THIS:

The price of a business class ticket versus the price of a ticket in economy in the airline industry; the price of admission for children versus the price of admission for an adult at the movie theatre—these are classic examples of price discrimination. However, as this study proves, as long as a market meets the basic conditions of: 1) monopoly power, 2) market segregation, and 3) the ability to prevent resale, price discrimination can and will occur—even in the most unlikely places.

of soft drinks for less than six single cans. Or the local bagel shop might sell you a baker's dozen, where you may get 13 bagels for the price of 12. This type of price discrimination allows the producer to charge a higher price for the first unit than for, say, the twentieth unit. This form of price discrimination is effective because a buyer's willingness to pay declines as additional units are purchased.

Section Check

1. When producers charge different prices for the same good or service when no cost differences exist, it is called price discrimination.
2. Price discrimination occurs if demand differs among buyers and the seller can successfully identify group members, because producers can make profits by charging different prices to each group.
3. Price discrimination would not work well if the person buying the product could easily resell the product to another customer at a higher, profitable price.

Summary

Section 9.1

- A pure monopoly exists where there is only one seller of a product for which no close substitute is available.
- Barriers to entry tend to be very high in monopoly.
- Sources of monopoly power include legal barriers, economies of scale, and control over important resources.
- A natural monopoly occurs when one firm can provide the good or service at a lower cost than two or more smaller firms.

Section 9.2

- The monopolist's demand curve is downward sloping because it is the market demand curve.
- To produce and sell another unit of output, the monopolist must lower its price on all units.
- The marginal revenue curve lies below the demand curve for the monopolist.

Section 9.3

- The monopolist maximizes profits at that output where marginal revenue equals marginal cost.
- If $P > ATC$ at the profit-maximizing level of output, the monopolist is earning economic profits.

- If $P < ATC$ at the profit-maximizing level of output, the monopolist is incurring economic losses.
- Monopolists' profits can last into the long run because in monopoly, there are barriers to entry.

Section 9.4

- Monopoly results in smaller output and a higher price than would be the case under perfect competition.
- Since the monopolist produces at an output where $P > MC$, the monopolist is not producing enough output from society's standpoint.

Section 9.5

- Anti-combine laws can reduce the profitability of a monopoly and push production closer to the social optimum.

Section 9.6

- Price discrimination occurs when producers charge different prices for the same good or service when no cost differences exist.
- Price discrimination occurs where: 1) monopoly power exists; 2) market segregation is possible; and 3) resale is difficult.

Key Terms and Concepts

For a complete glossary of chapter key terms, visit the textbook's Web site at http://www.sextonmicro2e.nelson.com.

monopoly 229
natural monopoly 230

allocative efficiency 243
average cost pricing 244

price discrimination 247

Review Questions

1. Which of the following could be considered a monopoly:

   a. DeBeers diamonds

   b. the only dentist in a small town

   c. Ford Motor Company

2. Given the data in the tables, determine the short-run profit-maximizing (loss-minimizing) level of output and price for the monopolist. Fixed cost equals $10.

Quantity	Price		Output	Total Cost
4	$35		4	$ 20
5	30		5	30
6	25		6	45
7	20		7	65
8	15		8	100

3. Is it optimal for the monopolist to operate on the inelastic portion of the demand curve? Why or why not?

4. If economic profits were zero, would a monopolist ever stay in business? Why might it be possible for a monopolist to earn positive economic profits in the long run?

5. What is meant by "the welfare loss" of monopoly? Why is there no welfare loss if a monopolist successfully practises perfect price discrimination?

6. Suppose an industry experiences decreasing average costs of production over the relevant range of market demand. Discuss the merits of a regulation requiring the natural monopolist to price where demand equals marginal cost and service all willing customers. What about where demand equals average cost? Are any practical difficulties likely to be encountered with either regulatory program?

7.

Price	Quantity	Fixed Cost	Variable Cost
$100	0	$60	$ 0
90	1	60	25
80	2	60	40
70	3	60	50
60	4	60	70
50	5	60	100
40	6	60	140
30	7	60	190
20	8	60	250

A simple monopolist with the fixed and variable cost schedules maximizes profits at what level of output?

8.

"Super Duper" Cuts Hair Salon

Permanent Price for Haircuts

Long Hair	$100
Short Hair	75

Does the above price schedule reflect price discrimination? Why or why not?

9. Explain why a computer store offering significant student discounts may require student buyers to sign an agreement not to purchase another computer from the store for a period of six months.

10. Explain how each of the following is a form of price discrimination.

  a. a student discount at a movie theatre

  b. long-distance phone service that costs 15 cents per minute for the first 10 minutes, and 5 cents per minute after 10 minutes

  c. a senior citizens' breakfast discount at a local restaurant

  d. coupon discounts on laundry detergent

11. In October 1999, Coca-Cola announced that it might test a new vending machine that was temperature sensitive. The price of the soft drinks in the machines would be higher on hot days. How is this a form of price discrimination? How can the placement of the vending machines create a monopoly? What if other vending machines are close by and are not owned by Coca-Cola?

Fill in the Blanks

Section 9.1

1. A true or pure monopoly exists where there is only _____ seller of a product for which no close substitute is available.

2. Monopolists are _____ rather than price takers.

3. A monopolist's barriers to entry can include _____, _____, and _____.

4. _____ include franchising, licensing, and patents.

5. The situation in which one large firm can provide the output of the market at a lower cost than two or more smaller firms is called a _____.

6. A barrier to entry is control over an important _____, such as DeBeers' control over much of the world's output of diamonds.

Section 9.2

7. In monopoly, the market demand curve may be regarded as the demand curve for the _____ because it is the market for that particular product.

8. If a monopolist reduces output, the price will _____; and if the monopolist expands output, the price will _____.

9. In monopoly, if the seller wants to expand output, it will have to lower its price on _____ units.

Section 9.3

10. The monopolist, like the perfect competitor, will maximize profits at that output where _____ = MC.

11. The monopolist, unlike the perfect competitor, will not maximize profits at that output where _____ = MC.

12. If at a monopolist's profit-maximizing price and output the price is less than _____, the monopolist is generating economic losses.

13. In monopoly, economic profits are not eliminated by entry because one of the conditions for monopoly is that _____ exist.

14. Patents and copyrights are examples of _____ power designed to provide an incentive to develop new products.

Section 9.4

15. The major efficiency objection to monopoly is that a monopolist charges _____ prices and produces _____ output than would exist under perfect competition.

16. A monopolist produces at an output where the price is _____ than its marginal cost, so the value to society from the last unit produced is _____ than its marginal cost.

17. An argument against monopoly is that a lack of competition tends to hinder _____ advance, but, in fact, many near-monopolists are important innovators.

Section 9.5

18. Two major approaches to dealing with the monopoly problem are commonly used: _____ laws and _____.

19. Under the Competition Act, criminal offences are handled by _____, whereas civil offences are handled by _____.

20. The goal of government regulation as an alternative approach to dealing with monopolies is to achieve the efficiency of large-scale production without permitting the _____ monopoly prices and _____ output that can cause allocative inefficiency.

21. From society's point of view, allocative efficiency occurs where the price of the good is equal to _____. But with natural monopoly, at the "optimal" level of output for allocative efficiency, _____ are incurred.

22. A compromise between unregulated monopoly and marginal cost pricing is _____ pricing, where the monopolist is permitted to price the product where price equals _____.

23. Average cost pricing _____ the incentives for a monopolist to find ways to reduce its costs.

Section 9.6

24. _____ occurs when sellers charge different customers different prices for the same good or service when the cost does not differ.

25. When there are a number of competing firms, price discrimination is _____ likely because competitors tend to undercut the _____ prices charged those discriminated against.

26. A profit-maximizing seller will charge a _____ price for more inelastic demanders and a _____ price for more elastic demanders.

27. The profit-maximizing rule for a price-discriminating monopolist is to price where _____ equals _____ for each different group of demanders.

28. For price discrimination to work, the person buying the product at a discount must have difficulty in _____ the product to customers being charged more.

29. _____, which allow sellers to charge a higher price for the first unit than for later units, are another form of price discrimination.

True or False

Section 9.1

1. For a pure monopoly, the firm and the industry are one and the same.

2. A monopoly firm is a price maker, and it will pick a price that is the highest point on its demand curve.

3. Pure monopolies are a rarity because few goods and services truly have only one producer.

4. The cost advantage of a natural monopoly is due to economies of scale throughout the relevant output range.

Section 9.2

5. As in perfect competition, in monopoly the demand curve for the firm's product is downward sloping.

6. The marginal revenue curve for a monopolist lies below the demand curve.

7. For a monopoly to get revenue from marginal customers, the firm has to lower the price so that marginal revenue is always less than price.

8. When a monopolist cuts price to attract new customers, its existing customers benefit.

9. Along the inelastic portion of the demand curve, when the price falls, total revenue rises, so that marginal revenue is positive.

10. Along the elastic portion of the demand curve, when the price falls, total revenue rises so that marginal revenue is positive.

11. A monopolist will never knowingly operate in the inelastic portion of its demand curve because increased output will lead to lower total revenue and higher total cost in that region.

Section 9.3

12. For a monopolist, the profit-maximizing price is indicated by the height of the demand curve at the profit-maximizing quantity of output.

13. If, at a monopolist's profit-maximizing price and output, the price is greater than average total cost, the monopolist is generating economic losses.

14. Economic profits cannot persist in the long run for a monopolist.

15. A monopolist will incur a loss if there is insufficient demand to cover average total costs at any price and output combination along its demand curve.

16. Having monopoly guarantees economic profits.

Section 9.4

17. Perfect competition leads to lower output and higher prices than would exist under monopoly.

18. Monopoly creates a welfare loss because a monopoly does not produce enough of a good from society's perspective.

19. There is widespread agreement among economists about the size of the welfare loss from monopoly.

Section 9.5

20. By imposing fines and possible jail terms on some monopoly practices, anti-combine laws aim to reduce the profitability of monopoly.

21. Government regulation of monopolies aims to achieve the efficiency of large-scale production without permitting the monopolists to charge monopoly prices, which would reduce output.

22. With natural monopoly, the efficient, or optimal, output is one that produces zero economic profits for the producer where price equals marginal cost.

23. Any regulated business that produced for long at the optimal, or efficient, output would go bankrupt.

24. Under average cost pricing, a regulated monopoly is permitted to earn a normal return, as firms experience in perfect competition in the long run.

Section 9.6

25. Price discrimination is possible only with monopoly or where members of a small group of firms follow identical pricing policies.

26. When different groups of customers have predictably different elasticities of demand, a monopolist could earn higher profits by charging those different buyers different prices, if it could prevent resale of the product among customers.

27. Price differentials between groups will erode if reselling is easy, which is why price discrimination is usually limited to services and to some goods where it is inherently difficult to resell or where the producer can effectively prevent resale.

Multiple Choice

Section 9.1

1. Pure monopoly is defined as
   a. an industry in which there is a single seller.
   b. a market structure in which there are many substitute products.
   c. a market in which there are many rival firms competing for sales.
   d. a market structure in which there is a single buyer.

2. For a true, or pure, monopoly,
   a. there is only one seller of the product.
   b. no close substitutes are available.
   c. the firm and the industry are the same.
   d. it must be virtually impossible for other firms to overcome barriers to entry.
   e. all of the above are true.

3. Which of the following is inconsistent with monopoly?
   a. a single seller
   b. economies of scale
   c. $MR < P$
   d. free entry and exit
   e. selling in the elastic portion of the demand curve in order to maximize profits

4. For a natural monopoly, which of the following is *false?*
   a. It is more efficient to have a single firm produce the good.
   b. Production of the good must involve economies of scale throughout the relevant output range.
   c. It would typically result from a firm's possession of an exclusive patent.
   d. One large firm can produce at lower cost than two or more smaller firms.

5. Which of the following is potentially a barrier to entry into a product market?
   a. patent protection on the design of the product
   b. economies of scale in the product market
   c. government licensing of the product's producers
   d. the control of a crucial input necessary to produce the product
   e. all of the above

6. A natural monopoly is defined as an industry in which
   a. one firm can produce the entire industry output at a lower average cost than can a larger number of firms.
   b. a single firm controls crucial inputs to the production process.
   c. one firm is very large relative to other firms that could enter the industry.
   d. a single seller exists as a result of patent protection.

Section 9.2

7. For a monopolist,
   a. its demand curve is downward sloping.
   b. its marginal revenue is less than price.
   c. existing economic profits can be sustained over time.
   d. all of the above are true.

8. If a profit-maximizing monopolist is currently charging a price on the inelastic portion of its demand curve, it should
   a. raise price and decrease output.
   b. lower price and increase output.
   c. reduce both output and price.
   d. hold output constant and raise price.
   e. do none of the above.

9. If a monopolist had a zero marginal cost of production, it would maximize profits by choosing to produce a quantity where
   a. demand was inelastic.
   b. demand was unit elastic.
   c. demand was elastic.
   d. it is impossible to determine where along a demand curve such a monopolist would choose to produce.

10. Tom is the monopoly provider of a town's cable-TV service, whose current subscription price is $20 per month. In order to attract one more subscriber, he has to lower his price to $19.95. What is true of Tom's marginal revenue from that additional subscriber?
   a. Tom's marginal revenue equals $19.95.
   b. Tom's marginal revenue is greater than $19.95.
   c. Tom's marginal revenue is less than $19.95.
   d. Tom's marginal revenue is between $19.95 and $20.

11. Rob owns the only ice-cream shop in the entire region. When he lowers his price, the shop attracts more customers, but its total revenue falls. Which of the following is true of Rob?
   a. He is a monopolist operating on the inelastic region of his demand curve.
   b. He is a monopolist operating on the elastic region of his demand curve.
   c. He would not choose to lower his price in such a situation.
   d. He is a price taker.
   e. Both a and c are true of Rob.

Section 9.3

12. A profit-maximizing monopolist sets
   a. the product price where marginal cost equals marginal revenue.
   b. output where marginal cost equals marginal revenue.
   c. output where marginal cost equals average revenue.
   d. output where demand equals average total cost.
   e. price equal to the highest dollar amount that any customer is willing to pay.

13. Which of the following is *not* true about a profit-maximizing monopolist?
    a. The monopolist faces the downward-sloping market demand curve.
    b. The monopolist always earns an economic profit.
    c. The price of output exceeds marginal revenue.
    d. The monopolist chooses output where marginal revenue equals marginal cost.
    e. All of the above are true.

14. Monopolists are like perfectly competitive firms in that
    a. both maximize profits at the output level where marginal revenue equals marginal cost.
    b. both could be earning either positive profits or losses in the short run.
    c. both are in industries with downward-sloping demand curves.
    d. all of the above are true of both of them.
    e. a and b are true of both of them, but not c.

15. A price-taking firm and a monopolist are alike in that
    a. price equals marginal revenue for both.
    b. both maximize profits by choosing an output where marginal revenue equals marginal cost, provided that price exceeds average variable cost.
    c. price exceeds marginal cost at the profit-maximizing level of output for both.
    d. in the long run, both earn zero economic profits.

16. Which of the following is true of perfect competition but not true of monopoly?
    a. The firm's average total cost curve is U-shaped.
    b. Marginal revenue is equal to price.
    c. A profit-maximizing firm chooses output where marginal revenue equals marginal cost.
    d. Profits may exist in the short run.

Section 9.4

17. Which of the following is true for a firm that is a monopolist?
    a. The firm will definitely make an economic profit in the short run.
    b. The firm will produce a smaller quantity of output than what would be best from the viewpoint of ideal economic efficiency.
    c. The additional revenue that can be generated from an increase in output will exceed the firm's price.
    d. The firm can charge whatever it wants for its product since consumers have no alternatives.

18. Objections to monopolies do *not* include which of the following?
    a. They reduce output below the efficient level of output that would be produced in perfect competition.
    b. They reduce the price below what would be charged in perfect competition.
    c. They charge a price that is greater than marginal cost.
    d. They create a welfare cost.
    e. All of the above are objections to monopolies.

19. Monopoly is unlike perfect competition in that
    a. a monopolist's price is greater than marginal cost.
    b. there are no barriers to entry into a monopoly industry.
    c. a monopolist earns an economic profit only if its price is greater than *ATC*.
    d. all of the above are ways monopoly is unlike perfect competition.
    e. a and b, but not c, are ways monopoly is unlike perfect competition.

Section 9.5

20. If regulators set a price according to marginal cost pricing, the firm will
- **a.** earn positive economic profits.
- **b.** make zero economic profits.
- **c.** suffer an economic loss.
- **d.** earn the same level of profits as it would absent regulation.

21. Average cost pricing for a natural monopoly will
- **a.** result in the socially efficient level of output.
- **b.** result in a less than socially efficient level of output.
- **c.** result in a greater than socially efficient level of output.
- **d.** result in the firm suffering economic losses.
- **e.** result in the firm earning economic profit.

22. Under average cost pricing by a natural monopoly,
- **a.** price is greater than marginal cost.
- **b.** there will be a welfare cost.
- **c.** the producer will earn a normal rate of return.
- **d.** there is little or no incentive for the producer to hold down costs.
- **e.** all of the above are true.

23. Which of the following is not a limitation that regulators face when they implement average cost pricing?
- **a.** Average cost pricing provides little or no incentive for firms to keep costs down.
- **b.** The accurate calculation of a firm's costs is difficult.
- **c.** Decisions are political and often influenced by special interests.
- **d.** All of the above are limitations faced by regulators implementing average cost pricing.

Section 9.6

24. A price-discriminating monopolist will
- **a.** price where marginal revenue equals marginal cost for each different group of demanders.
- **b.** charge a higher price for more inelastic demanders.
- **c.** have to face customers who have a difficult time reselling the good to others who were charged more.
- **d.** do all of the above.

25. A price-discriminating monopolist will tend to charge a lower price to students if it believes that student demand is
- **a.** more elastic than that of other demanders.
- **b.** more inelastic than that of other demanders.
- **c.** unit elastic.
- **d.** graphically represented by a vertical curve.

26. Which of the following is not true of successful price discriminators?
- **a.** They could make greater profits by charging everyone a higher, uniform price.
- **b.** Their customers must have different elasticities of demand.
- **c.** Their customers must have difficulty reselling the good to other customers.
- **d.** They must have some degree of monopoly power.

27. Price discrimination may be a rational strategy for a profit-maximizing monopolist when

  a. there is no opportunity for reselling across market segments.
  b. there is a substantial opportunity for reselling across market segments.
  c. consumers are unable to be segmented into identifiable markets.
  d. the elasticity of demand is the same across all customers.

Problems

1. [Section 9.2]

Fill in the missing data in the table below for a monopolist.

Quantity	Price	Total Revenue	Marginal Revenue	Demand Elastic or Inelastic?
1	$11			
2	10			
3	9			
4	8			
5	7			
6	6			
7	5			
8	4			
9	3			
10	2			
11	1			

2. [Section 9.3]

Assume that the monopolist in problem 1 had fixed costs of $10 and a constant marginal cost of $4 per unit. Add columns to the above table for Total Cost, Marginal Cost, and Profit. What is the profit-maximizing quantity of output? What price will the monopolist charge? What is the profit?

3. [Section 9.3]

Use the following diagram to answer a–c.

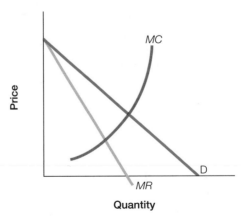

  a. Assuming the monopolist indicated in the diagram produced at all, indicate its profit-maximizing quantity and price.
  b. Add an *ATC* curve that would show this monopolist earning an economic profit.
  c. Add an *ATC* curve that would show this monopolist earning an economic loss.

4. [Section 9.5]

Use the following diagram to answer a-c.

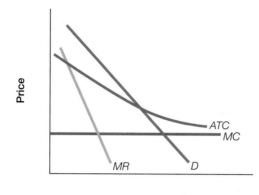

a. Indicate the efficient result on the graph above.
b. Illustrate the profits or losses from the efficient result in a.
c. Show the average cost-pricing solution. What profits are earned with that approach?

chapter 10

Monopolistic Competition and Oligopoly

section 10.1 Monopolistic Competition

- What are the distinguishing features of monopolistic competition?
- How can a firm differentiate its product?

WHAT IS MONOPOLISTIC COMPETITION?

monopolistic competition
a market structure with many firms selling differentiated products

Monopolistic competition is a market structure where many producers of somewhat different products compete with one another. For example, a restaurant is a monopoly in the sense that it has a unique name, menu, quality of service, location, and so on; but it also has many competitors—others selling prepared meals. That is, monopolistic competition has features in common with both monopoly and perfect competition, even though this may sound like an oxymoron—like "jumbo shrimp" or "press release." As with monopoly, individual sellers in monopolistic competition believe that they have some market power. But monopolistic competition is probably closer to competition than monopoly. Entry into and exit out of the industry is unrestricted, and consequently, there are many independent sellers. In virtue of the relatively free entry of new firms, the long-run price and output behavior, and zero long-run economic profits, monopolistic competition is similar to perfect competition. However, the monopolistically competitive firm produces a

In The **NEWS**

IS A BEER A BEER?

To show that some differentiation is perceived rather than real, blind taste tests on beer were conducted on 250 participants.

Four glasses of identical beer, each with different labels, were presented to the subjects as four different brands of beer. In the end, all the subjects believed that the brands of beer were different and that they could tell the difference between them. Another interesting result came out of the taste tests—most of the participants commented that at least one of the beers was unfit for human consumption.

SOURCE: R. Ackoff and J. Emshoff, *Sloan Management Review*, Spring 1976, p. 11.

CONSIDER THIS:
Product differentiation, whether perceived or real, can be effective. Take another example: In blind taste testing, very few people can consistently distinguish between Coca-Cola and Pepsi, yet there are many loyal customers of each brand. Sometimes the key to product differentiation is that consumers believe the brands are different.

© iStockphoto.com/Jill Chen

product that is different (that is, *differentiated* rather than identical or homogeneous) from others, which leads to some degree of monopoly power. In a sense, sellers in a monopolistically competitive market may be regarded as "monopolists" of their own particular brands; but unlike firms with a true monopoly, there is competition among many firms selling similar (but not identical) brands. For example, a buyer living in a city of moderate size and in the market for books, CDs, toothpaste, furniture, shampoo, video rentals, restaurants, eyeglasses, running shoes, and music lessons has many competing sellers from which to choose.

© Kristina Paul

THE THREE BASIC CHARACTERISTICS OF MONOPOLISTIC COMPETITION

The theory of monopolistic competition is based on three characteristics: (1) product differentiation, (2) many sellers, and (3) free entry.

Product Differentiation

One characteristic of monopolistic competition is **product differentiation**—the accentuation of unique product qualities, real or perceived, to develop a specific product identity.

The significant feature of differentiation is the buyer's belief that various sellers' products are not the same, whether the products are actually different or not. Aspirin

Restaurants can be very different. A restaurant that sells pizza competes with other Italian restaurants, but it also competes with restaurants that sell burgers and fries. Monopolistic competition has some elements of competition (many sellers) and some elements of monopoly power (differentiated products).

A great view and a romantic setting can differentiate one restaurant from another.

product differentiation
goods or services that are slightly different, or perceived to be different, from one another

and some brands of over-the-counter cold medicines are examples of products that are very similar or identical but have different brand names. Product differentiation leads to preferences among buyers dealing with or purchasing the products of particular sellers.

Physical Differences Physical differences constitute a primary source of product differentiation. For example, brands of ice cream (such as Chapmans and Breyers), or fast-food restaurants (such as Wendy's and Burger King) differ significantly in taste to many buyers.

Prestige Prestige considerations also differentiate products to a significant degree. Many people prefer to be seen using the currently popular brand, whereas others prefer the "off" brand. Prestige considerations are particularly important with gifts—Cuban cigars, Godiva chocolates, Rolex watches, and so on.

Location Location is a major differentiating factor in retailing. Shoppers are not willing to travel long distances to purchase similar items, which is one reason for the large number of convenience stores and service station mini-marts. Because most buyers realize there are no significant differences among brands of gasoline, the location of a gas station might influence their choice of gasoline. Location is also important for restaurants. Some restaurants can differentiate their products with beautiful views of city lights, ocean, or mountains.

Service Service considerations are likewise significant for product differentiation. Speedy and friendly service or lenient return policies are important to many people. Likewise, speed and quality of service may significantly influence a person's choice of restaurants.

The Impact of Many Sellers

When many firms compete for the same customers, any particular firm has little control over or interest in what other firms do. That is, a restaurant may change prices or improve service without a retaliatory move on the part of other competing restaurants because the time and effort necessary to learn about such changes may have marginal costs that are greater than the marginal benefits.

The Significance of Free Entry

Entry in monopolistic competition is relatively unrestricted in the sense that new firms may easily start the production of close substitutes for existing products; this is the case for restaurants, lawn care service, barbershops, and many forms of retail activity. Because of relatively free entry, economic profits tend to be eliminated in the long run, as is the case with perfect competition.

Section Check

1. The theory of monopolistic competition is based on three primary characteristics: product differentiation, many sellers, and free entry.
2. There are many sources of product differentiation, including physical differences, prestige, location, and service.

Price and Output Determination in Monopolistic Competition

- How are short-run economic profits and losses determined?
- How is long-run equilibrium determined?

DETERMINING SHORT-RUN EQUILIBRIUM

Because monopolistically competitive sellers are price searchers rather than price takers, they do not regard price as given by market conditions as do perfectly competitive firms.

Because each firm sells a slightly different product for which there are many close substitutes, the firm's demand curve is downward sloping but quite flat (elastic). In perfect competition, the demand curve is horizontal because each firm, one of a great many sellers, sells the same homogeneous product. Given the position of an individual firm's demand curve, we can determine short-run equilibrium output and price by using a method similar to that used to determine monopoly output and price.

The cost and revenue curves of a typical seller are shown in Exhibit 1; the intersection of the marginal revenue and marginal cost curves indicates that the short-run profit-maximizing output will be q^*. By observing how much will be demanded at that output level, we find the profit-maximizing price, P^*. That is, at the equilibrium quantity, q^*, we go vertically to the demand curve and read the corresponding price on the vertical axis, P^*, just as we did for monopoly.

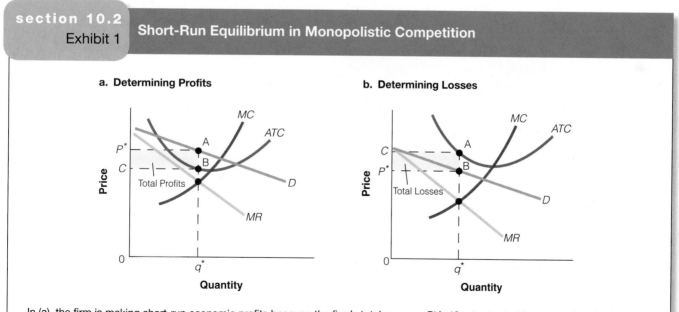

section 10.2
Exhibit 1   **Short-Run Equilibrium in Monopolistic Competition**

a. Determining Profits

b. Determining Losses

In (a), the firm is making short-run economic profits because the firm's total revenue, P^*Aq^*0, at output q^* is greater than the firm's total cost, CBq^*0. The firm has a total profit of area P^*ABC. In (b), the firm is incurring a short-run economic loss because at q^*, price is below average total cost. At q^*, total cost, CAq^*0, is greater than total revenue, P^*Bq^*0, so the firm incurs a total loss of $CABP^*$.

THREE-STEP METHOD FOR MONOPOLISTIC COMPETITION

Let us return to the same three-step method we used in Chapters 8 and 9. Determining whether a firm is generating economic profits, economic losses, or zero economic profits at the profit-maximizing level of output, q^*, can be done in three easy steps.

1. Find where marginal revenue equals marginal cost, and proceed straight down to the horizontal quantity axis to find q^*, the profit-maximizing output level.

2. At q^*, go straight up to the demand curve and then to the left to find the market price, P^*. Once you have identified P^* and q^*, you can find total revenue at the profit-maximizing output level, because $TR = P \times q$.

3. The last step is to find total cost. Again, go straight up from q^* to the average total cost (ATC) curve and then left to the vertical axis to compute the average total cost *per unit*. If we multiply average total cost by the output level, we can find the total cost ($TC = ATC \times q$).

If total revenue is greater than total cost at q^*, the firm is generating total economic profits. If total revenue is less than total cost at q^*, the firm is generating total economic losses. Remember, the cost curves include implicit and explicit costs—that is, even at zero economic profits, the firm is covering the total opportunity costs of its resources and earning a normal profit or rate of return.

SHORT-RUN PROFITS AND LOSSES IN MONOPOLISTIC COMPETITION

Exhibit 1(a) shows the equilibrium position of a monopolistically competitive firm. As we just discussed, the firm produces where $MC = MR$, at output q^*. At output q^* and price P^*, the firm's total revenue is equal to P^*Aq^*0, which is $P^* \times q^*$. At output q^*, the firm's total cost is CBq^*0, which is $ATC \times q^*$. In Exhibit 1(a), we see that total revenue is greater than total cost, so the firm has a total profit of area P^*ABC.

In Exhibit 1(b), at q^*, price is below average total cost, so the firm is minimizing its economic loss. At q^*, total cost, CAq^*0, is greater than total revenue, P^*Bq^*0, so the firm incurs a total loss of $CABP^*$. Other than the shape of the demand curve, this is no different from determining the monopolist's price and output in the short run.

DETERMINING LONG-RUN EQUILIBRIUM

The short-run equilibrium situation depicted in Exhibit 1, whether involving profits or losses, will probably not last long, because there is entry and exit in the long run. If market entry and exit are sufficiently free, new firms will enter when there are economic profits, and some firms will exit when there are economic losses.

When firms are making economic profits, new firms will enter the market. As a result of this influx, there are more sellers of similar products. This means that each new firm will cut into the demand of the existing firms. That is, the demand curve for each of the existing firms will fall. This decline in demand will continue to occur until the average total cost (ATC) curve becomes tangent (barely touching) to the demand curve and economic profits are reduced to zero, as shown in Exhibit 2.

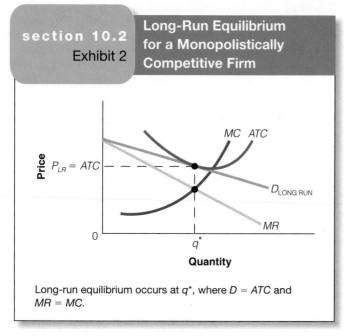

section 10.2
Exhibit 2

Long-Run Equilibrium for a Monopolistically Competitive Firm

Long-run equilibrium occurs at q^*, where $D = ATC$ and $MR = MC$.

When firms are making economic losses, some firms will exit the industry. As some firms exit, fewer firms remain in the market. This increases the demand for the remaining firms' products, shifting their demand curves to the right. The higher demand results in smaller losses for the existing firms, until all losses finally disappear where the *ATC* curve is tangent to the demand curve, as seen in Exhibit 2.

In short, long-run equilibrium occurs at a level of output at which each firm's demand curve is just tangent to its *ATC* curve. The point of tangency always occurs at the same level of output as that at which marginal cost is equal to marginal revenue, as shown in Exhibit 2. At this equilibrium point, there are zero economic profits and no incentives for firms to either enter or exit the industry.

Section Check

SECTION CHECK

1. A monopolistically competitive firm is making short-run economic profits when the equilibrium price is greater than average total costs at the equilibrium output; when equilibrium price is below average total cost at the equilibrium output, the firm is minimizing its economic losses.
2. In the long run, equilibrium price equals average total costs. With that, economic profits are zero, so there are no incentives for firms to either enter or exit the industry.

Monopolistic Competition versus Perfect Competition

- What are the differences and similarities between monopolistic competition and perfect competition?
- What is excess capacity?
- Why does the monopolistically competitive firm fail to meet productive efficiency?
- Why does the monopolistically competitive firm fail to meet allocative efficiency?

We have seen that both monopolistic competition and perfect competition have many buyers and sellers and relatively free entry. However, product differentiation enables a monopolistic competitor to have some influence over price. Consequently, a monopolistically competitive firm has a downward-sloping demand curve, but because of the large number of good substitutes for its product, the curve tends to be much more elastic than the demand curve for a monopolist.

THE SIGNIFICANCE OF EXCESS CAPACITY

Because in monopolistic competition the demand curve is downward sloping, its point of tangency with the *ATC* curve will not and cannot be at the lowest level of average cost. What does this mean? It means that even when long-run adjustments are complete, firms are not operating at a level that permits the lowest average cost of production—the efficient scale of the firm. The existing plant, even though optimal for the equilibrium

How much do you value variety in clothing? Imagine a world where everyone wore the same clothes, drove the same cars, and lived in identical houses. In other words, most individuals are willing to pay for a little variety, even if it costs somewhat more.

excess capacity

occurs when the firm produces below the level where average total cost is minimized

productive efficiency

output production that minimizes average total cost

volume of output, is not used to capacity; that is, **excess capacity** exists at that level of output. Excess capacity occurs when the firm produces below the level where average total cost is minimized.

Unlike a perfectly competitive firm, a monopolistically competitive firm could increase output and lower its average total cost, as shown in Exhibit 1(a). However, any attempt to increase output to attain lower average cost would be unprofitable because the price reduction necessary to sell the greater output would cause marginal revenue to fall below the marginal cost of the increased output. As we can see in Exhibit 1(a), to the right of q^*, marginal cost is greater than marginal revenue. Consequently, in monopolistic competition, there is a tendency toward too many firms in the industry, each producing a volume of output less than what would allow lowest cost. Economists call this tendency a failure to reach **productive efficiency.** For example, there may be too many grocery stores or too many service stations, in the sense that if the total volume of business were concentrated in a smaller number of sellers, average cost, and thus price, could in principle be less.

FAILING TO MEET ALLOCATIVE EFFICIENCY, TOO

Productive inefficiency is not the only problem with a monopolistically competitive firm. Exhibit 1(a) shows a firm that is not operating where price is equal to marginal costs. In the monopolistically competitive model, at the intersection of the *MC* and *MR* curves (q^*), we can clearly see that price is greater than marginal cost. This means that society is willing to pay more for the product (the price, P^*) than it costs society to produce it. In this case, the firm is failing to reach allocative efficiency, where price equals marginal cost. In short, this means that the firm is underallocating resources—too many firms are producing, each at output levels that are less than full capacity. Note that in Exhibit 1(b), the perfectly com-

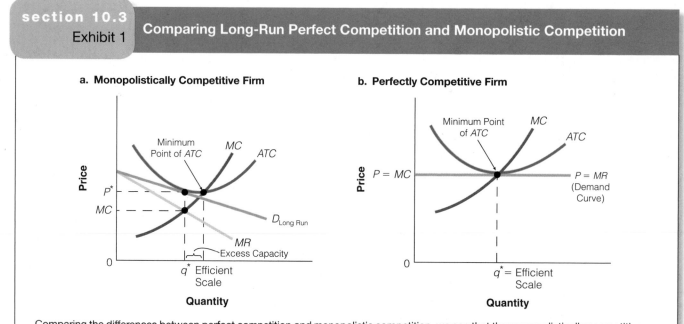

petitive firm has reached both productive efficiency ($P = ATC$ at the minimum point on the *ATC* curve) and allocative efficiency ($P = MC$). However, it is clear that these drawbacks in the monopolistically competitive market would be far greater in monopoly, where the demand curve is more inelastic (steeper).

Further, in defence of monopolistic competition, the higher average cost and the slightly higher price and lower output may simply be the price firms pay for differentiated products—variety. That is, just because monopolistically competitive firms have not met the conditions for productive and allocative efficiency, it is not obvious that society is not better off.

WHAT ARE THE REAL COSTS OF MONOPOLISTIC COMPETITION?

We have just argued that perfect competition meets the tests of allocative and productive efficiency and that monopolistic competition does not. Can we "fix" a monopolistically competitive firm to look more like an efficient, perfectly competitive firm? One remedy might entail using government regulation, as in the case of a natural monopoly. However, this process would be costly because a monopolistically competitive firm makes no economic profits in the long run. Therefore, asking monopolistically competitive firms to equate price and marginal cost would lead to economic losses because long-run average total cost would be greater than price at $P = MC$. Consequently, the government would have to subsidize the firm. Living with the inefficiencies in monopolistically competitive markets might be easier than coping with the difficulties entailed by regulations and the cost of the necessary subsidies.

We argued that the monopolistically competitive firm does not operate at the minimum point of the *ATC* curve, whereas the perfectly competitive firm does. However, is this a fair comparison? In monopolistic competition, there are differentiated goods and services, whereas in perfect competition, there are not. In other words, the excess capacity that exists in monopolistic competition is the price we pay for product differentiation. Have you ever thought about the many restaurants, movies, and gasoline stations that have "excess capacity"? Can you imagine a world where all firms were working at full capacity? After all, choice is a good, and most of us value some choice.

In short, the inefficiency of monopolistic competition is a result of product differentiation. Since consumers value variety—the ability to choose from competing products and brands—the loss in efficiency must be weighed against the gain in increased product variety. The gains from product diversity can be large and may easily outweigh the inefficiency associated with a downward-sloping demand curve.

ARE THE DIFFERENCES BETWEEN MONOPOLISTIC COMPETITION AND PERFECT COMPETITION EXAGGERATED?

The significance of the difference between the relationship of marginal cost to price in monopolistic competition and in perfect competition can easily be exaggerated. As long as preferences for various brands are not extremely strong, the demand for a firm's products will be highly elastic (very flat). Accordingly, the points of tangency with the *ATC* curves are not likely to be far above the point of lowest cost, and excess capacity will be small, as illustrated in Exhibit 2. Only if differentiation is strong will the difference between the long-run price level and the price that would prevail under perfectly competitive conditions be significant.

Remember this little caveat: The theory of the firm is like a road map that does not detail every gully, creek, and hill but does give directions to get from one geographic point to another. Any particular theory of the firm may not tell precisely how an individual firm will operate, but it does provide valuable insight into the ways firms will tend to react to changing economic conditions such as entry, demand, and cost changes.

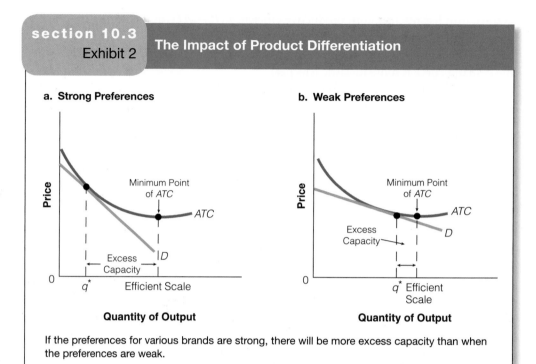

section 10.3
Exhibit 2   **The Impact of Product Differentiation**

a. Strong Preferences

Price

Minimum Point
of *ATC*

ATC

Excess
Capacity

D

0   *q**   Efficient Scale

Quantity of Output

b. Weak Preferences

Price

Minimum Point
of *ATC*

ATC

Excess
Capacity

D

0   *q** Efficient
Scale

Quantity of Output

If the preferences for various brands are strong, there will be more excess capacity than when the preferences are weak.

Section Check

1. Both the competitive firm and the monopolistically competitive firm may earn short-run economic profits, but these profits will be eliminated in the long run.
2. Because monopolistically competitive firms face a downward-sloping demand curve, average total cost is not minimized in the long run, after entry and exit have eliminated profits. Monopolistically competitive firms fail to reach productive efficiency, producing at output levels less than the efficient output.
3. The monopolistically competitive firm does not achieve allocative efficiency because it does not operate where the price is equal to marginal costs. This means that society is willing to pay more for additional output than it costs society to produce additional output.

section 10.4 Advertising

- Why do firms advertise?
- Is advertising good or bad from society's perspective?
- Will advertising always increase costs?
- Can advertising increase demand?

WHY DO FIRMS ADVERTISE?

Advertising is an important nonprice method of competition that is commonly used in monopolistic competition. Why do firms advertise? The reason is simple: By advertising, firms hope to increase the demand and create a less elastic demand curve for their products, thus enhancing revenues and profits. Advertising is part of our life, whether we are watching television, listening to the radio, reading a newspaper or magazine, or simply driving down the highway. Firms that sell differentiated products can spend between 10 and 20 percent of their revenue on advertising.

ADVERTISING CAN CHANGE THE SHAPE AND POSITION OF THE DEMAND CURVE

Consider Exhibit 1, which shows how a successful advertising campaign can increase demand and change elasticity. If an ad campaign convinces buyers that a firm's product is truly different, the demand curve for that good will become less elastic. Consequently, price changes (up or down) will have a relatively smaller impact on the quantity demanded of the product. The firm hopes that this change in elasticity, ideally coupled with an increase in demand, will increase profits.

The degree to which advertising affects demand will vary from market to market. For example, in the laundry detergent market, empirical evidence shows that it is very important to advertise because the demand for any one detergent critically depends on the amount of money spent on advertising. That is, if you don't advertise your detergent, you don't sell much of it.

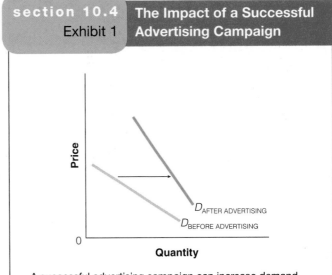

section 10.4
Exhibit 1

The Impact of a Successful Advertising Campaign

A successful advertising campaign can increase demand and lead to a less elastic demand curve, such as $D_{\text{AFTER ADVERTISING}}$.

IS ADVERTISING GOOD OR BAD FROM SOCIETY'S PERSPECTIVE?

What Is the Impact of Advertising on Society?

This question elicits sharply different responses. Some have argued that advertising manipulates consumer tastes and wastes billions of dollars annually creating "needs" for trivial products. Advertising helps create a demonstration effect, whereby people have new urges to buy products that were previously unknown to them. In creating additional demands for private goods, the ability to provide needed public goods (for which there is little advertising to create demand) is potentially reduced. Moreover, sometimes advertising is based on misleading claims, so people find themselves buying products that do not provide the satisfaction or results promised in the ads. Finally, advertising itself requires resources that raise average costs.

On the other hand, who is to say that the purchase of any product is frivolous or unnecessary? If one believes that people are rational and should be permitted freedom of expression, the argument against advertising loses some of its force.

Furthermore, defenders of advertising argue that firms use advertising to provide important information about the price and availability of a product, the location and hours of store operation, and so on. This allows for customers to make better choices and allows markets to function more efficiently.

Will Advertising Always Increase Costs?

Although it is true that advertising may raise the average total cost, it is possible that when substantial economies of scale exist, the average production cost will decline more than the amount of the per-unit cost of advertising. In other words, average total cost, in some situations, actually declines after extensive advertising. This can happen because advertising may

Advertising and Economies of Scale

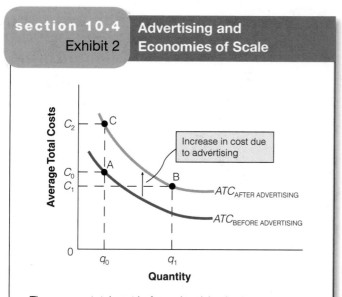

The average total cost before advertising is shown as $ATC_{BEFORE ADVERTISING}$. After advertising, the curve shifts to $ATC_{AFTER ADVERTISING}$. If the increase in demand resulting from advertising is significant, economies of scale from higher output levels may offset the advertising costs, lowering average total cost. The movement from point A to point B allows the firm to sell its product at a lower price. However, when two firms engage in an advertising war, it is possible that neither will gain market share (increased output) but each will incur higher advertising costs. This is shown as a movement from point A to point C in Exhibit 2—output remains at q_0, but average total cost rises from C_0 to C_2.

allow the firm to operate closer to the point of minimum cost on its *ATC* curve. Specifically, notice in Exhibit 2 that the average total cost curve before advertising is $ATC_{BEFORE ADVERTISING}$. After advertising, the curve shifts upward to $ATC_{AFTER ADVERTISING}$. If the increase in demand resulting from advertising is significant, economies of scale from higher output levels may offset the advertising costs. Average total cost may fall from C_0 to C_1, a movement from point A to point B, and allow the firm to sell its product at a lower price. Toys "R" Us versus a smaller, owner-operated toy store provides an example.

However, it also is possible that an advertising war between two firms, say Burger King and McDonald's, will result in higher advertising costs for both and no gain in market share (increased output) for either. This is shown as a movement from point A to point C in Exhibit 2. Output remains at q_0, but average total cost rises from C_0 to C_2.

Firms in monopolistic competition are not likely to experience substantial cost reductions as output increases. Therefore, they probably will not be able to offset advertising costs with lower production costs, particularly if advertising costs are high. Even if advertising does add to total cost, however, it is true that advertising conveys information. Through advertising, customers become aware of the options available to them in terms of product choice. Advertising helps customers choose products that best meet their needs, and it informs price-conscious customers about the costs of products. In this way, advertising lowers information costs, which is one reason that the Competition Bureau opposes bans on advertising.

What If Advertising Increases Competition?

If advertising reduces information costs, this leads to some interesting economic implications. For example, say that as a result of advertising, we know about more products that may be substitutes for the products we have been buying for years. That is, the more goods that are advertised, the more consumers are aware of "substitute" products, which leads to increasingly competitive markets. Studies in the eyeglass, toy, and drug industries have shown that advertising has increased competition and led to lower prices in these markets.

ACTIVE LEARNING EXERCISE

ADVERTISING

Q: Why is it so important for monopolistically competitive firms to advertise?

A: Owners of fast-food restaurants must compete with many other restaurants, so they often must advertise to demonstrate that their restaurant is

different. Advertising may convince customers that a firm's products or services are better than others, which then may influence the shape and position of the demand curve for the products and potentially increase profits. Remember, monopolistically competitive firms are different from competitive firms because of their ability, to some extent, to set prices.

SECTION CHECK

Section Check

1. With advertising, a firm hopes it can alter the elasticity of the demand for its product, making it more inelastic and causing an increase in demand that will enhance profits.
2. To some, advertising manipulates consumer tastes and creates "needs" for trivial products. However, if one believes that people act rationally, this argument loses some of its force.
3. Where substantial economies of scale exist, it is possible that average production costs will decline more than the amount of per-unit costs of advertising in the long run.
4. By making consumers aware of different "substitute" products, advertising may lead to more competitive markets and lower consumer prices.

section 10.5

Oligopoly

- What is oligopoly?
- What is mutual interdependence?
- Are economies of scale a major barrier to entry?
- Why is it so difficult for the oligopolist to determine its profit-maximizing price and output?

WHAT IS OLIGOPOLY?

As we stated in Chapter 8, an **oligopoly** exists where relatively few firms control all or most of the production and sale of a product (*oligopoly* = few sellers). The products may be either homogeneous or differentiated; but the barriers to entry are often high, which makes it difficult for firms to enter the industry. Consequently, long-run economic profits may be earned by firms in the industry. Examples of oligopolistic markets include commercial airlines, oil, automobiles, steel, breakfast cereals, computers, cigarettes, tobacco, and sports drinks. For all these products, the market is dominated by anywhere from a few to several big companies, although they may have many different brands (e.g., General Motors, General Foods, Dell Computers).

oligopoly
a market structure with only a few sellers offering similar or identical products

MUTUAL INTERDEPENDENCE

Oligopoly is characterized by **mutual interdependence** among firms; that is, each firm shapes its policy with an eye to the policies of competing firms. Oligopolists must strategize, much like good chess or bridge players, who are constantly observing and anticipating the moves of their rivals. Oligopoly is likely to occur whenever the number of firms in an industry is so small that any change in output or price on the part of one firm appreciably impacts the sales of competing firms. In this situation, it is almost inevitable that competitors will respond directly to each other's actions in determining their own policies.

mutual interdependence
when a firm shapes its policy with an eye to the policies of competing firms

WHY DO OLIGOPOLIES EXIST?

Primarily, oligopoly is a result of the relationship between the technological conditions of production and potential sales volume. For many products, a firm cannot obtain a reasonably low cost of production unless it is producing a large fraction of the market output. In other words, substantial economies of scale are present in oligopoly markets. Automobile and steel production are classic examples of this. Because of legal concerns such as patents, large start-up costs, and the presence of pronounced economies of scale, the barriers to entry are quite high in oligopoly.

ECONOMIES OF SCALE AS A BARRIER TO ENTRY

Economies of large-scale production make operation on a small scale during a new firm's early years extremely unprofitable. A firm cannot build up a large market overnight; in the interim, average total cost is so high that losses are heavy. Recognition of this fact discourages new firms from entering the market, as illustrated in Exhibit 1. We can see that if an automobile company produces quantity Q_{LARGE} rather than Q_{SMALL}, it will be able to pro-

In The **NEWS**

END WIRELESS "OLIGOPOLY"

BY BARBARA SHECTER

Pierre Karl Peladeau, the chief executive of Quebecor Inc., is urging the federal government to "throw off the regulatory yoke" to clear the way for development of a fourth wireless network that will drive the technology and pricing necessary for his television and newspaper holdings to survive in the digital age.

In a speech to a business crowd in Toronto yesterday, Mr. Peladeau said new technology, such as Apple Inc.'s iPhone, is being held back in Canada by the "oligopoly" of the three existing wireless operators owned by Rogers Communications Inc., Telus Corp. and Bell Canada Inc.

Combined with the high cost of data transmission relative to other countries such as the United States, the penetration of wireless devices is lagging behind demand to use the technology for accessing news and entertainment programming, he said.

"We are witnessing a profound revolution in the way we consume information," Mr. Peladeau said, adding that Quebecor's Sun newspaper holdings and TVA Inc. television network are "in the eye of the storm."

"Canada has to throw off the regulatory yoke and give the private sector the chance to be entrepreneurial," said Mr. Peladeau. "By restricting access to new media, we are condemning traditional media to mediocrity and decline."

His comments, which follow moves by technology giants Google Inc. and Apple Inc. to shake up the wireless world in the United States with similar arguments, drew laughter and derision from his would-be competitors in wireless service who came to hear the luncheon address. More than one criticized Mr. Peladeau for calling for less regulation at the same time his company is asking the government to set aside spectrum for new wireless players and regulate access to their competitors' infrastructure and networks for roaming.

"I think it's very funny that he wants all the regulations off and then he asks for what amounts to a subsidy," said Ken Engelhart, vice-president of regulatory affairs at Rogers.

Michael Hennessy, vice-president of wireless, broadband and content policy at Telus, echoed those remarks and added that a company with $10 billion in annual revenue, as well as major broadcast and newspaper holdings, has no reason to ask the federal government for assistance to get into a new business.

The wireless players also took pains to point out the fact that Quebecor was in the wireless business in 2000, but chose to sell a minority stake in the struggling Fido business owned by Microcell.

SOURCE: Material reprinted with the express permission of: "The National Post Company." a CanWest Partnership.

CONSIDER THIS:

Some oligopolies, markets in which a few sellers offer similar products, may not be entirely avoidable or undesirable. Particularly in industries characterized by significant economies of scale, an oligopolistic market structure can often generate the efficiencies necessary to produce better products at lower prices. However, an oligopoly can also allow select firms to earn excess profits at the expense of consumers and economic progress. The wireless sector in Canada is currently dominated by three major operators: Rogers Communications, Telus Corp., and Bell Canada. A wireless spectrum auction (involving more than 270 licences for radio waves across the country over which cellphone networks operate) will see additional competition introduced to this evolving industry.

duce cars at a significantly lower cost. If the average total cost to a potential entrant is equivalent to point A on the *ATC* curve and the price of automobiles is less than P_0, a new firm would be deterred from entering the industry.

EQUILIBRIUM PRICE AND QUANTITY IN OLIGOPOLY

It is difficult to predict how firms will react when there is mutual interdependence. No firm knows what its demand curve looks like with any degree of certainty, and therefore it has a very limited knowledge of its marginal revenue curve. To know anything about its demand curve, the firm must know how other firms will react to its prices and other policies. In the absence of additional assumptions, then, equating marginal revenue and marginal cost is relegated to guesswork. Thus, it is difficult for an oligopolist to determine its profit-maximizing price and output.

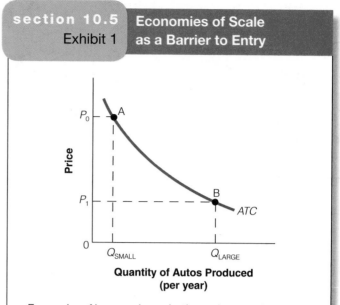

section 10.5
Exhibit 1
Economies of Scale as a Barrier to Entry

Economies of large-scale production make operation on a small scale more costly, *ceteris paribus.*

© ARTEKI/Shutterstock

Do you think economies of scale are important in this industry? Unlike home-cooked meals, few cars are "homemade." The barriers to entry in the auto industry are formidable. A new entrant would have to start out as a large producer (investing billions of dollars in plant, equipment, and advertising) to compete with existing firms, which have lower average total costs per unit because of economies of large-scale production.

Section Check

1. Oligopolies exist where relatively few firms control all or most of the production and sale of a product. The products may be homogeneous or differentiated, but the barriers to entry are often very high and, consequently, there may be long-run economic profits.
2. When firms are mutually interdependent, each firm shapes its policy with an eye to the policies of competing firms.
3. Economies of large-scale production make operation on a small scale extremely unprofitable. Recognition of this fact discourages new firms from entering the market.
4. Because in oligopoly the pricing decision of one firm influences the demand curve of competing firms, the oligopolist faces considerable uncertainty as to the location and shape of its demand and marginal revenue curves. Thus, it is difficult for an oligopolist to determine its profit-maximizing price and output.

section 10.6

Collusion and Cartels

- Why do firms collude?
- What is joint profit maximization?
- Why does collusion break down?

UNCERTAINTY AND PRICING DECISIONS

The uncertainties of pricing decisions are substantial in oligopoly. The implications of misjudging the behaviour of competitors could prove to be disastrous. An executive who makes the wrong pricing move may force the firm to lose sales or, at a minimum, be forced himself to back down in an embarrassing fashion from an announced price increase. Because of this uncertainty, some believe that oligopolists change their prices less frequently than perfect competitors, whose prices may change almost continually. The empirical evidence, however, does not clearly indicate that prices are in fact always slow to change in oligopoly situations.

COLLUSION

collude

when firms act together to restrict competition

Because the actions and profits of oligopolists are so dominated by mutual interdependence, the temptation is great for firms to **collude**—to get together and agree to act jointly in pricing and other matters. If firms believe they can increase their profits by coordinating their actions, they will be tempted to collude. Collusion reduces uncertainty and increases the potential for monopoly profits. From society's point of view, however, collusion has the same disadvantages monopoly does; namely, it creates a situation in which goods very likely become overpriced and underproduced, with consumers losing out as the result of a misallocation of resources.

IS COLLUSION LIKE A MONOPOLY?

From the standpoint of pricing and output decisions, a truly collusive oligopoly that involves all the firms in an industry could act as the equivalent of one large firm with several plants. Acting in this manner, the economic effect of the collusive oligopoly would be exactly the same as that of a monopoly; a single demand curve would exist for the group of companies. Once the profit-maximization price was determined, they could agree on how much output each firm in the group would offer for sale.

JOINT PROFIT MAXIMIZATION

cartel

a collection of firms that agree on sales, pricing, and other decisions

joint profit maximization

determination of price based on the marginal revenue derived from the market demand schedule and marginal cost schedule of the firms in the industry

Agreements between or among firms on sales, pricing, and other decisions are usually referred to as cartel agreements. A **cartel** is a collection of firms making an agreement.

Cartels may lead to what economists call **joint profit maximization:** Price is based on the marginal revenue function, which is derived from the product's total (or market) demand schedule and the various firms' marginal cost schedules, as shown in Exhibit 1. With outright agreements—necessarily secret because of anti-combine laws (in Canada, at least)—firms that make up the market will attempt to estimate demand and cost schedules and then set optimum price and output levels accordingly.

Equilibrium price and quantity for a collusive oligopoly, like those for a monopoly, are determined according to the intersection of the marginal revenue curve (derived from the market demand curve) and the horizontal sum of the short-run marginal cost curves for the oligopolists. As shown in Exhibit 1, the resulting equilibrium quantity is Q^* and the equilibrium price is P^*. Collusion facilitates joint profit maximization for the oligopoly. Like monopoly, if the oligopoly is maintained in the long run, it charges a higher price, produces less output, and fails to maximize social welfare, relative to perfect competition, because $P^* > MC$ at Q^*.

The manner in which total profits are shared among firms in the industry depends in part on the relative costs and sales of the various firms. Firms with low costs and large supply capabilities will obtain the largest profits because they have greater bargaining power. Sales, in turn, may depend in large measure on consumer preferences for various brands if there is product differentiation. With outright collusion, firms may agree on market shares and the division of profits. The division of total profits will depend on the relative bargaining strength of each firm, influenced by its relative financial strength, ability to inflict damage (through price wars) on other firms if an agreement is not reached, ability to withstand similar actions on the part of other firms, relative costs, consumer preferences, and bargaining skills.

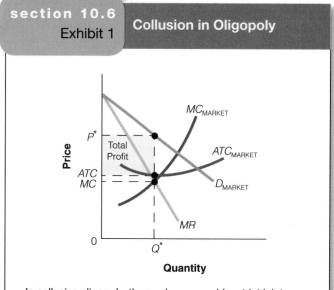

section 10.6
Exhibit 1 — **Collusion in Oligopoly**

In collusive oligopoly, the producers would restrict joint output to Q^*, setting their price at P^*. The price and output situation is identical to that for monopoly. The members of the collusive oligopoly would share the profits in the shaded area.

In The **NEWS**

QUEBEC GAS RETAILERS CAUGHT UP IN PRICE-FIXING SCHEME

BY ANONYMOUS

The federal Competition Bureau says criminal charges have been laid against 13 people and 11 companies for allegedly fixing gasoline prices in four Quebec markets.

"Today's announcement sends a clear message that the Competition Bureau will take action to stop price-fixers whenever we have evidence that they have broken the law," bureau commissioner Sheridan Scott told a news conference in Montreal.

"Price-fixing is a fraud against consumers. It deprives Canadians of the benefits of a competitive market, including a lower price and a greater choice."

Scott said the charges and guilty pleas are a result of an "extensive investigation" by the bureau.

She said gas retailers in Thetford Mines, Victoriaville, Magog and Sherbrooke allegedly phoned each other to agree on gasoline prices.

Scott said an "overwhelming majority" of businesses in these markets are accused of participating in the alleged scheme between 2005 and 2007.

SOURCE: Adapted from Anonymous, "Quebec Gas Retailers Caught Up in Price Fixing Scheme," *Telegraph-Journal*, Saint John, N.B., June 13, 2008, p. B1. Reprinted with permission of *The New Burnswick Telegraph-Journal*.

CONSIDER THIS:

In the four Quebec markets affected, the gas retailers involved in the collusive agreement produced the same economic effect as a single firm—a monopoly. The retailers would restrict joint output to achieve a desired price, sharing in the greater-than-normal profits—joint profit maximization at work.

WHY ARE MOST COLLUSIVE OLIGOPOLIES SHORT LIVED?

Collusive oligopolies are potentially highly profitable for participants but detrimental to society. Fortunately, most strong collusive oligopolies are rather short lived, for two reasons. First, in Canada and in some other nations, collusive oligopolies are strictly illegal under anti-combine laws. Second, for collusion to work, firms must agree to restrict output to a level that will support the profit-maximizing price. At that price, firms can earn positive economic profits. Yet there is a great temptation for firms to cheat on the agreement of the collusive oligopoly; and because collusive agreements are illegal, the other parties have no way to punish the offender. Why do they have a strong incentive to cheat? Because any individual firm could lower its price slightly and thereby increase sales and profits, as long as it goes undetected. Undetected price cuts could bring in new customers, including rivals' customers. In addition, there are nonprice methods of defection—better credit terms, rebates, prompt delivery service, and so on.

Section Check

1. The mutual interdependence of oligopolists tempts them to collude in order to reduce uncertainty and increase potential for monopoly profits.
2. Joint profit maximization requires the determination of price based on the market demand for the product and the marginal costs of the various firms.
3. Most strong collusive oligopolies are rather short lived, for two reasons: (1) Collusive oligopolies are strictly illegal under Canadian anti-combine laws, and (2) there is a great temptation for firms to cheat on the agreement of the collusive oligopoly.

---

section 10.7

Other Oligopoly Models

- What is the kinked demand curve model?
- What happens to the oligopolists' profits if entry is easy?
- How can existing firms deter potential entrants?

THE KINKED DEMAND CURVE MODEL—PRICE RIGIDITY

As we have seen, collusion tends to be fragile in oligopoly markets. Prices in some oligopolistic industries tend to be quite stable, or rigid. That is, even if demand or cost changes, firms will be reluctant to change their prices. For example, if demand or costs were to increase, a firm might be tempted to increase its prices but may not because it fears that rivals will not raise their prices and the firm will lose customer sales. The firm may also be reluctant to lower its prices for fear of setting off a round of price warfare. That is, once the collusion outcome has been reached, individual producers have an incentive to be cautious about changing their output—or price.

kinked demand curve
indicates the price rigidity in oligopoly when competitors show a greater tendency to follow price reductions than price increases

This idea of price rigidity in oligopoly is the basis of the **kinked demand curve** model. According to the kinked demand curve model, each firm faces a demand curve that is kinked at the collusive market price (P^*) and output (q^*). This kinked demand curve, illustrated in Exhibit 1, is produced by the greater tendency of competitors to follow price reductions than price increases. A price reduction takes business away from other firms and forces them to cut prices in order to protect their sales. A price increase does not necessitate a readjustment because other firms gain customers if one increases its price. At the point of the kink, the *MR* curve is discontinuous.

The profit-maximizing price, P^*, is indicated in Exhibit 1 by the point at which the demand curve changes slope. At prices higher than P^*, the firm's demand curve is very elastic. The reason for this elasticity is that a price increase would significantly cut revenues, as other rival firms fail to follow the price increase, causing the firm to lose sales and market share. If it lowers the price below P^*, reductions would yield little additional business because most of the other firms are presumed to follow price cuts. That is, sales will only increase if the total market quantity demanded increases due to the lower price. Below P^*, the firm does not capture many rivals' clients as rival firms match the price reduction, so the demand curve tends to be relatively inelastic below P^*. A slight decrease in price will not lead to a large increase in quantity demanded because rivals will lower their price to maintain their market share.

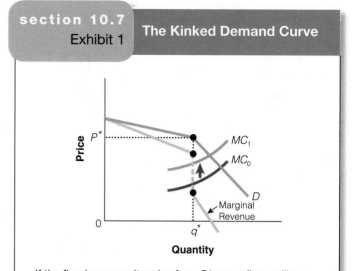

section 10.7
Exhibit 1 **The Kinked Demand Curve**

If the firm increases its price from P^*, most firms will not follow, and its demand curve is said to be relatively elastic (that is, a slight increase in price will lead to a more-than-proportionate fall in the quantity demanded). Conversely, below P^*, demand is relatively inelastic; a slight decrease in price will not lead to a large increase in the quantity demanded because rivals will also lower prices to hold on to their market share. Even if the marginal cost increases from MC_0 to MC_1, the firm will produce the same at the same price, P^*, and at the same output, q^*.

One important consequence of the kink in the demand curve is that the firm may be slow to adjust price in response to cost changes. Because of the kink in the demand curve, the marginal revenue curve is discontinuous. Therefore, the *MC* curve can move up or down over a substantial range without affecting the optimum level of output or price. For example, as the marginal cost increases from MC_0 to MC_1 in Exhibit 1, the firm will continue to produce at the same price, P^*, and at the same output, q^*.

The key feature of the kinked demand curve is that the shape of the firm's demand curve is dependent on the action of competing firms. In the real world, of course, when a firm raises its price, anticipating that other firms will also raise prices but they do not, then the price-raising firm will face the prospect of a major sales decline, and the firm that initiated the price increase will usually retreat from the price increase originally announced. The explanation for the price rigidity comes from the idea that firms do not want to engage in destructive price competition.

Not all oligopolies experience price rigidity. For example, during the high inflationary periods of the 1970s, some oligopolists increased their prices frequently. Oligopolists are more likely to experience price rigidity in situations of excess capacity—during a business downturn or a recession, for instance. In such cases, firms are likely to match a price cut but not a price hike—that is, they face a kinked demand curve. Also, if an oligopolist believes that other firms are faced with rising cost, then all the firms in the industry would respond to the change in marginal cost by adjusting their price and output accordingly to maintain their collusive position.

PRICE LEADERSHIP

Over time, an implied understanding may develop in an oligopoly market that a large firm is the **price leader,** sending a signal to competitors, perhaps through a press release, that they have increased their prices. This approach is not outright collusion because no formal

price leader
a large firm in an oligopoly that unilaterally makes changes in its product prices that competitors tend to follow

section 10.7
Exhibit 2 **Long-Run Equilibrium and Deterring Entry**

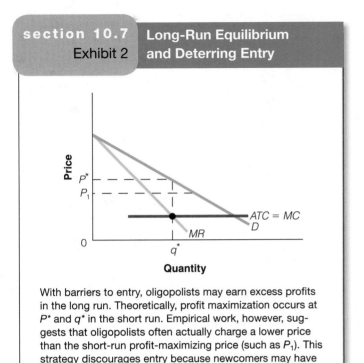

With barriers to entry, oligopolists may earn excess profits in the long run. Theoretically, profit maximization occurs at P^* and q^* in the short run. Empirical work, however, suggests that oligopolists often actually charge a lower price than the short-run profit-maximizing price (such as P_1). This strategy discourages entry because newcomers may have costs higher than P_1.

price follower
a competitor in an oligopoly that goes along with the pricing decision of the price leader

price leadership
when a dominant firm that produces a large portion of the industry's output sets a price that maximizes its profits, and other firms follow

predatory pricing
setting a price deliberately low in order to drive out competitors

cartel arrangement or formal meetings are used to determine price and output; but this is what is called tacit collusion. Any competitor that goes along with the pricing decision of the price leader is called a **price follower.**

Price leadership is most likely to develop when one firm, the so-called dominant firm, produces a large portion of the total output. The dominant firm sets the price that maximizes its profits, and the smaller firms, which would have little influence over price anyway, act as if they are perfect competitors—selling all they want at that price. In the past, a number of firms have been price leaders: General Motors (automobiles), Kellogg's (breakfast cereals), and Goodyear (tires).

WHAT HAPPENS IN THE LONG RUN IF ENTRY IS EASY?

Mutual interdependence is, in itself, no guarantee of economic profits, even if the firms in the industry succeed in maximizing joint profits. The extent to which economic profits disappear depends on the ease with which new firms can enter the industry. When entry is easy, excess profits attract newcomers. New firms may break down existing price agreements by undercutting prices in an attempt to establish themselves in the industry. In response, older firms may reduce prices to avoid excessive sales losses; as a result, the general level of prices will begin to approach average total cost.

HOW DO OLIGOPOLISTS DETER MARKET ENTRY?

If most firms reach a scale of plant and firm size great enough to allow lowest-cost operation, their long-run positions will be similar to that shown in Exhibit 2. To simplify, we have drawn *MC* and *ATC* constant. The equilibrium, or profit-maximizing, price in an established oligopoly is represented by P^*. Typically, the rate of profit in these industries is high, which would encourage entry. However, empirical research indicates that oligopolists often initiate pricing policies that reduce the entry incentive for new firms. Established firms may deliberately hold prices below the maximum profit point at P^*, charging a price of, say, P_1. This lower than profit-maximizing price may discourage newcomers from entering. Because new firms would likely have higher costs than existing firms, the lower price may not be high enough to cover their costs. However, once the threat of entry subsides, the market price may return to the profit-maximizing price, P^*.

Similarly, if the price is deliberately kept low (below average variable cost) to drive a competitor out of the market, it is called **predatory pricing.** However, both economists and the courts have a difficult time deciding whether the price is truly predatory. Even if the price is driven down below average variable cost (recall from Chapter 8, when price is below *AVC*, it is the shutdown point of a firm), the courts still have to determine whether the low price destroyed the rival and kept it out of business. Did the firm significantly raise its prices once the rival had been driven out of the industry? As a result, it is often difficult to distinguish predatory pricing from vigorous competition.

1. In the kinked demand curve model, if one firm cuts its price, rivals will follow, but rival firms will not follow the firm if it raises its price.
2. When market entry is easy, excess profits attract newcomers. They may break down existing price agreements, causing older firms to reduce their prices and, ultimately, drive the general level of prices toward average total cost.
3. Firms in an oligopoly may deliberately hold prices below the short-run profit-maximizing point in order to discourage newcomers from entering the market.

Summary

Section 10.1
- The theory of monopolistic competition is based on three primary characteristics: product differentiation, many sellers, and free entry.
- Product differentiation has many sources, including physical differences, prestige, location, and service.

Section 10.2
- A monopolistically competitive firm makes short-run economic profits when equilibrium price is greater than average total cost at the equilibrium output; when equilibrium price is below average total cost at the equilibrium output, the firm is minimizing its economic losses.
- In the long run, equilibrium price equals average total cost, economic profits are zero, and there is no incentive for firms to either enter or exit the industry.

Section 10.3
- Both the competitive firm and the monopolistically competitive firm may earn short-run economic profits; these profits are eliminated in the long run.
- Because monopolistically competitive firms face a downward-sloping demand curve, average total cost is not minimized in the long run, after entry and exit have eliminated profits.
- Monopolistically competitive firms fail to reach productive efficiency—producing at output levels lower than the efficient output.
- Monopolistically competitive firms do not achieve allocative efficiency because they do not operate where price is equal to marginal cost.

Section 10.4
- With advertising, a firm hopes that it can alter the elasticity of demand for its product, making it more inelastic and causing an increase in demand that will enhance profits.
- Product differentiation leads monopolistically competitive firms to advertising.

- Critics of advertising argue that advertisers attempt to manipulate tastes and create brand loyalty to reduce competition.
- Defenders of advertising argue that where substantial economies of scale exist, production costs may actually fall, and by making customers aware of different "substitute" products, advertising may actually lead to more competitive markets and lower consumer prices.

Section 10.5
- Oligopolies exist where relatively few firms control all or most of the production and sale of a product.
- Products may be homogeneous or differentiated, but the barriers to entry are often very high; consequently long-run profits are possible.
- Oligopoly is characterized by mutual interdependence among firms.
- Because the pricing decision of one firm influences the demand curve of competing firms in oligopoly, the oligopolist faces considerable uncertainty as to the location and shape of its demand and marginal revenue curves.
- It is difficult for an oligopolist to determine its profit-maximizing price and output.

Section 10.6
- Joint profit maximization requires the determination of price on the basis of the market demand for the product and the marginal costs of the various firms.
- The two primary reasons that most strong collusive oligopolies are rather short lived: 1) Collusive agreements are strictly illegal under Canadian anti-combine laws, and 2) there is a great temptation for firms to cheat on the agreement of the collusive oligopoly.

Section 10.7
- In the kinked demand curve model, if one firm cuts its price, rivals will follow, but rival firms will not follow a price increase.
- Oligopoly firms may deliberately hold prices below the profit-maximizing price in order to discourage new firms from entering the market.

Key Terms and Concepts

For a complete glossary of chapter key terms, visit the textbook's Web site at http://www.sextonmicro2e.nelson.com.

monopolistic competition 262
product differentiation 264
excess capacity 268
productive efficiency 268
oligopoly 273

mutual interdependence 273
collude 276
cartel 276
joint profit maximization 276
kinked demand curve 278

price leader 279
price follower 280
price leadership 280
predatory pricing 280

Review Questions

1. List three ways in which a grocery store might differentiate itself from its competitors.

2. What might make you choose one gas station over another?

3. If Frank's hot-dog stand was very profitable when he first opened, why should he expect those profits to fall over time?

4. Can you explain why there are some restaurants that are highly profitable while other restaurants in the same general area are going out of business?

5. Suppose that half the restaurants in a city are closed so that the remaining eateries can operate at full capacity. What "cost" might restaurant patrons incur as a result?

6. Why is advertising more important for the success of chains such as Toys "R" Us and Staples than for the corner barbershop?

7. What is meant by the price of variety? Graph and explain.

8. Think of your favourite ads on television. Do you think that these ads have an effect on your spending? These ads are very expensive; do you think they are a waste from society's standpoint?

9. Which of the following markets are oligopolistic?
   a. corn
   b. funeral services
   c. airline travel
   d. hamburgers
   e. oil
   f. breakfast cereals

10. Which of the following are characteristic of oligopolistic industries?
    a. a large number of firms
    b. few firms
    c. a high degree of product differentiation
    d. high barriers to entry
    e. free entry and exit
    f. mutual interdependence

11. Suppose Farmer Smith from Alberta and Farmer Jones from Saskatchewan agree to restrict their combined output of wheat in an attempt to increase the price and profits. How likely do you think the Smith–Jones cartel is to succeed? Explain.

12. Explain how the joint profit-maximizing price of colluding firms under oligopoly is determined? How about output?

13. Explain how the long-run equilibrium under oligopoly differs from that of perfect competition.

14. Which of the following are barriers to entry?
    a. an expired patent
    b. copyrights
    c. monopoly of crucial inputs
    d. economies of scale
    e. the presence of an existing firm in an industry
    f. exclusive government licence

Fill in the Blanks

Section 10.1

1. Monopolistic competition is similar to both _____ and perfect competition. As in monopoly, firms have some control over market _____, but as in perfect competition, they face _____ from many other sellers.

2. Due to the free entry of new firms, long-run economic profits in monopolistic competition are _____.

3. Firms in monopolistic competition produce products that are _____ from those produced by other firms in the industry.

4. In monopolistic competition, firms use _____ names to gain some degree of control over price.

5. The theory of monopolistic competition is based on three characteristics: (1) product _____, (2) many _____, and (3) free _____.

6. Product differentiation is the accentuation of _____ product qualities to develop a product identity.

Section 10.2

7. Monopolistic competitive sellers are price _____ like monopolists, and they do not regard price as given by the market. Because products in the industry are slightly different, each firm faces a(n) _____ -sloping demand curve.

8. In the short run, equilibrium output is determined where marginal revenue equals marginal _____. The price is set equal to the _____ the consumer will pay for this amount.

9. When price is greater-than-average total costs, the monopolistic competitive firm will make an economic _____.

10. Barriers to entry do not protect monopolistic competitive firms in the _____ run. Economic profits will _____ new firms to the industry. Similarly, firms will leave when there are economic _____.

11. Long-run equilibrium in a monopolistic competitive industry occurs when there are _____ economic profits or losses, so there is no incentive for firms to _____ or _____ the industry.

Section 10.3

12. Because it faces competition, a monopolistically competitive firm has a(n) _____ -sloping demand curve that tends to be more _____ than the demand curve for a monopolist.

13. Even in the long run, monopolistically competitive firms do not operate at levels that permit the full realization of _____ of scale.

14. Unlike a perfectly competitive firm in long-run equilibrium, a monopolistically competitive firm will produce with _____ capacity. The firm could lower average costs by increasing output, but this would reduce _____.

15. In monopolistic competition there is a tendency toward too _____ firms in the industry. Monopolistically competitive industries will not reach _____ efficiency, since firms in the industry do not produce at the _____ per-unit cost.

16. In monopolistic competition, firms operate where price is _____ than marginal cost, which means that consumers are willing to pay _____ for the product than it costs society to produce it. In this case, the firm fails to reach _____ efficiency.

17. Although average costs and prices are higher under monopolistic competition than they are under perfect competition, society gets a benefit from monopolistic competition in the form of _____ products.

Section 10.4

18. Advertising is an important type of _____ competition that firms use to _____ the demand for their products.

19. Advertising may not only increase the demand facing a firm, it may also make the demand facing the firm more _____ if it convinces buyers the product is truly different. A more inelastic demand curve means price changes will have relatively _____ effects on the quantity demanded of the product.

20. Critics of advertising assert that it _____ average total costs while manipulating consumers' tastes. However, if people are _____ , this argument loses some of its force.

21. When advertising is used in industries with significant economies of _____, per-unit costs may decline by more than per-unit advertising costs.

22. An important function of advertising is to lower the cost of acquiring _____ about the availability of substitutes and the _____ of products.

23. By making information about substitutes and prices less costly to acquire, advertising will increase the _____ in industries, which is good for consumers.

Section 10.5

24. Oligopolies exist when only a(n) _____ firms control all or most of the production and sale of a product.

25. In oligopoly, products may be either homogeneous or _____.

26. In oligopoly, _____ to entry are often very high, preventing competing firms from entering the market.

27. In oligopoly, firms can earn long-run _____ profits.

28. Oligopoly is characterized by mutual _____ among firms. Oligopolists must _____ because the number of firms in the industry is so small that changes in one firm's price of output will affect the sales of competing firms.

29. In oligopoly, barriers to entry in the form of large start-up costs, economies of scale, or _____ are usually present.

30. The economy of large-scale production _____ new firms from entering a market, because high initial average total costs impose heavy losses on new entrants.

31. Mutual interdependence means that no firm knows with _____ what its demand curve looks like. The demand curve and the profit-maximizing price and output will depend on how others _____ to the firm's policies.

Section 10.6

32. Because they are mutually interdependent, oligopolists are tempted to get together and agree to act jointly, or to _____ , in order to reduce uncertainty and raise profits.

33. Collusion has the same results that monopoly does: goods that are priced too _____ and outputs that are too _____.

34. Agreements between firms regarding sales, pricing, and other decisions are called _____ agreements.

35. Although collusive oligopolies may be profitable for participants, they are often short lived because firms have a great temptation to _____ on their fellow colluders.

Section 10.7

36. In oligopoly, an understanding may develop under which one large firm will play the role of price _____, sending signals to competitors that they have changed their prices.

37. Competitors that go along with the pricing decisions of a price leader are called price _____.

38. The idea of price _____ in oligopoly is the basis of the kinked demand curve model.

39. Under the assumptions of the kinked demand curve model, a firm's demand curve is _____ elastic for price increases than for price decreases.

40. The kinked demand curve model implies that firms may be slow to adjust price in response to changes in _____.

True or False

Section 10.1

1. Monopolistic competition is a mixture of monopoly and perfect competition.

2. Like pure monopolists, firms in monopolistically competitive industries can earn economic profits in the long run.

3. By differentiating their products and promoting brand-name loyalty, firms in monopolistic competition can raise prices without losing all their customers.

Section 10.2

4. In monopolistic competition, as in perfect competition, all firms in an industry charge the same price.

5. Monopolies, competitive firms, and monopolistic competitive firms all follow the same general rule when deciding how much to produce.

6. A monopolistic competitor's demand curve is relatively more inelastic than a monopolist's demand curve.

Section 10.3

7. Unlike perfectly competitive firms, firms in monopolistic competition will operate with excess capacity, even in the long run.

8. Although there are certain inefficiencies associated with monopolistic competition, society receives a benefit from monopolistic competition in the form of differentiated goods and services.

Section 10.4

9. Although advertising will add to the cost of production, when there are significant economies of scale, advertising may lower the per-unit total cost.

10. Misleading claims and preposterous bragging about products is a type of advertising that will result in increased demand for a firm's products.

Section 10.5

11. Under oligopoly, individual firms produce only an infinitesimal share of total output.

12. The auto industry is an example of oligopoly.

13. Under oligopoly, as in perfect competition and monopolistic competition, firms cannot earn economic profits in the long run.

Section 10.6

14. When firms in an oligopolistic industry collude, the effects are the same as under monopoly.

15. When firms collude to set prices, their individual demand curves become relatively more elastic.

16. Although they are difficult to establish, most collusive oligopolies last indefinitely.

Section 10.7

17. The new diamond industry in northern Canada will not threaten the economic profits earned by members of the international diamond cartel.

18. Collusion tends to be quite resilient in oligopoly markets.

19. In the kinked demand curve model, other firms are assumed to match price reductions because price reductions take business away from rivals, forcing them to cut price to protect their sales.

20. In the kinked demand curve model, an oligopoly firm's marginal revenue is discontinuous (has a gap in it).

Multiple Choice

Section 10.1

1. Which of the following is *not* a source of product differentiation?
   a. physical differences in products
   b. differences in quantities that firms offer for sale
   c. differences in service provided by firms
   d. differences in location of sales outlets

2. Which of the following characteristics do monopolistic competition and perfect competition have in common?
   a. Individual firms believe that they can influence market price.
   b. Firms sell brand-name products.
   c. Firms are able to earn long-run economic profits.
   d. Competing firms can enter the industry easily.

Section 10.2

3. Firms in monopolistically competitive industries cannot earn economic profits in the long run because
   a. government regulators, whose first interest is the public good, will impose regulations that limit economic profits.
   b. the additional costs of product differentiation will eliminate long-run economic profits.
   c. economic profits will attract competitors whose presence will eliminate profits in the long run.
   d. whenever one firm in the industry begins making economic profits, others will lower their prices, thus eliminating long-run economic profits.

4. Maria's West Side Bakery is the only bakery on the west side of the city. She is a monopolistic competitor and she is open for business. Which of the following *cannot* be true of Maria's profits?
   a. She is making an economic profit.
   b. She is making neither an economic profit nor loss.
   c. She is making an economic loss that is less than her fixed cost.
   d. She is making an economic loss that is greater than her fixed cost.

5. Claire is considering buying the only Hungarian restaurant in Sudbury, Ontario. The restaurant's unique food means that it faces a negatively sloped demand curve, and is currently earning an economic profit. Why shouldn't Claire assume that the current profits will continue when she makes her decision?
   a. Claire will not earn those profits right away because she doesn't know much about cooking.
   b. The firm is a monopolist, and this will attract government regulation.
   c. Current economic profits will be eliminated by the entry of competitors.
   d. Although economic profits are positive, accounting profits may be negative.

Use the accompanying diagram to answer questions 6–7.

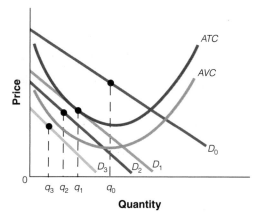

6. Which of the demand curves represents a long-run equilibrium for the firm?
   a. D_0
   b. D_1
   c. D_2
   d. D_3

7. Which of the demand curves will result in the firm shutting down in the short run?
   a. D_0
   b. D_1
   c. D_2
   d. D_3

Section 10.3

8. In the long run, firms in monopolistic competition do not attain productive efficiency because they produce
   a. at a point where economic profits are positive.
   b. at a point where marginal revenue is less than marginal cost.
   c. at a point to the left of the low point of their long-run average total cost curve.
   d. where marginal cost is equal to long-run average total cost.

9. In the long run, firms in monopolistic competition do not attain allocative efficiency because they
   a. operate where price equals marginal cost.
   b. do not operate where price equals marginal cost.
   c. produce more output than society wants.
   d. charge prices that are less than production costs.

10. Compared to perfect competition, firms in monopolist competition in the long run produce
   a. less output at a lower cost.
   b. less output at a higher cost.
   c. more output at a lower cost.
   d. more output at a higher cost.

Section 10.4

11. If Rolf wants to use advertising to reduce the elasticity of demand for his chiropractic services, he must make sure the advertising
   a. clearly states the prices he charges.
   b. shows that he is producing a product like that of the other chiropractors in town.
   c. shows why his services are truly different from the other chiropractors in town.
   d. explains the hours and days that he is open for business.

12. Advertising about prices by firms in an industry will make an industry more competitive because it
   a. reduces the cost of finding a substitute when one producer raises his price.
   b. assures the consumers that prices are the same everywhere.
   c. increases the cost for all firms because of the existence of economies of scale.
   d. reduces the number of firms because of the existence of economies of scale.

Section 10.5

13. Which of the following is *not* a characteristic of oligopoly?
   a. A few firms control most of the production and sale of a product.
   b. Firms in the industry make price and output decisions with an eye to the decisions and policies of other firms in the industry.
   c. Competing firms can enter the industry easily.
   d. Substantial economies of scale are present in production.

14. Under oligopoly, a few large firms control most of the production and sale of a product because
    a. economies of scale make it difficult for small firms to compete.
    b. diseconomies of scale make it difficult for small firms to compete.
    c average total costs rise as production expands.
    d. marginal costs rise as production expands.

15. In an oligopoly such as the Canadian domestic airline industry, a firm such as Air Canada would
    a. carefully anticipate Air Transat, and WestJet's likely responses before it raised or lowered fares.
    b. pretty much disregard Air Transat and WestJet's likely responses when raising or lowering fares.
    c. charge the lowest fare possible in order to maximize market share.
    d. schedule as many flights to as many cities as possible without regard to what competitors do.

Section 10.6

16. One of the reasons that collusive oligopolies are usually short lived is that
    a. they are unable to earn economic profits in the long run.
    b. they do not set prices where marginal cost equals marginal revenue.
    c. they set prices below long-run average total costs.
    d. parties to the collusion often cheat on one another.

17. In a collusive oligopoly, joint profits are maximized when a price is set based on
    a. its own demand and cost schedules.
    b. the market demand for the product and the summation of marginal costs of the various firms.
    c. the price followers' demand schedules and the price leader's marginal costs.
    d. the price leader's demand schedule and the price followers' marginal costs.

18. During the 1950s, many profitable manufacturing industries in Canada, such as steel, tires, and autos, were considered oligopolies. Why do you think such firms work hard to keep imports from other countries out of the Canadian market?
    a. Without import barriers, excess profits in Canada would attract foreign firms, break down existing price agreements, and reduce profits of Canadian firms.
    b. Without import barriers, foreign firms would be attracted to Canada and cause the cost in the industry to rise.
    c. Without import barriers, foreign firms would buy Canadian goods and resell them in Canada, causing profits to fall.
    d. Without import barriers, prices of goods would rise, so consumers would buy less of the products of these firms.

Section 10.7

19. Over the past 20 years, Dominator Inc. a large firm in an oligopolistic industry, has changed prices a number of times. Each time it does so, the other firms in the industry follow suit. Dominator Inc. is a
    a. monopoly.
    b. perfect competitor.
    c. price leader.
    d. price follower.

20. In the kinked demand curve model, starting from the initial price, the demand curve assumed to face a firm is relatively _____ for price increases and relatively _____ for price decreases.

a. elastic; elastic
b. elastic; inelastic
c. inelastic; elastic
d. inelastic; inelastic

21. The kinked demand curve model illustrates

a. how price rigidity could characterize some oligopoly firms, despite changing marginal costs.
b. how price increases and price decreases can elicit different responses from rival firms, in oligopoly.
c. why price rigidity may be more common when firms have excess capacity than when operating near capacity.
d. the importance of expectations about rival behaviour in oligopoly.
e. all of the above.

Problems

1. [Section 10.1]

Product differentiation is a hallmark of monopolistic competition, and the text lists four sources of such differentiation: physical differences, prestige, location, and service. How do firms in the industries listed below differentiate their products? How important is each of the four sources of differentiation in each case? Give the most important source of differentiation in each case.

a. fast-food restaurants
b. espresso shops/carts
c. hairstylists
d. soft drinks
e. wine

2. [Sections 10.2 and 10.3]

How are monopolistically competitive firms and perfectly competitive firms similar? Why don't monopolistically competitive firms produce the same output in the long run as perfectly competitive firms, which face similar costs?

3. [Section 10.3]

As you know, there are important differences between perfect competition and monopolistic competition. Show your understanding of these differences by listing the following terms under either "Perfect Competition" or "Monopolistic Competition."

		Perfect Competition	Monopolistic Competition
standardized product	productive efficiency		
differentiated product	horizontal demand curve		
allocative efficiency	downward-sloping demand curve		
excess capacity	no control over price		

4. [Section 10.4]

In what way is the use of advertising another example of Adam Smith's "Invisible Hand," according to which entrepreneurs pursuing their own best interest make consumers better off?

5. [Section 10.5]

Important differences exist between perfect competition and oligopoly. Show your understanding of these differences by listing the following terms under either "Perfect Competition" or "Oligopoly."

		Perfect Competition	Oligopoly
allocative efficiency	large economies of scale		
many small firms	productive efficiency		
high barriers to entry	horizontal demand curve		
few large firms	mutual interdependence		
downward-sloping demand curve	no control over price		

6. [Section 10.6]

One of the world's most successful cartels has been the Central Selling Organization (CSO), which controls about three-quarters of the world's diamonds. This collusive oligopoly has kept diamond prices high by restricting supply, like a monopolist. The CSO has also promoted the general consumption of diamonds through advertising and marketing. New supplies of diamonds have been found in Canada and Russia. These new mines, which are outside the direct control of the CSO, want to sell their diamonds on the open market.

a. What would you predict will happen in the market for diamonds if these new mines do not cooperate with the cartel?

b. What do you think will happen to CSO diamond advertising?

11

Labour Markets and the Distribution of Income

section

11.1 Labour Markets

- How is income distributed among workers?
- What is derived demand?

MARKETS FOR LABOUR

Approximately 70 percent of net national income goes to wages and salaries for labour services. After labourers take their share, the remaining 30 percent of net national income is compensation received by the owners of land and capital and the entrepreneurs who employ those resources to produce valued goods and services. In this chapter, we will see how supply and demand in the labour market determines the salary levels, among different workers.

In labour markets, actor Jim Carrey can make over $10 million a film. Singer Shania Twain's income is many times larger than that of the average college professor or medical doctor. Female models make more than male models, yet male basketball players make more than female basketball players. Why is this the case? To understand why some workers receive such vastly different compensation for their labour than others we must focus on the workings of supply and demand in the labour market.

DETERMINING THE PRICE OF A PRODUCTIVE FACTOR: DERIVED DEMAND

Input markets are the markets for the factors of production used to produce output. Output (goods and services) markets and input markets have one major difference. In input or

In The **NEWS**

NHL PLAYER SALARIES

BY WILLIAM WATSON

In 1930, when Babe Ruth was asked why he deserved to be paid more ($80,000) than then-president Herbert Hoover ($75,000), he replied: "I had a better year."

He was right. He hadn't had a great year—only 46 home runs in 1929 compared to 60 in 1927—but he'd definitely bested Hoover, who'd presided over the biggest crash in stock-market history. Perhaps spurred on by his (for those days) stupendous salary, Ruth did better in 1930—49 homers to lead the league—while Hoover fell into the long slump that eventually ended his major-league political career.

The Ruth–Hoover comparison came to mind as I read columnist Don Martin's gripe in the *National Post* ... that NHL hockey players make more money than the Prime Minister.

True, he was comparing the $455,000 earned by the worst-paid player in the league—the Buffalo Sabres' Chris Taylor—to the Prime Minister's $282,000. With just six goals in 54 games, Taylor is clearly no Ruth.

But what of it if, as Don Martin notes, Peter Forsberg earns more in one season than the 99-member Conservative caucus?

Forsberg provides a lot more entertainment value to a lot more people.

In a market economy, what people earn is determined not by the inherent moral worth of what they do (whoever might decide that) but by supply and demand. It may be sad that hockey players earn so much more than registered nurses. But the supply of people who can play hockey at the professional level is a lot smaller than the supply of registered nurses.

And the demand for them is greater. Millions of people are willing to pay lots of money to watch NHL hockey. On CBC two nights ago, league president Gary Bettman said fully 40 million people had watched the nine lowest-drawing teams in his league. Knowing that, large corporations pay millions of dollars per year to advertise on hockey telecasts. If the life-saving work registered nurses do could command audiences like that, then registered nurses would be paid as much as hockey players and other pro athletes.

Don Martin's point, and it's widely shared, is that because players make a lot they should back off and give the owners their salary cap. The unfairness in that is that we don't actually know what the owners make. I suspect many are much richer than even the richest players. The owners supposedly have lost hundreds of millions of dollars in the past several years and yet none has gone out of business. Only deep-pocketed people can do that.

Conservative commentators don't often favour unions. But unlike most unions, which generally want all workers to be paid the same regardless of their productivity, the NHL players' union is trying to maintain an open auction market in which free agents are rewarded according to their performance. (And it's a market, remember, that the best players can't freely enter until they are 31 years old.) If some teams are spoiling that market by bidding more than other teams can afford, it's not clear why that's a problem the players should fix.

SOURCE: Adapted from William Watson, "Filthy Rich-and Rightly So," *National Post*, September 23, 2004, p. A18. Reprinted with permission from the author.

CONSIDER THIS:
Hockey salaries are a derived demand. It is the customers' demand for a hockey game that drives hockey player salaries.

---

factor markets, the demand for an input is called a **derived demand.** That is, the demand for an input like labour is derived from the demand for the good or service. So consumers do *not* demand the labour directly—it is the goods and services that labour produces that consumers demand. For example, the chef at a restaurant is paid, and her skills are in demand, because she produces what the customer wants—a meal. The "price" of any productive factor is directly related to consumer demand for the final good or service.

derived demand
the demand for an input is derived from the consumer's demands for a good or service

Section Check

1. Supply and demand determine the prices paid to workers.
2. In factor or input markets, demand is derived from consumers' demand for the final good or service that the input produces.

Supply and Demand in the Labour Market

- What is the marginal revenue product for an input?
- What is the marginal resource cost of hiring another worker?
- Why is the demand curve for labour downward sloping?
- What is the shape of the supply curve of labour?

WILL HIRING THAT EXTRA INPUT ADD MORE TO REVENUE THAN COSTS?

marginal revenue product (MRP)

marginal product times the price of the product

marginal resource cost (MRC)

the amount that an extra input adds to the firm's total costs

Because firms are trying to maximize their profits, they try (by definition) to make the *difference* between total revenue and total cost as large as possible. An input's attractiveness, then, varies with what the input can add to the firm's revenues relative to what the input adds to costs. The demand for labour is determined by its **marginal revenue product (MRP),** which is the additional revenue that a firm obtains from one more unit of input. Why? Suppose a worker adds $500 per week to a firm's sales by his productivity; he produces 100 units that add $5 each to firm revenue. In order to determine if the worker adds to the firm's profits, we would need to calculate the marginal resource cost associated with the worker. The **marginal resource cost (MRC)** is the amount that an extra input adds to the firm's total costs. In this case, the marginal resource cost is the wage the employer has to pay to entice an extra worker. Assume that the marginal resource cost of the worker, the market wage, is $350 per worker a week. In our example, the firm would find its profits growing by adding one more worker, because the marginal benefit (*MRP*) associated with the worker, $500, would exceed the marginal cost (*MRC*) of the worker, $350. So we can see that just by adding another worker to its labour force, the firm would increase its weekly profits by $150 ($500 − $350). Even if the market wage were $490 per week, the firm could slightly increase its profits by hiring the employee because the marginal revenue product, $500, is greater than the added labour cost, $490. At wage payments above $500, however, the firm would not be interested in the worker because the marginal resource cost would exceed the marginal revenue product, making additional hiring unprofitable.

THE DEMAND CURVE FOR LABOUR SLOPES DOWNWARD

The downward-sloping demand curve for labour indicates a negative relationship between the wage and the quantity of labour demanded. Higher wages will decrease the quantity of labour demanded, whereas lower wages will increase the quantity of labour demanded. But why does this relationship exist?

The major reason for the downward-sloping demand curve for labour (illustrated in Exhibit 1) is the law of

section 11.2	The Marginal Revenue
Exhibit 1	Product of Labour

The marginal revenue product of labour curve shows how the marginal revenue product depends on the number of workers employed. The curve is downward sloping because of the diminishing marginal product of labour.

diminishing marginal product. Remember that the law of diminishing marginal product states that as increasing quantities of some variable input (say, labour) are added to fixed quantities of another input (say, land or capital), output will rise, but at some point it will increase by diminishing amounts.

Consider a farmer who owns a given amount of land. Suppose he is producing wheat, and the relationship between his output and his labour force requirements is that indicated in Exhibit 2. Output expands as more workers are hired to cultivate the land, but the growth in output steadily slows, meaning the added output associated with one more worker declines as more workers are added. For example, in Exhibit 2 when a third worker is hired, total wheat output increases from 5500 bushels to 7000 bushels, an increase of 1500 bushels in terms of marginal product. However, when a fourth worker is added, total wheat output only increases from 7000 bushels to

section 11.2 Exhibit 2	Diminishing Marginal Productivity on a Hypothetical Farm	
Units of Labour Input (workers)	**Total Wheat Output (bushels per year)**	**Marginal Product of Labour (bushels per year)**
0	–	
1	3000	3000
2	5500	2500
3	7000	1500
4	8000	1000
5	8500	500
6	8800	300
7	9000	200

8000 bushels, or a marginal increase of 1000 bushels. Note that the reason for this is *not* that the workers being added are steadily inferior in terms of ability or quality relative to the first workers. Indeed, for simplicity, we assume that each worker has exactly the same skills and productive capacity. But as more workers are added, each additional worker has fewer of the fixed resources with which to work and marginal product falls. For example, the fifth worker might just cultivate the same land more intensively. The work of the fifth worker, then, might only slightly improve output. That is, the marginal product (*MP*)— the number of physical units of added output from the addition of one additional unit of input—falls.

As we discussed earlier, the marginal revenue product (*MRP*) is the change in total revenue associated with an additional unit of input. The marginal revenue product is equal to the marginal product, the units of output added by a worker, multiplied by marginal revenue, in this case the price of the output (e.g., $10 per bushel of wheat).

$$MRP = MP \times P$$

(Note that in this case the price of the output, wheat, is the same at all levels of output because the farmer is a price taker in a competitive wheat market.)

The marginal revenue product of labour declines because of the diminishing marginal product of labour when additional workers are added. This is illustrated in Exhibit 3, which shows various output and revenue levels for a wheat farmer using different quantities of labour. We see in Exhibit 3 that the marginal product, or the added physical volume of output, declines as the number of workers grows because of diminishing marginal product. Thus, the fifth worker adds only 60 bushels of wheat per week, compared with 100 bushels for the first worker.

HOW MANY WORKERS WILL AN EMPLOYER HIRE?

Profits are maximized if the firm hires only to the point where the wage equals the expected marginal revenue product. Because the demand curve for labour and the value of the marginal revenue product show the quantity of labour that a firm demands at a given wage in a competitive labour market, we say that the marginal revenue product (*MRP*) is the same as the demand curve for labour for a competitive firm.

Using the data in Exhibit 3, if the market wage is $500 per week, it would pay for the grower to employ six workers. The sixth worker's marginal revenue product ($500)

section 11.2
Exhibit 3 — Marginal Revenue Product, Output, and Labour Inputs

Quantity of Labour	Total Output (bushels per week)	Marginal Product of Labour (bushels per week)	Product Price (dollars per bushel)	Marginal Revenue Product of Labour	Wage Rate (*MRC*) (dollars per week)
0	0				
1	100	100	$10	$1000	$500
2	190	90	10	900	500
3	270	80	10	800	500
4	340	70	10	700	500
5	400	60	10	600	500
6	450	50	10	500	500
7	490	40	10	400	500
8	520	30	10	300	500

equals the wage, so profits are maximized. Adding a seventh worker would be unprofitable, though, as that worker's marginal revenue product of $400 is less than the wage of $500. Hiring the seventh worker would reduce profits by $100.

But what if the market wage increases from $500 to $700? In this case, the firm would employ only four workers, since the fourth worker's marginal revenue product ($700) equals the wage ($700), and thus profits are maximized. That is, a higher wage rate, *ceteris paribus,* lowers the employment levels of individual firms.

In a competitive labour market, many firms are competing for workers and no single firm is big enough by itself to have any significant effect on the level of wages. The intersection of the market supply of labour and the market demand for labour determines the competitive market wage, as shown in Exhibit 4(a). The firm's ability to hire all the

section 11.2
Exhibit 4 — The Competitive Firm's Hiring Decision

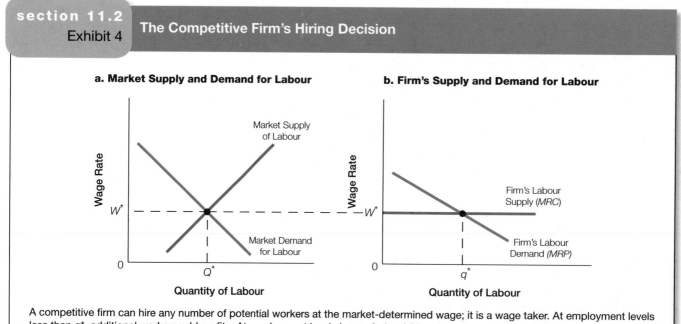

A competitive firm can hire any number of potential workers at the market-determined wage; it is a wage taker. At employment levels less than q^*, additional workers add profits. At employment levels beyond q^*, additional workers are unprofitable; at q^*, profits are maximized.

workers it wishes at the prevailing wage is similar to perfect competition in output markets, where a firm could sell all it wanted at the going price.

In Exhibit 4, when the firm hires fewer than q^* workers, the marginal revenue product exceeds the market wage, so adding workers expands profits. With more than q^* workers, though, the "going wage" exceeds marginal revenue product, and hiring additional workers lowers profits. With q^* workers, profits are maximized.

In this chapter, we assume that labour markets are competitive—there are many buyers and sellers of labour, with no individual firm or no individual worker having an impact on wages. This is generally a realistic assumption because in most labour markets firms compete with each other to attract workers, and workers can choose from many possible employers.

THE MARKET LABOUR SUPPLY CURVE

How much work effort are individuals collectively willing and able to supply in the marketplace? This is the essence of the market supply curve. Just as was the case in our earlier discussion of the law of supply, a positive relationship exists between the wage rate and the quantity of labour supplied. As the wage rate rises, the quantity of labour supplied increases, *ceteris paribus;* as the wage rate falls, the quantity of labour supplied falls, *ceteris paribus.* This positive relationship is consistent with the actual empirical evidence that the total quantity of labour supplied by *all* workers increases as the wage rate increases, as shown in Exhibit 5.

section 11.2
Exhibit 5
The Market Supply Curve of Labour

An increase in the wage rate, from A to B, leads to an increase in the quantity of labour supplied, *ceteris paribus.* A decrease in the wage rate, from B to A, leads to a decrease in the quantity of labour supplied, *ceteris paribus.*

Section Check

1. The demand curve for labour is downward sloping because of diminishing marginal product. That is, if additional labour is added to a fixed quantity of land or capital equipment, output will increase, but eventually by smaller amounts.
2. The marginal revenue product of labour is the marginal product times the price of the output.
3. Along a market supply curve, a higher wage rate will increase the quantity supplied of labour and a lower wage rate will decrease the quantity supplied of labour.

Labour Market Equilibrium

section 11.3

- How are the equilibrium wage and employment determined in labour markets?
- What shifts the labour demand curve?
- What shifts the labour supply curve?

section 11.3
Exhibit 1
Supply and Demand in the Labour Market

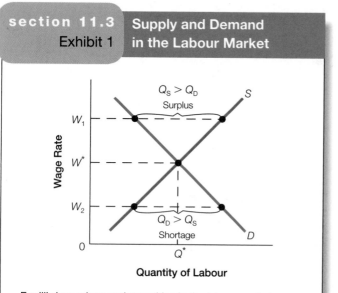

Equilibrium prices and quantities in the labour market are determined in the same way that prices and quantities of goods and services are determined: by the intersection of demand and supply. At wages above the equilibrium wage, like W_1, quantity supplied exceeds quantity demanded, and potential workers will be willing to supply their labour services for an amount lower than the prevailing wage. At a wage lower than W^*, like W_2, potential demanders will overcome the resulting shortage of labour by offering workers a wage greater than the prevailing wage. In both cases, wages are pushed toward the equilibrium value.

DETERMINING EQUILIBRIUM IN THE LABOUR MARKET

The equilibrium wage and quantity in the labour market is determined by the intersection of labour demand and labour supply. Referring to Exhibit 1, the equilibrium wage, W^*, and equilibrium employment level, Q^*, are found at that point where the quantity of labour demanded equals the quantity of labour supplied. At any wage higher than W^*, like at W_1, the quantity of labour supplied exceeds the quantity of labour demanded, resulting in a surplus of labour. In this situation, unemployed workers would be willing to undercut the established wage in order to get jobs, pushing the wage down and returning the market to equilibrium. Likewise, at a wage below the equilibrium level, like at W_2, quantity demanded would exceed quantity supplied, resulting in a labour shortage. In this situation, employers would be forced to offer higher wages in order to hire as many workers as they would like. Note that only at the equilibrium wage are both suppliers and demanders able to exchange the quantity of labour they desire.

SHIFTS IN THE LABOUR DEMAND CURVE

In Chapter 3, we demonstrated that changes in the determinants of demand can shift the demand curve for a good or service. In the case of an input such as labour, two important factors can shift the demand curve: increases in labour productivity, such as due to technological advances; or changes in the output price of the good, such as due to increased demand for the firm's product. Exhibit 2 highlights the impact of these changes.

section 11.3
Exhibit 2
Shifts in the Labour Demand Curve

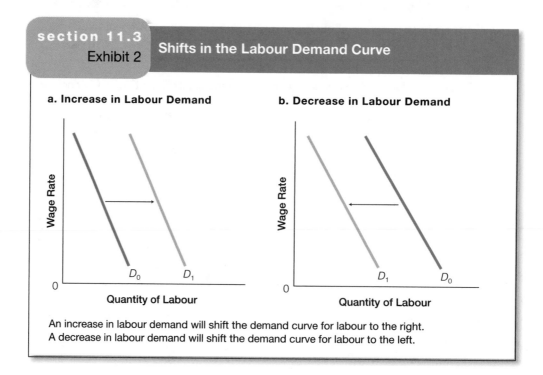

An increase in labour demand will shift the demand curve for labour to the right. A decrease in labour demand will shift the demand curve for labour to the left.

Changes in Labour Productivity

Workers can increase productivity if they have more capital or land with which to work, if technological improvements occur, or if they acquire additional skills or experience. This increase in productivity will increase the marginal product of the labour and shift the demand curve for labour to the right from D_0 to D_1 in Exhibit 2(a). However, if labour

ACTIVE LEARNING EXERCISE

LABOUR SUPPLY AND DEMAND

Q: Why do elementary and high-school teachers, who provide a valuable service to the community, make millions and millions of dollars less than star hockey players?

A: It is the marginal revenue product of teachers and the supply of teachers that determine the market wage (regardless of how we perceive the job's importance). A teacher's marginal revenue product is well below $1 million a year. Most people probably think that teachers are more important than star hockey players, yet teachers make a lot less money. Of course, the reason for this is simple supply and demand. A lot of people enjoy watching star hockey players but only a few individuals have the skill to perform at that level. Although demand for teachers is also large, there is also a relatively large number of potential suppliers. As seen in Exhibit 3, this translates into a much lower wage for teachers than for star hockey players.

© REUTERS/CORBIS

section 11.3
Exhibit 3

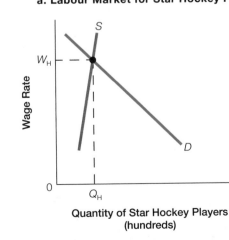

a. Labour Market for Star Hockey Players

Wage Rate

Quantity of Star Hockey Players
(hundreds)

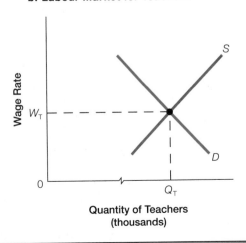

b. Labour Market for Teachers

Wage Rate

Quantity of Teachers
(thousands)

productivity falls, then marginal product will fall and the demand curve for labour will shift to the left, as shown in Exhibit 2(b).

Changes in the Demand for the Firm's Product

The greater the demand for the firm's product, the greater the firm's demand for labour or any other variable input (the "derived demand" discussed earlier). The reason for this is that the higher demand for the firm's product increases the firm's marginal revenue, which increases marginal revenue product. That is, the greater demand for the product will cause prices to rise, and the price of the product is part of the value of the labour to the firm ($MRP = MP \times P$)—so the rising product price shifts the labour demand curve to the right. Of course, if demand for the firm's product falls, the labour demand curve will shift to the left as marginal revenue product falls.

SHIFTING THE LABOUR SUPPLY CURVE

In Chapter 3, we learned that changes in the determinants of supply can shift the supply curve for goods and services to the right or left. Likewise, several factors can cause the labour supply curve to shift. These factors include immigration and population growth, the number of hours workers are willing to work at a given wage (worker tastes or preferences), nonwage income, and amenities. Exhibit 4 illustrates the impact of these factors on the labour supply curve.

Immigration and Population Growth

If new workers enter the labour force, it will shift the labour supply curve to the right, as from S_0 to S_1 in Exhibit 4(a). Of course, if workers leave the country or the labour force population declines, it will cause the supply curve to shift to the left, as shown in Exhibit 4(b).

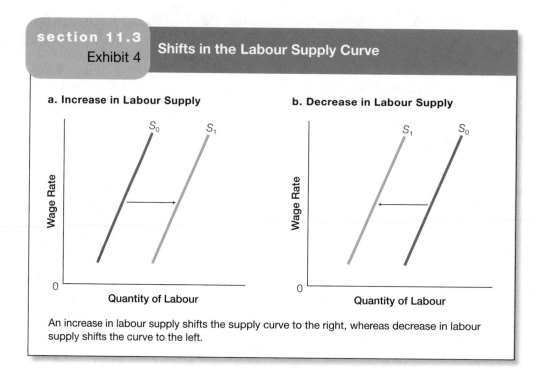

section 11.3
Exhibit 4   **Shifts in the Labour Supply Curve**

a. Increase in Labour Supply

b. Decrease in Labour Supply

An increase in labour supply shifts the supply curve to the right, whereas decrease in labour supply shifts the curve to the left.

Number of Hours People Are Willing to Work (Worker Preferences)

If people become willing to work more hours at a given wage (due to changes in worker tastes or preferences), the labour supply curve will shift to the right, shown in the movement from S_0 to S_1 in Exhibit 4(a). If they become willing to work fewer hours at a given wage (for example, as they approach retirement age), then the labour supply curve will shift to the left, as shown in Exhibit 4(b).

Nonwage Income

Increases in income from other sources than employment can cause the labour supply curve to shift to the left. For example, if you just won $20 million in the lottery, you might decide to take yourself out of the labour force. Likewise, a decrease in nonwage income (say, pension benefits were reduced) might push a person back into the labour force, thus shifting the labour supply curve to the right.

Amenities

Amenities associated with a job or a location—like good fringe benefits, safe and friendly working conditions, a child-care centre, and so on—will make for a more desirable work atmosphere, *ceteris paribus.* These amenities would cause an increase in the supply of labour, resulting in a rightward shift, such as from S_0 to S_1 in Exhibit 4(a). If job conditions deteriorated, it would lead to a reduction in the labour supply, shifting the labour supply curve to the left, as shown in Exhibit 4(b).

In The **NEWS**

CAUSE, CONSEQUENCE, AND CURE OF CHILD LABOUR

In 1995, at least 120 million children aged between 5 and 14 performed full-time work, many in excess of ten hours a day. When part-time work is included, the number of working children in the world rises to a staggering 250 million! In 1995, the proportion of working children aged 10–14 was 26 percent in Africa and 13 percent in Asia. To make matters worse, many children work in hazardous or unhygienic conditions, risking accident, injury, or health deterioration. Full-time work also prevents children from obtaining an education, trapping them in a vicious circle of despair.

While the incidence of child labour is at least headed in the right direction, it still is a very serious problem, and has outraged many developed countries. A natural reaction to this plight has been to seek different kinds of bans of child labour. For example, *"Harkin's bill"*—passed in the United States in 1997—bans the import of goods produced using child labour. Other initiatives have placed the decision in consumers' hands, by requiring that product labels specify the absence of child labour in the production of imported goods. While these initiatives are often well intended, many developing countries have criticized them on the basis that

they disguise an ulterior motive: protectionism against cheap labour.

In several articles, Kaushik Basu of Cornell University and the World Bank claims that many proposed initiatives at curbing child labour do not adequately consider the impact on working children themselves whose welfare they are imtended to improve. . . . His research shows that the popular sector-specific ban—in which industries that use child labour are prevented from exporting their goods to developed countries—can make working children worse off. Children who are unable to work in export-related industries may turn to welding or, worse, prostitution. Sadly, a UNICEF study has found that 5000–7000 young Nepalese girls moved from the carpet industry to prostitution as a result of such bans. . . .

The problem in many poor countries today is that families depend on their children's wages for survival. A ban on child labour could push many families to the brink of starvation, given that social programs are nonexistent. The author believes that while isolated cases of child abuse do exist—where children are sent to work, so that parents do not have to—parents generally send their children to work only when compelled by poverty, not due to malice. There is no other way to explain the prevalence of child labour as a mass phenomenon. . . .

(continued)

IN THE NEWS (continued)

According to Basu, the long-run consequences of child labour have largely been neglected. Having forgone schooling, a working child will generally be less productive in his adult life. Consequently, his wages will be low as an adult, increasing the likelihood that he will be compelled to send his children to work as well. Basu refers to this vicious cycle as a "child labour trap." In light of this dreadful possibility, he suggests that "if an economy is caught in a child labour trap, what is needed is a large effort to educate one generation. . . ."

Basu believes that a labour market can be in a "good" or "bad" equilibrium. In a "good" equilibrium—characteristic of developed countries—children do not work, and adult wages are relatively high. This is so because children are poor substitutes for adults as jobs require high levels of skill. This is not true of developing countries, where jobs are menial, and children are good substitutions for adults, such as in making hand-knotted carpets. . . .

The author cautions that the impact of banning child labour in a given country has to be studied empirically before jumping to conclusions. Remember that an outright ban can sometimes result in starvation instead. In the latter circumstance, the interest of the working children may be better served by combining light work with schooling. In fact, a study of Peruvian families has shown that, in some cases, a limited amount of part-time work makes it possible for children to attend school.

SOURCE: *Economic Intuition*, Spring 2000, pp. 5–6. © 2000 *Economic Intuition*, Montreal, Quebec.

CONSIDER THIS:
If developing countries can aquire more capital and better technology (either through foreign aid, or developed countries lending them funds), worker productivity will rise, wages for adult workers will rise, and thus the necessity of child labour as a means for survival will diminish.

Section Check

1. The intersection of the labour demand curve and the labour supply curve determines wages in the labour market.
2. The labour demand curve can shift if there is a change in productivity or a change in the demand for the final product.
3. The labour supply curve can shift if there are changes in immigration or population growth, workers' preferences, nonwage income, or amenities.

section
11.4   Labour Unions

- Why do labour unions exist?
- What is the impact of unions on wages?
- Can unions increase productivity?

WHY ARE THERE LABOUR UNIONS?

The supply and demand curves for labour can help us better understand the impact of labour unions. Labour unions like the Canadian Auto Workers (CAW) and the United Food and Commercial Workers (UFCW) were formed to increase their members' wages and to improve working conditions. On behalf of the union members, the union negotiates with firms through a process called **collective bargaining.** Why is this necessary?

collective bargaining
negotiations between representatives of employers and unions

The argument is that when economies begin to industrialize and urbanize, firms become larger and often the "boss" becomes more distant from the workers. In small shops or on farms, workers usually have a close relationship with an owner–employer, but in larger enterprises, the workers may only know a supervisor, and have no direct contact with either the owner or upper management. Workers realize that acting together, as a union of workers, gives them more collective bargaining power than acting individually.

WHERE ARE LABOUR UNIONS FOUND?

Approximately 4.1 million Canadian workers belonged to unions in 2005. With a labour force of 13.8 million paid employees, that means about 30 percent of employees were unionized. Employees in the public sector (government, Crown corporations, schools, hospitals) were four times as likely to belong to a union than employees in the private sector (71 percent versus 18 percent). Low union rates were found for 15- to 24-year-olds (14 percent) compared to 45- to 54-year-olds (40 percent). Geographically, the highest union rate was in Quebec (37 percent), whereas the lowest union rate was in Alberta (22 percent).

Wide variation in union rates is observed across different industries. Industries with high rates of unionization include education (68 percent), public administration (68 percent), utilities (67 percent), health care and social assistance (54 percent), and transportation and warehousing (43 percent). Low rates of unionization are found in agriculture (5 percent); professional, scientific, and technical industries (5 percent); accommodation and food (6 percent); and finance, insurance, and real estate industries (8 percent). The size of the firm also has an impact on union rates, with small firms (those with under 20 employees) having a 13 percent union rate, and large firms (those with over 500 employees) having a 51 percent union rate.

UNION IMPACT ON LABOUR SUPPLY AND WAGES

Labour unions influence the quantity of union labour hired and the wages at which they are hired primarily through their ability to alter the supply of labour services from what would exist if workers acted independently. One way to do this, of course, is by raising barriers to entry into a given occupation. For example, by restricting membership, unions can reduce the quantity of labour supplied to industry employers from what it otherwise would be, and as a result, wages in that occupation would increase from W_0 to W_1, as shown in Exhibit 1(a). As you can see in the shift from Q_0 to Q_1 in Exhibit 1(a), although some union workers will now receive higher wages, others will become unemployed. Many economists believe that this is why wages are approximately 10–25 percent higher in union jobs, even when nonunion workers have comparable skills. Of course, some of these gains will be appropriated by the unions in the form of union dues, initiation fees, and the like, so the workers themselves will not receive the full benefit.

WAGE DIFFERENCES FOR SIMILARLY SKILLED WORKERS

Suppose you had two labour sectors: the union sector and the nonunion sector. If unions are successful in obtaining higher wages either through bargaining, threatening to strike, or by restricting membership, wages will rise and employment will fall in the union sector, as seen in Exhibit 1(a). With a downward-sloping demand curve for labour, higher wages mean that less labour is demanded in the union sector. Those workers that are equally skilled but are unable to find union work will seek nonunion work, thus increasing supply in that sector and, in turn, lowering wages in the nonunion sector. This effect is shown in Exhibit 1(b). Thus, comparably skilled workers will experience higher wages in the union sector (W_1) than in the nonunion sector (W_2).

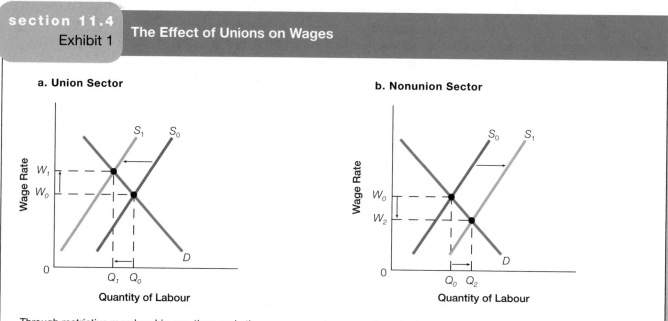

a. Union Sector

b. Nonunion Sector

Through restrictive membership practices and other means, a union can reduce the labour supply in its industry, thereby increasing the wage rate they can earn (from W_0 to W_1) but reducing employment (from Q_0 to Q_1), as shown in Exhibit 1(a). However, as workers unable to get jobs in the union sector join the nonunion sector, the supply of labour in the nonunion sector increases (from Q_0 to Q_2), lowering wages in those industries (from W_0 to W_2), as shown in Exhibit 1(b).

CAN UNIONS LEAD TO INCREASED PRODUCTIVITY?

Harvard University economists Richard Freeman and James Medoff argue that unions might actually increase worker productivity. Their argument is that unions provide a collective voice that workers can use to communicate their discontents more effectively. This might lower the number of union workers that quit their jobs. Resignations can be particularly costly for firms, because they have often invested in training and job-specific skills for their employees. In addition, by handling workers' grievances, unions may increase worker motivation and morale. The combined impact of fewer resignations and improved morale could boost productivity.

However, this improvement in worker productivity in the union sector should show up on the bottom line—the profit statement of the firm. Although the empirical evidence is mixed, it appears that unions may lower the profitability of firms, not raise it.

In The **NEWS**

UNIONS PLAY A LARGER ROLE IN LIVES OF WOMEN

BY ERIC BEAUCHESNE

The labour movement has undergone dramatic shifts in recent decades, including a quadrupling in the proportion of union members who are women to nearly one-half.

"The biggest and most profound transformation in membership occurred in the mix of men and women," Statistics Canada said in a report published [in 2004] entitled The Union Movement in Transition.

In 1977, women represented just 12 per cent of total union membership, it noted. By 2003, their share had surged to 48 per cent.

The increasing representation of women in unions reflects a variety of changes in society in general and the workplace in particular, according to the study, appearing in

IN THE NEWS *(continued)*

the latest edition of the agency publication, *Perspectives on Labour and Income*.

Those changes include the growing proportion of women in the workforce, their increased presence in the heavily unionized public sector, as well as traditionally male-dominated and heavily unionized industries, rising unionization among part-time workers, many of whom are women, and the expansion of unions into traditionally female-dominated workplaces, especially in the service sector.

The increasing "feminization" of the labour movement is in contrast to another trend which is the decline in the proportion of workers who are unionized.

Union membership rose to just above four million in 2003 from 2.8 million in 1977, the report noted.

That more than 40-per-cent growth is not surprising in light of the advantages of union membership, the report said.

And "certainly" unionized women workers have shared in those benefits, Ernest Akyeampong, the report's author said in an interview.

For example, unionized women working full time earned 92 per cent as much in hourly earnings as their male coun-terparts, while non-unionized women workers earned about 80 per cent as much as their non-unionized male counterparts, he noted.

However, the report noted that the growth in total union membership has failed to keep pace with increases in employment, resulting in a unionization rate that has slowly declined.

After reaching 34.2 per cent in 1987, the rate fluctuated between 30 and 31 per cent over most of the past decade.

SOURCE: Adapted from Eric Beauchesne, "Unions Play Larger Role In Lives of Women: Four-Fold Increase In Representation," *The Gazette* (Montreal), September 1, 2004, p. B5. Materials reprinted with the express permission of: "CANWEST NEWS SERVICE," a CanWest Partnership.

CONSIDER THIS:
In 2006, the unionization rate for both men and women declined, the decrease was larger for men. At 30.1 percent, the rate for women continued to exceed the rate for men (29.4 percent).

Section Check

1. Workers realize that acting together gives them collective bargaining power.
2. Labour unions try to increase their members' wages and improve working conditions.
3. Through restrictive membership, a union can reduce the labour supply in the market for union workers, thus reducing employment and raising wages. This increases the supply of workers in the nonunion sector, shifting supply to the right and lowering wages for nonunion workers.

Income Distribution

section 11.5

- What has happened to the income distribution since 1951?
- Are the income distribution statistics accurate?
- How much income inequality exists in other countries?

The ultimate purpose of producing goods and services is to satisfy the material wants of people. Up to this point, we have examined the process by which society decides which wants to satisfy in a world characterized by scarcity; we have examined the question of how goods are produced; and we have examined the question of how society can fully

section 11.5
Exhibit 1
Mean Household Income by Quintile (Year 2006)

Quintile	Income
Lowest Quintile	$ 13 800
Second Quintile	31 800
Third Quintile	51 800
Fourth Quintile	77 800
Highest Quintile	152 600

SOURCE: Statistics Canada, Income in Canada, Catalogue no. 75-202-X, 2006.

section 11.5
Exhibit 2
Before-Tax Income Shares (Percentage)

Year	Lowest Fifth	Second Fifth	Third Fifth	Fourth Fifth	Highest Fifth
1951	4%	11%	18%	23%	43%
1971	4	11	18	25	43
1991	4	10	17	25	44
2001	4	10	16	24	45
2006	4	10	16	24	47

SOURCE: Statistics Canada, Income in Canada, Catalogue no. 75-202-X, 2006.

utilize its productive resources. We have not, however, looked carefully into the question of for whom society produces consumer goods and services. Why are some people able to consume much more than others? Exhibit 1 shows a breakdown of mean (average) household income before tax. Economists rank Canadian households by income and then divide them into five groups (quintiles) based on their income levels. The average income of the richest fifth of Canadian households, at $152 600, is over ten times greater than that of the poorest fifth of Canadian households, at $13 800.

THE RECORD SINCE 1951

Exhibit 2 illustrates the distribution of income in Canada since 1951. The figures in the table represent the shares of the total before-tax income in Canada going to each fifth (quintile) of Canadian households. As you can see from this table, in 2006 the fifth of Canadian households with the lowest incomes received only 4 percent of the total before-tax income in Canada. The highest fifth (20 percent) of Canadian households received 47 percent of the total before-tax income. In other words, the income share of the highest fifth of Canadian households is over ten times greater than the income share of the lowest fifth of households.

Looking at the figures since 1951, it is interesting to note that the income shares have remained relatively stable over that period. The share of income going to the lowest fifth of households is about 4 percent over the whole period, whereas the share of income going to the middle fifth of households is roughly 16 to 18 percent over the same period. One does notice, however, that the share of income going to the highest fifth of Canadian households has risen from 43 percent to 47 percent, suggesting that "the rich are getting richer."

INCOME DISTRIBUTION IN OTHER COUNTRIES

Is Canada typical of advanced, industrialized nations with respect to the distribution of income among its population? This is a difficult question to answer with absolute certainty, given international differences in defining income, difficulties in measuring the impact of taxes, the problem of nonmonetary payments, and so on. Despite these obstacles, international comparisons of income distribution have been made.

Exhibit 3, constructed with data from the World Bank, shows that income inequality is greater in Canada and the United States than in Sweden and Japan. However, the table also shows that some of the greatest disparities in income are found in developing countries such as Mexico, Chile, and Brazil.

Although income inequality within nations is often substantial, it is far less than income inequality among nations. The majority of global income inequality comprises differences in living standards among countries rather than disparities within nations.

Global Income Inequalities

Country	Lowest 10%	Highest 10%
Japan	4.8%	21.7%
Sweden	3.7	20.1
Germany	3.3	23.7
India	3.5	33.5
Canada	2.8	23.8
France	2.8	25.1
United Kingdom	2.3	27.7
China	2.4	30.4
United States	1.8	30.5
Russia	1.7	38.7
Mexico	1.3	41.7
Chile	1.3	45.6
South Africa	1.1	45.9
Brazil	0.7	48.0

This table shows the percentage of income for the lowest 10 percent of the population and the highest 10 percent of the population.

SOURCE: The World Bank Group, World Development Report, 2003.

Note: The income inequality differences are approximations, because the data vary according to survey year, and different methods are used for computing the distribution of income in different countries.

ARE WE OVERSTATING THE DISPARITY IN THE DISTRIBUTION OF INCOME?

Failing to take into consideration differences in age, certain demographic factors, and government taxation and transfer programs, which have all been identified as elements that influence income distribution data, suggests that we might be overstating inequality.

Differences in Age

At any moment in time, middle-aged people tend to have higher incomes than both younger and older people. At middle age most people are at their peak in terms of productivity, and participate in the labour force to a greater extent than the very old or very young. Put differently, if every individual earned exactly the same total income over his or her lifetime, there would still be some observed inequality at any given moment in time, simply because people earn more in middle age.

Other Demographic Trends

Other demographic trends, like the increased number of divorced couples and the rise of two-income families, have also caused the measured distribution of income (which is measured in terms of household income) to appear more unequal. For example, in the 1950s, the majority of families had single incomes. Today, many households have two breadwinners instead of one. Suppose their incomes rise from $50 000 a year to roughly $100 000; these households thus move into a higher-income quintile and create greater apparent income inequality. At the same time, divorces create two households instead of

The contrasts between rich and poor are more extreme in Brazil than in almost any other country in the world. According to the UN Development Program, nearly half of Brazil's population lives in absolute poverty. Those who are unable to make a living as vendors of newspapers or lottery tickets, shoeshine boys, guards for parked cars, or the like are often forced to earn a living illegally. The number of children who work on the streets, or even live there permanently, is estimated to have reached 10 million.

in-kind transfers

transfers given in goods and services rather than cash

one, lowering income per household for divorced couples; thus, they move into lower-income quintiles, also creating greater apparent income inequality.

Government Activities

The impact of government activity should be considered in evaluating the measured income distribution. Government-imposed taxes burden different income groups in different ways. Most importantly, Canada has a progressive income tax system, which means that higher-income individuals pay a larger proportion of their income in tax than lower-income individuals. The progressivity of the tax system results in the after-tax income distribution being more equal than the before-tax income distribution. In 2006, for example, the shares of after-tax income going to each of the five quantiles were 5 percent, 11 percent, 16 percent, 24 percent, and 44 percent, respectively. As you can see when comparing to the before-tax shares in Exhibit 2, the share of after-tax income going to each of the lower two quantities is greater, whereas the after-tax share of the quantities is lower.

Also, government programs benefit some groups of income recipients more than others. For example, it has been argued that government-subsidized higher education has benefited the high- and middle-income groups more than the poor (because far more students from these income groups go to university), as have such things as government subsidies to airports, operas, and art museums. Some programs, though, clearly aid the poor more than the rich. Food banks, school lunch programs, housing subsidies, daycare subsidies, and several other programs provide recipients with **in-kind transfers**—that is, transfers given in a nonmonetary form. When these in-kind transfers are included, many economists conclude that they have served to reduce levels of inequality from the levels suggested by aggregate income statistics.

WHY DO SOME EARN MORE THAN OTHERS?

There are many reasons why some people make more income than others. Some reasons for the differences in income include differences in age, skill, education and training, preferences with respect to risk and leisure, and discrimination.

Age

The amount of income people earn varies over their lifetimes. Younger people with few skills tend to make little income when they begin their working careers. Income rises as workers gain experience and on-the-job training. As productivity increases, workers can command higher wages. These wage earnings generally increase up to the age of 50 and fall dramatically at retirement age, around 65.

Skills and Human Capital

Some workers are just more productive than others and therefore earn higher wages. The greater productivity may be a result of innate skills or of improvements in human capital, such as training and education. Still others, like star athletes and rock stars, have specialized talents that are in huge demand, so they make more money than those with fewer skills or with skills that are in less demand.

Worker Preferences

Aside from skills, education, and training, people have different attitudes about and preferences regarding their work. Workaholics (by definition) work longer hours and so they earn more than others with comparable skills. Some earn more because they work more intensely than others. Still others may choose jobs that pay less but have more amenities—flexible hours, favourable job location, generous benefit programs, child care, and so on. And some may choose to work less and spend more time pursuing leisure activities, like travelling, hobbies, or spending time with family and friends. It is not for us to say that one preference is better than another but simply to recognize that these choices lead to differences in earnings.

Job Preferences

Some of the differences in income are the result of the risks or undesirable features of some occupations. Police officers and firefighters are paid higher wages because of the dangers associated with their jobs. Nickel miners and garbage collectors are paid more than other workers with comparable skill levels because of the unpleasantness of the jobs. In short, some workers have higher earnings because they are compensated for the difficult, risky, or unappealing nature of their jobs.

Discrimination

Finally, some of the differences in income result from employment and wage discrimination. Employment discrimination occurs when a worker is denied employment or promotion on the basis of some feature, such as gender, age, religion, or race, without any regard to his or her productivity. Wage discrimination occurs when a worker is given employment at a wage lower than that of other workers based on an attribute other than productivity. These types of discrimination are illegal but, because they can be difficult to detect, still sometimes occur.

Discrimination is one factor in explaining why men, on average, earn more than women. Studies have shown that even after accounting for a wide range of factors that determine incomes, such as education, training, experience, seniority, and hours worked, a male–female wage gap remains that can be attributed to discrimination in the labour market. Moreover, it is important to note that discrimination outside of the labour market may also contribute to male–female wage inequality. Because women, on average, perform a greater share of household responsibilities' especially childrearing, this impacts the labour market choices women make in areas such as occupational choice, mobility, training, absenteeism, and hours worked.

REMEDYING DISCRIMINATION

In Canada, the problem of employment discrimination is addressed primarily through the Employment Equity Act (1996). This federal legislation requires or encourages Canadian employers to give preferential treatment in employment practices to a list of designated groups—specifically women, persons with disabilities. Aboriginal peoples, and visible minorities.

Applying only to companies in federally regulated industries (such as banking, telecommunications, and the airline industry, to name a few) and those corporations that are controlled by two or more provincial governments, the act ultimately has limited coverage.

In The **NEWS**

LITERACY SKILLS AND EARNINGS

BY ERIC BEAUCHESNE

Immigrants earn less than Canadian-born workers in part because their literacy skills are lower, Statistics Canada says in a [2004] report.

It also found "no evidence" of discrimination against immigrant workers, at least in terms of those skills.

"Literary skills have a significant impact on earnings," concludes the report…. "If immigrants had the same average literacy scores as the native-born, the earnings differential between immigrants and the native-born would narrow by about 20 per cent."

Among university-educated workers, it would eliminate just over half of the immigrants' earnings disadvantage, it adds.

The study found that, on average, literacy and numeracy skills among immigrants are significantly below the averages of non-immigrants with equivalent educational credentials and other observable characteristics.

That, it says, may explain in part what has been a decline in the relative job market success of immigrants over the past decade.

A Statistics Canada study released earlier [in 2004] found that recent immigrants were up to three times more likely than non-immigrants to suffer low incomes, regardless of sex, level of education, family type or province of residence.

The latest study, however, found that there is no evidence that immigrants receive a lower return from their literacy skills than Canadian-born workers with the same skills levels, it said. The lower earnings of immigrants cannot be explained by discrimination—defined as equally productive workers being paid unequally—in terms of their literacy skills.

"In other words, Canadian labour markets appear to reward the literacy and numeracy of immigrants to Canada in exactly the same way that they do non-immigrants," it said.

However, Canadian employers place little value on immigrants' foreign work experience, with highly educated immigrants realizing markedly lower returns for that experience, it said.

SOURCE: Adapted from Eric Beauchesne, "Immigrants Earning Less, Report Says: No Evidence of Discrimination," *Windsor Star*, September 8, 2004, p. E6. Materials reprinted with the express permission of: "CAN-WEST NEWS SERVICE", a CanWest Partnership.

CONSIDER THIS:
Literacy skills have a significant impact on earnings. On average, literacy skills of immigrants are below the averages of equivalent nonimmigrants. This explains, in part, why immigrants earn less than Canadian-born workers.

Although some provincial governments have chosen to incorporate employment equity standards into their provincial-level human rights legislation, no province has preferential employment practices equivalent to those in the Employment Equity Act.

Policies designed around the concepts of *pay equity* and *pay equality* are intended to address the existence of wage discrimination in Canada. Pay equality, or equal pay for equal work, is required by law in Canada. The principle of pay equality works as follows: suppose an organization employs both male and female truck drivers, with reasonable allowances for differences in skill or seniority, the female truck drivers would have to be paid the same as the male truck drivers.

Alternatively, pay equity legislation, or equal pay for work of equal value, only exists in certain jurisdictions in Canada (for example, in Ontario, pay equity is guaranteed through the Ontario Pay Equity Act). The principle of pay equity works as follows: suppose an organization's nurses are seen as doing a job that is equal in importance to its plumbers; they must all then be paid the same.

Employment equity programs are controversial. Employment equity may increase the probability that someone will be hired on some basis other than productivity. Although this may be desirable from the standpoint of equalizing opportunities among demographic groups, it also can serve to lower society's output and firms' profits. Furthermore, some critics have raised the "reverse discrimination" equity argument. For example, with respect to productivity, a firm may be forced to hire a worker from one of the designated groups with a marginal revenue product of $80 instead of a nondesignated worker whose marginal revenue product may be $100 (perhaps because of more years of schooling). Society ultimately loses $20 of output (the difference in the value of marginal output). Moreover, if the firm that hires the worker from one of the designated groups has to pay the prevailing wage (say, $90) to avoid wage discrimination charges, hiring that worker will lower profits. With that, the firm might decide not to hire anyone, knowing that employment equity will prevent them from hiring the profitable nondesignated worker (whose marginal revenue product exceeds the prevailing wage by $10) instead of the worker from one of the designated groups (whose hiring will reduce profits by $10).

Employers' actions to protect profits, then, might negate some or all of the expected gains from employment equity. One alternative to using implicit quotas would be to subsidize employers for hiring members from one of the designated groups. Opponents to this approach regard it as a gift or bailout for business enterprise more than a help to underrepresented workplace groups. The subsidy approach would, however, provide employers with greater incentives to increase job opportunities for designated group members.

Section Check

1. From 1951 to 2006 the distribution of income has been relatively stable.
2. Demographics and government programs affect the disparity in income inequality.
3. Income inequality between nations is substantial.

Poverty

- How do we define poverty?
- How many people live in poverty?
- What government programs help to reduce poverty?

At several points in this chapter, the words "rich" and "poor" have been used without being defined. Of particular interest is the question of poverty. Our concern over income distribution largely arises because most people believe that those with low incomes have lower satisfaction than those with higher incomes. Thus, the "poor" people are those who, in a material sense, suffer relative to other people. It is desirable, therefore, to define and measure the extent of poverty in Canada.

DEFINING POVERTY

In Canada, poverty is measured on a relative income basis. Statistics Canada has determined that an average Canadian household spends 43 percent of its after-tax income on food, clothing, and shelter. A household that spends 63 percent or more of its after-tax income (an additional 20 percentage points) on these three necessities is defined as low income.

Based on the above definition, Statistics Canada is able to create what is called a **low-income cut-off (LICO),** which is the income level at which a household spends 63 percent of its income on food, clothing, and shelter. These low-income cut-offs depend on

low-income cut-off (LICO)
the income level at which a household spends 63 percent of its income on food, clothing, and shelter

Low-Income After-Tax Cut-Offs, 2006

		Community Size			
	Rural Area	Urban Areas			
		Less than 30 000	30 000–99 999	100 000–499 999	500 000 and over
Size of Family Unit		$			
1 person	11 492	13 152	14 671	14 857	17 568
2 persons	13 987	16 008	17 857	18 082	21 381
3 persons	17 417	19 932	22 236	22 516	26 624
4 persons	21 728	24 867	27 741	28 091	33 216
5 persons	24 742	28 317	31 590	31 987	37 823
6 persons	27 440	31 404	35 034	35 474	41 946
7 or more persons	30 138	34 491	38 477	38 962	46 070

SOURCE: Statistics Canada, Income in Canada, Catalogue no. 75-202-X, 2006.

the number of people that live in the household as well as the size of the community that the household lives in. Exhibit 1 shows the low-income cut-offs for various household sizes and various community sizes. The LICO for a single-person household living in a large Canadian city is $17 568, whereas the LICO for a four-person family living in a rural area is $21 728.

At this point, it is important to emphasize that Statistics Canada's low-income cut-off is a relative measure of poverty, not an absolute measure of poverty. For example, a household right at the low-income cut-off would still have approximately 37 percent of its after-tax income to spend on goods and services other than food, shelter, and clothing. Thus, it would not be poor in an absolute sense, especially when compared to households in countries such as Pakistan or Ethiopia. It is poor, however, in the sense that its income falls to a specified degree below the income of an average comparable household. An absolute measure of poverty is based on whether a household's income is sufficient to provide the basic necessities of life in minimum quantities.

HOW MANY PEOPLE LIVE IN POVERTY?

Based on Statistics Canada's low-income cut-offs, we can measure the incidence of poverty as the percentage of households whose income falls below the low-income cut-off. Exhibit 2 provides a summary of poverty rates among households based on selected characteristics of the household.

Unattached individuals have a 29.2 percent incidence of low income, whereas only 6.6 percent of married couples with children are poor. The most likely family to be poor is a single-parent family headed by a female, with a poverty rate of 28.2 percent.

The age of the head of the household makes a significant difference to a household's income and to the risk of poverty. Households headed by an 18- to 24-year-old have a 29.2 percent incidence of low income, considerably higher than the 17.4 percent of households that are headed by a 25- to 54-year-old.

The Incidence of Low Income by Selected
Household Characteristics, 2006

Characteristic	Percentage of Households Below LICO
Married couples with children	6.6
Single-parent families (female head)	28.2
Unattached individuals	29.2
Age of household head 18–24 years	29.2
Age of household head 25–54 years	17.4
Household head has less than a high school education	23.7
Household head has university degree	11.1

SOURCE: Statistics Canada, Income in Canada, Catalogue no.75-202-X, 2006.

Education also makes a huge impact on the incidence of poverty. Households headed by someone with a university degree have a poverty rate of 11.1 percent, whereas those headed by someone with less than a high-school education have a 23.7 percent incidence of low income.

POLICIES TO REDUCE POVERTY

There are a variety of government programs designed to reduce poverty and redistribute income. We examine several of them here.

Taxes

One way to redistribute income to reduce disparities among individuals is through federal and provincial income tax. The federal income tax (and the majority of provincial income tax) is designed to be a **progressive tax system**—one that imposes higher marginal tax rates on higher incomes. For example in 2008 (federally), an individual would pay 15 percent tax on the first $37 885 of taxable income, 22 percent on the next $37 884 of taxable income, 26 percent on the next $47 415 of taxable income, and 29 percent of taxable income over $123 184.

progressive tax system
as a person's income rises, the amount of his or her tax as a proportion of income rises

Social Insurance Programs

A second means by which income redistribution can be carried out by the government is through social insurance programs operated by the federal government, the provinces, and municipalities. These programs are often referred to as Canada's social safety net and consist of both in-kind transfers and cash transfers. In-kind transfers are direct transfers of goods and services such as food banks and school lunch programs, whereas **cash transfers** are direct cash payments such as low-income support, pension payments, and employment insurance (EI) benefits.

Public pension payments are a cash transfer program that provides income to persons over the age of 65. Health care is an in-kind transfer that covers medical care and hospitalization—financed by the provincial governments with funding from the federal government. Neither of these programs are considered welfare programs because one does not have to be poor to receive benefits. Benefits for the unemployed in the form of

cash transfer
direct cash payment such as public pensions, social assistance, and employment insurance

Employment Insurance are also a cash transfer payment. All three of these social insurance programs are event based—old age, illness, or job loss.

Known by such names as "social assistance," "income support," "income assistance," and "welfare assistance," these programs of last resort are targeted toward people with little or no income suffering from poverty. For example, the Ontario Child Benefit program is designed to help low-income families in Ontario provide for their children, and the Guaranteed Income Supplement (GIS) is a program that provides additional money (above that provided by the Old Age Security pension) to low-income seniors.

Government Subsidies

A third way that governments can help the less affluent is by using government revenues to provide low-cost public services. Inexpensive public housing, subsidized public transportation, and even public parks are services that probably serve the poor to a greater extent than the rich. "Free" public education is viewed by many as an equalizing force in that it opens up opportunities for children of less prosperous members of society to obtain employment that could improve their economic status. Of course, not all government programs benefit the relatively poor at the expense of the rich. For example, provincial government subsidies to universities may help middle-income and upper-income groups more than the poor. In addition, there are agricultural subsidies that often provide large benefits to farmers who may already have sufficient incomes.

Minimum Wage

Can a higher minimum wage ease the burden on the poor? We discussed the minimum wage in Chapter 4. You may recall that the minimum-wage law forbids employers from paying a wage less than the minimum wage. In Canada, provinces administer their own minimum-wage legislation—for example, the minimum-wage in Ontario is $8.75 (2008).

Almost all economists would agree that a large increase in the minimum wage — say, to $20 — would have a devastating effect on the unskilled labour market; many unskilled workers would lose their jobs, and many small businesses would have to shut their doors. There is some debate among economists over the elasticity of the demand curve for labour. If the demand curve for labour is relatively inelastic, an increase in the minimum wage leads to only a small reduction in employment. However, if the demand curve for labour is relatively elastic, the reduction in employment is larger.

Critics of a higher minimum wage argue that it is poorly targeted if its object is to reduce poverty, because many of the recipients of the minimum wage are teenagers living in households that are not facing poverty. Some argue that a policy focusing on subsidizing the wages of the poor would go much further in reducing poverty. That is, society needs to find more effective policy for low-wage workers—perhaps job-training programs.

Section Check

1. In Canada, poverty is defined on a relative income basis. A household that spends 63 percent or more of its after-tax income on food, shelter, and clothing is classified as poor.
2. The incidence of low income varies depending on the characteristics of the household, such as family type, age, and education.
3. There are a variety of programs designed to reduce poverty: progressive income tax, cash transfer, in-kind transfers, social assistance, and minimum wages.

Summary

Section 11.1

- Input markets are the markets for the factors of production used to produce output.
- In factor or input markets, demand is derived from consumers' demand for the final good or service that the input produces.

Section 11.2

- The marginal revenue product of an input is the marginal product times the price of the output.
- The demand curve for labour is downward sloping because of the diminishing marginal product of labour—as additional labour is added to a fixed quantity of land or capital equipment, output will increase, but eventually by smaller amounts.

Section 11.3

- Wages in the labour market are determined by the intersection of the labour demand curve and the labour supply curve.
- The labour demand curve can shift if there is a change in productivity or a change in the demand for the final product.
- The labour supply curve can shift if there are changes in immigration or population growth, workers' preferences, nonwage income, or amenities.
- Real wages are determined by the intersection of the labour demand and labour supply curves.

- If the demand for labour rises more rapidly than the supply of labour, real wages will rise.
- If the supply of labour rises more rapidly than the demand for labour, real wages will fall.

Section 11.4

- Through restrictive membership, a union can reduce the labour supply in the market for union workers, thus reducing employment and raising wages.
- With unionization, the supply of workers in nonunion sectors typically increases, shifting supply to the right and lowering wages for nonunion workers.

Section 11.5

- From 1951 to 2006, the distribution of income remained relatively stable.
- Demographics and government programs affect the disparity in income inequality.
- Income inequality between nations is substantial.

Section 11.6

- In Canada, poverty is defined on a relative income basis—a household that spends 63 percent or more of its after-tax income on food, shelter, and clothing is classified as poor.
- The incidence of low income varies by household type, age, and education.

Key Terms and Concepts

For a complete glossary of chapter key terms, visit the textbook's Web site at http://www.sextonmicro2e.nelson.com.

derived demand 293
marginal revenue product
(*MRP*) 294

marginal resource cost (*MRC*) 294
collective bargaining 302
in-kind transfers 308

low-income cut-off (LICO) 311
progressive tax system 313
cash transfer 313

Review Questions

Use the following table to answer questions 1 and 2.

Quantity of Labour	Total Output	Marginal Product of Labour	Marginal Revenue Product of Labour
0	—	_____	_____
1	250	_____	_____
2	600	_____	_____
3	900	_____	_____
4	1125	_____	_____
5	1300	_____	_____
6	1450	_____	_____
7	1560	_____	_____

1. The table shows the Total Output each week of workers in a perfectly competitive apple orchard. The equilibrium price of a kilogram of apples is $4. Complete the Marginal Product of Labour and the Marginal Revenue Product of Labour columns in the table.

2. Using the same table, how many workers will the owner hire if the equilibrium wage rate is $550 per week? $650 per week?

3. What happens to the demand curve for labour when the equilibrium price of output increases?

4. Which of the following groups are likely to benefit from legislation substantially increasing the minimum wage? Explain why.

   a. unskilled workers seeking jobs but lacking experience and education

   b. skilled workers whose current wages are above the minimum wage

   c. manufacturers of machinery that saves labour in industries employing large amounts of unskilled labour

   d. unskilled workers who have a criminal record

   e. teenagers seeking their first job

   f. unskilled workers who retain employment after the minimum wage is raised

   g. regions where almost everybody already earns substantially more than the minimum wage

5. If a competitive firm is paying $8 per hour (without fringe benefits) to its employees, what would tend to happen to its equilibrium wage if the company began to give on-the-job training or free dental insurance to its workers? What would happen to its on-the-job training and dental insurance for its workers if the government mandated a minimum wage of $9 an hour?

6. Would the owner of University Pizza Parlour hire another worker for $60 per day if that worker added 40 pizzas a day and each pizza added $2 to University Pizza Parlour's revenues? Why or why not?

7. What would happen to the demand for unskilled labour if there was an increase in the demand for hamburgers and fries?

8. Professional athletes command and receive higher salaries than teachers. Yet teachers, not athletes, are considered essential to economic growth and development. If this is in fact the case, why do athletes receive higher salaries than teachers?

9. The availability of jobs at higher real wages motivates many people to migrate to Canada. Other things equal, what impact would a large influx of immigrants have on Canadian real wages?

10. The dean at Acadia University knows that poets generally earn less than engineers in the private market; that is, the equilibrium wage for engineers is higher than that for poets. Suppose that all colleges and universities, except Acadia University, pay their professors according to their potential private market wage. The administration at Acadia University believes that salaries should be equal across all disciplines because its professors work equally hard and because all of the professors have similar qualifications. As a result, Acadia University opts to pay all of its professors a mid-range wage. What do you think is likely to happen to the engineering and poetry programs at Acadia University?

11. How might each of the following affect the distribution of income in the near term:

    a. a massive influx of low-skilled immigrants

    b. a new baby boom occurs

    c. the babies in (b) enter their twenties

    d. the babies in (b) reach age 65 or older

12. How might a significant reduction in the divorce rate affect the distribution of income?

Fill in the Blanks

Section 11.1

1. In input or factor markets, the demand for an input is a _____ demand _____ from consumers' demand for the good or service.

2. _____ markets are the markets for the factors of production used to produce _____.

Section 11.2

3. The demand for labour is determined by its _____, which is the additional revenue that a firm obtains from one more unit of input.

4. The _____ is the amount that an extra input adds to a firm's total costs.

5. A firm would find its profits growing by adding one more worker when the _____ associated with the worker exceeds the _____ of the worker.

6. The law of diminishing marginal product reflects the fact that by adding increasing quantities of a _____ input (for example, labour) to fixed quantities of another input, output will rise, but at some point it will increase by _____ amounts.

7. Profits are maximized if a firm hires only to the point where the wage equals the expected _____.

8. As the wage rate rises, the quantity of labour supplied _____, *ceteris paribus;* as the wage falls, the quantity of labour supplied _____, *ceteris paribus.*

Section 11.3

9. At a wage below the equilibrium level, quantity _____ would exceed quantity _____, resulting in a labour _____. In this situation, employers would be forced to offer higher wages in order to hire as many workers as they would like.

10. Increases in the demand curve for labour may arise from _____ in labour productivity or from _____ in the price of the good.

11. Workers can increase productivity if they have more _____ or land with which to work, if _____ improvements occur, or if they acquire additional _____ or experience.

12. If labour productivity falls, then the demand curve for labour will shift to the _____.

13. If new workers enter the labour force, the labour supply curve will shift to the _____.

Section 11.4

14. If unions are successful in raising union wages, the result will be _____ wages in the nonunion sector.

15. Labour unions were formed to _____ members wages and _____ working conditions.

16. The province of _____ has the lowest union rate.

17. The rate of unionization is greater in the _____ sector of the Canadian economy.

Section 11.5

18. Differences in _____, certain _____ factors, and government _____ activities have all been identified as elements that influence the income distribution data and suggest that we might be overstating inequality.

19. At any moment in time, middle-aged persons tend to have _____ incomes than younger and older persons because they are at an age when their _____ is at a peak and they are participating in the _____ to a greater extent.

Section 11.6

20. The low-income cut-off for Canada is set at the income level at which a household spends 63 percent of its income on _____, _____, and _____.

21. In Canada, poverty is defined on a _____ basis.

22. The incidence of poverty declines as the level of education attainment of the household head _____.

True or False

Section 11.1

1. By far the largest fraction of national income goes to wages and salaries for labour services.

2. The "price" of a productive factor is directly related to consumer demand for the final good or service.

Section 11.2

3. In a competitive labour market, a firm's marginal resource cost is the market wage.

4. Hiring an additional worker would lower profits when the marginal resource cost is less than the marginal revenue product.

5. The law of diminishing marginal product states that as increasing quantities of a variable input (for example, labour) are added to fixed quantities of another input, output will rise, but at some point it will increase by diminishing amounts.

6. The marginal revenue product of labour declines, even in the case of competitive output markets, because of the diminishing marginal product of labour.

7. A profit-maximizing firm will hire up to the last unit of input for which the wage is expected to exceed the marginal revenue product.

8. In a competitive labour market, a firm can hire all the labour it wishes at the prevailing wage.

Section 11.3

9. Only at the equilibrium wage are both suppliers (workers) and demanders (employers) of labour able to exchange the quantity of labour they desire.

10. Decreases in the demand curve for labour may arise from decreases in labour productivity or from increases in the price of the good produced by that labour.

11. An increase in the demand for a good will increase the demand for labour.

12. A decrease in the nonwage income of workers would shift the labour supply curve to the right.

Section 11.4

13. The wage premium paid to union workers shows that all workers benefit from the activity of unions.

14. If unions are successful in obtaining higher wages, it causes employment to rise in the union sector but to fall in the nonunion sector.

Section 11.5

15. The distribution of measured income has remained relatively stable.

16. Even if every individual earned exactly the same income over his or her lifetime, there would still be inequality at any given moment in time.

17. The increased proportion of the population that is either very young or very old has tended to decrease the observed inequality in the distribution of income.

18. Both the increased number of divorced couples and the rise of two-income families have caused the measured distribution of income to appear more unequal.

19. The impact of increased government activity should be considered in evaluating the measured income distribution because government-imposed taxes burden different income groups differently and many government programs benefit some groups of income recipients more than others.

20. The income distribution is considerably more unequal than it appears.

Section 11.6

21. The poverty rate reflects a relative standard for poverty.

22. Many "poor" individuals in Canada, using the official definition, would be considered well off, even "rich," in many less-developed countries.

Multiple Choice

Section 11.1

1. Which of the following is *false* about labour markets?
   a. The greatest fraction of national income goes to wages and salaries for labour services.
   b. The price and quantity of labour depends on its supply and demand.
   c. The demand for labour is a derived demand.
   d. The price of labour tends to increase when the demand for the output produced by the labour increases.
   e. All of the above are *true*.

2. Which of the following statements best describes the concept of *derived demand*.
   a. Input demand comes from the supply of other inputs.
   b. Input demand comes from government legislation.
   c. Input demand comes from the consumer demand for outputs.
   d. Input demand does not exist.

Section 11.2

3. Marginal revenue product
   a. is the additional revenue that a firm obtains by employing one more unit of an input.
   b. will increase if an input's productivity increases.
   c. will decrease if the price of the output produced by the input falls.
   d. is characterized by all of the above.

4. The marginal resource cost of an input
   a. is the amount an added unit of an input adds to a firm's total cost.
   b. exceeds the market wage in a competitive industry.
   c. is less than the market wage in a competitive industry.
   d. is characterized by both a and b.
   e. is characterized by both a and c.

5. If an additional salesclerk is hired to work in a furniture store, the clerk's sales efforts will contribute $700 to the store's total revenue. The store's profits will rise if the additional salesclerk is hired whenever the cost of hiring the clerk is _____ in wages and other costs.
   a. $700
   b. less than $700
   c. more than $700
   d. There is not enough information to make a determination.

6. A firm will increase its profits by adding one more unit of an input when
   a. $MRP < MRC$.
   b. $MRP = MRC$.
   c. $MRP > MRC$.
   d. none of the above

7. Assuming competitive markets, a worker's contribution to revenue is given by
   a. the production function.
   b. the marginal revenue product of labour.
   c. the marginal resource cost of labour.
   d. the marginal product minus marginal cost.

8. In a competitive labour market,
   a. a firm is a wage taker.
   b. a firm can hire all the labour it wishes to at the market wage.
   c. a firm hires a small fraction of the total market quantity of labour supplied.
   d. a firm hires a substantial fraction of the total market quantity of labour supplied.
   e. all of the above except d are true.

9. MRP falls as more labour is hired in a perfectly competitive market because
   a. MRC increases as more labour is hired.
   b. the price of the output produced falls as more inputs are hired and more output is produced.
   c. of the law of diminishing marginal product.
   d. of all of the above.

10. In a competitive labour market in equilibrium,
    a. a firm's $MRP = MP \times MR$.
    b. a firm's $MRP = MP \times P$.
    c. a firm's $MRP = MRC$.
    d. a firm's *wage* $= MRC$.
    e. all of the above are true.

Section 11.3

11. At any wage higher than the equilibrium wage, the quantity of labour supplied
    _____ the quantity of labour demanded, resulting in a _____ of labour.
    a. exceeds; surplus
    b. exceeds; shortage
    c. is less than; surplus
    d. is less than; shortage

12. An increase in the demand for labour can result from
    a. increases in the price of the good produced by the labour.
    b. technological improvements.
    c. improvements in labour productivity.
    d. an increase in the amount of capital available for use by workers.
    e. any of the above.

13. Which of the following results in a rightward shift of the market demand curve for
    labour?
    a. an increase in labour productivity
    b. an increase in demand for the firm's product
    c. an increase in a firm's product price
    d. all of the above

14. The market supply of labour resources is affected by
    a. the number of hours workers are willing to work.
    b. the amount of immigration allowed.
    c. changes in a nation's working-age population.
    d. all of the above.

Section 11.4

15. If labour unions successfully negotiate wage increases for their members,
    a. the wages of nonunion workers increase as well.
    b. the wages in nonunion sectors decrease.
    c. employment likely falls in the union sector.
    d. both a and c occur.
    e. both b and c occur.

16. Approximately what percentage of Canadian workers belong to unions?
    a. about 16 percent
    b. about 30 percent
    c. about 47 percent
    d. about 80 percent

17. Unionization provides _____ in given occupations, and as a result, wage rates in
    these occupations have a tendency to _____ .
    a. barriers to entry; decrease
    b. barriers to entry; increase
    c. ease of entry; decrease
    d. ease of entry; increase

18. According to economists Medoff and Freeman, unions might make workers more productive by _____ .
   a. improving morale
   b. reducing the amount of employee turnover
   c. providing a forum for communication of worker grievances
   d. all of the above

Section 11.5

19. Which of the following is true?
   a. There is substantial income inequality in Canada, and there has been little change in the distribution of measured income in the past few decades.
   b. There is substantial income inequality in Canada, but there have been significant changes in the distribution of measured income in the past few decades.
   c. There is very little income inequality in Canada, and there has been little change in the distribution of measured income in the past few decades.
   d. There is very little income inequality in Canada, but there have been significant changes in the distribution of measured income in the past few decades.

20. The measured distribution of income may appear more unequal as a result of
   a. an increased number of divorced couples.
   b. an increased proportion of young people in the population.
   c. an increased proportion of older people in the population.
   d. an increase in the number of two-income families.
   e. all of the above.

21. Which of the following is likely to improve a person's income?
   a. increasing productivity
   b. investing in human capital
   c. possessing a special talent or skill
   d. being highly motivated to succeed
   e. all of the above

Section 11.6

22. The poverty rate
   a. is the proportion of the persons who fall below the low-income cut-off.
   b. is set at two times the cost of providing a nutritionally adequate diet.
   c. may understate the degree of poverty by not counting noncash government benefits as income.
   d. All of the above are true.
   e. None of the above are true.

23. The official low-income cut-off for Canada is currently set at the income level at which a household spends _____ percent of its after-tax income on food, clothing, and shelter.
   a. 20
   b. 43
   c. 63
   d. 83

Problems

1. [Section 11.2]

Fill in the missing data on the following chart.

Workers	Total Corn Output	Marginal Product of Labour
1	4 000	
2	10 000	
3	15 000	
4		3 000
5		1 000
6		−1 000

2. [Section 11.2]

Fill in the missing data on the following chart for a perfectly competitive firm.

Workers	Total Output	Marginal Product	Price	Marginal Revenue Product
1	200		20	
2	380		20	
3	540		20	
4	680		20	
5	800		20	
6	900		20	
7	980		20	
8	1040		20	

3. [Section 11.3]

Indicate which point could correspond to the equilibrium wage and quantity hired

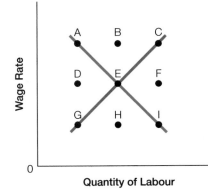

Quantity of Labour

a. at the initial equilibrium.
b. if the price of the output produced by the labour increased.
c. if the price of the output produced by the labour decreased.
d. With an increase in immigration.
e. With a reduction in the quality of workplace amenities.
f. if worker productivity increased and an increase in workers' nonwage incomes.
g. if worker productivity decreased and a decrease in population.
h. if there were an increase in the price of output produced by the labour and an increase in the number of hours workers were willing to work.
i. if there were a decrease in the price of output produced by the labour and a decrease in workers' nonwage incomes.

4. [Section 11.4]

Use the following diagram to answer a–c.

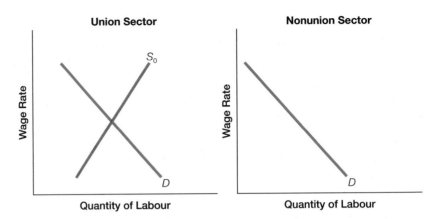

a. If unions were unable to have any effect on wages, draw the supply curve for the nonunion sector.

b. If unions were able to restrict the supply of labour in the union sector, indicate what would happen in both the union and nonunion sectors.

c. What happens to the union wage and the number of union workers hired in b? What happens to the nonunion wage and the number of nonunion workers hired in b?

5. [Section 11.5]

Explain at least three reasons why the official data on the distribution of income may overstate the actual degree of income inequality.

6. [Section 11.6]

Can economic growth reduce poverty? How does the answer depend on whether we are using an absolute or relative measure of poverty?

chapter 12

The Environment

12.1 NEGATIVE EXTERNALITIES AND POLLUTION
How are negative externalities internalized?

12.2 PUBLIC POLICY AND THE ENVIRONMENT
What forms of intervention can be taken to protect the environment?

12.3 PROPERTY RIGHTS
What is the connection between property rights and the environment?

Negative Externalities and Pollution

- What are social costs?
- How are negative externalities internalized?

In the 1970s, fish were mysteriously disappearing from thousands of lakes in central and eastern Canada. The culprit was coal-burning power plants in the United States that were releasing sulphur dioxide and nitric oxide into the atmosphere, which then travelled north to Canada; when combined with water, it created acid rain. Acid rain was not only killing fish, but also destroying crops and trees. Today, acid rain is no longer an environmental problem.

The Acid Rain Program in the United States has been responsible for the dramatic reduction in sulphur dioxide and nitric oxide emissions. The program uses an allowance trading system (cap and trade) which is a dramatic departure from traditional environmental regulatory methods. In this chapter, we will examine the economics of pollution, and those government policies that can be used to reduce pollution.

WHAT ARE SOCIAL COSTS?

As we learned in Chapter 6, whenever an economic activity has benefits or costs that are shared by individuals other than the demanders or suppliers of a good or service, an externality is involved. If the activity imposes costs on individuals other than the demanders or suppliers of a good or service, it is said to have negative externalities. Put another way, negative externalities exist anytime the social costs of producing a good or service exceed the private costs. Social costs refer to costs that spill over to other members of society. Private costs refer to costs incurred only by the producer of the good or service.

section 12.1
Exhibit 1
The Effect of a Negative Externality

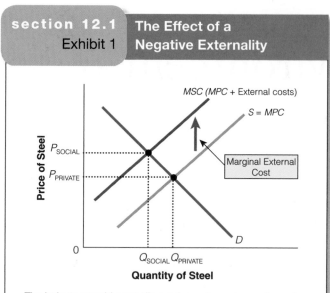

The industry would normally produce where demand equals supply (where supply is equal to the marginal private costs), at output $Q_{PRIVATE}$ and charging price $P_{PRIVATE}$. If, however, the industry were forced to also pay those external costs imposed on others, the industry would produce where demand equals marginal social costs, at output Q_{SOCIAL} and price P_{SOCIAL}. Where firms are not forced to pay for negative externalities, output tends to be larger and prices lower than at the optimal output, where the marginal benefits to society (as measured by demand) equal the marginal costs to society.

internalized externalities *when an industry is forced to compensate those enduring some negative externality caused by its production*

This factory is clearly polluting the water downstream, creating a negative externality for those who fish downstream. It is possible that the people who fish could try to bargain with the factory, perhaps even pay it to pollute less. However, sometimes private bargaining does not work and the government can provide a solution through regulation or pollution taxes.

© Nagy Melinda/Shutterstock

NEGATIVE EXTERNALITIES AND POLLUTION

The classic example of a negative externality is pollution. When a steel mill puts soot into the air as a by-product of making steel, it imposes costs on others not connected with the steel mill or with buying or selling steel. The soot requires nearby homeowners to paint their houses more often, entailing costs. Studies show that respiratory diseases are greater in areas with high air pollution, imposing substantial costs, often the shortening of life itself. In addition, the steel mill might discharge chemicals or overheated water into a stream, thus killing wildlife, ruining business for those who make a living fishing, spoiling recreational activities for the local population, and so on.

In deciding how much to produce, the steel makers are governed by demand and supply. They do not worry (unless forced to) about the external costs imposed on members of society, and in all likelihood, the steel makers would not even know the full extent of those costs.

Consider the hypothetical steel industry in Exhibit 1. It produces where demand and supply intersect, at output $Q_{PRIVATE}$ and $P_{PRIVATE}$. Let us assume that the marginal social cost of producing the product is indicated by the marginal social cost (MSC) curve, lying above the supply curve, which represents the industry's marginal private costs (MPC). The marginal social costs of production are higher at all output levels, as those costs include all of the industry's private costs plus the costs that spill over to other members of society from the pollution produced by the industry—that is, the external costs.

At output Q_{SOCIAL}, the marginal social costs to society equal the marginal social benefits (as indicated by the demand curve) from the sale of the last unit of steel. At that output, the price of steel is P_{SOCIAL}. If the firm were somehow forced to compensate people who endure the costs of its pollution, the firm would produce at output Q_{SOCIAL} and price steel at P_{SOCIAL}. In that case, we would say that the externalities were **internalized,** because each firm in the industry would now be paying the entire cost to society of making steel. When negative externalities are internalized, steel firms produce less output (Q_{SOCIAL} instead of $Q_{PRIVATE}$) and charge higher prices (P_{SOCIAL} instead of $P_{PRIVATE}$). Optimal output occurs where the marginal social costs are equal to the marginal social benefits. When firms do not pay all of the social costs they incur, and therefore produce too much output, the result is too much pollution. The output of pollution is directly related to the output of the primary goods produced by the firm.

MEASURING EXTERNALITIES

It is generally accepted that in the absence of intervention, the market mechanism will underproduce goods and services with positive externalities, such as education, and overproduce those with negative externalities, such as pollution. But the exact extent of these market misallocations is quite difficult to establish in the real world because the divergence between social and private costs and benefits is often difficult to measure. For example, exactly how much damage at the margin does a steel mill's air pollution do to nonconsumers of the steel? No one really knows because no market fully measures those costs. Indeed, the costs are partly nonpecuniary, meaning that no outlay of money occurs. Even though we pay dollars to get medicine for respiratory ailments and pay dollars for paint to repair pollution-caused peeling, we do not make explicit money payments for the visual pollution and undesirable odours that the mill might produce as a by-product of making steel. Nonpecuniary costs

Are cellular phones a negative or positive externality? Some would say a negative externality because cellphones can distract drivers and cause accidents. On the other hand, cellphones may be a positive externality because drivers with cellphones can report accidents, crimes, stranded motorists, or drunk drivers.

are real costs and potentially have a monetary value that can be associated with them, but assessing that value in practical terms is immensely difficult. You might be able to decide how much you would be willing to pay to live in a pollution-free world, but no current mechanism allows anyone to express the perceived monetary value of having clear air to breathe and smell. Even some pecuniary, or monetary, costs are difficult to truly measure: How much respiratory disease is caused by pollution and how much by other factors such as secondhand cigarette smoke? Environmental economists continue to make progress in valuing these difficult damages.

ACTIVE LEARNING EXERCISE

NEGATIVE EXTERNALITIES

Q: After months of looking at houses he could not afford, Dean recently bought a home near the airport. After living in his house for only a week, Dean was so fed up with the noise that he decided to organize a group of local homeowners in an effort to stop the noise pollution. Should Dean be compensated for bearing this negative externality?

A: Because few people want to live in noisy areas, housing prices and rents in those areas are lower, reflecting the cost of the noise in the area. As a result, fewer people competed with Dean for the purchase of his house relative to houses in quieter neighborhoods, so it is likely he did not pay as much as he might have in another area. Because Dean paid a lower price for living in a noisier area, he has already been compensated for the noise pollution.

Section Check

1. Social costs are those costs that accrue to the total population; private costs are incurred only by the producer of the good or service.
2. If the industry were somehow forced to compensate people who endure the costs of pollution, we would say that the industry had internalized the externality.
3. When negative externalities are internalized, the industry produces less output at a higher price.
4. Optimal output occurs when marginal social benefits are equal to marginal social costs.

Public Policy and the Environment

- What is the "best" level of pollution?
- What is a pollution tax?
- What are transferable pollution rights?

Even though measuring externalities, both negative and positive, is often nearly impossible, it does not necessarily mean that it is better to ignore the externality and allow the market solution to continue. As already explained, the market solution will almost certainly result in excessive output by polluters unless some intervention occurs. What form should the intervention take?

ENVIRONMENTAL REGULATION

One approach to dealing with externalities is to regulate behaviour in response to the externality. The range of environmental regulations is significant, as the government can choose to prohibit certain activities that cause pollution, dictate maximum permissible levels of pollution, or require producers to adopt certain pollution-control technology. In Canada, environmental policy is the joint responsibility of all three levels of government (federal, provincial, and municipal), with Environment Canada as the central department responsible for developing and enforcing regulations designed to protect the environment.

Evidence suggests that pollution levels have declined in recent years (see In the News), although these statistics do not measure exactly what Environment Canada's impact has been, as other things were also changing. However, it does appear that the regulatory approach adopted by Environment Canada to limit key pollutants has led to a reduction in pollution levels. For example, the phasing-out of leaded gasoline, which started in the 1980s, has dramatically reduced the levels of lead in the atmosphere.

WHY IS A CLEAN ENVIRONMENT NOT FREE?

In many respects, a clean environment is no different from any other desirable good. In a world of scarcity, we can increase our consumption of a clean environment only by giving up something else. The problem that we face is choosing the combination of goods that does the most to enhance human well-being. Few people would enjoy a perfectly clean environment if they were cold, hungry, and generally destitute. On the other hand, an individual choking to death in smog is hardly to be envied, no matter how great his or her material wealth.

Only by considering the additional cost as well as the additional benefit of increased consumption of all goods, including clean air and water, can decisions on the desirable combination of goods to consume be made properly.

THE COSTS AND BENEFITS OF POLLUTION CONTROL

It is possible, even probable, that pollution elimination, like nearly everything else, is subject to diminishing returns. Initially, a large amount of pollution can be eliminated fairly inexpensively, but getting rid of still more pollution may prove more costly. Likewise, it is

In The **NEWS**

PROGRESS IS HAPPENING ON OUR ENVIRONMENTAL FRONT

BY NIGEL HANNAFORD

As we prepare for Earth Day, let the record show that cleaning up the environment may carry unintended consequences.

Years ago, I lived in a coastal community where effluent from paper mills had made the end of the inlet near the docks into a life-depleted zone. This was clearly not good, so the mill was ordered to clean up.

It did so at vast expense, but with great success. Life returned, a veritable seaweed Serengeti on the West Coast. Unfortunately, amid this proliferation of biological abundance was the hole-boring, wood-chewing teredo worm, scourge of wooden ships in days of yore. It promptly attacked the wooden dock pilings that had sat there in sterile safety for decades. More vast expense. But, it's progress, and there's more of it than we think.

For, if polls are any guide, Canadians seem to love the environment more than they know about it, and are broadly unaware that things are getting better, not worse.

For instance, an Environment Canada poll taken last year found 76 per cent of Canadian respondents thought environmental regulations were too weak, and favoured various green levies on manufacturers for the purpose of fighting pollution. On the other hand, a 2006 poll revealed that although 89 per cent of Canadians had heard of the Kyoto Protocol—it was much in the news in the run-up to the election—more than two-thirds of them said they knew nothing about it. This despite a widespread belief reported by Leger, that global warming "will destroy the Earth."

And in 2004, the Fraser Institute noted what it termed "a strong disconnect between Canadian student perceptions of environmental trends (mostly negative) and the reality of environmental trends (mostly positive)."

A certain amount of the Canadian split personality about the environment is just human nature. Some people consider themselves realists, and heaven knows, realists are happiest when the facts are least appetizing. Others just enjoy a good scare; I have often wondered if the gene that makes you like slasher movies doesn't also rev you up when NASA says an asteroid is closing in on the Earth, or Al Gore says we're all going to drown.

And, of course, if you're looking for government funds, the tap opens wider to the degree government thinks people are anxious. All of this leads to increased public interest, but not necessarily accurate perception.

So, a few encouraging factoids for Earth Day.

According to Environment Canada's National Environmental Indicator Series, industry is cleaning up its noxious emissions. For example, between 1990 and 2000, mercury to air was cut 77 per cent, and sulphur dioxide emissions in Eastern Canada dropped to about half what they were 30 years ago. More generally, Environment Canada's National Pollutant Release Inventory covering 907 facilities and 160 substances shows an eight per cent decrease in pollutant releases to air, water and land between 1996 and 2006; in the latter year, over one million tonnes of this variegated crap were sent for recycling and energy recovery. And this, from the list of Canadian Environmental Sustainability Indicators in 2007:

- —Between 1990 and 2002, Canadian manufacturers cut by a third the amount of energy needed to produce a unit of goods and services.
- —Nearly 60 per cent of Canadian households are using compact fluorescent bulbs, three times as many as in 1994.
- —Low-flow showerheads are in use in 60 per cent of Canadian households, up from 42 per cent in 1994.
- —According to Environment Canada's Municipal Water Use Report, in 2004, we all used six litres of water less per person on average than we did in 2001.
- —The Fraser Institute quotes Statistics Canada that thanks to improvements to vehicle exhaust systems, there was an 82.6 per cent decrease in ambient levels of carbon monoxide between 1974 and 2001—despite a 30 per cent increase in total vehicle registrations—and ambient lead levels in the atmosphere are now too small to be worth measuring.

Plus, you no longer need your stomach pumped if you fall into Lake Erie, and when did you last hear about acid rain?

Progress is happening. Altogether, the Fraser study found 31 out of 37 primary indicators of environmental quality were stable, or improved.

"Things are, in fact, improving dramatically in the developed world as improvements in technology, higher incomes and democratic systems have created an ever-increasing ability to protect the environment," the 2004 report concluded. "There is every reason to believe that similar improvements will be seen globally as developing countries open to international trade and have access to advanced technologies. And locally, while many Canadians are unaware of it, the majority of environmental trends in Canada have been positive for decades."

Even in Ottawa. The last time the roof of one of the buildings on Parliament Hill was redone, it took unprecedented ages for the copper to acquire the customary shade of corroded green to match the other roofs. Maybe they should paint it. Just as on the coast, you can't rely on pollution the way you used to.

SOURCE: Nigel Hannaford, "Progress is happening on our environmental front," *Calgary Herald,* April 19, 2008, p. A30. Material reprinted with the express permission of: "Calgary Herald Group, Inc.", a CanWest Partnership.

CONSIDER THIS:

In recent years, a host of environmental regulations have combined to dramatically improve Canada's air, water, and land quality. These changes will lead to improved health, longevity, and quality of life for all Canadians.

Costs and Benefits of Pollution Controls

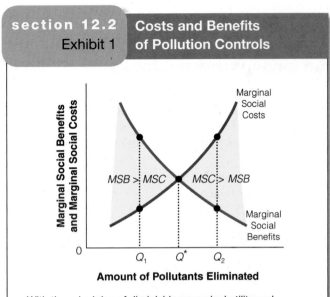

With the principles of diminishing marginal utility and increasing marginal cost at work, the marginal benefits of further expenditures on pollution control will, at some point, fall below the marginal costs to society imposed by still stricter controls. At output Q_1, pollution control is inadequate; on the other hand, elimination of Q_2 pollution will entail costs that exceed the benefits. Only at Q^* is pollution control expenditure at an optimum level. Of course, in practice, it is difficult to know exactly the position and slope of these curves.

also possible that the benefits from eliminating soot from the air might decline as more and more pollution is eliminated. For example, perhaps some pollution elimination initially would have a profound impact on health costs, home repair expenses, and so on, but as pollution levels fall, further elimination of pollutants brings fewer marginal benefits.

The cost–benefit trade-off just discussed is illustrated in Exhibit 1, which examines the marginal social benefits and marginal social costs associated with the elimination of air pollution. In the early 1960s, we had few regulations as a nation on pollution control, and as a result, private firms had little incentive to eliminate the problem. In the context of Exhibit 1, we may have spent Q_1 on controls, meaning that the marginal social benefits of greater pollution control expenditures exceeded the marginal costs associated with having the controls. Investing more capital and labour to reduce pollution is efficient in such a situation.

Optimum pollution control occurs when Q^* of pollution is eliminated. Up to that point, the marginal benefits from the elimination of pollution exceed the marginal costs, both pecuniary and nonpecuniary, of the pollution control. Overly stringent regulations force companies to control pollution to the level indicated by Q_2 in Exhibit 1, where the additional costs from the controls far outweigh the additional environmental benefits. It should be stated, however, that increased concerns about pollution have probably caused the marginal social benefit curve to shift to the right over time, increasing the optimal amount of pollution control. Because of measurement problems, however, it is difficult to state whether we are generally below, at, or above the optimal pollution level.

HOW MUCH POLLUTION?

It is practically impossible to get widespread agreement on what the appropriate level of pollution should be. Indeed, if we *did* have the appropriate level, about half of the people would think it too little and half would think it too much. People with different preferences and situations are simply going to have different ideas about the costs and benefits of pollution abatement. For example, consider a community that contains a college and an oil refinery, the latter emitting large quantities of nauseating and potentially noxious fumes into the atmosphere. Who do you think is most likely to participate in a protest favouring stringent pollution controls on the refinery: the college students or the townspeople? It is a safe bet that the answer is the college students. In fact, the college students may want to shut down the refinery altogether. Why? One may think that college students are more aware of and sensitive to the environmental quality of the community. Maybe. But the long-term residents of the community, those who plan to stay there and raise their children there, are certainly at least as concerned about the air quality in their community. Indeed, they may well be more concerned about local pollution than the college students who, after all, will typically live in the community only until they graduate. The primary difference between the townspeople and the students is probably not in the desire for a clean environment but the fact that the cost of cleaning up the environment will fall almost entirely on the townspeople. It is their jobs, incomes, and retirement

ACTIVE LEARNING EXERCISE

RELATIVE COSTS AND BENEFITS OF POLLUTION CONTROL

Q: Pete drives a 1948 pickup truck that has no smog equipment and gets poor gas mileage. He lives and does most of his driving in a sparsely populated area of Alberta. Do you think Pete should be required to install the same smog equipment on his car as someone with a similar vehicle living in downtown Toronto or Montreal?

A: The economic benefits of pollution control vary by location. In the wide-open, low-population-density areas of Alberta, the marginal benefit of pollution cleanup is lower than it would be in a large metropolitan area that already has a large amount of smog. Why? Alberta has so much space and so few people that the marginal benefit of pollution abatement is quite low. The same would certainly not be true in Toronto, where the air is already more polluted by cars and factories. Because so many people are affected and the air is already so saturated with pollutants, the marginal benefit of pollution elimination is much higher in Toronto than it would be in rural Alberta. That is, if a uniform standard is applied, regardless of loca-

tion, then the car in Alberta would be overcontrolled and the car in Toronto would be undercontrolled. Unfortunately, many of our environmental laws contain this "uniformity" flaw.

© JIM SUGAR/CORBIS

plans that will be jeopardized by strict pollution control requirements or the closing of the refinery. The students will not have to pay this cost because their job prospects and current income will be quite independent of the profitability of the local refinery. Not surprisingly, then, it is the students who will be most eager to either shut down the refinery or clean it up because they will reap many of the benefits and pay few of the costs. The townspeople will be a little less enthusiastic about environmental purity because they are likely to pay for much of it.

The point is not to decide which group is right or wrong. Both the students and the townspeople are quite rational, given the different situations they face. The purpose here is to emphasize that controversy is sure to arise when a community of people share a common, or public, good (or bad). Conflicts are inevitable because different people have different preferences and face different costs. This explains much of the controversy that surrounds environmental issues. Controversy over environmental protection would largely disappear if everyone could pay for and consume a preferred level of environmental quality, independent of the level paid for and consumed by others, in much the same way that individuals can choose either beer or wine—each getting the private goods they want. But there is no way to completely avoid this type of controversy for public goods such as air quality or national defence. It should be recognized, however, that one way people often moderate controversies of this type is by sorting themselves into relatively homogeneous groupings. Communities that contain people with similar backgrounds, preferences, and circumstances are more likely to avoid socially divisive controversies than are communities containing more diverse populations.

POLLUTION TAXES

Another means of solving the misallocation problem (relatively too many polluting goods) posed by the existence of externalities is for the government to create incentives for firms to internalize the external costs resulting from their activities. For example, returning to the case of pollution, suppose that the marginal private cost of making steel was $150 a tonne. Suppose further that at the margin, each tonne of steel caused $40 in environmental damages per tonne. If the government were then to levy a **pollution tax**—a tax levied on a firm for environmental pollution—on the steelmaker equal to $40 per tonne, the manufacturer's marginal private cost would rise from $150 to $190; the $190 figure would then be equal to the true marginal social cost of making steel. The firm would accordingly alter its output and pricing decisions to take into account its higher marginal cost, leading ultimately to reduced output (and pollution) and higher prices. The firm also has an incentive to seek new, less pollution-intensive methods of making steel.

pollution tax

tax levied by government on a firm for environmental pollution

Using taxes to internalize external costs is appealing because it allows the relatively efficient private sector to operate according to market forces in a manner that takes socially important spillover costs into account. A major objection to the use of such taxes is that, in most cases, it is difficult to measure externalities with any precision. Choosing a tax rate involves some guesswork, and poor guessing might lead to a solution that is far from optimal. But it is likely to be better than ignoring the problem. In spite of the severe difficulties in measurement, however, many economists would like to see greater effort made to force internalization of externalities through taxes rather than using regulation. Why? We know that firms will seek out the least expensive (in terms of using society's scarce resources) approaches to cleanup because they want more profits. This plan is good for them and good for society because we can have more of everything that way, including environmental quality.

TRANSFERABLE POLLUTION RIGHTS

transferable pollution rights

a right given to a firm to discharge a specified amount of pollution; its transferable nature creates incentive to lower pollution levels

Economists see an opportunity to control pollution through a government-enforced system of property rights. In this system, the government issues **transferable pollution rights** that give the holder the right to discharge a specified amount (smaller than the uncontrolled amount) of pollution into the air. In this plan, firms have an incentive to lower their levels of pollution because they can sell their permits if they go unused. Specifically, firms that can lower their emissions at the lowest costs will do so and trade their pollution rights to firms that cannot reduce their pollution levels as easily. That is, each polluter—required either to reduce pollution to the level allowed by the number of rights it holds or buy more rights—will be motivated to eliminate all pollution that is cheaper than the price of pollution rights. The crucial advantage to the pollution rights approach comes from the fact that the rights are private property and can be sold.

It is worth emphasizing that this least-cost pattern of abatement does not require any information about the techniques of pollution abatement on the part of the government—more specifically, Environment Canada. Environment Canada does not need to know the cheapest abatement strategy for each and every polluter. Faced with a positive price for pollution rights, each polluter has every motivation to discover and use the cheapest way to reduce pollution. Nor does Environment Canada need to know anything about the differences in abatement costs among polluters. Each polluter is motivated to reduce pollution as long as the cost of reducing one more unit is less than the price of pollution rights. The information and incentives generated by private ownership and market exchange of these pollution rights automatically leads to the desirable pattern of pollution abatement—namely, having those best at cleaning up doing all the cleanup.

The pollution rights approach also creates an incentive for polluters to develop improved pollution abatement technologies. Our economic history is full of examples of technological development that has allowed more output to be produced with less land and labour. Conspicuously absent until recently have been technological developments designed for output to be produced with less pollution. Market prices on land and labour have always provided a strong incentive to conserve these resources. The absence of prices for the use of our atmosphere and waterways, however, made it privately unprofitable to worry about conserving their use. Marketable pollution rights could remedy this neglect.

The prospect of buying and selling pollution permits would allow firms to move into an area that is already as polluted as allowed by Environment Canada standards. Under the tradable permits policy, the firm can set up operation by purchasing pollution permits from an existing polluter in the area. This type of exchange allows the greatest value to be generated with a given amount of pollution. It also encourages polluters to come up with cheaper ways of reducing pollution, because the firm that reduces pollution is able to sell its pollution credits to others, making pollution reduction profitable.

Pulp and paper mills pollute our environment. The pulp and paper industry is one of the largest and most polluting industries in North America. One of the primary environmental concerns is the use of chlorine-based bleaches and resultant toxic emissions to air, water, and soil.

WHAT IS AN IDEAL POLLUTION CONTROL POLICY?

What would be the objectives of an ideal pollution control policy? First, and most obviously, we want pollution reduced to the efficient level—the level that maximizes the value of all of our resources. This goal would involve continuing to reduce pollution by one more unit only as long as the value of the improved environmental quality is greater than the value of ordinary goods that are sacrificed.

A second related objective is to reduce pollution as cheaply as possible. Two separate considerations are important here. If pollution is to be reduced as cheaply as possible, it is obvious that each pollution source has to abate at minimum cost. Of the many ways to cut back on pollution, not all are equally costly. But even if all polluters are abating as cheaply as possible, it does not necessarily mean that pollution overall is being reduced at least cost.

The pattern of pollution abatement over all sources is of great importance here. Because some polluters will be more efficient at pollution reduction than others, the least-cost abatement pattern will require some polluters to clean up more than others.

A third objective of a pollution control policy is to establish incentives that will motivate advances in pollution abatement technology. Over the long run, this objective may be even more important than the first two. For example, the cost of controlling pollution can be significantly reduced over time, even if the second objective is not fully realized, if consistent advances are made in the technology of pollution control.

It should be clear that these three objectives—(1) achieving the efficient level of pollution, (2) achieving pollution reduction at least cost, and (3) motivating advances in abatement technology—may never be fully realized, especially the first objective.

Because we cannot own and control identifiable and separate portions of the atmosphere, we are not in a position to require that a price be paid in exchange for fouling clean air we each consider ours alone. Without such exchanges and prices, we have no way of knowing the value people place on clean air. Without this information, it is not possible to determine the efficient level of air pollution. Likewise, private ownership of identifiable and separate portions of water in our lakes, rivers, and oceans is not possible, leaving no precise ways of determining the efficient level of water pollution. In the absence of market exchange, we rely on the political process to determine the efficient level of pollution.

In a democratic political order, the presumption is that the information provided by voting and lobbying will keep the political process at least somewhat responsive to the preferences of the citizens. To the extent that this presumption is justified, the hope is that political decision makers will arrive at a level of pollution near the efficient level.

ACTIVE LEARNING EXERCISE

INCENTIVES AND POLLUTION

Q: Brad and Angelina were horrified with the number of abandoned automobiles in their community. Attempting to come up with a solution for this form of visual pollution, they thought maybe something along the lines of deposits on bottles might work. Can you help? How would deposits on autos work? How would it affect the incentives of the litterer and the recoverer?

A: It is estimated that 15 percent of all automobiles in the United States are abandoned at the end of their useful lives along streams, fields, highways, and streets. However, mandatory deposits would provide incentives for both recovery and against the littering of abandoned automobiles. That is, if the deposit is set sufficiently high, people would be less likely to abandon their autos because they would lose their deposits. On the other hand, if someone did decide to abandon an auto, someone else has the incentive to tow it to a recycling centre and receive the deposit. This example emphasizes the essential economic reasoning that incentives matter.*

*For more details, see D. Lee, P. Graves, and R. Sexton, "Controlling the Abandonment of Automobiles: Mandatory Deposits Versus Fines," *Journal of Urban Economics* 31, no. 1 (January 1992).

© easyshoot/Shutterstock

Section Check

1. Environmental regulations force companies to find less pollution-intensive ways of producing goods and services.
2. Pollution taxes can be used to force firms to internalize externalities and allow the relatively efficient private sector to operate according to market forces in a manner that takes socially important spillover costs into account.
3. Transferable pollution rights create incentives for the firms that are best at cleaning up to do so.
4. The transferable pollution rights policy encourages polluters to come up with cheaper ways of reducing pollution because the firm that reduces pollution is able to sell its remaining pollution credits to others.
5. The objectives of pollution control policies are to achieve the efficient level of pollution, achieve pollution reduction at least cost, and motivate advances in abatement technology.

section

12.3 Property Rights

- What is the relationship between externalities and property rights?
- What is the Coase theorem?

PROPERTY RIGHTS AND THE ENVIRONMENT

The existence of externalities and the efforts to deal with them in a manner that will enhance the social good can be considered a question of the nature of property rights. If Environment Canada limits the soot that a steel company emits from "its" smokestack, then the property rights of the steel company with respect to its smokestack have been altered or restricted. Similarly, zoning laws restrict how property owners can use their property. Sometimes, to deal with externalities, governments radically alter arrangements of property rights.

Indeed, the entire matter of dealing with externalities ultimately evolves into a question of how property rights should be altered. If no externalities existed in the world, reasons for prohibiting property owners from using their property in any manner they voluntarily chose would be few. Ultimately, then, externalities involve an evaluation of the legal arrangements under which we operate our economy and thus illustrate one area where law and economics merge.

If a rancher lives downstream from a polluting factory and the courts have given the rights to the factory to pollute, economists say that the property rights to pollute are well defined. However, the rancher may be able to negotiate privately and pay the polluting firm to reduce the amount of pollution—and make both parties better off.

THE COASE THEOREM

In a classic paper, Nobel laureate Ronald Coase observed that when the benefits are greater than the costs for some course of action (say, environmental cleanup), potential transactions can make some people better off without making anyone worse off. This idea is known as the **Coase theorem.** To appreciate this important insight, consider the following problem: A cattle rancher lives downstream from a paper mill. The paper mill dumps waste into the stream, which injures the rancher's cattle. If the rancher is not compensated, an externality exists. The question is, why does the externality persist? Suppose the courts have established (perhaps because the paper mill was there first) that the property rights to use (or abuse) the stream reside with the mill. If the benefits of cleanup are greater than the costs, the rancher should be willing to pay the mill owner to stop polluting. Let's assume that the rancher's benefits (say $10 000) from the cleanup undertaken by the mill are greater than the cost (say $5000). If the rancher were to offer $7500 to the mill owner to clean up the stream, both the rancher and the mill owner would be better off than with continued pollution. If, on the other hand, the rancher had the property rights to the stream, and the mill owner received a sufficiently high benefit from polluting the river, then it would be rational for the mill owner to pay the rancher up to the point where the marginal benefit to the mill owner of polluting equalled the marginal damage to the rancher from pollution.

Coase theorem
states that where property rights are defined in a clear-cut fashion, externalities are internalized

TRANSACTION COSTS AND THE COASE THEOREM

The mill owner and rancher example hinges critically on low transaction costs. Transaction costs are the costs of negotiating and executing an exchange, excluding the cost of the good or service bought. For example, when buying a car, it is usually rational for the buyer to spend some time searching for the "right" car and negotiating a mutually agreeable price.

Suppose instead that the situation involved 1000 ranchers and 10 mill owners. Trying to coordinate the activity between the ranch owners and mill owners would be almost impossible. Now imagine the complexities of more realistic cases: over 6 million people live in the Greater Toronto Area (locally abbreviated as the GTA). Each of them is damaged a little by a large number of firms and other consumers (for example, automobile drivers) in the GTA.

In The **NEWS**

BARS PLAN LAST-GASP PARTIES AS TOUGH SMOKE LAWS BEGIN

BY CHRISTINE SISMONDO

The Habs' flag is at half-mast at Kilgours' Bar Meets Grill these days—and not because the Canadiens failed to reach the Stanley Cup finals. This time it's lowered to honour the passing of an old friend: the awning that covered their Bloor Street patio for 11 years.

At midnight on Tuesday, Peter Kilgour will roll up the awning for the very last time. To mark the occasion, trumpeter Patrick McGroarty will play Taps for the folks gathering for the Rolling-Up-the-Awning bash, held to mark the passing of the Ontario Smoke-Free legislation prohibiting smoking in all public places, including previously exempted designated smoking rooms and covered patios.

"The concept of legislating the outdoors is so absurd that I thought we might as well have a laugh," Mr. Kilgour said.

Kilgours' isn't the only last-gasp party that night. At Mitzi's Sister in Parkdale, owner Lesli Gaynor is planning an open stage where performers will only be performing smoky sad songs, preferably containing the words "cigarette" and "smoke."

"We're going to gather and say goodbye to the smoking room," explains Ms. Gaynor. "It's been a real social hub and a really nice place for people to meet one another."

At night's end, every bar regular (smoker and non, alike) will pile into the tiny glass-enclosed, separately ventilated Queen West street-facing smoking room (larger regulars first, smaller folks on top), to see just how many people they can fit. A photographer will be on hand.

The Artful Dodger, a pub on Isabella Street near Yonge, is grappling with losing both its smoking room and at least part of its covered patio. "The final night, we'll throw a blast for the regulars and see just how smoky we can get it before we wind the fans down," manager Leanne Garvie said.

Spirits on Church is planning a special open-mike session called "A Laugh to Your Last Smoke," featuring smoking comedians. Master of Ceremonies Jo-Anna Downey will be joining owner Helli Donaldson in handing out Popeye candy cigarettes to commemorate the demise of their smoking room.

George Milbrandt, owner of Front Street's C'est What is hosting what he refers to as a wake. He has invited people to come and pay their respects to the soon-to-be defunct smoking room. If you bring a friend, your friend gets a free meal.

"We're calling our party The Great Ontario Smoke-In," said Mr. Milbrandt, "to celebrate the day that righteousness triumphed over reason."

Ontario's provincewide legislation, which takes effect on Tuesday, will replace a patchwork of rules and put an end to designated smoking rooms in bars and restaurants.

Edgar Mitchell, president of the Pub and Bar Coalition of Canada, with 3500 members in Ontario, said more than 700 establishments will be forced to close designated smoking rooms. Businesses will suffer even more losses, he predicted, because the new legislation extends the smoking ban to any patio that has a canopy. "There is no rational scientific air risk necessitating such a ban," Mr. Mitchell said.

SOURCE: Christine Sismondo, "Bars Plan Last-Gasp Parties as Tough Smoke Laws Begin," *National Post,* Toronto Edition, May 27, 2006, p. A13. Reprinted with permission from the author.

CONSIDER THIS:

Who has the right to the air—the smokers or the nonsmokers? Why are property rights important in understanding the pollution problem? The classic dilemma in this situation is that smokers believe that it is their right to be able to dump their smoke into the air without added costs to them because nobody really owns the air. On the other hand, nonsmokers believe they have the right to breathe fresh air. Who is right? The issue is one of property rights. If only a few individuals were involved and therefore the cost of negotiating relatively low, then it is possible that an exchange could take place that might make both parties better off. For example, if the property rights were assigned to smokers, then nonsmokers could bribe smokers for the right to clean air.

It thus becomes apparent why the inefficiencies resulting from pollution control are not eliminated by private negotiations. First is the issue of ambiguity regarding property rights in air, water, and other environmental media. Firms that have historically polluted resent controls, giving up their rights to pollute only if bribed, yet consumers feel they have the right to breathe clean air and use clean bodies of water. These conflicting positions must be resolved in court, with the winner being, of course, made wealthier. Second, transaction costs increase greatly with the number of transactors, making it next to impossible for individual firms and citizens to negotiate private agreements. Finally, the properties of air or water quality (and similar public goods) are such that additional people can enjoy the benefits at no additional cost and cannot be excluded from doing so. Hence, in practice, private agreements are unlikely to solve many problems of market failure.

It is, however, too easy to jump to the conclusion that governments should solve any problems that cannot be solved by private actions. No solution may be possible, or all solutions may involve costs that exceed benefits. In any event, the ideas developed in this chapter should enable you to think critically about such problems and the difficulties in formulating appropriate policies.

Section Check

1. In a world with no externalities, property owners with only a few exceptions, could use their property in any manner they desired. Ultimately, then, externalities involve an evaluation of the legal arrangements in which we operate our economy.
2. The Coase theorem states that where property rights are defined in a clear-cut fashion, externalities are internalized. This condition holds where information and transaction costs are close to zero.

Summary

Section 12.1
- When an activity imposes costs on individuals other than the demanders or suppliers of a good or service, it is said to have negative externalities.
- An externality can be internalized when the producer of the externality is forced to compensate those enduring some negative impact caused by its production.
- Optimal output occurs where marginal social benefits are equal to marginal social costs.
- When externalities are internalized, the industry produces less output at a higher price.

Section 12.2
- Environmental regulations force companies to find less pollution-intensive ways to produce goods and services.
- The government can use pollution taxes to force firms to internalize externalities.
- A transferable pollution right policy encourages polluters to come up with cheaper ways to reduce pollution,

because the firm that reduces pollution is able to sell its remaining pollution credits to others.
- An ideal pollution control policy achieves the efficient level of pollution, achieves pollution reduction at least cost, and motivates the advancement of abatement technology.

Section 12.3
- In a world with no externalities, with a few exceptions, property owners could use their property in any manner they desired.
- Ultimately, externalities involve an evaluation of the legal arrangements in which we operate our economy.
- The Coase theorem states that where property rights are defined in a clear-cut fashion, externalities are internalized. This condition holds where information and transaction costs are close to zero.

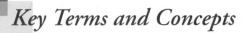

Key Terms and Concepts

For a complete glossary of chapter key terms, visit the textbook's Web site at http://www.sextonmicro2e.nelson.com.

internalized externalities 326   transferable pollution rights 332   Coase theorem 335
pollution tax 332

Review Questions

1. Why can a homeowner make a better argument for compensation for noise pollution if a local airport was built after he moved in than if it was already there when he moved in? Would it matter whether or not he knew it was going to be built?

2. A newly released study demonstrates that populated areas with significant air pollution caused by diesel engines experience a much higher incidence of cancer. If diesel engines were banned, what sorts of results would you expect?

3. A factory releases air pollutants that have a negative impact on the adjacent neighbourhood (populated by 2000 households). If the government could assign property rights to the air to either the factory or the residents of the neighbourhood, would this make a difference in the quantity of pollution generated?

4. Compare a pollution reduction program that permits a certain level of pollution using emission standards with one that permits the same level of pollution using transferable pollution rights.

5. Many communities have launched programs to collect recyclable materials but have been unable to find buyers for the salvaged materials. If the government were to offer a subsidy to firms using recycled materials, how might this affect the market for recycled materials? Illustrate using a demand and supply diagram.

6. Evaluate the following toll charges for a stretch of highway frequented by commuters: a toll of $2 between 7 A.M. and 10 A.M. and between 3 P.M. and 6 P.M., and a $4 toll at all other times of the day. Do you think these toll charges will help reduce traffic congestion?

7. Evaluate the following statement: "If people do not use paper or if they recycle paper, there is less incentive for lumber companies to plant trees on private land."

Fill in the Blanks

Section 12.1

1. _____ are costs imposed on people other than the suppliers or demanders of a good or service.

2. When a factory puts soot in the air as a by-product of its production, it is imposing _____ on others.

3. With external costs, the marginal _____ costs of production are greater than the marginal _____ costs of production.

4. Pollution policy from an efficiency perspective largely seeks ways for external costs to be _____ by decision makers.

5. Where firms are not forced to pay for negative externalities, their output is _____ and their prices are _____ than they would otherwise be.

6. Forcing producers to internalize external costs would _____ their costs of production.

7. Many of the costs of negative externalities are _____ to measure, especially the _____ costs that have no market prices.

Section 12.2

8. The goal of environmental regulations is to force companies to find less _____-intensive ways to produce.

9. Air quality has _____ in most Canadian cities since 1970.

10. Pollution reduction, like other forms of production, is subject to _____ returns.

11. The optimal quantity of pollution occurs where the _____ of pollution abatement equals the _____ from pollution abatement.

12. Eliminating nearly all pollution would be economically _____, because the marginal _____ would exceed the marginal _____.

13. The economically ideal tax to impose on a polluter would be _____ the marginal external costs imposed on others by its production.

14. Compared to emission standards, pollution taxes lead to abatement by firms who can do so at the _____ cost.

15. Under a system of transferable pollution rights, firms with high costs of abatement would likely be _____, and firms with low costs of abatement would be _____.

Section 12.3

16. Problems of external costs are largely a question of how _____ should be assigned.

17. _____, the costs of negotiating and executing exchanges, must be low for well-defined property rights to allow externalities to be internalized.

18. According to the Coase theorem, markets can internalize externalities as long as _____ are well defined and _____ costs are low.

19. When large numbers of individuals are affected by an external cost, the transactions costs of using voluntary negotiation to internalize it are likely to be _____.

True or False

Section 12.1

1. Activities that impose costs on people other than the suppliers or demanders of a good or service are negative externalities.

2. In markets where negative externalities are created, the marginal social cost of production exceeds the marginal private cost of production.

3. In markets where negative externalities are created, the marginal private cost of production equals the marginal social cost of production.

4. The marginal social cost of production equals the marginal private cost of production plus the marginal external cost of production.

5. A poultry-packing firm breeds, raises, and slaughters chickens for market. The firm's chicken yards and processing plant emit foul odours into the air, which affects surrounding residential neighbourhoods. If the poultry-packing firm is a perfectly competitive firm producing at a level of output such that the price of a kilogram of chicken equals the firm's marginal cost, it will produce a socially optimal quantity of chicken.

6. The nonpecuniary (or nonmonetary) costs associated with negative externalities are, in practice, very difficult to assess.

Section 12.2

7. The goal of Environment Canada regulations is to force companies to find less pollution-intensive ways of producing goods and services.

8. Available evidence suggests that since 1970, environmental regulations have not succeeded in reducing Canadian pollution levels.

9. Compliance standards can create situations where the marginal cost of eliminating pollution exceeds the marginal benefit from doing so.

10. Eliminating nearly all pollution would lead to economic efficiency and healthier lifestyles for all.

11. Economists believe that pollution reduction is likely subject to diminishing returns.

12. In practice, it is very difficult to determine the appropriate pollution tax to levy to correct for a negative externality.

13. Under a system of transferable pollution rights, firms with relatively high abatement costs will sell rights to pollute to firms with relatively low abatement costs.

14. In order for a transferable pollution rights system to work, Environment Canada needs to know the cheapest way for each polluter to reduce pollution.

Section 12.3

15. Transaction costs must be low for well-defined property rights to lead to the internalization of externalities.

16. The problem of externalities can be viewed as a question of how property rights should be assigned.

17. According to the Coase theorem, if transaction costs are high it is unlikely that private negotiations can resolve an externality problem and achieve social efficiency.

Multiple Choice

Section 12.1

1. Many harmful externalities occur because
  a. persons do not pay the full social cost of using a resource.
  b. persons do not pay the full private cost of using a resource.
  c. companies do not pay the market price for natural resources.
  d. companies pay more than the full social cost of using a resource.

2. A firm is generating harmful externalities when
  a. marginal social cost is less than marginal private cost.
  b. marginal social cost is the same as marginal private cost.
  c. marginal social cost is greater than marginal private cost.
  d. the firm is not producing at the level of output where the *MPC* is minimized.

3. Pollution
  a. is an example of a positive externality.
  b. should be reduced to zero, the socially efficient level.
  c. is not an economic problem.
  d. is an example of a negative externality.
  e. is characterized by both b and d.

4. Pollution control costs lead to
  a. lower prices for goods and services produced by polluting firms.
  b. higher prices for goods and services produced by polluting firms.
  c. a decrease in the cost of production by polluting firms.
  d. an increase in production of output by polluting firms.

5. The true extent of a negative externality may be difficult to measure because
  a. firms often keep poor records of their cash outlays.
  b. of the intricacies of accounting rules.
  c. certain costs may be nonpecuniary.
  d. none of the above.

6. If the government were able to force a firm to internalize the external cost of its production, we would expect
  a. the firm to produce more to make up for incurring a higher private cost.
  b. the marginal social cost curve to shift up and the firm to produce more and charge a higher price as a result.
  c. the firm to produce less and charge a higher price as a result of incurring higher marginal private costs.
  d. the firm to lower its price to compensate for incurring a higher private cost.

7. If significant external costs are imposed on third parties by a polluting firm,
   a. the marginal private cost curve overstates the relative importance of the product to society and output should increase.
   b. the marginal private cost curve understates the relative importance of the product to society and output should increase.
   c. the marginal private cost overstates the cost to society and output should increase.
   d. the marginal private cost curve understates the cost to society and output should decrease.
   e. the marginal private cost curve accurately reflects the cost to society and output should not change.

8. External costs created by polluting firms
   a. are paid by no one in society.
   b. are typically paid by the consumer purchasing the product.
   c. may be paid by society in the form of nonpecuniary costs, higher medical bills, and/or cleanup costs.
   d. are typically paid by the producer of the pollution.
   e. are typically paid for by the government.

Section 12.2

9. It is likely that the marginal cost of pollution abatement
   a. falls the more pollution is reduced.
   b. rises the more pollution is reduced.
   c. is constant as pollution is reduced more.
   d. equals zero.

10. Taxes on the emissions of polluting firms are primarily intended to
    a. encourage firms to reduce product prices.
    b. encourage firms to increase production of output.
    c. raise revenue for general spending needs.
    d. encourage firms to pollute less.

11. An ideal pollution tax
    a. does not affect the quantity of the good produced.
    b. forces a firm to internalize the externality.
    c. causes a polluting firm to increase production to the socially efficient level of output.
    d. leads to a reduction in price to the consumer of the polluting firm's output.

12. If regulations are too stringent,
    a. the marginal social benefit of pollution reduction may outweigh the marginal social cost of pollution reduction.
    b. the marginal social cost of pollution reduction may outweigh the marginal social benefit of pollution reduction.
    c. the marginal social cost of pollution reduction will just equal the marginal social benefit from pollution reduction.
    d. none of the above is correct.

13. An advantage that pollution taxes and transferable pollution rights have over regulations is that the former
    a. work well even if pollution output cannot be accurately measured.
    b. result in equal levels of pollution abatement across all firms.
    c. make it in the interests of firms to reduce pollution in the most efficient manner possible.
    d. reduce pollution to zero.

14. A transferable pollution right
    a. would command a price of zero in the free market since pollution is "bad" for society.
    b. could never be resold.
    c. gives a firm the right to emit a certain quantity of pollution.
    d. gives a firm the right to emit an unlimited amount of pollution.

15. Which of the following is *not* an advantage of transferable pollution rights?
    a. They create incentives for polluters to develop cheaper ways to reduce pollution.
    b. They allow the greatest value of output to be produced with a given amount of pollution.
    c. They require polluters to reduce emissions, regardless of the cost.
    d. The rights are private property and may be bought or sold freely.

16. Under a system in which the government grants a fixed number of transferable pollution rights, an increase in demand for the output of firms would
    a. decrease the resale price of pollution rights.
    b. increase the resale price of pollution rights.
    c. increase overall pollution levels.
    d. decrease overall pollution levels.

Section 12.3

17. Pollution in a free market is more likely when
    a. property rights are not well defined.
    b. property rights are difficult to enforce.
    c. transaction costs of negotiating private market solutions are high.
    d. All of the above are true.

18. According to the Coase theorem, one way to deal with an externality problem when transaction costs are low is
    a. for the government to impose pollution taxes.
    b. for the government to make certain that property rights are well defined.
    c. for the government to issue transferable pollution permits.
    d. for the government to impose compliance standards.

19. The Coase theorem suggests that private solutions to externality problems
    a. can lead to an optimal allocation of resources if private parties can bargain at relatively low cost.
    b. result in the efficient outcome under all conditions.
    c. will result in the same distribution of wealth no matter how property rights are assigned.
    d. will result in different efficiency levels of production, depending crucially on how property rights are assigned.

20. In the case of a private solution to the externality problem, the distribution of rights
   a. restricts the ability of private parties to properly price the externalities.
   b. enhances the market incentive to reach an efficient solution.
   c. determines who bears the cost of the solution but does not affect the efficient result.
   d. affects the efficiency of the outcome but does not determine who bears the cost.

Problems

1. [Section 12.1]
   Say that the last tonne of steel produced by a steel company imposes three types of costs: labour costs of $25; additional equipment costs of $10; and the cost of additional soot dumped into the air of $15. What costs will the steel company consider in deciding whether to produce another tonne of steel?

2. [Section 12.1]
   Draw a standard supply and demand diagram for widgets, and indicate the equilibrium price and output.

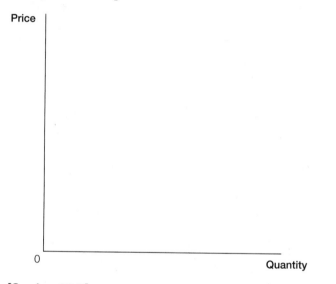

3. [Section 12.1]
   Assuming that the production of widgets generates external costs, illustrate the effect of the producer being forced to pay a tax equal to the external costs generated, and indicate the equilibrium output.

4. [Section 12.1]
   If instead of generating external costs, widget production generates external benefits, illustrate the effect of the producer being given a subsidy equal to the external benefits generated, and indicate the equilibrium output.

5. [Section 12.2]
   If a firm can reduce its sulphur dioxide emissions for $30 per tonne, but it owns transferable pollution rights that are selling for $40 per tonne, what will the firm want to do if it is trying to maximize profits?

6. [Section 12.3]
   A chemical factory dumps pollutants into a nearby river (permissible under the existing laws). In lieu of dumping into the river, the factory could pay for the pollution to be hauled to a toxic-waste dump site at a cost of $125 000 per year. A vacation resort located downstream from the factory suffers damages estimated at $200 000 per year. Evaluate whether a change in law is necessary to achieve an efficient outcome in this situation.

Study Guide Answers

CHAPTER 1

Fill in the Blanks

1. limited; unlimited **2.** scarcity **3.** inputs **4.** scarcity; value **5.** trade-offs
6. macroeconomics; microeconomics **7.** theories; explain; predict **8.** hypothesis
9. *ceteris paribus* **10.** correlation **11.** fallacy of composition **12.** positive
13. wants; resources **14.** labour; land; capital; entrepreneurship **15.** knowledge
and skill; education and on-the-job training **16.** production techniques; products; profits **17.** competition **18.** wants and desires **19.** choices; wants and desires **20.** opportunity cost **21.** how much **22.** marginal; marginal; adding to;
subtracting from **23.** expected marginal benefits; expected marginal costs
24. rise; fall; fall; rise **25.** positive **26.** specialize; lower **27.** comparative advantage **28.** skill; wasted; best **29.** language; relative availability of products; relative value; less; more **30.** voluntary; price **31.** market failure

True or False

1. T **2.** F **3.** F **4.** T **5.** F **6.** F **7.** T **8.** F **9.** T **10.** T **11.** F **12.** T **13.** T **14.** T
15. T **16.** F **17.** T **18.** T **19.** T **20.** F **21.** T **22.** F **23.** F **24.** T **25.** T **26.** F
27. T **28.** T **29.** T **30.** T **31.** T **32.** T

Multiple Choice

1. b **2.** d **3.** d **4.** d **5.** b **6.** d **7.** d **8.** c **9.** c **10.** c **11.** d **12.** c **13.** d **14.** d **15.** d
16. e **17.** e **18.** d **19.** b **20.** d **21.** b **22.** d **23.** b **24.** b **25.** c **26.** b **27.** b **28.** a
29. b **30.** e **31.** b **32.** b **33.** c **34.** c

Problems

1.
  a. microeconomics
  b. macroeconomics
  c. microeconomics
  d. macroeconomics
  e. microeconomics
2.
  a. both normative and positive statements
  b. normative statements
  c. positive statements
  d. both normative and positive statements
  e. positive statements
3.
  a. $50; $25
  b. 3; 5; Mark would go as long as his marginal benefit was greater than the admission price.
  c. Yes; 6; Mark would buy the pass because his total benefits exceed his total cost. Once he has the pass, the marginal cost of attending one more day becomes zero, so he will go as long as his marginal benefits exceed zero.
4.
  a. $57; $88
  b. 43; 44; He would produce as long as the price (marginal benefit) exceeded the marginal cost.

CHAPTER 2

Fill in the Blanks

1. what; how; for whom **2.** decentralized **3.** mixed **4.** least **5.** labour intensive;
capital intensive **6.** product **7.** inputs; firms; factor; input **8.** circular flow;
product; factor; firms **9.** production possibilities **10.** resources; technology
11. inefficiently; potential **12.** unemployed; better **13.** efficiency; most
14. concave; increasing **15.** opportunity cost; increases **16.** fewer; more
17. technology; labour productivity; natural resource finds **18.** scarcity; trade-offs **19.** scarcity; choice; opportunity costs; efficiency; economic growth

True or False

1. T **2.** T **3.** T **4.** F **5.** T **6.** T **7.** F **8.** T **9.** F **10.** T **11.** F **12.** T **13.** T **14.** T
15. T **16.** F **17.** F **18.** F

Multiple Choice

1. a **2.** c **3.** d **4.** c **5.** a **6.** d **7.** e **8.** e **9.** e **10.** c **11.** d **12.** c **13.** c **14.** e **15.** b
16. b **17.** c **18.** d **19.** a **20.** c **21.** c **22.** e **23.** b

Problems

1.

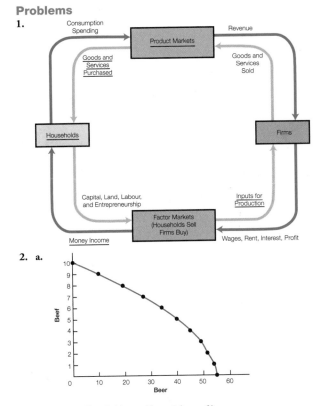

2. a.

b. 1 side of beef; 6 kegs of beer; 9 kegs of beer
c. 35 kegs of beer
d. No; that combination is inside the production possibilities curve, which means more of one good could be produced without giving up any production of the other good.
e. No; that combination is beyond the production possibilities curve and therefore unattainable.
3. a. Yes; the bowed-outward shape of the production possibilities curve indicates increasing opportunity costs.
  b. Zero; because point I is inside the production possibilities curve, moving from point I to point D means that the output of food can increase with no decrease in the output of shelter.
  c. 10 units of food
  d. All of the points on the production possibilities curve are efficient because at any of those points more of one good could be produced only by sacrificing some output of the other good. However, the curve does not tell us which of those points is best from the perspective of society.
  e. N; additional resources or new technology (shifting the PPC outward).
  f. I; economy must ensure that all resources are being utilized to their fullest extent, no wasted resources.

CHAPTER 3

Fill in the Blanks

1. market; exchanging **2.** trade **3.** buyers; sellers **4.** competitive **5.** quantity demanded **6.** substitution **7.** individual demand schedule **8.** market demand curve
9. money (or absolute or nominal); relative **10.** a good's price; moving along
11. prices of related goods; income; number; tastes; expectations
12. rightward; leftward **13.** substitutes **14.** increase; decrease **15.** increase
16. quantity supplied; quantity supplied **17.** profits; production; higher
18. positive **19.** willing; able **20.** input; expectations; number; technology; regulation; taxes and subsidies; weather **21.** lower; right **22.** increases **23.** decreases

True or False
1. T 2. F 3. T 4. T 5. F 6. T 7. T 8. T 9. T 10. F 11. F 12. T 13. F 14. T
15. F 16. T 17. F 18. T 19. F 20. F

Multiple Choice
1. e 2. d 3. d 4. b 5. d 6. d 7. b 8. b 9. c 10. b 11. d 12. c 13. d 14. c

Problems

1. a.

P	Q_D
$5	4
4	8
3	12
2	16
1	20

b.

P	Q_D
$5	6
4	12
3	18
2	24
1	30

c.

P	Q_D
$5	5
4	10
3	15
2	20
1	25

2.

3. a.

b.

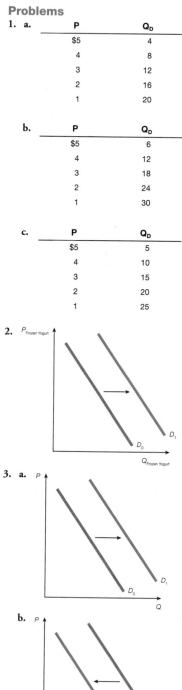

c.

d.

e.

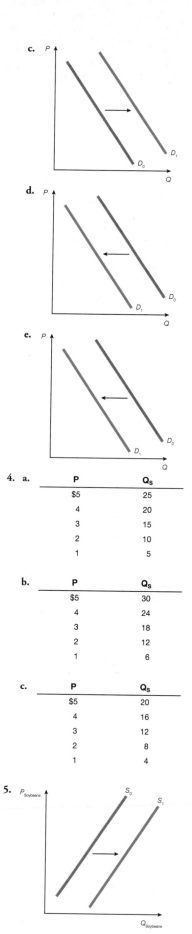

4. a.

P	Q_S
$5	25
4	20
3	15
2	10
1	5

b.

P	Q_S
$5	30
4	24
3	18
2	12
1	6

c.

P	Q_S
$5	20
4	16
3	12
2	8
1	4

5.

6. **a.**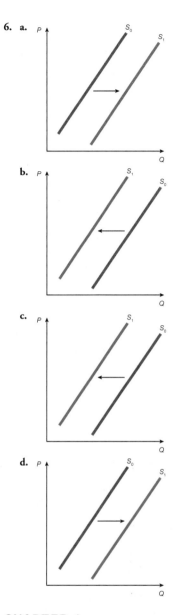

CHAPTER 4

Fill in the Blanks

1. equilibrium; equilibrium **2.** surplus **3.** shortage **4.** surplus; more; cut back; more **5.** greater; greater **6.** higher; lower **7.** decrease **8.** increase; be indeterminate **9.** ceiling; floor **10.** shortages **11.** decline **12.** additional **13.** unintended consequences

True or False

1. F **2.** T **3.** F **4.** T **5.** T **6.** F **7.** T **8.** T **9.** F **10.** F

Multiple Choice

1. c **2.** d **3.** a **4.** d **5.** c **6.** b **7.** a **8.** c **9.** b **10.** a **11.** a **12.** c **13.** e **14.** e **15.** a **16.** c

Problems

1. **a.**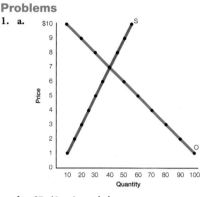

b. $7; 40 units traded
c. Surplus; at $9, above the equilibrium price, there will be a surplus of 30 units of Z (the quantity supplied at $9 [50] minus the quantity demanded at $9 [20]).
d. Shortage; at $3, below the equilibrium price, there will be a shortage of 60 units of Z (the quantity demanded at $3 [80] minus the quantity supplied at $3 [20]).
e. $8, with 45 units traded (at the new supply and demand intersection)
f. $6, with 50 units traded (at the new supply and demand intersection)

2. **a.** To get to point A would require a decrease in supply; to get to point B would require a decrease in supply and an increase in demand; to get to point C would require an increase in demand; to get to point D would require a decrease in supply and a decrease in demand; point E is the current equilibrium; to get to point F would require an increase in supply and an increase in demand; to get to point G would require a decrease in demand; to get to point H would require an increase in supply and a decrease in demand; to get to point I would require an increase in supply.
b. B; because it indicates a decrease in supply and an increase in demand.
c. Indeterminate; because one of the changes decreases supply and the other increases supply, we don't know what the net effect is on supply. If the effects were of the same magnitude, the result would be E; if the increase in supply were greater than the decrease in supply, the answer would be I; if the decrease in supply were greater than the increase in supply, the answer would be A.
d. C; A; A
e. G; I; G

3.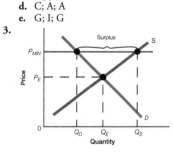

a. If the price floor is raised, the quantity supplied increases, the quantity demanded decreases, and the surplus increases; if the price floor is lowered, the quantity supplied decreases, the quantity demanded increases, and the surplus decreases.
b. The quantity supplied does not change, the quantity demanded increases, and the surplus decreases.
c. The quantity supplied increases, the quantity demanded does not change, and the surplus increases.

4.

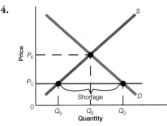

a. If the price ceiling is raised, the quantity supplied increases, the quantity demanded decreases, and the shortage is reduced; if the price ceiling is lowered, the quantity supplied decreases, the quantity demanded increases, and the shortage is increased.

b. The quantity supplied does not change, the quantity demanded increases, and the shortage is increased.

c. The quantity supplied increases, the quantity demanded does not change, and the shortage is decreased.

CHAPTER 5

Fill in the Blanks

1. demanded **2.** larger **3.** smaller **4.** close substitutes; proportion of income; time **5.** more **6.** greater; substitutes **7.** midpoint method **8.** rise; quantity demanded **9.** fall; quantity demanded **10.** elastic; inelastic **11.** income **12.** quantity demanded; price **13.** substitutes **14.** supplied **15.** quantity supplied; price **16.** elastic **17.** less than **18.** more **19.** elasticity of supply and demand **20.** more

True or False

1. T **2.** T **3.** T **4.** T **5.** T **6.** F **7.** T **8.** T **9.** F **10.** F **11.** F **12.** T **13.** T **14.** F **15.** T **16.** T **17.** F **18.** T **19.** F **20.** F **21.** T

Multiple Choice

1. b **2.** d **3.** b **4.** a **5.** b **6.** b **7.** a **8.** a **9.** d **10.** b **11.** b **12.** b **13.** a **14.** d **15.** c **16.** b **17.** b **18.** a

Problems

1. $E_D = \dfrac{\dfrac{500}{850}}{\left|\dfrac{-3}{4.5}\right|} = 0.88$

2. The demand is relatively elastic at prices above the midpoint of a straight-line demand curve and relatively inelastic below the midpoint, so it is relatively elastic for a price change from $12 to $10 but relatively inelastic for a price change from $6 to $4.

3. Demand is inelastic because an increase in price increases total revenue; demand is elastic because an increase in price decreases total revenue.

4. A good is normal when an increase in income increases the quantity of the good demanded at a given price. If a higher income increases the quantity of the good demanded, it has a positive income elasticity. A good is inferior when an increase in income decreases the quantity of the good demanded at a given price. If a higher income decreases the quantity of a good demanded, it has a negative income elasticity.

5. 20 percent ÷ −10 percent = −2

CHAPTER 6

Fill in the Blanks

1. consumer surplus **2.** demand curve; market price **3.** increase **4.** producer surplus **5.** already; output **6.** maximum, minimum **7.** consumer surplus; producer surplus **8.** externalities **9.** negative externality; positive externality **10.** lowers; true **11.** internalize (bear) **12.** positive externalities **13.** overallocation **14.** underproduce **15.** nonexcludable, nonrivalrous **16.** nonexcludable **17.** nonrivalrous **18.** free rider **19.** free rider **20.** providing **21.** asymmetric information **22.** adverse **23.** Moral hazard **24.** common **25.** tragedy of the commons

True or False

1. T **2.** T **3.** F **4.** F **5.** T **6.** T **7.** T **8.** T **9.** T **10.** T **11.** T **12.** F **13.** T **14.** F **15.** F **16.** T **17.** F **18.** T **19.** T **20.** T

Multiple Choice

1. b **2.** b **3.** c **4.** d **5.** c **6.** b **7.** a **8.** b **9.** b **10.** d **11.** b **12.** b **13.** d **14.** a **15.** e **16.** a **17.** a **18.** c **19.** a **20.** b

Problems

1. a. $30; He will produce 3 units.

b. Producer surplus will increase from $30 to $60; he will now produce 4 units.

2.

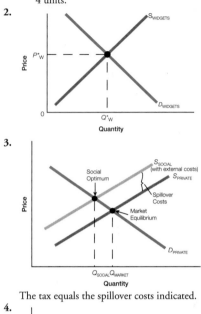

3.

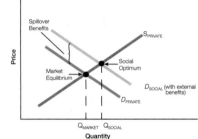

The tax equals the spillover costs indicated.

4.

The subsidy equals the spillover benefits indicated.

CHAPTER 7

Fill in the Blanks

1. total revenues; total costs **2.** most valuable **3.** monetary **4.** opportunity **5.** maximize **6.** implicit **7.** implicit; explicit **8.** sunk **9.** short; long **10.** all **11.** variable **12.** output **13.** small **14.** diminishing marginal product **15.** fixed; variable **16.** do not vary **17.** going out of business **18.** variable **19.** fixed; variable **20.** total cost; level of output **21.** average variable cost **22.** additional **23.** horizontal **24.** average fixed **25.** diminishing marginal **26.** less; more **27.** short; variable **28.** planning **29.** economies; constant returns; diseconomies **30.** minimum efficient **31.** input; technology **32.** diseconomies of scale

True or False

1. F **2.** F **3.** T **4.** T **5.** F **6.** T **7.** T **8.** T **9.** F **10.** T **11.** F **12.** T **13.** T **14.** T **15.** T **16.** F **17.** T **18.** T **19.** T **20.** T **21.** F **22.** T **23.** T **24.** T **25.** T **26.** F **27.** F **28.** T **29.** T **30.** T **31.** T **32.** T **33.** F **34.** T **35.** T

Multiple Choice

1. d **2.** e **3.** d **4.** a **5.** d **6.** a **7.** b **8.** d **9.** d **10.** d **11.** c **12.** d **13.** b **14.** b **15.** c **16.** d **17.** b **18.** c **19.** c **20.** e **21.** d **22.** a **23.** e **24.** d **25.** b **26.** c **27.** c **28.** a **29.** c **30.** a **31.** d

Problems

1.

Labour (workers)	Total Product (kilograms)	Marginal Product (kilograms)
0	0	0
1	20	20
2	44	24
3	62	18
4	74	12
5	80	6
6	78	−2

a. Candy's Candies begins to experience diminishing marginal product with the third worker, the first one for whom marginal product begins to fall.

b. Candy's Candies experiences a negative marginal product beginning with the sixth worker.

2. a. Average Fixed Cost (AFC)
b. Average Variable Cost (AVC)
c. Average Total Cost (ATC)
d. Marginal Cost (MC)
e. Where MC is less than AVC, AVC is falling; when MC equals AVC, AVC does not change; and when MC exceeds AVC, AVC is rising; thus the intersection of MC and AVC is at the minimum point of AVC. Where MC is less than ATC, ATC is falling; when MC equals ATC, ATC does not change; and when MC exceeds ATC, ATC is rising; thus the intersection of MC and ATC is at the minimum point of ATC.
f. The point where MC equals AFC has no economic significance.

3.

Output	Total Fixed Costs	Total Variable Costs	Total Costs	Average Fixed Cost	Average Variable Cost	Average Total Cost	Marginal Cost
1	$200	$ 60	$ 260	$ 200	$ 60	$ 260	$ 60
2	200	100	300	100	50	150	40
3	200	120	320	66.66	40	106.66	20
4	200	128	328	50	32	82	8
5	200	158	358	40	32	72	30
6	200	218	418	33	36	70	60
7	200	326	526	29	47	75	108
8	200	480	680	25	60	85	154

CHAPTER 8

Fill in the Blanks

1. perfect competition; monopoly; monopolistic competition; oligopoly **2.** large; homogenous (standardized); easy **3.** price takers **4.** pure monopoly **5.** differentiated; so many **6.** a few **7.** many; small **8.** identical (homogenous) **9.** small **10.** horizontal; entire **11.** total revenues; total costs **12.** market price; quantity of units sold **13.** average revenue **14.** marginal revenue **15.** marginal revenue **16.** marginal; total cost−total revenue **17.** total revenue; total costs; marginal revenue; marginal costs **18.** average total cost; the market price **19.** economic profits; economic losses; zero economic profits **20.** variable **21.** fixed costs **22.** average total costs; average variable costs **23.** marginal cost; average variable cost **24.** input prices **25.** enter the industry; expand **26.** exceeds; equals **27.** zero economic profits **28.** per-unit total costs **29.** input costs **30.** do not change **31.** rise **32.** efficient

True or False

1. T **2.** T **3.** T **4.** F **5.** T **6.** F **7.** T **8.** T **9.** T **10.** T **11.** F **12.** F **13.** T **14.** T **15.** T **16.** F **17.** F **18.** T **19.** F **20.** T **21.** F **22.** T **23.** T **24.** T **25.** T **26.** F **27.** T **28.** T

Multiple Choice

1. a **2.** e **3.** d **4.** c **5.** d **6.** b **7.** c **8.** c **9.** b **10.** d **11.** b **12.** a **13.** e **14.** b **15.** d **16.** e **17.** b **18.** c **19.** d **20.** a **21.** c **22.** b **23.** a **24.** a

Problems

1. a.

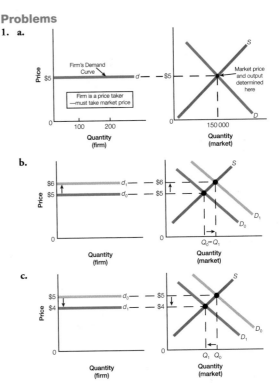

b.

c.

2.

Quantity	Price	Total Revenue	Marginal Revenue	Total Cost	Marginal Cost	Total Profit
6	10	60	10	30	3	30
7	10	70	10	35	5	35
8	10	80	10	42	7	38
9	10	90	10	51	9	39
10	10	100	10	62	11	38
11	10	110	10	75	13	35
12	10	120	10	90	15	30

Its profit-maximizing output is 9 units.

3.

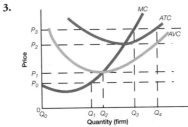

a. at P_0, zero units; at P_1, Q_2 units; at P_2, the unmarked quantity where $MC = ATC$; at P_3, Q_3 units
b. any price above P_2; P_2; any price below P_2
c. any prices below P_1
d. The firm's supply curve would be its MC curve above the minimum point of the AVC curve.

4. If firms are currently earning economic profits, that will attract new firms to enter the industry, shifting the industry supply curve right. That will lower price and reduce economic profits. If firms are currently earning economic losses, firms will exit the industry. That will raise the price and reduce economic losses.

5.

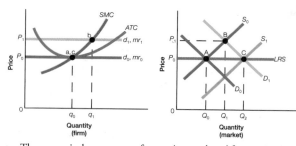

a. The answer is the movement from point a to b and from point A to B.
b. The answer is the movement from point b, returning to point c (same as point a), and from point B to point C.

CHAPTER 9

Fill in the Blanks

1. one 2. price makers 3. legal barriers; economies of scale; control of important inputs 4. legal barriers to entry 5. natural monopoly 6. input 7. firm 8. rise; fall 9. all 10. *MR* 11. *P* 12. average total cost 13. barriers to entry 14. monopoly 15. higher; less 16. greater; greater 17. technological 18. anti-combine; regulation 19. the courts; the Competition Tribunal 20. high; low 21. marginal cost; losses 22. average cost; average total cost 23. reduces 24. price discrimination 25. less; high 26. higher; lower 27. marginal revenue; marginal cost 28. reselling 29. quantity discounts

True or False

1. T 2. F 3. T 4. T 5. F 6. T 7. T 8. T 9. F 10. T 11. T 12. T 13. F 14. F 15. T 16. F 17. F 18. T 19. F 20. T 21. T 22. F 23. T 24. T 25. T 26. T 27. T

Multiple Choice

1. a 2. e 3. d 4. c 5. e 6. a 7. d 8. a 9. b 10. c 11. e 12. b 13. b 14. d 15. b 16. b 17. b 18. b 19. a 20. c 21. b 22. e 23. d 24. d 25. a 26. a 27. a

Problems

1.

Quantity	Price	Total Revenue	Marginal Revenue	Demand Elastic or Inelastic?
1	$11	$ 11	$ 11	elastic
2	10	20	9	elastic
3	9	27	7	elastic
4	8	32	5	elastic
5	7	35	3	elastic
6	6	36	1	elastic
7	5	35	−1	inelastic
8	4	32	−3	inelastic
9	3	27	−5	inelastic
10	2	20	−7	inelastic
11	1	11	−9	inelastic

2.

Quantity	Price	Total Revenue	Marginal Revenue	Demand Elastic or Inelastic?	Total Cost	Marginal Cost	Profit
1	11	$ 11	$ 11	elastic	14	4	−3
2	10	20	9	elastic	18	4	2
3	9	27	7	elastic	22	4	5
4	8	32	5	elastic	26	4	6
5	7	35	3	elastic	30	4	5
6	6	36	1	elastic	34	4	2
7	5	35	−1	inelastic	38	4	−3
8	4	32	−3	inelastic	42	4	−10
9	3	27	−5	inelastic	46	4	−19
10	2	20	−7	inelastic	50	4	−30
11	1	11	−9	inelastic	54	4	−43

The profit-maximizing quantity of output is 4 units. The demand curve tells the monopolist that she can charge a price of $8. The profit is $6.

3. a.

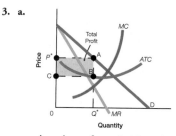

where the profit-maximizing price is P^* and the profit-maximizing quantity is Q^*

b.

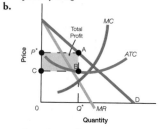

where the profit-maximizing price is P^*, the profit-maximizing quantity is Q^*, and P^* exceeds *ATC* at Q^*

c.

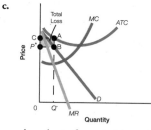

where the profit-maximizing price is P^*, the profit-maximizing quantity is Q^*, and P^* is less than *ATC* at Q^*

4. a.

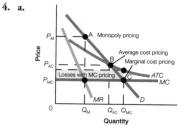

The efficient result is at point C, where price equals marginal cost.

b.

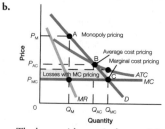

The losses with marginal cost pricing equal the shaded area in the diagram above.

c.

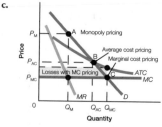

The average cost pricing solution is at point B, where economic profits are zero.

CHAPTER 10

Fill in the Blanks

1. monopoly; price; competition **2.** zero **3.** differentiated **4.** brand **5.** differentiation; sellers; entry **6.** unique **7.** searchers; negatively **8.** cost; maximum
9. profit **10.** long; attract; losses **11.** zero; enter; exit **12.** downward; elastic
13. economies **14.** excess; profits **15.** many; productive; lowest **16.** greater;
more; allocative **17.** differentiated **18.** non-price; increase **19.** inelastic; smaller
20. raises; rational **21.** scale **22.** information; prices **23.** competition **24.** few
25. differentiated **26.** barriers **27.** economic **28.** interdependence; strategize
29. patents **30.** discourage **31.** certainty; react **32.** collude **33.** high; low
34. cartel **35.** cheat **36.** leader **37.** followers **38.** rigidity **39.** more **40.** marginal
cost

True or False

1. T **2.** F **3.** T **4.** F **5.** T **6.** F **7.** T **8.** T **9.** T **10.** F **11.** F **12.** T **13.** F **14.** T
15. F **16.** F **17.** F **18.** F **19.** T **20.** T

Multiple Choice

1. b **2.** d **3.** c **4.** d **5.** c **6.** b **7.** d **8.** c **9.** b **10.** b **11.** c **12.** a **13.** c **14.** a **15.** a
16. d **17.** b **18.** a **19.** c **20.** b **21.** e

Problems

1. a. Physical differences are probably most important. Big Macs, Whoppers, tacos, and various sorts of pizza all rely on physical differences to attract customers. Location of restaurants is important as well.

b. A convenient location is very important, although service is considered an important aspect by many espresso drinkers.

c. Service is number one, but location is important as well. How far are you willing to drive to get a great cut or perm?

d. Physical qualities, including taste and the look of the container, are most important although location is important too. Coca-Cola gained market leadership years ago by making Coke available everywhere—at movie theaters, at lunch counters, and in ubiquitous vending machines.

e. Physical differences is probably the most important, but prestige is important as well.

2. Both types of firms operate in industries with many other sellers and with no real barriers to entry or exit. They follow similar rules when choosing the level of output. Both types of firms also will experience zero economic profits in the long run.

In the short run monopolistic competitors and perfectly competitive firms follow similar rules for choosing the profit maximizing output. They produce where marginal revenue equals marginal cost. Monopolistic competitors will produce less than perfectly competitive firms will, because the relation between price and marginal revenue differs between these types of firms. Since firms that are monopolistic competitors face a negatively sloped demand curve, they are price makes and price is greater than marginal revenue. They produce an output less than the output where price equals marginal cost. A perfectly competitive firm will produce where price equals marginal cost since they are price takers.

In the long run, entry will force both types of firms to the output where economic profits are equal to zero, which occurs where the demand curves are tangent to the average total cost curve. Because the monopolistic competitor faces a negatively sloped demand curve, this point will be at a level of output less than the perfect competitor.

3.

Perfect Competition	Monopolistic Competition
standardized product	differentiated product
allocative efficiency	downward-sloping demand curve
productive efficiency	excess capacity
horizontal demand curve	
no control over price	

4. Producers use advertising to increase the demand for their products and reduce the elasticity of the demand facing their firm. They do this to increase their profits. If all firms advertise, the results are often not those anticipated by the firm. Advertising by firms will make consumers more aware of the prices charged by other firms and the availability of substitutes for the goods and services they buy. This type of information will increase the elasticity of demand facing firms as well as making the industry more competitive. Advertising may result in lower prices and more output and lower profits.

5.

Perfect Competition	Oligopoly
many small firms	mutual interdepence
allocative efficiency	downward-sloping demand curve
productive efficiency	high barriers to entry
horizontal demand curve	few large firms
no control over price	large economies of scale

6. a. If the Canadian and Russian mines provide a significant share of the world's supply, increasing the supply will result in the price of diamonds falling. This will be the result of the breakdown of the cartel.

b. CSO will no longer be willing to advertise to increase the demand for diamonds in general. This type of advertising might only sell more Canadian or Russian diamonds and generate no profit for CSO. If CSO continues to advertise diamonds they will try to distinguish the diamonds they are selling. They might try to establish a brand to differentiate their product from the others.

CHAPTER 11

Fill in the Blanks

1. derived; derived **2.** Input; output **3.** marginal revenue product **4.** marginal resource cost **5.** marginal revenue product; marginal resource cost **6.** variable; diminished **7.** marginal revenue product **8.** increases; falls **9.** demanded; supplied; shortage **10.** increases; increases **11.** capital; technological; skills **12.** left **13.** right **14.** lower **15.** increase; improve **16.** Alberta **17.** public **18.** age; demographic; redistributive **19.** higher; productivity; labour force **20.** food; shelter; clothing **21.** relative **22.** increases

True or False

1. T **2.** T **3.** T **4.** F **5.** T **6.** T **7.** F **8.** T **9.** T **10.** F **11.** T **12.** T **13.** F **14.** F
15. T **16.** T **17.** F **18.** T **19.** T **20.** F **21.** T **22.** T

Multiple Choice

1. e **2.** c **3.** d **4.** a **5.** b **6.** c **7.** b **8.** e **9.** c **10.** e **11.** a **12.** e **13.** d **14.** d **15.** e
16. b **17.** b **18.** d **19.** a **20.** e **21.** e **22.** a **23.** c

Problems

1.

Workers	Total Corn Output	Marginal Product of Labour
1	4 000	4 000
2	10 000	6 000
3	15 000	5 000
4	18 000	3 000
5	19 000	1 000
6	18 000	−1 000

2.

Total Workers	Total Output	Marginal Product	Price	Marginal Revenue Product
1	200	200	20	4000
2	380	180	20	3600
3	540	160	20	3200
4	680	140	20	2800
5	800	120	20	2400
6	900	100	20	2000
7	980	80	20	1600
8	1040	60	20	1200

3. a. E **b.** C **c.** G **d.** I **e.** A **f.** B **g.** D **h.** F **i.** H

4. a., b.

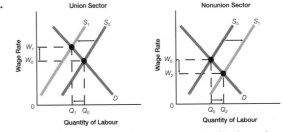

c. Union wages go up and the number of union workers hired goes down; nonunion wages go down and the number of nonunion workers hired goes up.

5. The official data may overstate the actual degree of income inequality because it fails to take into consideration differences in age, demographic factors such as the increasing number of both divorced couples and double-income families, and government redistributive activities (by ignoring the effects of taxes and in-kind subsidies).

6. Economic growth could potentially reduce absolute measures of poverty by increasing real incomes. However, economic growth by itself cannot eliminate relative measures of poverty because there will always be some with lower real incomes than others.

CHAPTER 12

Fill in the Blanks

1. Negative externalities **2.** external costs **3.** social; private **4.** internalized **5.** larger; lower **6.** raise **7.** difficult; nonpecuniary (nonmonetary) **8.** pollution **9.** improved **10.** diminishing **11.** marginal benefit; marginal cost **12.** inefficient; costs; benefits **13.** equal to **14.** lowest **15.** buyers; sellers **16.** property rights **17.** Transaction costs **18.** property rights; transaction costs **19.** large

True or False

1. T **2.** T **3.** F **4.** T **5.** F **6.** T **7.** T **8.** F **9.** T **10.** F **11.** T **12.** T **13.** F **14.** F **15.** T **16.** T **17.** T

Multiple Choice

1. a **2.** c **3.** d **4.** b **5.** c **6.** c **7.** d **8.** c **9.** b **10.** d **11.** b **12.** b **13.** c **14.** c **15.** c **16.** b **17.** d **18.** b **19.** a **20.** c

Problems

1. The steel firm will only consider its marginal private costs (*MPC*) in deciding whether to produce another tonne of steel. In this case $35 (labour costs + additional equipment costs).

2.

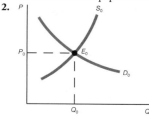

3.

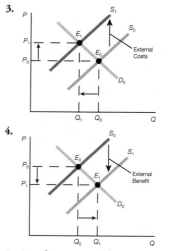

4.

5. A profit-maximizing firm will choose to reduce its sulphur dioxide emissions, thus enabling it to sell the transferable pollution right. In this case, since the firm can sell the right for $40 per tonne (the marginal benefit from the reduced sulphur dioxide emissions), but the marginal cost of reducing the emissions is only $30 per tonne, the firm stands to make $10 per tonne.

6. If the factory has the property rights, then the resort pays the factory between $125 000 and $200 000 not to pollute. Both are better off than with continued pollution. If the resort has the property rights, then the factory will choose not to pollute since the disposal fee ($125 000) is less than the cost of compensating the resort ($200 000).

Glossary

accounting profits total revenues minus total explicit costs

adverse selection a situation where an informed party benefits in an exchange by taking advantage of knowing more than the other party

aggregate the total amount—such as the aggregate level of output

allocative efficiency production where the price of a good equals marginal cost

asymmetric information occurs when the available information is initially distributed in favour of one party relative to another in an exchange

average cost pricing to set the price equal to average total cost

average fixed cost (AFC) a per-unit measure of fixed costs; fixed costs divided by output

average revenue (AR) total revenue divided by the number of units sold

average total cost (ATC) a per-unit cost of operation; total cost divided by output

average variable cost (AVC) a per-unit measure of variable costs; variable costs divided by output

bar graph represents data using vertical bars rising from the horizontal axis

capital the equipment and structures used to produce goods and services

capital intensive production that uses a large amount of capital

cartel a collection of firms that agree on sales, pricing, and other decisions

cash transfer direct cash payment such as public pensions, social assistance, and employment insurance

causation when one event brings on another event

ceteris paribus holding all other things constant

change in demand the prices of related goods, income, number of buyers, tastes, and expectations can change the demand for a good. That is, a change in one of these factors shifts the entire demand curve

change in quantity demanded a change in a good's price leads to a change in quantity demanded, a move along a given demand curve

circular flow model of income and output an illustration of the continuous flow of goods, services, inputs, and payments between firms and households

Coase theorem states that where property rights are defined in a clear-cut fashion, externalities are internalized

collective bargaining negotiations between representatives of employers and unions

collude when firms act together to restrict competition

command economies economies where the government uses central planning to coordinate most economic activities

common resource a rival good that is not excludable

comparative advantage occurs when a person or a country can produce a good or service at a lower opportunity cost than others

competitive market a market where the many buyers and sellers have very little market power—each buyer's and seller's effect on market price is negligible

complement an increase (a decrease) in the price of one good shifts the demand curve for another good to the left (right)

constant-cost industry an industry where input prices (and cost curves) do not change as industry output changes

constant returns to scale occur in an output range where LRATC does not change as output varies

consumer sovereignty consumers vote with their dollars in a market economy; this explains what is produced

consumer surplus the difference between the price a consumer is willing and able to pay for an additional unit of a good and the price the consumer actually pays; for the whole market it is the sum of all the individual consumer surpluses

correlation two events that usually occur together

cross-price elasticity of demand a measure of the impact that a price change of one good will have on the quantity demanded of another good at a given price

deadweight loss the loss of total surplus that results from an action that alters a competitive market equilibrium

derived demand the demand for an input derived from consumers' demand for the good or service produced with that input

diminishing marginal product as a variable input increases, with other inputs fixed, a point will be reached where the additions to output will eventually decline

diseconomies of scale occur in an output range where LRATC rises as output expands

the economic problem scarcity forces us to choose, and choices are costly because we must give up other opportunities that we value

economic profits total revenues minus explicit and implicit costs

economics the study of the allocation of our limited resources to satisfy our unlimited wants

economies of scale occur in an output range where LRATC falls as output increases

efficiency getting the most from society's scarce resources

elastic demand segment a portion of the demand curve where the percentage change of quantity demanded is greater than the percentage change in price ($E_D > 1$)

empirical analysis the use of data to test a hypothesis

entrepreneurship the process of combining labour, land, and capital together to produce goods and services

equilibrium price the price at the intersection of the market supply and demand curves; at this price the quantity demanded equals the quantity supplied

equilibrium quantity the quantity at the intersection of the market supply and demand curves; at the equilibrium quantity, the quantity demanded equals the quantity supplied

excess capacity occurs when the firm produces below the level where average total cost is minimized

explicit costs the opportunity costs of production that require a monetary payment

externalities a benefit or cost from consumption or production that spills over onto those that are not consuming or producing the good

factor (or input) markets the market where households sell the use of their inputs (capital, land, labour, and entrepreneurship) to firms

fallacy of composition the incorrect view that what is true for the individual is always true for the group

fixed costs costs that do not vary with the level of output

free rider deriving benefits from something not paid for

goods items we value or desire

goods and services flow the continuous flow of inputs and outputs in an economy

human capital the productive knowledge and skill people receive from education and on-the-job training

hypothesis a testable proposition

implicit costs the opportunity costs of production that do not require a monetary payment

income effect at higher prices, buyers feel poorer, causing a lowering of quantity demanded

income elasticity of demand a measure of the responsiveness of the quantity demanded of a good to a change in income

income flow the continuous flow of income and expenditure in an economy

increasing-cost industry an industry where input prices rise (and cost curves rise) as industry output rises

increasing opportunity cost the opportunity cost of producing additional units of a good rises as society produces more of that good

individual demand curve a graphical representation that shows the inverse relationship between price and quantity demanded

individual demand schedule a schedule that shows the relationship between price and quantity demanded

individual supply curve a graphical representation that shows the positive relationship between the price and the quantity supplied

inelastic demand segment a portion of the demand curve where the percentage change in quantity demanded is less than the percentage change in price ($E_D < 1$)

inferior good if income increases, the demand for a good decreases; if income decreases, the demand for a good increases

in-kind transfers transfers given in goods and services rather than cash

internalized externalities when an industry is forced to compensate those enduring some negative externality caused by its production

joint profit maximization determination of price based on the marginal revenue derived from the market demand schedule and marginal cost schedule of the firms in the industry

kinked demand curve indicates the price rigidity when competitors show a greater tendency to follow price reductions than price increases

labour the physical and human effort used in the production of goods and services

labour intensive production that uses a large amount of labour

land the natural resources used in the production of goods and services

law of demand the quantity of a good or service demanded varies inversely (negatively) with its price, *ceteris paribus*

law of supply the higher (lower) the price of the good, the greater (smaller) the quantity supplied

long run a period over which all production inputs are variable

low-income cut-off (LICO) the income level at which a household spends 63 percent of its income on food, clothing, and shelter

macroeconomics the study of the whole economy including the topics of inflation, unemployment, and economic growth

marginal cost (MC) the change in total costs resulting from a one-unit change in output

marginal product (MP) the change in total output of a good that results from a unit change in input

marginal resource cost (MRC) the amount that an extra input adds to the firm's total costs

marginal revenue (MR) the increase in total revenue resulting from a one-unit increase in sales

marginal revenue product (MRP) marginal product times the price of the product

marginal thinking focusing on the additional, or marginal, choices; marginal choices involve the effects of adding or subtracting from the current situation, the small (or large) incremental changes to a plan of action

market the process of buyers and sellers exchanging goods and services

market demand curve the horizontal summation of individual demand curves

market economy an economy that allocates goods and services through the private decisions of consumers, input suppliers, and firms

market failure when the economy fails to allocate resources efficiently on its own

market supply curve a graphical representation of the amount of goods and services that suppliers are willing and able to supply at various prices

microeconomics the study of household and firm behaviour and how they interact in the marketplace

minimum efficient scale the output level where economies of scale are exhausted and constant returns to scale begin

mixed economy an economy where government and the private sector determine the allocation of resources

money price the price that one pays in dollars and cents, sometimes called an absolute or nominal price

monopolistic competition a market structure with many firms selling differentiated products

monopoly a market with only one supplier of a product that has no close substitute and there are natural and legal barriers to entry that prevent competition

moral hazard taking additional risks because you are insured

mutual interdependence when a firm shapes its policy with an eye to the policies of competing firms

natural monopoly a firm that can produce at a lower cost than a number of smaller firms could

negative externality occurs when costs spill over to an outside party that is not involved in producing or consuming the good

negative incentives incentives that either increase costs or reduce benefits resulting in a decrease in the activity or behaviour

negative relationship when two variables change in opposite directions

normal good if income increases, the demand for a good increases; if income decreases, the demand for a good decreases

normative analysis a subjective, nontestable statement—how the economy should be

oligopoly a market structure with only a few sellers offering similar or identical products

opportunity cost the value of the best forgone alternative that was not chosen

perfect competition a market with many buyers and sellers, selling homogeneous goods, easy market entry and exit, and no firm can affect the market price

pie chart a circle subdivided into proportionate slices that represent various quantities that add up to 100 percent

pollution tax tax levied by government on a firm for environmental pollution

positive analysis an objective testable statement—how the economy is

positive externality occurs when benefits spill over to an outside party that is not involved in producing or consuming the good

positive incentives incentives that either reduce costs or increase benefits resulting in an increase in the activity or behaviour

positive relationship when two variables change in the same direction

predatory pricing setting a price deliberately low in order to drive out competitors

price ceiling a legally established maximum price

price controls government-mandated minimum or maximum prices

price discrimination the practice of charging different consumers different prices for the same good or service

price elasticity of demand a measure of the responsiveness of quantity demanded to a change in price

price elasticity of supply the measure of the sensitivity of the quantity supplied to changes in price of a good

price floor a legally established minimum price

price follower a competitor in an oligopoly that goes along with the pricing decision of the price leader

price leader a large firm in an oligopoly that unilaterally makes changes in its product prices that competitors tend to follow

price leadership when a dominant firm that produces a large portion of the industry's output sets a price that maximizes its profits, and other firms follow

price taker a perfectly competitive firm takes the price that it is given by the intersection of the market demand and market supply curves

private good a good with rivalrous consumption and excludability

producer surplus the difference between what a producer is paid for a good and the cost of producing that unit of the good; for the market, it is the sum of all the individual sellers' producer surpluses—the area above the market supply curve and below the market price

product differentiation goods or services that are slightly different, or perceived to be different, from one another

product markets the market where households are buyers and firms are sellers of goods and services

production possibilities curve the potential total output combinations of any two goods for an economy

productive efficiency output production that minimizes average total cost

profit-maximizing output rule a firm should always produce at the output where $MR = MC$

profits the difference between total revenue and total cost

progressive tax system the amount of an individual's tax rises as a proportion of income, as the person's income rises

public good a good that has two properties: nonrivalous in consumption and nonexcludability

relative price the price of one good relative to other goods

resources inputs used to produce goods and services

rule of rational choice individuals will pursue an activity if the expected marginal benefits are greater than the expected marginal costs

scarcity exists when human wants (material and nonmaterial) exceed available resources

service an intangible act that people want, like treatment from a doctor or a dentist

shortage a situation where quantity demanded exceeds quantity supplied

short run a period too brief for some production inputs to be varied

short-run market supply curve the horizontal summation of the individual firms' supply curves in the market

short-run supply curve as a cost relation, this curve shows the marginal cost of producing any given output; as a supply curve, it shows the equilibrium output that the firm will supply at various prices in the short run

slope the ratio of rise (change in the Y variable) over the run (change in the X variable)

specializing concentrating in the production of one, or a few, goods

substitute an increase (a decrease) in the price of one good causes the demand curve for another good to shift to the right (left)

substitution effect at higher prices, buyers increasingly substitute other goods for the good that now has a higher relative price

sunk costs costs that have been incurred and cannot be recovered

surplus a situation where quantity supplied exceeds quantity demanded

tax incidence the analysis of the effect of a particular tax on the distribution of economic welfare

theory statements or propositions used to explain and predict behaviour in the real world

time-series graph a type of line chart that plots data trends over time

total cost (TC) the sum of the firm's total fixed costs and total variable costs

total fixed costs (TFC) the sum of the firm's fixed costs

total product (TP) the total output of a good produced by the firm

total revenue (TR) the product price times the quantity sold

total variable cost (TVC) the sum of the firm's variable costs

total welfare gains the sum of consumer and producer surplus

transferable pollution rights a right given to a firm to discharge a specified amount of pollution; its transferable nature creates incentive to lower pollution levels.

unintended consequences the secondary effects of an action that may occur after the initial effects

unit elastic demand demand with a price elasticity of 1; the percentage change in quantity demanded is equal to the percentage change in price

variable something that is measured by a number, such as your height

variable costs costs that vary with the level of output

X-axis the horizontal axis on a graph

Y-axis the vertical axis on a graph

Index